WOMEN, MARRIAGE
AND POLITICS
1860–1914

Women, Marriage and Politics
1860–1914

PAT JALLAND

CLARENDON PRESS · OXFORD
1986

Oxford University Press, Walton Street, Oxford OX2 6DP
London New York Toronto
Delhi Bombay Calcutta Madras Karachi
Petaling Jaya Singapore Hong Kong Tokyo
Nairobi Dar es Salaam Cape Town
Melbourne Auckland
and associated companies in
Beirut Berlin Ibadan Mexico City Nicosia

Oxford is a trade mark of Oxford University Press

Published in the United States
by Oxford University Press, New York

British Library Cataloguing in Publication Data
Jalland, Pat
Women, marriage and politics 1860–1914.
1. Women – Great Britain – Social conditions
2. Politicians – Great Britain – History – 19th century
3. Politicians – Great Britain – History – 20th century
I. Title
305.4'32   HQ1593
ISBN 0–19–822668–3

Library of Congress Cataloging in Publication Data
Jalland, Patricia.
Women, marriage, and politics, 1860–1914.
Bibliography: p.
Includes index.
1. Women – Great Britain – History – 19th century.
2. Politicians' wives – Great Britain – History – 19th century.
3. Women in public life – Great Britain – History – 19th century.
4. Family – Great Britain – History – 19th century.
I. Title.
HQ1593.J34 1986   305.4'0941   85–28406
ISBN 0–19–822668–3

Set by Hope Services, Abingdon
Printed in Great Britain
at the University Printing House, Oxford
by David Stanford
Printer to the University

FOR JOHN

Acknowledgements

THE preparation of this book has depended heavily on the help of other people and institutions. John Hooper shared my enthusiasm for this project from its inception, and his constant support, informed criticism and practical assistance were invaluable at every stage. I am deeply indebted to several good friends and colleagues who took the time and trouble to read and comment on my chapters, and gave me the benefit of their knowledge and judgement: Peter Clarke, Oliver MacDonagh and Barry Smith generously read the entire manuscript, offering detailed and thoughtful suggestions for improvement, and providing encouragement and advice whenever needed. Barbara Caine and Allan Martin contributed helpful comments on particular chapters. The responsibility for any errors or omissions remains my own.

Dee Cook was an enthusiastic and splendidly efficient graduate research assistant for this project. In particular, her aid in the laborious task of tracing MSS collections was indispensable, as was her help in transcribing longhand notes from masses of primary materials in archives scattered across the United Kingdom. Dee made a major contribution by compiling the excellent index. Alan Milburn, Simon Ville and Patricia Wilkie also assisted in transcribing material from large MSS collections, mainly in Newcastle-on-Tyne and Edinburgh.

Helen Macnab skilfully and cheerfully bore the principal burden of transferring my manuscript to the word processor, aided by Bev Gallina, Barbara Hawkins, Anthea Bundock, Janice Aldridge, and especially Ronni Neil in the final stages. Their work is appreciated all the more because they were using word processors while the problems of repetitive strain injury were only beginning to be recognised.

My thanks are also due to the Australian Research Grants Committee for a three year research grant from 1980–1983, which funded part-time research assistants and enabled me to work far more extensively on the numerous MSS collections in the U.K. The Australian National University awarded me a Visiting Fellowship in the History Department of the Research School of social Sciences from 1983 to 1986, thus providing the ideal environment for writing this book.

I am grateful to all those who allowed me access to their family archives. I should particularly like to acknowledge the courtesy and helpfulness of the Earl of Balfour, Sir William Gladstone Bt., Mrs Helen Pease, the Samuel family, and Mrs R. T. Sneyd. Dr Pauline Dower's interest and assistance in my research and her generous hospitality at Cambo House and Wallington are warmly appreciated. I owe a special debt to all the librarians and archivists who facilitated the research for this book, especially Dr B. S. Benedikz (Birmingham University Library), Mr

Alistair Elliot (formerly of the University Library, Newcastle-upon-Tyne), Mr D. S. Porter (Bodleian Library, Oxford), Dr Angela Raspin (British Library of Political and Economic Science), Miss Marion Stewart (Churchill College, Cambridge) and Mr Christopher Williams and Mr A. G. Veysey (Clwyd Record Office).

The staff at Oxford University Press have been a pleasure to work with, notably Ivon Asquith, Robert Faber, Dorothy McLean and John Waś.

Permissions

Copyright permissions for quotations from manuscript collections have been kindly granted by Sir Richard and Lady Acland (Acland MSS); Mr Mark Bonham-Carter (Margot Asquith's letters); the Duke of Atholl (Atholl MSS); the Earl of Balfour (Balfour MSS); the British Library (the Papers of A. J. Balfour, Sir Henry Campbell-Bannerman, Sir Charles Dilke, Mary Drew, A. G. Gardiner, W. E. Gladstone); the Bodleian Library (Acland, Bryce, Carrington, Harcourt and Selborne Papers); Warren Murton, Solicitors (Bryce MSS); Brigadier A. W. A. Llewellen Palmer (Carrington Papers); the University of Birmingham (Chamberlain Archive); Viscount Chandos and the Master, Fellows and Scholars of Churchill College in the University of Cambridge (Chandos Papers); the British Library of Political and Economic Science (Courtney Collection; Graham Wallas MSS); Lord Craigmyle (Craigmyle Papers); Sir William Gladstone Bt. (W. E. Gladstone, Glynne-Gladstone and Mary Drew Papers); the Librarian, Liverpool University Library (Glasier and Rathbone Papers); Viscount Hambleden (Hambleden MSS); the Public Record Office, on behalf of Mrs Sheila Lochhead (Ramsay MacDonald Papers); the Trustees of the National Library of Scotland (Haldane and Minto Papers); The London School of Economics and Political Science, in association with the Virago Press Ltd (the Passfield Papers, and Beatrice Webb's diary); the Earl of Selborne (Selborne Papers); the Administrative Trustees of the Chevening Estate (Stanhope MSS); Mr T. G. Talbot (Talbot MSS); Dr Pauline Dower and the Trevelyan family (Trevelyan MSS); the Principal of Pusey House, Oxford (Ward Papers).

The following publishers have kindly granted copyright permissions for extracts from printed sources: Jonathan Cape Ltd (Sybil Lubbock, *The Child in the Crystal*, 1939; Lady Constance Malleson, *After Ten Years*, 1931); Croom Helm Limited (Leonore Davidoff, *The Best Circles*, 1973; Brian Harrison, *Separate Spheres*, 1978); Methuen & Co. (Lucy Masterman, ed., *Mary Gladstone: Her Diaries and Letters*, 1930); John Murray (Publishers) Ltd. (Sir Edward Cadogan, *Before the Deluge*, 1961); Weidenfeld and Nicolson Ltd. (Lawrence Stone, *The Family, Sex and Marriage in England 1500–1800*, 1977; Kenneth Rose, *The Later Cecils*, 1975). I offer my apologies to any copyright owners I have been unable to locate.

Contents

PART FOUR: SPINSTERHOOD

List of Illustrations

Aims and Sources

THIS book explores the lives of women in more than fifty families involved in British politics from about 1860 to 1914. The evidence is drawn mainly from the correspondence and diaries of large numbers of these women who were highly literate and self-conscious even if not formally educated. Though not a homogeneous group, they were linked by class and sex, while their families were often associated by marriage, friendship, or political alliances. Their family papers provide an unusually rich source of personal testimony on the lives of upper-middle- and upper-class women over several generations. This evidence is used to investigate important private and social experiences—including courtship, marriage, childbirth and spinsterhood—and to analyse the roles and attitudes of politicians' wives.

Substantial advances have been made over the past twenty years in the study of the history of women and the family. Scholars of the Victorian period have questioned the simple stereotype of the idle, passive female idealized in some Victorian novels and prescriptive manuals. As Martha Vicinus recognized in 1977, research is now increasingly concerned with 'the relationship . . . between the prescribed ideal of womanhood and the actual reality'.[1] But it has been easier to identify misleading stereotypes and questionable generalizations than to recapture this 'actual reality'. Scholars exploring women's history have often regretted that 'the most significant gap in the primary sources is the lack of autobiographical data'.[2] This misleading complaint recurs, whether the focus is childbirth, spinsterhood, marriage, or any other area of personal rather than public life. Perhaps this is because social historians have tended to pay more attention to the working classes, for whom the literary sources are more limited.

It is wrong to assume that all women are 'hidden from history' and that women's history is necessarily the story of the inarticulate. Women of the upper-middle and upper classes sometimes left substantial personal records, which have been largely neglected.

Yet historians have long accepted the significant role of the upper
and middle classes in determining the attitudes and values of the
Victorian age, and the women of these privileged classes deserve
more historical attention. Brian Harrison noted in 1978 that the
social and political role of upper-class women was an important
and unexplored subject.[3] Recently Jeanne Peterson has illustrated
how this gap might be filled, with an illuminating essay on the
women in the Paget family. Her conclusions are based on 'a
microscopic' study of women's lives in a single family, because 'a
systematic, statistical survey of Victorian women of the upper-
middle class is perhaps an impossible task'.[4] However, manuscript
sources do permit an analytical study of an extensive group of
families which includes many dozens of women in its scope.

My book explores the 'actual reality' of the lives of upper-class
women in Britain from about 1860 to 1914 through the substantial
personal testimony of the women in politicians' families. These
families have been chosen as my focus for two reasons. First,
politicians have more vanity and ambition than most other
occupational groups and a corresponding tendency to justify
themselves to posterity by preserving their papers. Secondly, the
political élite of the Victorian and Edwardian eras was closely
identified with the social and intellectual aristocracy of the
country—it was far from being a narrow occupational group.
Victorian politicians were also landowners, country gentlemen,
industrialists, lawyers and intellectuals; their sons and brothers
were often doctors, diplomats, businessmen, academics or clergymen. Thus the family papers of a Victorian 'political family' can
reveal much about the broad spectrum of the upper levels of
society. There is no reason to suppose that the fifty or so families
in this study were unrepresentative of the upper-middle and upper-
class as a whole. 'Political families' are usually interpreted here
in this broad sense—except in the two chapters on political wives
per se.

My sources have been drawn as widely as possible from dozens
of family archives, rather than from a small sample. Since the
evidence for women's lives is so widely and thinly scattered, the
only satisfactory method of research was to examine all politicians'
papers which preserved relevant material about women. My
search for women's papers therefore initially included all manuscript collections for British Members of Parliament from the

1860s to 1914. As far as possible I checked all family papers which have survived, to discover the nature and extent of material relating to women. This laborious procedure eliminated numerous collections, since many families preserved only political material, which they regarded as historically significant. The public achievements of the men were saved for posterity while the personal correspondence of the women was frequently burned. Women's records tended to be kept by accident, sentiment or default, revealing fragments of the lives of obscure sisters and nieces as well as the more famous wives.

Nevertheless, about fifty family collections finally yielded useful material on women's experience. These were scattered throughout the United Kingdom, in private archives and public repositories. There were about twenty massive collections, while the remainder were more random and patchy. Two general decisions were necessary about priorities. American women who married into British political families were excluded since their American background would have confused the picture (except for Mary Chamberlain, whose efforts to become a good British political wife are very revealing). Secondly, priority has been given, wherever possible, to previously neglected women who saw themselves primarily as wives, mothers, and daughters. I have placed less emphasis on those women who were famous in their own right, whether as suffragist leaders, society hostesses, or prime ministers' wives. Thus Catherine Gladstone receives less attention than her two daughters, Mary and Helen. Similarly, Margot Asquith secures far less space than she would have expected, whereas her sister, Laura Tennant, is the subject of a case study on courtship. Published memoirs, biographies and diaries have also been consulted but they were often less valuable than family papers, given the emphases of this book.

Many women in these families corresponded regularly—sometimes daily over many years—with sisters, parents and close female friends. For women who left home to marry, these letters were a lifeline to their own family and their past. If they were separated from their husbands during parliamentary sessions, their letters often contained a running commentary on the minutiae of family life. Most of these letters were the equivalent of today's telephone conversations—they were not written with an eye to possible publication. But their importance to family members was

often profound. Lady Constance Malleson described her mother's
desire to escape from the 'prison' of her husband's home in the
1890s: 'She would sometimes walk for miles—usually on the
strength of letters received from the living world of London or
Dublin. Letters made up her whole existence . . . They were the
backbone of her life at Castlewellan.'[5] Meriel Talbot's diary
illustrates the crucial importance of such correspondence to young
married women: '[letters] received in 1860: 255. Wrote 268. Excess
of written over received 13'. Her output increased to 398 letters in
1863 and 425 the following year.[6] In 1879 the newly married
Maggie Acland explained to her sister-in-law: 'since I became your
sister and Harry's wife my own correspondence has greatly
increased, with Father, Mother, Aunt Mary and Maude to write
to, besides the 9 brothers and Nellie . . . I never seem to have half
enough time to write all the letters I want to'.[7]

Correspondence provides the most important source for this
book, but diaries have also contributed—though only a small
number of women kept diaries of significant value for the
historian. The majority of extant diaries are essentially appoint-
ment books intended as *aide-mémoires*, but some became more
ambitious, recording thoughts and descriptions in an unsystematic
manner. Other diaries were used as confessionals, often started by
lonely adolescent girls like Margaret King and continued, perhaps
out of habit, to affirm their identity or sort out their ideas. In 1883
Beatrice Potter saw her diary as a confidante which served as 'the
more or less perfect reflection of one's own little Ego'.[8] These
diaries often repeat the information sent out in letters to close
female friends and sisters, usually in a condensed form which is
less revealing than the letters. Even 'confessional' diaries do not
necessarily tell the whole truth, if only because of the danger
of family members reading the entries at some point. Mary
Gladstone's enormous correspondence with close friends, sisters
and cousins provides more intimate evidence about her private life
than does her diary. On 29 December 1883, for example, she fell
in love with Harry Drew, but her diary merely notes: 'A most
tremendous anxious day in a way that must not be revealed even to
this book.'[9] These female diarists usually had no thought of
publication precisely because of the distinction they made between
the public and private worlds. Mary Gladstone and Beatrice Webb
were exceptions, since they were among the few Victorian women

to be involved directly in public life. Mary Gladstone regarded her diary as worthy of ultimate (but selective) publication because it recorded her father's political career and her own role in it.

I shall concentrate on the four aspects of women's experience which are most richly recorded in these family papers: marriage, childbirth, spinsterhood, and the roles of political wives *per se*. The focus and the structural treatment of these four main themes vary according to the nature of the subject and the sources. Since marriage and motherhood were major phases in the life cycle of Victorian and Edwardian women, the focus in these sections is on their personal life. The fact that most of these women came from political families is incidental, for they experienced marriage and childbirth in similar fashion to upper-middle- and upper-class women in general. The focus of the two chapters on 'Political Wives', however, is quite different; there it is essential that these women were wives of politicians, and their special roles and attitudes are examined in depth. The focus alters again in the final chapter on spinsters, whose private lives did not follow the usual pattern of the Victorian female life cycle because they failed to become wives and mothers. Their experiences illuminate the deficiencies of Victorian theories about women's roles and, in some respects, point to a future for women which would involve greater choices. The overall emphasis of the book is placed on aspects of women's personal lives, which have been seriously neglected, rather than on women's public involvement in areas such as the suffrage movement, local government, royal commissions, or philanthropy.

The treatment of most themes in the book combines a general analysis, drawing on widely dispersed evidence, with a series of individual case studies illustrating the variety of behaviour within the general patterns. Thus the section on courtship and marriage includes three thematic chapters analysing the rituals of courtship and motives for marriage, followed by a fourth chapter which examines the experiences of five women in more depth. Similarly, the section on 'Political Wives' comprises one chapter which analyses the roles and attitudes of politicians' wives, followed by a chapter focusing on five detailed case studies. The sections on childbirth and spinsterhood depart from this structure to some extent. The emphasis in the two childbirth chapters is placed on the analysis of common patterns of experience, with relevant

6 *Aims and Sources*

examples. Conversely, spinsterhood is best explored through individual case studies which examine the experiences of unmarried women within their family settings. The special character of this book lies in the combination of general patterns drawn from the private papers of a large number of families, with detailed case studies of individual women. As Oliver MacDonagh has observed: 'generality is valid, not to say necessary, to organise experience in the mind or on the page. But every phenomenon, every stretch of past reality, has its own inimitable form and markings, and every human actor his own "particular glimpse".'[10]

The Education of Good Wives and Mothers

VICTORIAN social thought emphasized the 'natural' separation of the spheres between the sexes, and a rigid sexual division of labour. It was widely accepted, even by many suffragists, that physiological and intellectual differences between the sexes fitted males for the public sphere and females for their domestic world. Even a feminist like Frances Power Cobbe accepted that women's domestic role was the logical corollary of the capacity for reproduction:

So *immense* are the claims on a Mother, physical claims on her bodily and brain vigour, and moral claims on her heart and thoughts, that she cannot, I believe, meet them all, and find any large margin beyond for other cares and work. She serves the community in the very best and highest way it is possible to do, by giving birth to healthy children . . . This is her *Function*, Public and Private, at once—The *Profession* which she has adopted. No higher can be found; and in my judgment it is a misfortune . . . when a woman . . . is lured by any generous ambition to add . . . any other systematic work; either as breadwinner to the family, or as philanthropist or politician . . .[1]

Females were seen as ordained by God to be dutiful wives and mothers, guardians of the home and family. Most Victorian political families shared sincere religious beliefs based on genuine commitment rather than mere obedience to social convention. Daily family prayers and frequent attendance at church services were an important part of their lives. Protestantism reinforced traditional views of the female role and encouraged individual philanthropy as a proper social activity for upper-class women.

The expectations of young girls growing up in Victorian Britain were circumscribed by these dominant ideas, which they assimilated from childhood. Their mothers were their role models, since their brothers were treated differently and their fathers' lives were remote. The vast majority of middle- and upper-class women did

8   *Introduction*

not question the conventional wisdom of 'separate spheres' and
the translation of female gender into domesticity. Mrs Henry
Fowler was typical, as her daughter recalled: 'My mother's
vocation was her home-life and all its radiating branches.
Wifehood, as she exemplified it, was a profession in itself,
and anything which it did not absorb was consumed in motherhood . . .'[2]

Popular advice manuals and medical texts reinforced the
prevailing attitudes about the role of women and the proper
methods for raising them. Biology was identified as the key to
female function, since the woman 'is an admirably constructed
apparatus for the most mysterious and sublime of nature's
mysteries—the reproductive process.'[3] Puberty was perceived as
the most critical stage in the female life cycle, for 'the future
woman is moulded at this time.'[4] The commencement of menstruation was a time of great disturbance, marking the advent of
womanhood and the 'perfect subordination of self to another'.
Therefore such education as girls received should train them in the
noble arts of service and self-sacrifice, transforming devoted
daughters into perfect wives and mothers.[5] A classical education
such as their brothers received was not only unnecessary, but also
positively harmful. If women's energies were diverted from
reproductive to intellectual ends, the human race would suffer:
'During the crisis of puberty . . . there should be a general
relaxation from study, which might otherwise too forcibly engross
the mind and the energies required by the constitution to work out
nature's ends.'[6] Writers deplored excessive mental application and
intellectual stimulation at the 'dawn of womanhood', between the
ages of thirteen and sixteen.[7] Fashionable society and emotional
excitement were equally condemned during the early years of
puberty as likely to 'produce a condition of physical and moral
instability, ill-fitted for the grave responsibilities of wifehood and
motherhood'.[8] The postponement of young womanhood until the
formal 'coming out' at seventeen was seriously recommended; for
example, in 1888 one doctor advised: 'Probably the most successful mode of rearing girls, so as to bring them to the full perfection
of womanhood, is to retard the period of puberty as much as
possible, at least until the 14th or 16th year.' Cold baths, exercise
in the open air, a plain diet and a strict regimen were suggested to
encourage this process of retardation.[9]

It is impossible to generalize very far about the upbringing of
Victorian upper-class children; diversity was the outstanding
characteristic. Some parents were undoubtedly tyrannical disci-
plinarians, quite remote from their offspring. Many children were
expected to be seen and not heard: 'signs of individuality in the
young, if observed, were firmly nipped in the bud . . . the child was
only permitted to think under supervision'.[10] Stories abound of
children brought up by nannies, governesses and servants, having
little contact with their parents except for formal daily visits.
B. L. Booker recalled her London childhood in the 1890s, reared
by expensive nannies and meeting her mother once a day in the
drawing room after tea: 'We lived upstairs in a different world and
were at the mercy of our nurses', one of whom 'terrorised and
starved me when she got me to herself'.[11] Many parents were strict
with adolescent daughters. Beatrice Potter received stern advice
from her mother before visiting a friend in 1870: 'the same spirit of
obedience to God should guide you in every position, and no
indulgence or luxury should cause you to avoid self-denial when
that is your duty.'[12]

By contrast, the upbringing of the Tennant sisters in their
isolated Scottish castle was far removed from the traditional
picture of Victorian childhood: 'We were wild children and, left to
ourselves, had the time of our lives.'[13] Lady Leith appeared to be
almost as casual as Sir Charles Tennant; she allowed 'her family to
grow up as best they may while she goes to London with one
daughter or two and brings them out'.[14] Nor were young girls
always relegated to the nursery, as Mrs Louise Creighton
confirmed in 1879: 'I think that the more one can have a common
life with one's children the better for all parties.' She also
recommended a particular 'ABC of Arithmetic' to Mrs Humphry
Ward to assist in teaching Dorothy—it avoided multiplication
tables and developed the child's mind.[15] There were many
references to loving relationships, parental tolerance and even
spoilt children. Kate Potter remarked on the upbringing of her
sister's children in 1873:

The little Holts are really charming dispositioned children but decidedly
spoilt which makes them the most wilful, disobedient little monkeys. It is
funny that Lallie [Laurencina Holt] with all her determination in most
things should be so soft to her children.[16]

Excessive authority and excessive freedom coexisted in Victorian children's upbringing. There were marked differences even between closely related families which spent considerable time together; the young Lytteltons were 'impatient of restraint' while their cousins, the Gladstones, were 'diffident and mindful of authority'.[17]

Female adolescence was prolonged, and the role of the adolescent girl was ill-defined, since she was no longer a child nor yet a marriageable woman. Some Victorian girls suffered agonizing boredom in the aimless years between childhood and marriage. Elizabeth Haldane remembered adolescence as 'the least happy part' of an otherwise contented life and the only time she endured 'what is now called frustration'.[18] Beatrice Potter's diary featured regular complaints of deadly boredom and ill-health as she grew up. At twenty she suffered from headaches, a 'weak liver' and anaemia, but most of all from 'want of employment, which makes life almost a torture, a silent misery, all the more painful because apparently causeless.' She believed that her poor health and self-disgust sprang from 'deadly ennui', loneliness and the 'absence of any occupation'.[19] Helen Gladstone became vividly aware of the futility of her previous home life when she went to study at Cambridge at the age of twenty-eight. The female students at Newnham were purposeful: 'a refreshing change from the aimlessness of most girls' lives'.[20]

Throughout the Victorian period the vast majority of girls in upper-middle- and upper-class families were educated entirely at home.[21] Even the educational reforms of the last two decades of the nineteenth century had little impact on upper-class girls until the Edwardian era. Most were taught at home by governesses whose academic training was often very limited, and their social status uncertain.[22] Some governesses did earn the affection and respect of pupils and parents; the Ribblesdale family regretted the departure of their French governess in 1881 after 'eight years of uninterrupted confidence and support; loved and depended on by us all'.[23] But many governesses were remembered for their severity as well as their ignorance—like Millicent Fawcett's governess who was 'incompetent to the last degree'.[24] Maggie Harkness commented to Beatrice Potter in 1879 on the education of their contemporaries: 'girls brought up at home in a schoolroom, and shut up all day long with a woman who perhaps

possesses no mind whatsoever' were not equipped for any
independent life.[25]

The experience of the Lyttelton, Gladstone an: Bell girls
illustrates some characteristic features of female upbringing in
these political families. Lucy Lyttelton was the gentle, sweet-
tempered daughter of Lord Lyttelton, an affectionate father and
fine scholar. At the age of thirteen Lucy wrote an account of her
childhood, recalling a governess who stayed with them until 1848,
when Lucy was seven:

I was not happy in Miss Nicholson's time . . . She managed me ill; over-
severe and apt to whip [slap] me for obstinacy when I was only dense, and
punishing too often. So I was always labouring under a sense of injustice
. . . At Brighton I used to be taken out walking on the parade with my
hands tied behind me . . . At home my usual punishment was being put
for a time into a large, deep, old-fashioned bath that was in one corner of
the schoolroom.

The next governess was over-indulgent and taught them little for
three years, but she was followed by 'a woman of stern and upright
mind' who exposed Lucy's faults unsparingly. Even so, Miss
Pearson was unsystematic, frequently ill, and the children were
often left to work on their own at poetry, the 'Christian Year' and
'bits of Shakespeare and Milton'. Not until 1856, when Lucy was
fifteen, did a new governess impose some regularity on the
schoolroom routine. Two days each week were reserved for
Italian, two for French and two for English, interspersed with
some music, drawing, arithmetic, and the 'repetition of Cornwall's
geography and Reed's English History'. The severity of Lucy's
treatment was mitigated by the knowledge of her mother's loving
care, though Lady Lyttelton interfered little between her children
and their governesses.[26]

Mary Gladstone, daughter of the great Liberal leader, was born
in 1847, six years after her cousin, Lucy Lyttelton. She wrote in old
age that 'a lifelong depreciation started in my childhood when old
Mrs Talbot gave me the impression that I was "wanting" i.e. half-
witted. My governess, from 10–17 years, continued to treat me as
half-witted, so I grew up as a nonentity. I have never outgrown
it.'[27] Mary received no praise or encouragement from her
governess, only criticism and assumed disapproval. She and her
two sisters never learned to concentrate, to study systematically or

think analytically. Lucy Masterman commented years later on Mary's education at the age of seventeen:

She could speak French and read Dante in Italian, and later was able to speak and read German. Otherwise her knowledge seems to have had no sort of framework and her studies no aim whatever. When emancipated from the schoolroom she read furiously, but inconsequently . . . Her mind was kept like a kind of domestic pet, to be fed upon literary tit-bits.[28]

A generation later, matters had not improved significantly for Molly Bell, daughter of a millionaire iron-master. She grew up with 'a never-ending regret that I happened to be a girl'. She and her sister, Elsa, were taught by an uninspired governess from the time Molly was five:

For more than ten years I was bored to death all the time . . . My mother's idea of the equipment required for her two daughters was that we should be turned out as good wives and mothers and be able to take our part in the social life of our kind. We must speak French and German perfectly, and be on friendly if not intimate terms with Italian. We must be able to play the piano and sing a bit, we must learn to dance well, and know how to make small talk. The more serious side of education did not take any part in the plans my mother made for us. Science, mathematics, political economy, Greek and Latin—there was no need for any of these. No girl that we knew was trained for any career or profession, nor did girls of our class go to school.

The governess killed Molly's interest in formal education, leaving her unreceptive when she briefly attended Queen's College, London, at the age of fifteen. But after the governess left she developed an appetite for books ranging from 'the great classics' to Rider Haggard and regretted that she had discovered a love of learning too late. When she wistfully perused the Girton College syllabus at the age of eighteen she knew that she could never compensate for all the wasted years at home, but must continue her self-education in the great literature of Europe.[29] Like Mary Gladstone she was an accomplished pianist, and they both passed through 'a deeply religious phase'—an experience they shared with many adolescent Victorian girls.

Governesses continued to be employed to teach girls at home up to 1914, though the standard of their training did improve from the 1880s. Mary Drew noted in 1898 that her nine-year-old daughter had 'started well with the new Governess'.[30] In 1902 Mildred

Buxton employed a governess who stayed with the children for the next twenty years and was a great support to the family.[31] As late as 1912 May Harcourt engaged a French 'daily governess' to help one daughter with her reading: 'The other girls are full of drawing, elocution, fencing, dancing, German, singing and skating. So education is in full swing.'[32] Among the upper classes some parents evidently still equated ladylike accomplishments with education, even at this late date. Young ladies were trained for courtship but not for the more practical requirements of marriage. As Cynthia Asquith remarked:

Our helplessness equalled our want of independence; one engendered the other. Everything was done for us. I was never so much as taught how to mend or wash—let alone make—my clothes. I couldn't even pack for myself. Of cooking I knew no more than the art of navigation. Absurd upbringing, for even had conditions remained as they were how can you criticise a cook if you know nothing of her craft?[33]

Very few girls in these families received any formal education outside the home. Private boarding schools were usually only patronized in exceptional domestic circumstances—they seem to have been generally the preserve of the middle levels of the middle class.[34] Olive and Violet Maxse attended a private school for young ladies in Paris for some years in the 1880s, presumably because their parents were separated. The school specialized in ladylike refinements such as music, drawing and needlework, with an hour's rest each afternoon. Cecilia Maxse warned her adolescent daughter, Violet, in 1887: 'the chief thing now is for you to keep your health—and build up tastes and resources during this chrysalis state'.[35] A generation earlier Mrs Humphry Ward spent nine years as a young girl at three different boarding schools, characterized by poor teaching and ignorance of the physical needs of growing girls: 'As far as intellectual training was concerned, my nine years from seven to sixteen were practically wasted. I learnt nothing thoroughly or accurately.' She compared her experience most unfavourably with her brothers' six years at Rugby.[36] Louise Childers went to a private boarding school in Brighton from 1867 to 1874. At the cost of £67 per term she learned English, music, French, German, Italian, singing, riding and callisthenics.[37]

It was rather more common for girls from these political families to spend a year in a finishing school which offered a similar range

of accomplishments to the boarding schools. In 1875 Beatrice
Potter's preparation for 'coming out' was a year at an establishment called Stirling House, where she hated the 'continual din of
the piano and the want of interesting conversation'.[38] Janet Ward
was 'finished' in Paris in 1898, with instruction in piano, singing
and history, and excursions with an aristocratic chaperone who
was neither knowledgeable nor helpful.[39] In 1900 Miriam Pease's
French finishing school featured English, history, literature,
'natural sciences', music, German and drawing, all conducted in
French. At least her French improved and she was obliged to learn
how to look after her own clothes.[40]

A fortunate minority of girls in these political families were able
to take advantage of the new secondary and higher education
developing from the 1880s in response to the women's movement.
But very few of these girls were allowed this opportunity, and
many enjoyed it for too short a time. After several years of home
education by a governess, fourteen-year-old Mildred Hugh Smith
was sent in 1880 for three years at Kensington High School—'a
revolutionary idea in those days'.[41] In 1895 Lady Carrington
'drove to Kensington Square to King's College for Ladies to find
out about classes for girls'; and arranged for her daughters to begin
instruction.[42] Molly and Elsa Bell briefly attended lectures at
Queen's College, London, in the year or so before 'coming out'. If
these families gave their daughters a good education at all, it was
usually too little and too late. Katharine Wallas condemned this
practice about 1910:

The Balfour girl arrived [at Cambridge]—A pretty looking creature of
about 18 knowing nothing beyond $(a + b)^2$ and with an idea that she'll get
through Matric. in June. Parents in these circles are pretty cruel to their
children without meaning harm. [They] keep the poor things without a
chance of doing serious work and are then suddenly seized with the idea
that it would be 'nice for Ruth to go to College'.[43]

Margaret Gladstone, daughter of a chemistry professor and
subsequently wife of Ramsay MacDonald, was unusually fortunate
in her education—perhaps partly because her mother died when
she was born, and also because she came from the professional
ranks of the middle-class, below the social level of many families in
this study. Margaret spent five years at Doreck College in London
in the 1880s, moving on to 'the Ladies Classes' at King's College in

Kensington Square for several more years. Her courses at King's College included physiology, Greek, moral philosophy, architecture and ethics, besides the more traditional female subjects such as modern European languages.[44] A generation later Margaret MacDonald's three daughters attended the City of London Junior School, the Tremarth School and the renowned North London Collegiate School.

Girls in upper-class families were well aware that their upbringing was inferior to the public school and university education of their brothers. Maud Selborne recalled the mid-Victorian decades: 'Boys went to preparatory schools and then on to public schools, just as they do now, but it was not at all usual for girls of the upper class to go to boarding schools.'[45] Girls also fully understood the rationale for their inferior education: 'It was generally thought that girls were less capable of being educated than boys, and that any but a smattering of accomplishments made them less likely to be good wives and mothers.'[46] Yet despite occasional regrets, most of these girls accepted the domestic ideology of the separate spheres, which they learned from their own families from an early age. Consequently, even the most talented girls had expectations which were lower as well as different from their brothers'. Elizabeth Haldane had to live frugally in the country with her mother in the 1870s so that her brothers could be 'set up in life'. She considered herself uneducated, and life 'looked black and grim':

I should have loved going to college, but college in those days was unusual for girls, and the idea was not encouraged. It was also expensive . . . I should, of course, have liked to study for a profession, but that was an impossible idea unless one were in the sad position of 'having to work for one's bread' . . . I had no special reason to concentrate, as a young man would have had.[47]

When Margaret Gladstone visited Balliol College, Oxford, in 1891 she was torn between envy and acquiescence: 'I should like to spend three years at such a place if I were a man; but being a girl, I think I prefer being at home.'[48]

The adult correspondence of these political wives and daughters may suggest to the modern reader that they were not ill educated. One explanation for their level of literacy is the extent of their self-education. Molly Trevelyan and many others regretted their lack of formal learning and attempted to compensate as best they could. Some asked brothers to help them in school holidays, though this often caused resentment and frustration, underlining their inadequate educational opportunities. It was fairly common for elder sisters to instruct younger sisters; Margaret King noted in 1869 that 'ever since I was a wee thing I have taught the others'.[49] Mary Gladstone helped her sister, Helen, in 1877, by 'reading Chaucer and doing Butler's "Analogy"' together.[50] Elizabeth Haldane participated in the new movement for correspondence classes and read widely in philosophy and the classics, encouraged and advised by her aunt and mother.[51] Beatrice Potter was fortunate in winning the guidance of Herbert Spencer, who provided her with reading lists and discussed her ideas. In her thirties Mary Gladstone gained an eminent tutor in Lord Acton, her father's friend. She noted in 1883: 'began going steadily through Lord Acton's list of the hundred books that have had the most effect on the world's history'—including works by Plato, Aristotle, Dante, Liebnitz, Rousseau, Spencer, Pascal, Hooker, Coleridge and Darwin.[52]

More important than self-education, however, was the influence of the family culture which these girls unconsciously absorbed from childhood. Vera Brittain subsequently envied 'the incalculable advantages of heredity and early environment that are involved in merely being born a member of such families as the Huxleys, the Haldanes, the Frys, the Darwins or the Arnolds'.[53] The same point could be made about the Trevelyans, the Cecils, the Balfours, the Gladstones and the Lytteltons, and many other families in this study. Politics, 'Society' and the intellectual élite were closely bound together in the Victorian and Edwardian years. A prime minister could be a philosopher or a theologian, and public service was still the counterpart of privilege. Political families entertained distinguished guests from all walks of life and the women heard erudite discussions of literature, philosophy and the arts, as well as politics. Lucy Masterman said of the Gladstone household: 'it was a happy family atmosphere, brimful of affection and mental activity, and responsive to most of the intellectual interests of the day'.[54] Families played music together, visited art exhibitions and concerts, and often read aloud from the classics in the evening. Daughters usually had the free run of their fathers' libraries, even if they received little guidance as to their

reading. The Cecil children learned while very young to participate in incessant family debates on philosophy, metaphysics,
politics, and every other subject except religion. Lord Salisbury
treated all his children as intellectual equals with opinons to be
respected and arguments to be countered.[55] Not all daughters in
political families had the ability or inclination to utilize these
opportunities to the full, but those who did emerged with a
confidence and knowledge which bore little relation to the efforts
of their governesses.

The long-term results of this haphazard and inadequate female
education were the product of accident as much as individual
talent, environment and training. Scholars of the intellectual
calibre of Gladstone and Lord Lyttelton considered an abysmal
education adequate for their daughters, while their sons went to
public school and university. These parents saw no reason to
develop their daughters' intellectual potential in any structured
manner since the girls were destined to become dutiful wives and
mothers. For girls without a formal education or alternative career
prospects, their future life was entirely determined by their
particular experience of courtship, marriage and motherhood.

Recent scholarship has contributed greatly to our knowledge of
women in the vanguard of the women's movement, who often
questioned contemporary social theory and tried to transform
women's roles and enlarge their expectations. We know far less
about the women who accepted the ideology of their times and
lived within its confines. This book explores the experiences of
that more passive majority—as lovers, wives, mothers and
spinsters—through the lives of women in Victorian and Edwardian
political families.

PART ONE

COURTSHIP AND MARRIAGE

I

The Rituals of Courtship and Marriage

ELABORATE social conventions were created to restrict and regulate young love and courtship among the upper-middle and upper-class. The London Season, 'coming out', country house parties and balls—all operated to ensure that young people only met others of desirable social background. Leonore Davidoff in *The Best Circles* has provided a perceptive analysis of the significance, functions and operation of 'Society'. She argues that Society was developed from the eighteenth century in the fluid and expanding situation created by industrialization to control access to aristocratic ranks by the upwardly mobile new rich. Regulation of the marriage market through the elaborate code of social etiquette remained vital in the Victorian period:

> One of the most essential points of access to high status group membership is through marriage. This avenue of advancement took on new significance during our period. It often provided status legitimacy through one partner and new capital through the other. Throughout the nineteenth century arranged marriages were no longer acceptable so that individual choice had to be most carefully regulated to ensure exclusion of undesirable partners and maximum gain for both sides.[1]

It seems to be impossible to give any precise estimate of the numbers of young ladies 'doing the Season' in London in any one year. Society was too fluid an entity to be precisely defined and counted at any one moment. There were constant complaints about the dilution of Society by upstarts and the *nouveaux riches*, but no statistical evidence. The magazine, the *Queen*, for example, protested in 1861:

> The crowning mischief, as we take it, is the way in which presentation at Court is now so vulgarised, that it has lost all value and meaning as a title to social distinction. Formerly, presentations were confined to the true aristocracy of the country, the peerage, the superior landed gentry, persons of distinction in art, science and letters and the holders of offices

of dignity under the Crown . . . It is now no longer so. Presentations are now so vulgarised that literally ANYBODY who has sufficient amount of perseverance or self confidence may be presented. The wives of all Members of Parliament are presented and they in turn present the wives and daughters of local squires and other small magnates. There is no knowing where this is to stop.

But no numbers were provided. Society was evidently expanding all the time. Davidoff writes of eighteenth-century Society as numbering between three and four hundred families. By contrast Society in the 1890s comprised about four thousand active families, though thirty thousand were listed in the Court Guide.[2] Perhaps the best we can do is to accept the 'top ten thousand' so frequently mentioned as Society's size in the late Victorian period, though that figure naturally includes all the families, not merely the girls 'coming out' in any one year. The families examined in this book, however, extend in social range well beyond this mythical top ten thousand.

The London Season was certainly perceived by young girls as a marriage market and they knew that only two or at most three Seasons were allowed to achieve their goal of matrimony. The girl's first Season, known as 'coming out', marked her entry into Society and her change in status from girl to marriageable young lady, usually at the age of seventeen. The newly married Blanche Cripps wrote to her sister, Beatrice Potter, in 1877: 'you will be in the whirl of the London season again soon. I only hope it may end as happily for you as it did for me last year.'[3] Sybil Lubbock vividly described the perils and pitfalls of 'coming out':

The conditions of a girl's first season at the end of the last century were such as to daunt any but the most assured. To stand upright in front of your mother, in a line with a row of other girls all in front of *their* mothers, obviously waiting to be asked to dance, and yet to wear on your face an expression of happy indifference—that surely was a test of demeanour hard to exact of the socially inexperienced . . . A strong flow of partners once ensured, another difficulty soon presented itself. To dance continuously, to be a success—yes, every mother wished that for her daughter, but not that she should dance continuously with the same person, nor sit out too long or too often, nor above all, seem too pleased to see any one man in particular.[4]

Daughters of the social and political élite also had to undergo the ritual of being presented at Court. Constance Battersea described the drive in the family's 'grand chariot' to the 'execution' at St James's Palace. She and her mother joined a mass of other débutantes and mothers, looking rather like a flock of sheep in long white veils, ostrich feathers and trailing trains. After a long wait in the ante-room, their names were finally announced, allowing them entry into the Queen's chamber where the débutante kissed the royal hand after a deep curtsey.[5] Cynthia Asquith also remembered the ritual with wry amusement:

The metamorphosis called Coming Out was supposed to be effected when you were presented at Court, where the wand was officially waved over your head. The picturesque rites of this social baptism were preceded by weeks of trepidation—weeks busied with long lessons in deportment . . . and panic-stricken rehearsals of my curtsey . . . then there were endless wearisome hours of trying-on.[6]

Many girls enjoyed their first Season and some even succeeded in catching a good husband, usually after meeting at a dance or ball. But there were inevitable disappointments, as with Alice Stanley's second Season in 1847. Her grandmother, Lady Stanley, warned Alice's mother: 'I am afraid you will be obliged to bring her again out of Town without a husband . . . You had better make up your mind quickly, expect nothing—either husbands or partners but let her enjoy her dances as well as she *can* and as she *will* if she does not see you *too* anxious.' Other young girls were like Betty Lytton in 1887: 'she was not an easy girl to please and disliked the common routine of balls etc.' It was all the more of a relief to her family when she captured Gerald Balfour.[7] Kate Courtney remarked on her Potter sisters: 'they go in for the "Season" but are rather cynical over it.' Kate commented on her own final London Season that 'many mistakes had been made, much trouble endured and some lessons learnt'. She was most thankful that she had not married either of the men who proposed to her during that troubled year. Even at sixteen, Beatrice Potter noticed that her clever sister Dorothea was 'totally unadapted to the shams and conventionalities of society and therefore not a favourite generally at balls etc.'[8] Lady Constance Malleson later described her own experience in 1905: 'the same people, the same talk, the same eternal round of so-called gaiety . . .I'll swear I never met an intelligent man during my whole London season.'[9]

For the aristocratic élite, country house weekends provided the

most favourable opportunities for getting to know potential
suitors. Victoria Dawnay in 1885 recalled their 'nice summer
parties at Panshanger, Castle Ashby and Wilton. I think of all the
people who have married since . . . they were always meant to be
marrying parties, and they often succeeded.'[10] In 1863, Lady
Cowper decided that more country house visiting would further
her daughters' prospects, and she hoped for invitations to
Chatsworth, Lord Ailesbury's seat at Tottenham, and 'other
places of public resort'.[11] But not all country house 'marrying
parties' were quite so successful, and Mary Gladstone had a low
opinion of them: 'I still think its a delusion for daughters . . . going
in to dinner each night hooked to a new person, it came to be tiring
work always to be digging in untried ground . . . dining in company
with 20 or 30 palls after a bit.'[12] In 1876, Mary visited her cousin
Gertrude's country seat, Penrhyn Castle:

What a great dull party it is . . . Gertrude is out of sight and Harry
[Gladstone] out shooting all day long . . . there are the 12 Miss Pennants
in the house. That of course makes at once a large proportion
of petticoats—shrivelled Lady Louisa Howard and her short-sighted
daughter, a pinched looking Miss Adeane, a fierce Mrs Hillyard with a
very long cadaverous husband, who preaches. The hope of the party is a
man called Mr Campbell who has luckily left his wife behind him . . . Lady
and Lord and Miss Harlech are coming, we hope they will be more
exciting than they sound . . . Gertrude and Ella are 'marching' after their
husbands shooting in spite of rain and wind.[13]

This contemporary account provides a useful corrective to the
golden memories which selectively recall only the beautiful people
and the matrimonial fantasies realized.

The restrictions and conventions of Society were designed to
make courtship difficult. 'An unmarried woman under thirty could
not go anywhere or be in a room even in her own house with an
unrelated man unless accompanied by a married gentlewoman or a
servant.'[14] Young girls could certainly not go unchaperoned to the
theatre, dances or restaurants. Few public places were open to
women alone, especially those below the critical age of thirty, so
that meetings with young men were usually restricted to the
home, under careful observation. Daughters paid social calls only
in the company of parents or chaperones and while suitable young
men might be permitted to call on Sundays, such visits inevitably
implied that their intentions were serious. A young girl also had to

be careful not to appear to encourage any one man unless she was willing to marry him. As one marriage manual commented, even in 1908 the continuation of such conventions still made it very difficult for single young men and women to make close friendships: 'even now, if a man shows a decided preference for a girl's company his name is at once coupled with hers in a manner which can but alarm'.[15]

Strict chaperonage hindered natural conversation throughout the period, though it was relaxed slightly after the turn of the century. In the 1850s, Lady Chesterfield 'never allowed her daughter to go unescorted by herself into society'. Forty years later, Mrs Humphry Ward wrote to her daughter, Dorothy: 'Of *course* I should not think of letting you go to a big public ball without your mother or some near relation . . . a large ball at your age, without me, is quite out of the question.'[16] Shortly before her marriage to Lord Carrington in 1877, Lily Harbord coyly described a shopping expedition with two other young women: 'alone as there was nobody to take us out. Oh! we were in such a fright.'[17] Even in 1910, when Neville Chamberlain was forty-one years old, his stepmother was anxious about arrangements for escorting his fiancée to a meeting:

Are you providing a chaperone for her? perhaps your Aunt Alice is going? If so, all right—If not, I think 'les convenances' require that she should have one, and if you will let us know one of the girls shall go down in time to accompany you. Much as it may seem the most natural thing in the world to be going off together there are occasions when one has to remember that you are not married yet.[18]

The established aristocracy could perhaps afford to be slightly more relaxed about the rules than the rising middle class, but they had to be careful too. Lady Frances Balfour, daughter of the Duke of Argyll, recalled that in the 1880s 'young men were supposed to be met with in their proper social place, the ball room, and acquaintance was formed there'. The male acquaintances of the Campbell girls were restricted to sons of their parents' friends. Sitting on the same sofa with a young man was regarded as unduly familiar and cause for reprimand.[19]

The aristocracy could not expect to ignore Society's rules without risking the sanction of exclusion from desirable drawing-rooms and from sources of alliance and power. This point is well illustrated by the correspondence between Lady Minto and her son, Bertie Viscount Melgund, from 1864 to 1873. When Bertie was nineteen, Lady Minto was most disturbed at reports that her son and heir was mixing in disreputable company. Her letters of advice are most instructive about Society's code of behaviour. She endeavoured to persuade Bertie to lead a responsible life befitting the heir to the earldom and allowing him to meet suitable potential wives:

[there is] a wide distinction between casual meetings with people in general society and pre-arranged meetings which lead to intimacy with persons of whose character and habits you have no knowledge. You may meet a dozen ladies every day at croquet parties and balls without supposing that you would care to meet one more than another but if you single out any particular person to visit, walk or dance with, the case is altered and you must remember that there are many inconveniences to be avoided besides the grand snare of matrimony.

She pointed out that people who were 'jolly' acquaintances on holiday at a watering place might quickly become objectionable and inconvenient friends in London. Before new acquaintances were admitted to the exclusive circle of friendship, their credentials must be checked to ensure they could happily mix with all other friends and family in all places. She cautioned him against Lady Limerick and her daughter, because some members of the family were disreputable, 'and the fact of a lady being separated from her husband never tells in her favour . . . there are a good many ladies in the world who like to draw young gentlemen on to a point from where it is difficult to retreat with honour'.[20]

Lady Minto's concern increased as Bertie gained a reputation (according to the *DNB*) first as a gentleman jockey, followed for twelve years by 'a curiously adventurous life, playing a part in many wars in many lands'.[21] She hinted to him broadly but vainly in 1869 that Minto House would hold 'yourself and wife, 14 children and 6 horses without difficulty'.[22] The following year, Lady Macgregor wrote from Hampton Court to inform Lady Minto of an unspecified indiscretion in the relationship between her own daughter and Lord Melgund, which both mothers agreed not to discuss further.[23] In 1873, when Bertie was twenty-eight and had already embarked on his adventurous career in foreign parts, Lady Minto again lectured him on his responsibilities as the heir:

'you are at the head of a family which has *ties to the soi*—traditions —and a reputation . . . You can't live a life of mere personal gratification much longer without doing yourself harm.'[24]

Lady Minto had every justification for anxiety, but Bertie ultimately reformed after sowing his wild oats for twenty years. In 1883, at the mature age of thirty-eight, Lord Melgund made an exceedingly suitable marriage to Lord Grey's niece and they had five children. Unfortunately, Lady Minto died too soon to see her efforts rewarded by Bertie's marriage and his subsequent career as Governor-General of Canada and Viceroy of India. Lady Minto's letters not only illustrate the concern to uphold the social conventions, but also the double standard which made a mother merely reproach a son who ignored the rules, whereas she would have intervened far more decisively with a daughter. Lady Frances Balfour's account of the unconventional start to her own engagement in 1878 provides an interesting contrast:

a fresh episode began, startling enough, in our social world This was an invitation from Eustace Balfour asking my brother and myself to luncheon. It transpired that he was a bachelor . . . The invitation was a shock to our conventional ideas, and my parents were quite at a loss what to make of such a proceeding. They had never met the youth still less had they made his acquaintance . . . Great were the heart-searchings and consultations.[25]

If a gentleman had serious intentions towards a lady of his own class, then he usually followed Society's rules closely enough to win the support of the lady's parents. No doubt Lord Melgund was far more careful than Eustace Balfour when he finally sought the hand of Lord Grey's niece.

ENGAGEMENT

The length of an engagement was expected to vary inversely according to the time the couple had previously known each other, but this convention was frequently ignored. Marriage manuals advised long friendships followed by short engagements, on the grounds that sincere affection could be killed by the restraints and irritations of long engagements.[26] Annie Swan's marriage manual argued that a long engagement was superfluous when the couple had known each other for many years and there were 'no obstacles in the way', but it was desirable after only a brief acquaintance.[27] An American manual of 1893 was a little more open on this question than its British counterparts:

Short engagements do not give sufficient time for the parties to get acquainted or to be sure of their own minds. Long engagements may be very unjust to either, especially to the lady, who thereby loses years of bloom that are her endowment of value far above a money estimate; and such long continued courting is apt to have a bad effect by uselessly extending an excited and dissatisfied condition of the affections and passions.[28]

The tensions and frustrations of a two-year engagement are well illustrated by the correspondence between Katharine Ramsay and Lord Tullibardine, later the eighth Duke of Atholl. An early letter of Kitty's in July 1897 shows the misunderstandings so easily produced by frequent absences after hesitant embraces:

How have I managed to give you the impression I don't like what you did on Sunday—that isn't true—I like every proof you can give me that you care for me—it was only that it was a shock at first. Don't think me an awful ass for writing like this—I feel I must write real letters to you as I see you so seldom and hardly ever alone—these letters have to take the place of talks and give me more confidence in it all.[29]

A few days later, Kitty was bold enough to address him by his first name, since 'these plunges must be made some time'. At another meeting a week later, the lovers vowed to give up everything for each other, and Kitty wrote: 'This was quite one of the happiest afternoons, I think, though it came to an abrupt conclusion.' Over a year later, Kitty wrote wistfully that if all went well everything would be quite openly acknowledged in about four months, and 'when we *are* married it won't be in secret'.[30] But the delay continued for reasons not revealed in the correspondence. In September 1898 they experienced problems in arranging meetings: 'but I dare say we will manage and it won't be long before we meet and make up arrears'. Seven months later, Kitty came closer to a daring admission of emotional longing and sexual frustration than was common in the letters of unmarried Victorian girls:

I have a big room here and wish you was [sic] next door—Do you think me dreadful for saying so—Please forgive me if you do . . . I do long for you so and am getting very impatient. I quite got the fidgits yesterday thinking of you and wanting you so much.[31]

Some parents preferred a lengthy courtship in the hope that time and closer acquaintance would 'wash away the magic'. In 1911 Maggie Cowell-Stepney reassured her recently widowed friend, Mary Drew, that she was right to advocate delay in the engagement of her only daughter, Dossie, to Mr Parish while visiting South Africa:

The thing I like *best of all* about him, is his not wanting to bind her—! and I do so hope you will keep to that plan,—and neither announce the engagement or let her wear a ring (except round her neck *inside!*) till she has come back to England and seen lots of other Englishmen.[32]

Other parents learnt from bitter experience that long engagements could end in disaster. Austen Chamberlain's fiancée, Ivy Dundas, had previously endured one of these endless engagements which came to nothing. Her father explained that 'for long years the poor child has been hoping on, where there seems but small chance of realization'. Mary Chamberlain was indignant on Ivy's behalf: 'How could they let that engagement run on for years in such a hopeless way?' Ivy did not make the same mistake twice. She was engaged to Austen within ten days of their first meeting in Algiers, and they were married two months later.[33]

Longer courtships and engagements seem to have been more common than whirlwind marriages among these families, but there were also many examples of the latter. Girls were trained for marriage and fearful of spinsterhood, while their mothers were usually concerned about the matrimonial prospects of several other children. Where there were no impediments, most parents were unlikely to object to short engagements for their daughters. For example, Kate Courtney invited Henry Hobhouse to a private dance at her family's London home. She introduced Henry to her sister, Maggie Potter: 'sudden fancy and after a week or two they are engaged—we all like him'.[34] The man usually sought a speedier courtship if he was already mature in years, had several children by a first wife who needed a mother, or had experienced previous rejection. Even the Gladstone family condoned the lightning courtship and engagement of the Revd Stephen Gladstone and Annie Wilson. Mary Gladstone noted in her diary on 20 December 1884: 'Stephy has been going it like a house on fire having only really known her during this one week.' Even a family death, after much 'wretched discussion', was not allowed to defer

the wedding, which took place a month later. The prime minister
and his wife were, no doubt, relieved, since Stephen was now
forty-one and had had four years to recover from an abortive
courtship of Constance West. But the speedy marriage was only
possible because his new love was eminently suitable, as the
beautiful daughter of a Liverpool doctor: 'so good, so charming,
young, tall, fair and healthy'.[35]

However, people often expressed serious reservations about
whirlwind marriages, either at the time or with the benefit of
hindsight. Violet Maxse met Lord Edward Cecil in February 1894,
became engaged in March and married in June. Although Lady
Salisbury had misgivings about the wisdom of Edward's marriage
to an exuberant atheist of limited means and separated parents,
she gave her blessing: 'I am quite against a long engagement and
so is your father, and we are quite ready for your wedding at any
time! Especially as I see you won't be quite sane till it is over!!!'[36]
But fourteen years later, Edward's sister, Lady Selborne, had
learned from their estranged marriage: 'The experience of Nigs
[Edward] and Violet always makes me anxious that people should
really know each other before they take the desperate step of
matrimony, and a month, even of constant visiting, is not
enough'.[37] Maggie Cowell-Stepney echoed these views in 1902
when Ben Bathurst, MP, brought his young lady over for the day,
both 'wildly in (what they call) love':

. . . but oh how easily and lightly they plunge—a little London
acquaintance [and] 3 delicious balls running—at the third he proposed and
she accepted *at once*, and broke it to her parents who hardly knew him by
sight—and now its done for ever and ever.[38]

INITIATION INTO THE NEW FAMILY AND LOSS OF THE OLD

It was the custom for the female members of the groom's family to
welcome the prospective bride into their family as a new sister and
daughter. The apprehensions of many young girls were painfully
clear in Helen Fox's letter to her prospective sister-in-law, Sarah
Angelina Acland: 'I hope when we meet you will not be
disappointed with me. I am sure you will feel with me that it is
rather trying for a girl being introduced to her future husband's
family.'[39] Angie Acland's reponse to news of the betrothal of her

first brother, Harry, in 1875 was typical of her generous nature: 'I have always longed for a sister and now you will be the first of my brothers to bring me one.'[40] The ordeal was made easier for the brides-to-be in the Acland clan by the warmly welcoming letters which were an essential part of this ritual. Mrs Acland commented on their reception of Margaret Rogers, in 1876: 'I think Maggie is happily settled in now. At first, of course it was strange for her—but you may be sure we did all in our power to prevent that feeling lasting.'[41]

Letters of welcome from the mother and sisters effectively conferred a blessing upon the proposed union and accepted the son's fiancée into their own family. Lady Cowper expressed this process of initiation in a letter to her son on his engagement in 1870: 'You know how I love Katie, and that from the first day I knew her, I felt she could really be a daughter to me.'[42] Laura, Lady Selborne was equally sympathetic when she welcomed her future sister-in-law, Miss Henrietta Riddell, in 1867: 'my position is exactly what I trust yours will be one day—that of one introduced into the family by the most sacred of ties. I have been married now nineteen years . . . I feel quite and absolutely as if they were my own flesh and blood.'[43] The sparkling Tennant sisters had a special talent for affection and passed through this ritual with flying colours. The mischievous Laura wrote to her prospective brother-in-law, Spencer Lyttelton, in January 1885:

Do you know I feel quite 'entered' in the Lyttelton Inventory; and all they have to do now is to dust one a little and see to repairs! I have seen five new relations in 24 hours and feel quite strong and well in spite of it. I think you are a divine family.[44]

Lady Ribblesdale's reaction to her son's betrothal to Charty Tennant in 1876 was highly favourable: 'we shall all love her, for her own sake as well as his'. Charty's mother was naturally relieved, since Lady Ribblesdale's approval was 'of paramount necessity, and without it we must have withheld our consent'.[45] The ritual of welcome combined the themes of the sanctity of marriage with the extension of the circle of family love.

In some cases the ritual of seeking approval was even more daunting because the girl was afraid she might not be welcome. May Burns was well aware that the relationship between Sir William Harcourt and his only son, Loulou, was exceptionally close. She was perceptive when she begged Sir William for his blessing: 'I feel a dreadful intruder but please Sir William, will you like me a little for Loulou's sake and if you will let me you will only find one more person to love you in your very affectionate May.'[46] The new bride was particularly anxious when marrying an older man whose daughter or sister had adopted the role of surrogate wife. The young American, Mary Endicott, was concerned about the reaction of Joseph Chamberlain's daughters to the news that she was to become his third wife. She was well aware that she would usurp Beatrice's place as mistress of the household and mother to her brothers and sisters. Mary was:

touched by the absolute readiness with which you all accepted the change which is to come into your lives . . . Can you appreciate the difference it makes to me to know that you are ready to receive me so warmly? . . . I now feel I indeed have a friend in you already, and have no fear for our relations in the future.[47]

If marriage generally brought a gain to the husband's family, it carried an equivalent loss to the wife's family. This was inevitable when a woman was perceived as actually leaving her parental family on marriage to be incorporated into her husband's family. Disruption of the former family life was often accompanied by a profound sense of loss for the new bride, her sisters and her mother. A year before her wedding in 1899, Katharine Ramsay wrote to her fiancé, Lord Tullibardine:

I get in such funks sometimes about it all and wonder how I can think of leaving my own people and the home I love and all the things with which I have been brought up. It is an awful thing to do when one sits and thinks about it but, of course, every woman who marries does it.[48]

W. E. Gladstone's newly married daughter, Agnes Wickham, wrote to her brother in 1874 that it was strange to be in a new place, away from 'my old belongings, with only one—and that a somewhat new—friend', but she concluded stoically that 'these things are natural'.[49] Most new brides accepted that their duty to their husband entailed the loss of their own family. Mary, Lady Minto, was most distressed when she had to leave for Canada six weeks after her marriage to Bertie, the reformed Lord Melgund, in 1883: 'I had never been away from home and felt the parting

The Rituals of Courtship and Marriage

from my mother and father acutely'.[50] More independent women
like Margaret Mackay, a generation later, were able to say: 'I have
no fears or regrets at leaving home. My home is *you*.'[51] But that
was a most unusual response.

The greatest disruption was experienced by the bride, but her
mother usually felt the deepest sense of loss. An earlier Lady
Minto wrote to Lord John Russell, her new son-in-law, in 1842:
'you have not lived with her five-and-twenty years, and therefore
memory has no place in your affection for her, and you cannot
even now comprehend the' blank she makes to me'.[52] Mrs Maria
Rogers mourned the loss of her 'right-hand' in 1875: 'the first note
of parting wakens rather a tumult in the Mother's heart—and I
must have time to think it over and reconcile myself to the flitting
of another from the home nest'.[53] Louisa, Lady Antrim, was
devastated by the marriage of her daughter in 1897: 'my heart is
very, very heavy . . . at present every day seems to make the pain
of having parted with Sybil deeper . . . I suppose it is realising all
the past is quite over and done and she does not need me any
more!' Lady Antrim tried to pull herself together by acknowledg-
ing that she did not want Sybil to remain a spinster, but it was hard
to stem the waves of jealousy.[54]

The sense of loss was all the greater if the daughter was an only
child or the mother a widow. Mrs Burns wrote to Lady Harcourt
on the engagement of her daughter to Lewis Harcourt in 1898: 'I
can hardly realize the change that has come into my life . . . I shall
be dreadfully lonely without her, for since her father's death we
have been very near.'[55] For Maggie Cowell-Stepney the loss of her
daughter in 1911 was like widowhood. She had brought up her
only daughter, Alcy, on her own, since her husband deserted her
during her pregnancy. Six months before the blow fell, Maggie
discussed her fears with Mary Drew, recently widowed and
likewise afraid of losing her only daughter. Maggie told her
friend that she had dreaded their separation since Alcy was
seventeen: 'the possible son-in-law (changing many times in
personality), always looming over me—and the bewildering
feeling of whether to love or to hate him'. Maggie faced the actual
engagement with despair: 'The whole world is just *wiped out* with
all its interests, and there *is* nothing left—except the Past.' She
tried to be thankful for the years they enjoyed together, but it did
not ease the heartbreak. She described Alcy's marriage as 'the day

of her happiness, and of my sorrow . . . One's life having suddenly all fallen down on one's head, like a pack of cards house—and there being no special reason for building it up again.'[56]

Female bonding between sisters, cousins and childhood friends who grew up together was often strong in this period. Inevitably, many single girls were 'ridiculously fearful about the marriages of one's friends altering the old affections.'[57] Mary Drew admitted that marriage 'does make a huge difference' to female friendships, while Frances Balfour confessed that: 'My friends' marriages always touch me very closely, and I am accused of never liking them to marry! I confess I have a momentary selfish pang when I hear of them withdrawing into the right and inevitable *oneness* of life.'[58] Margaret Ashton was so resentful of her sister's courtship with James Bryce in 1889 that Marion delayed the engagement. Margaret eventually acquiesced in 'the worst', though she warned her new brother-in-law that he would hardly be a welcome visitor.[59]

Beatrice Potter married in her thirties and had many opportunities to mourn the loss of her close friends and all but one of her sisters. In 1881 Beatrice noted: 'The last of the sisterhood, at least of those of my generation, pledged herself! . . . it is sad this last final breakup of the home life with all its ups and downs, through which we have been loving companions—Now I am left alone.' That same year, twenty-three year old Beatrice confessed in the privacy of her diary to feeling rather bitter at the marriage of her sister Maggie to Henry Hobhouse. She did not enjoy a visit to Italy in their company: 'since the necessary break in our absolute intimacy, it is rather painful to me to be with her. She was such a complete companion to me, and as such she is not to be replaced.' Beatrice commented rather sourly that Maggie was 'seedy and miserable, the natural result of the conditions of married existence'. Eight years later the situation repeated itself with the marriage of her close friends, Mary and Charles Booth. Mary was 'absorbed in a new friend for whom she has the same feeling she used to have for me', and the warm affection between them was cooling. Beatrice sadly concluded that 'it is doubtful whether warm sentimental friendships even with women are desirable' for women who must face life alone.[60]

Margot Tennant was intensely unhappy at the loss of her beloved sister Laura to Alfred Lyttelton in 1885:

. . . no one can take Laura's place in my heart but oh! *how* many I ask you will take my place—how many Lytteltons, Gladstones, Talbots . . . this can't be realized and even if she is faithful to me nothing takes the place of a bedroom–bathroom intimacy.[61]

The loss of Laura through marriage was made final by her death in childbirth the following year and Margot was desolate. Determined that in her own case the exclusive relationship of marriage would not alter her friendships, she informed her close friends accordingly when she married Asquith in 1894. Margot wrote to Violet Cecil:

You are a loyal, loving and stimulating friend and I beg you never to let me go—never *never*. Life is horribly sad and difficult even when fixed and illuminated by marriage . . . [I] should *hate* to lose what I have found so sweet in you and your friendship.[62]

Margot begged Lady Ribblesdale: 'you must never withdraw your love. I think in early married life one wants to feel all the old ties of love and encouragement.'[63]

Feelings of loss and resentment by mother, sisters and female friends of the bride were scarcely surprising. Marriage often involved a move to a location closer to the groom's family or occupation. This upheaval was harder for the bride than it would have been for the groom who had usually formed a wider circle of friendships and ties outside family and immediate friends, through his school, university or occupation. The bride was far more dependent on those domestic and family bonds of 'bedroom–bathroom intimacy' which were so often disrupted on marriage. A medical manual of 1892 provided helpful guidance to the bride on the extent of the transformation she should expect in her life:

Marriage is followed by a very much greater change in the circumstances and habits of the wife than in those of the husband. The latter still pursues the daily occupation to which he has been accustomed for years . . . on the other hand, the wife will most commonly find herself in a completely novel position. Her family ties are more completely broken . . . while she will often find herself separated by distance from old friends . . .[64]

WEDDINGS AND HONEYMOONS

The end of the Season was the time for weddings in London among the upper classes. Most weddings took place on Saturdays,

but Sundays and Mondays were also popular. A few marriage and
health manuals mentioned delicately that it was the lady's privilege
to select the actual day of the month: 'it is to her advantage to
select a wedding day from fifteen to eighteen days after the close
of menstruation in the month chosen', apparently to avoid
conception on the honeymoon.[65] But the evidence suggests that
these political families were more concerned about the political
calendar than the menstrual cycle, though the latter may have
been a hidden factor in the bride's suggestions. Weddings in
political families were generally planned for the parliamentary
recesses. May Harcourt was concerned in August 1909 that Robert
Harcourt's wedding 'will not be long delayed so that they can have
the Recess to enjoy themselves in'; Winston Churchill was married
on 15 September 1908 to allow 'a fortnight's joy' before Parliament resumed.[66]

The bridegroom's formal duties were minimal, mainly involving
arrangements for the ecclesiastical part of the ceremony. He had
to buy the gold wedding ring, apply for the license from the
clergyman in his fiancée's parish and pay the fee of £2. 13s. 6d.,
and arrange for the banns to be published on three Sundays prior
to the marriage. It was also customary for the bridegroom
to present his bride and her bridesmaids with their bouquets and
with a piece of jewellery each. Far more onerous were the duties
of the bride and her parents, who were responsible for the
wedding breakfast or feast, the invitations, and all other aspects
of the organization. It was usual to invite only family and close
friends to the post-wedding festivities, though others might be
invited to witness the wedding ceremony. The ceremony had to
take place between 8 a.m. and 3 p.m., though 2.30 p.m. was the
fashionable time. By the 1890s the breakfast banquet was less
common, and was often replaced by an elaborate afternoon tea at
4 p.m.[67]

The bride had to organize her trousseau, her bridesmaids and
the reception of the wedding presents. The usual problems arose
over gifts, as Caroline Philips discovered when she received two
'best' tea services but no dinner service. She asked her fiancé
George Trevelyan: 'Have you any Uncles or Aunts who will give
us a dinner set? . . . give out that we want a dinner service.'[68] The
extravagance of the wedding presents was frequently noted in this
period. Cynthia and Herbert Asquith received hundreds from

strangers as well as friends, since the groom's father was prime minister.[69] Many shared Maud Cecil's sense of guilt at the generosity of their gifts in 1883: 'The upper servants have given me a most lovely silver looking glass and brushes—my thoughts keep running on the curious fact that all these superfluities keep pouring in on me, while so many want bread and coals.'[70] Lady Tullibardine had similar moral qualms in 1899: 'I think it perfectly awful what a lot of people give wedding presents and how much they spend on them.'[71] Elizabeth Haldane commented more caustically on the vast quantities of expensive presents on show at an 1885 wedding where the minister said the couple were starting out in life 'amid great temporal miseries'.[72] The extravagance of such wedding gifts may be partly explained by the custom of exhibiting them at the wedding feast with donor's names attached.

The extent of the wedding trousseau is illustrated by Mary Trevelyan's list of her 'going away' clothes in 1904:[73]

Ball gown	6 combinations
dinner gown	6 nighties
tea gown	2 big stays
every evening gown	2 little stays
every morning gown	3 vests
big cloak	3 spencers
going away hat	1 stiff pants
travelling hat	4 pants summer
dinner jacket	
boots, shoes	
slippers	
12 stockings (4 silk, 4 wool etc.)	

Her fiancé's remark to his mother was interesting: 'I dissuade her from much jewellery, and we have chosen better things than much of the lesser trash which brides get.'[74] Austen Chamberlain's bride, Ivy Dundas, was delighted in 1906 when Mary Chamberlain insisted that she buy her trousseau from her own *haute couturier*, Mr Worth in Paris. But since Ivy's parents were not rich, she was alarmed at the possible expense. Mary Chamberlain accordingly engaged in extensive bargaining with Mr Worth, arranging that the wedding dress would not cost more than 650–800 francs. Ivy also ordered one day and one evening dress from Worth's, as well as stays, blouses, belts and three sets of underlinen. 'Think of me in

Worth dresses!' she proudly told her mother, 'Shan't be able to live up to it at all!'[75]

Later Victorian and Edwardian weddings were generally less spectacular than formerly. Lady Colin Campbell's etiquette manual confirmed that 'altogether, not so much stir is now made at a wedding'. She particularly noticed the change from the formal wedding breakfast to 'afternoon tea and light refreshments', combined with the abolition of 'the tedious custom of proposing a series of toasts'.[76] Lady Muriel Beckwith was convinced that weddings in this period were more subdued than they were to become again by the 1930s: 'the Victorians and Edwardians were more intimate, more serious, more stately, and above all less theatrical. Broadcasting, photographs in the Press, snapshots of the bride and bridegroom, a thousand and one details of publicity now extant, would have been disdained as bad form in the past.'[77]

These views are substantiated by the majority of weddings described in these family papers. Of course, a large minority did indulge in the traditional lavish Society wedding. Many prominent politicians probably felt this was unavoidable, since they could not afford to offend people. The wedding of H. H. Asquith and Margot Tennant in 1894 was celebrated with all the trappings at St George's Church, Hanover Square, the favourite church for Society weddings. Catherine Gladstone described it as 'a very astonishing wedding, full of *ministers*, Prime and Ex', including Balfour, Rosebery and Gladstone. Mrs Gladstone was characteristically unperturbed by their own late arrival, even though 'the tumult of cheering *outside* somewhat disturbed the first words of the marriage Service!'[78] A few weddings were ostentatiously extravagant. The first wedding to be celebrated in Westminster Abbey for many centuries was that between Lord Carnarvon and Lady Evelyn Stanhope in 1861.[79] Lord and Lady Carrington had their wedding in 1878 at the Chapel Royal, Whitehall, with 'all the dear sisters' as bridesmaids, followed by a 'tremendous reception' with a triumphal arch and 'heaps of flowers'.[80] Cynthia Charteris and Herbert Asquith were married at Holy Trinity Church, Sloane Square, in 1910, with 'a formidable retinue—twelve bridesmaids and two pages'.

The majority of weddings in these political families were, however, quite different, with the emphasis on sentiment rather than ostentation. Some expressed a dislike of weddings which involved display for its own sake. In 1869 when Caroline Philips married G. O. Trevelyan she thought 'a wedding and all the paraphernalia is the most absurd and horrid thing in the world, and quite a remnant of barbarism'. She and her father wanted to restrict the invitations to the two families, numbering about forty on the Philips side. When she discovered that G. O. Trevelyan had found an uncle 'to *do the deed*', she asked him to cut it short: 'With due deference to the Prayer-Book, it really wants doctoring and weeding, though part of the marriage service is very fine—though not as good as the Burial service.'[81] Maud Cecil told her fiancé, Willy Palmer, just before their own marriage: 'What a nuisance weddings are—I sincerely pity you to have to assist at two in one month. I think one quite bad enough!'[82]

The desire for quiet weddings with the minimum of fuss was well illustrated by the marriage of Viscount Amberley and Kate Stanley at Alderley in 1866: 'both families had a great objection to a fashionable wedding, with paragraphs in the papers, and photographs of the bride and bridegroom, and lists of guests, and the presents they gave, so a great deal of trouble was taken to keep it a quiet country wedding'.[83] Margaret Potter and Henry Hobhouse also wanted 'a quiet wedding, free from crowds and ceremony and excitement', in 1880. The ideal site for such a wedding was Mr Potter's residence, Rusland Hall, in the Lake District. The bride's sister, Kate Courtney, considered the result was quaint: 'all wedding dresses prohibited and we all came out in old finery—Maggie in short white dress and large white hat, very funny little bride—Henry with coat full of creases seen last at a funeral'.[84] Implicit in these comments was the belief that a wedding should be measured in terms of personal commitment and sincerity of feeling, rather than grandeur and ceremonial. This was illustrated by Mary Chamberlain's description of her own quiet ceremony as 'very solemn and impressive', and her step-son Neville's as 'full of hope, full of seriousness, and the bright promise of the future'.[85]

Some couples carried the reaction against religious ceremonial and conspicuous consumption a stage further. It was customary in Victorian Scotland for the wedding ceremony to be performed in the home. Lord John Russell and Lady Fanny Elliot were married in 1841 in the drawing room at Minto, and over forty years later Elizabeth Haldane attended a wedding in the library of a friend's home.[86] Some people preferred to dispense with the blessing of the church entirely. Sidney Olivier described the 'hurricane' that raged in 1889 'when it became evident that we were not going through a parson's hands. If I had had my freedom I would not have gone through a registrar's either.'[87] Mrs Humphry Ward in 1903 feared that, since George Trevelyan was 'so wholly non-Christian, he looks forward to a civil marriage'.[88] Kate Courtney evidently shared Mrs Humphry Ward's distaste for such a proceeding: 'Our Beatrice is married to Sidney Webb at the St Pancras Vestry Hall—a prosaic almost sordid ceremony—our civil marriages are not conducted with much dignity and seem rather to suggest a certain shadiness in the contracting partners.' Kate was relieved that the next wedding she attended was 'a proper one in a church'.[89]

The marriage of the two socialists John Bruce Glasier and Katharine Conway, in 1893, was by far the most unconventional. Glasier did not want the marriage to follow the rites of any church: 'we will have a quite new and beautiful ceremony. We will inaugurate the new era.' Katharine was entirely sympathetic to this idea, and did not want John even to write to her family:

. . . my relations would kill all they could *see* of our joy—and therefore it were best they saw it not at all till it were complete—A congregationalist parson with a rich bourgeois wife must be spared the agony of a boundless love that laps over all his miserable canons and rate of respectability and scales of income.

So they were married in the presence of two witnesses, with neither priest nor notary-public: 'standing close by the sea-shore with the fair moon shedding her tenderest light upon us I placed a ring upon Katharine's finger . . . and took each other for man and wife. We are therefore wedded according to the simple and beautiful manner of old Scotch custom and common law.'[90]

Wedding rituals were altered by the crises of life, death and war. Lady Frances Balfour's marriage in 1879 took place in the year of her mother's death, and the family were still in mourning: 'My father would never have stood anything like a party, so only relatives were asked . . . There was no formal sit-down meal', but only tea and the cutting of the wedding cake.[91] Pregnant ladies nearing their confinement were not expected to attend weddings; Gertrude Gladstone was excluded from the wedding of her sister-in-law, Mary Gladstone, for that reason in 1886. War also altered matrimonial expectations. During the Boer War, when Ivor Maxse was ordered to return to the Cape, Mary Wyndham

> got into a state of feverish anxiety and said she *must* be married to him before he left. This has made things very difficult to arrange as he may only have two days in England and may not like such a scrummagy [sic] marriage. However I do most deeply sympathize with her after all the horrors of these battles and awful loss of life.

Mary had her way and the wedding took place two weeks later, as Eleanor Cecil noted: '[it was] quite unlike any other I ever went to, and I rather think very much the most attractive—no fuss or snobbery and nothing to take one's attention from the married people themselves'.[92]

Lawrence Stone has sketched the development of the honeymoon from the sixteenth century:

> First, it was no more than a description of the first weeks after marriage, which consisted of a non-stop, sex-segregated public party with the wedding guests, taking place in the home. Next, it became a time of travel, but in the company of others, either a group or the sister of the bride. Finally, in the late-eighteenth and very early nineteenth centuries, it became a time of withdrawal and isolation away from home for private mutual exploration.[93]

Stone overstates the speed and timing of this move to the third stage of the private honeymoon among the upper classes. The Victorian evidence suggests that stages two and three continued to coexist. It was still customary to spend some time on honeymoons with family and friends. May and Loulou Harcourt spent the first week of their honeymoon in 1899 at the family home, Nuneham Park, accompanied for several days by May's mother. May was delighted with the 'gloriously happy week' at Nuneham and found it 'such a joy having Mother with us'. Undeterred by the company, the Harcourt honeymoon then 'migrated to Malvern to Aunt Emma's'.[94] A generation earlier, Loulou had accompanied his father, Sir William Harcourt, and his new stepmother on their 1876 honeymoon in Paris. The honeymoon of Sibell, Lady Grosvenor and George Wyndham in 1887 included visits to his parents at Clouds in Wiltshire and then to Sibell's mother at Lumley Castle.[95] This sort of honeymoon did have the distinct advantage of providing continuity and saving some couples from a sudden, artificial isolation which might have put a strain on an immature relationship.

There were two distinct types of honeymoon among these families. For those honeymoon couples with appropriate social connections, it was common practice to borrow a stately home or country house from wealthy friends or relatives. Louise Childers in 1885 borrowed Bedwell Park in Hertfordshire. Catherine Gladstone a year earlier offered Hawarden Castle for a week to an engaged couple who already had the option of Althorp.[96] The Duke of Buccleuch lent Bowhill to Lord John and Lady Fanny Russell in 1841, and the Countess Waldegrave lent Strawberry Hill to Sir William Harcourt in 1876.[97] The Balfour family honeymooned at Whittingehame, the family home in Scotland. Lady Georgiana Peel described the typical upper-class Victorian honeymoon of this type in 1867:

> we proceeded to Woburn Abbey for the honeymoon, which was very kindly put at our disposal by my cousin Hastings . . . He most kindly left a whole staff of servants to look after us, besides horses, carriages, and everything we could want . . . My uncle, Charles Russell, lived close by, and would often drop in to see us . . .[98]

A honeymoon of this nature was scarcely private or isolated. Lady Cowper warned her son Francis in 1870: 'I think you are right not to honeymoon at Panshanger; for judging by the state of excitement there, respecting your marriage, I think you would live in a constant state of triumphal arches.'[99] New brides must often have been self-conscious in the presence of inquisitive servants and well aware that this was a trial period for their own capacities as household manager. Annie Gladstone wrote to her formidable new mother-in-law, from her honeymoon at Halkyn Castle, Holywell, in 1885. After thanking Catherine dutifully for all her good advice, she continued: 'I hope that this holiday will not only be a happy one; but a useful one in preparing me for the many duties which as you say are waiting for me at Hawarden'.[100]

Those couples who preferred to avoid servants and family, or who were less well-endowed with available country seats, chose to travel in Europe. Even there, they sometimes had to insist on their desire for privacy, as did Margaret Mackay in a letter to her fiancé, Alex Shaw, in 1913:

> The thought of going to Alba and visiting your sister and husband's people

alarms me very much, just then I mean. I'd love to go afterwards. It is a comfort to remember that Louise is sure to understand my feelings as *she* put not only the Channel but the length of France between herself and relations for *her* honeymoon!!![101]

No doubt Caroline Philips and George Trevelyan could have found a suitable country house for loan, but they also preferred a European travelling holiday, moving from Brussels down the Rhine to Switzerland and back through Paris.[102]

Honeymoons ranged from the sublime to the mundane, but few reached the idyllic heights described by Laura Lyttelton in 1885: 'We are on the top of the cloud bars, and behind the stars . . . It is all like a dream one wants never to awaken from, and For Ever and for Ever seems too short for such wonderful stillness of storms, such rest and peace and complete drinking up of the wine of Love.'[103] Laura's husband echoed her sentiments, though more prosaically:

barring just an hour or two of strangeness and perhaps of depression (begotten of fatigue and reaction from the unnatural riot of the few days preceding the wedding) the time is a noble one full of tranquil harmony, fruitful in blessed hopes for the future founded on the sure experiences which only solitude can give.[104]

Maggie Cowell-Stepney believed such experiences were rare indeed, commenting in 1901: 'so many people have confessed to me that their honeymoons were miserable'.[105] For most couples the truth may have been somewhere between these two extremes. Some seemed to settle very quickly into relaxed contentment, especially if they were left to themselves. Mary Gladstone learned from her cousin, Gertrude, in 1875 that her two-week honeymoon with George Pennant had flown: 'their manners were very cosy—she has not felt shy over anything but has enjoyed the whole thing.'[106] Blanche Cripps wrote in 1877 that 'Willie and I are on such perfectly easy terms together that we might have been married for centuries and the time when we were not husband and wife seems already quite traditional, there is no doubt that we are very happily suited to each other'.[107]

Accounts of honeymoons tended to concentrate on literary and cultural activities, as if they gave some public purpose to the whole ritual—or perhaps the emphasis on the ordinary provided a cover for self-consciousness. James Bryce taught Marion some botany, 'but geology and Dante still slumber in our trunks. We read a little Virgil one day.'[108] Caroline Philips's idea of a perfect honeymoon with George Trevelyan was that he should read to her a great deal from 'suitable books' while she sketched.[109] Herbert Gladstone's ideal honeymoon consisted of 'music, gardening, golfing, singing —such delicious oneness of interests'.[110] Beatrice and Sidney Webb read at intervals during the first day of their honeymoon, 'by way of relieving the preoccupation of the first hours of married life'. Later in Dublin they conducted an 'unsuccessful investigation into that ramshackle race and its affairs . . . Hence to Belfast. Here we did some serious work.'[111] Meriel Talbot was less intense and perhaps more typical. Her diary entry for the second day of her honeymoon noted six letters received and five written. She continued: 'Pouring most of the day. Went out a little. Began the White Lady by Wilkie Collins.' Lady Sherbrooke's diary noted numerous letters written and received, long walks whenever it was not raining, and frequent games of billiards.[112]

These rituals of courtship and marriage were the public face of a largely concealed and complex process of marital selection among the upper-middle and upper classes in Victorian and Edwardian Britain. The continuation of ruling-class 'Society' was based on economic power as well as political influence, and the question of capital was fundamental in any prospective upper-class marriage. The role of these economic and social interests in marriage will be explored in the next chapter.

2

Money and Marriage

MARRIAGE was the most important social institution for the great majority of women in Victorian and Edwardian Britain. Yet the history of marriage is one of the more neglected fields of Victorian social history, especially the history of marriage as a social and personal experience. It has generally been studied in Britain in the context of the history of the family with an emphasis on earlier centuries. For example, Lawrence Stone in *The Family, Sex and Marriage in England, 1500–1800* (1977) and Edward Shorter in *The Making of the Modern Family* (1976) have developed important arguments about the evolution of marriage and the family over several centuries. They see the family in the sixteenth century as patriarchal and authoritarian, with members tied by deference and obligation rather than affection. Marriage was formal and distant, involving limited emotional commitment and maximum emphasis on economic and reproductive interests. Stone and Shorter argue that during the next four centuries, family relationships were increasingly determined by affection rather than economic interest, as the family became a closed and private unit.[1]

These general trends were reflected in the changing criteria used for selection of marriage partners over the centuries. Stone emphasizes two major factors involved in making the marriage choice. Up to 1660, the predominant motive at the top and bottom of the social scale was the economic or social interest of the family, so that marriage was a contract for the exchange of concrete benefits to the parents. After 1660 there was a change in 'emphasis on motives away from family interest and towards well-tried personal affection', which at its best could mean a marriage of long-term companionship and compatibility. Stone further argues that before 1660 the choice of spouse among substantial property owners was made entirely by the parents, though increasingly the children were granted some right of veto. The major transformation took place between 1660 and 1800, 'with the children now normally making their own choices, and the parents being left with no more than the right of veto over socially or economically unsuitable candidates'.[2]

The works of Stone and Shorter are stimulating, pioneer attempts to chart the development of the family over centuries. Inevitably both books suffer at times from sweeping generalizations based on limited evidence, scattered in time and location. Such ambitious surveys over three centuries restrict sources to random printed material, which tends to be dominated by notable males.[3] But, as Michael Anderson concludes, 'these scholars almost alone have published work on these issues of meaning and, on many themes, the body of evidence that they have assembled is strong enough at least to pose a challenge to others to find new sources and develop new ways of undertaking this essential task.'[4] My aim here is to examine significant aspects of Victorian and Edwardian marriage, using extensive primary material for a specific class group over a more limited period of time. My focus is on women, who have little place in Stone's work, and on a period which has been surprisingly neglected by family historians. The primary factors of social and economic interest and affection isolated by Stone will be analysed, and also subsidiary factors such as health, religion, politics and age.

PARENTAL CONTROL AND INFLUENCE

By the mid-nineteenth century middle- and upper-class British marriages were no longer strictly arranged and controlled by parents. However, informal regulation was vital, since the British upper class still sought to prevent undesirable alliances while permitting controlled access to social advancement by deserving new wealth. It was possible to allow children greater freedom of choice because a series of complex social institutions had been developed during the eighteenth century to control the courting process. County balls and assemblies combined with the elaborate ritual of the London Season to provide a safe national marriage market for the élite.

In addition to the careful regulation of the national market, most parents exercised some influence in guiding their daughter's choice. From the mid-nineteenth century outright veto was rare, because it was not often needed. Those who did apply the veto were usually very rich industrialists or members of the higher echelons of the aristocracy; it was they who had the greatest property or social status at stake. Hugh Bell, the wealthy son and heir of the millionaire ironmaster, Sir Lowthian Bell, was exceptionally fussy about his daughter's choice of a husband. The younger son of an earl was not considered good enough for Molly Bell in 1903 and she married instead the heir to a baronetcy. Molly's half-sister Gertrude was more unfortunate. In 1892 during a visit to Persia, Gertrude Bell, traveller and scholar, fell in love with Henry Cadogan, a secretary at the British Legation in Tehran. After several months in Cadogan's company in Persia, twenty-four-year-old Gertrude wrote to inform her parents of her engagement and asked their permission to marry. They strongly disapproved of her engagement to 'an impecunious diplomat', doubting whether Mr Cadogan could make her happy, especially as they understood he had gambling debts. They insisted that Gertrude return alone to England and her father remained obdurate in his veto. Mr Cadogan died of pneumonia nine months later and Gertrude Bell never married.[5]

A direct veto was also imposed in 1907 on the *bon affaire* between Lady Eileen Elliot, eldest daughter of the fourth Earl of Minto, and a man named Ross, whom the family considered unsuitable. This relationship developed when Lady Eileen was twenty-three and separated from her parents during her father's term as Viceroy of India. Eileen reacted to the veto by taking refuge in illness, drugs and drink. She was living with her aunt, Louisa Lady Antrim, who was shocked at the verdict of a consultant:

Eileen has been living on sleeping draughts and stimulants. 2 nights out of every 3 she has had draughts and also burgundy at luncheon and dinner—no wonder she felt faint. It accounts for everything—ill health, palpitations, hysteria and all.

Eileen subsequently 'staggered the Doctors, when she told them how much gin she used to drink', and they also found that 'one of her kidneys is loose and it drags at its moorings'. The family sent her to a nursing home for a 'rest cure', to be looked after by a nurse and a doctor; she was allowed no visitors and no letter-writing. Louisa Antrim described the home as a prison.[6] Eight years later, at the age of thirty-one, Eileen married Lord Francis

Montagu-Scott, sixth son of the Duke of Buccleuch and a captain in the Grenadier Guards. He had served as ADC to her father in India and was presumably more acceptable to the Minto family than the unfortunate Ross.

A year before Eileen's ill-fated affair, Lady Minto's propensity for influencing the marriage market was all too clear. She wrote to her sister, Louisa Antrim, in 1906, asking her to 'scan the peerage' for suitable young men to meet her daughters. Louisa obligingly replied:

Why not Lord Glamis—nearly 22—he is quite delightful in every way and has the most charming parents. I believe the Alfred Fitzroy son is nice—I don't know what age but he might be worth thinking of. Zena also says Lord Compton is so perfectly delightful. Why not ask him out as a cousin. Lord Lucas I know you are prejudiced against and also I think he is surly and sober and has only one leg. All the same I like the sound of him. I suppose Ed Wood is no good . . . Young Curzon I should certainly ask—I like his face.[7]

Lady Minto was highly effective in securing gentlemen of appropriate social status for her daughters; Ruby married the Earl of Cromer, while Violet's two husbands were Lord Lansdowne's younger son and Lord Astor of Hever.

Many parents managed to discourage unsuitable suitors before a formal veto became necesary. In 1892 Mr John Wallop, brother of the sixth Earl of Portsmouth, became fond of Katherine, second daughter of the sixth Earl of Stanhope. They met during a European holiday, which provided a more relaxed environment for the formation of unsuitable alliances. Evelyn, Lady Stanhope, described to her husband her efforts to discourage the young man:

Mr Wallop has attached himself more and more to us lately, in a way difficult to avoid; he is better off than most younger sons (a thousand p.a. now, and more to come), and has brains; he is rather taken by Katie but it would not do, and I think we shall steer clear of its complications.

Mr Wallop told Lady Stanhope so confidentially about his position and income that she felt he must have an ulterior motive. He emphasized particularly that his brother, Lord Portsmouth, had no children. But though he was nicer and cleverer than his brother, 'he has no set purpose in life at present, and he is 32'.[8] *Who's Who 1916* does not suggest that John Wallop acquired any special direction in life, but then his real sin was his failure to be the eldest son. Neither he nor Katherine ever married and their lives might have been very different if Lady Stanhope had been less ambitious in the marriage stakes.

Parental influence was usually more subtle and more akin to the powers attributed by Bagehot to Queen Victoria—to encourage, to warn and to be consulted. Lady Antrim interfered less with her own daughter's choice of husband than did her sister but she tried to hurry matters along. In 1896 she hoped the engagement of her daughter, Sybil, to Vivian, Baron Bicester, would shortly be announced. She now appreciated the depth of Lord Bicester's affection for Sybil and was ashamed at dismissing it so lightly a year earlier. But Sybil was keeping her ardent suitor 'dangling in suspense'. Lady Antrim 'did not like to pledge' Sybil, but encouraged Lord Bicester to hope: 'I think she is sure to have to care for him on further acquaintance and will be happy.' Lady Antrim wanted grandchildren badly and assured Lord Bicester that Sybil adored children: 'So I feel sure he will do *his* best to accommodate her with a family!!'[9] They married three months later and had seven children, which should have pleased Lady Antrim.

Where a girl married against her parents' wishes, there were occasional instances of parental retribution. One such example took place in 1874: 'the Osbornes are so irrevocably angry with their eldest daughter who married a Mr Blake that Mrs O has entirely cut her out, settled the estate on the Duchess of St Albans and her children.'[10] But it was more common for parents to acquiesce in their daughter's choice, however reluctantly. Lady Jeune argued that by the 1890s the women's movement had encouraged women to become more independent and voice their opinions, making 'maternal coercion an impossibility . . . any mother would find it very difficult . . . to force her [daughter] to marry a man solely because he was hugely rich.'[11] There was some truth in this, though the rules of Society generally restricted choice to the suitable candidates and reduced the possibility of dissent.

Sometimes parents opposed a match because the correct courtship procedure had not been followed; they resented not being consulted more than they objected to the candidate. Lady Frances Balfour described the reaction of her father, the Duke of Argyll, when Eustace Balfour proposed to her in 1878:

The Duke was much puzzled. Here was a youth with whom he was as yet unacquainted. This young man had asked his daughter to marry him, his competence was modest, and he had chosen architecture as his profession, I think there was some confusion in the Duke's mind between an Architect and a Builder and Contractor. My mother did the sensible thing, and asked Eustace to call on her, and that at once solved the personal difficulty.[12]

Jeannette Beveridge likewise aroused parental resentment over her engagement in 1908 to Richard Henry Tawney, her brother William's friend. Her main fault was to announce her 'good fortune' to her friends before her parents heard about it, and the news came as a great shock to them. She had been in love with Tawney since 1901, but kept her secret from her family because she was unsure of Tawney's feelings. She had even upset her mother by rejecting two good proposals in the interim. Her parents considered Tawney unsuitable; his prospects as a university lecturer were uncertain and there was some history of insanity in his family. William helped to reconcile their parents to the match, while Jeannette protested to her mother: 'The parents cannot surely under such circumstances refuse assent because of their own personal likes or dislikes or any ground except absolutely definite ones of health or character.'[13]

Mothers of young daughters could be powerfully offended if outsiders intervened in matrimonial management, thereby contravening the unwritten code of courtship and usurping the maternal role. Lady Vernon was furious when she discovered that Lady Cairns had stage-managed the courtship of her own daughter, Alice, in 1895. Alice's sister, Mildred Stanhope, related the saga:

Alice's engagement has caused much agitation for my Mother knew nothing of the man or any of his family; and was more than vexed with Lady Cairns for promoting and arranging the whole matter when the girls were staying with her in Scotland without giving Mama even a hint of what was taking place or Alice having an idea he cared for her; in fact Lady Cairns invited him back on purpose to propose; it came like a bombshell upon Mama in August and has been simmering ever since. Alice is certainly radiantly happy and Mama seems satisfied now with his excellence.[14]

In some cases parental opposition took a more nebulous form which, in the case of widows, revealed a natural reluctance to lose a child and be left alone. Herbert Samuel's sister, May, was most concerned about their mother's hostility to Herbert's forthcoming marriage in 1897:

> It is most distressing that she should have taken it so to heart . . . From what I can conclude I think you should have spoken to her earlier of your intentions—she is getting old now and I think the suddenness must have upset her . . . We must see how the Mother can be fixed up in the future as she will feel lonely in that big house.

Their mother's 'nervous and anxious condition of mind' led to considerable family misunderstanding and tension until Clara Samuel finally relented, saying that she would be content if Herbert was happy.[15] Mary Drew experienced similar misgivings in 1911 about her daughter's engagement to Francis Parish, a 60th Rifleman, but at least Mary kept her reservations from her daughter. She sadly confided to her friend, Maggie Cowell-Stepney, that Francis Parish 'was not quite big enough, out of the way enough' for her only daughter, who might suddenly wake up to see him as a 'commonplace very plain young man'. Maggie sympathized: 'you feel that it is really *too* flat that he shouldn't be a Fairy Prince instead of a Parish.'[16]

Parents interfered most when they had great social status or family fortunes at stake, especially if they were ambitious, upwardly mobile families. But few used the direct veto on their child's choice of partner since it was rarely necessary. Society's elaborate rules of courtship enabled children of the élite to choose a partner from a reasonably wide national range of socially acceptable candidates.

SOCIAL CONSIDERATIONS: THE UNSPOKEN ASSUMPTIONS

The two interrelated factors of social and economic interest, which traditionally determined marriage choice, remained dominant in upper-class Victorian and Edwardian society. At first sight it seems surprising that there was little discussion of social status and class background when these families considered potential partners for their daughters. But class compatibility was so fundamental that the rules of Society ensured that it rarely did become an explicit issue. It could usually be taken for granted that the couple came from similar social background, since young people in these political families would move only in the appropriate circles. Girls would have little or no opportunity to meet men of inferior class status in a situation conducive to courtship. At the highest social level, as Sir Edward Cadogan regretted later, 'the old English aristocracy were a very circumscribed community. If any of its members married outside the charmed circle, it was not looked upon with favour by our relatives. That circumstance by itself restricted the choice of partner for life.' Also, as Stone argues, in most cases 'close parent-child bonding has developed, so that parents are reasonably satisfied that their own values have been internalized in their children and the latter will therefore make their selection from within the socially appropriate group.'[17]

Yet Society's courtship rules were sufficiently flexible to allow some social mobility to deserving new wealth and occasionally to outstanding female beauty. Cadogan overstated the exclusiveness of the male members of the aristocracy; it has recently been calculated that 'if all male members of peerage families are taken together, then their marriages were predominantly outside the peerage group' since the seventeenth century. There was some scope for ambitious families with social aspirations to marry off their daughters to younger sons of the aristocracy.[18] By the later nineteenth century an alliance between an aristocrat and a successful industrialist's daughter was considered perfectly suitable. Indeed, wealthy industrialists' daughters and American heiresses could afford to pick and choose among the sons of the aristocracy, with so many landowners suffering from the depression. It was also recognized that a certain degree of elevation was possible for beautiful women with money. More unusual were some of the women in the exclusive social group known as the Souls, who achieved social elevation through their beauty, wit and brains rather than their money. But social mobility was kept within careful limits by the rules of Society.

When these elaborate social rules were broken or ignored, the couples who had crossed the class barriers in marriage risked the scorn of Society. Few did so. Lord Aldenham's daughter, Edith Gibbs, commented in 1890: 'Charlie Shaw Stewart has married a German Governess older than himself and not a lady. A Winchester friend of Herbert's [her brother] has married his cook, which is worse!' Lady Stanhope was horrified in 1889 to learn that

Lord Wenlock's sister was marrying a Venetian librarian. When Lord Carnarvon's daughter, Winifred, married beneath her in 1886, a typical response came from Lady Stanhope: 'I am disappointed at Winifred's marriage, but we must hope she will be happy.'[19] Winifred's unsuitable first husband died within a year of the marriage, and in 1890 she married Lord Gardiner's son, Herbert, later Lord Burghclere, who was considered 'much better suited to Winifred than his predecessor'. But even then poor Winifred did not quite satisfy the arbiters of social class. Lady Abercromby had her doubts about the match, since Herbert Gardiner was the illegitimate son of an actress whom Lord Gardiner subsequently married; moreover, 'Mr Gardiner has been a good deal in the Breadalbane set which is not a very good one.'[20]

The courtship of Henry Fowler, later Lord Wolverhampton, and Ellen Thorneycroft, daughter of a very wealthy Staffordshire ironmaster, also illustrates the problems in crossing the class barriers. On her father's death in the 1850s Ellen was left rich: 'much sought after for worldly as well as personal considerations, and [was] expected by her family to make a good match'. The family was horrified when Ellen showed her preference for the poor son of a Wesleyan minister 'who had no possessions but his brains and no heritage'. Fowler had determined from childhood to marry Ellen Thorneycroft and also to become MP for Wolverhampton. Their courtship was marred by the perpetual pressure exercised by her family to separate them, and by the inevitable misunderstandings when 'a woman's home-life and her heart-life are entirely out of tune'.[21]

By the rules of Society, Beatrice Potter accepted that Sidney Webb's humble social status meant that she could not marry him during her father's lifetime 'without grieving the old man past endurance'. On her father's death, Beatrice shocked her sisters with the sudden news of her intended marriage. One sister, Mary Playne, pointed out that it was as much the responsibility of Mr Webb as of the Potter family to bridge the social gulf: 'If he thoroughly dislikes and disparages the class to which we belong and the traditions we think have a real value, it is not likely there will be much sympathy between us.' Beatrice herself was only too well aware of the social irregularity: 'On the face of it it seems an extraordinary end to the once brilliant Beatrice Potter . . . to marry an ugly little man with no social position and less means.'[22]

But Beatrice overcame her dread of meeting Sidney's family in a dingy and crowded lower-middle-class house, and determined to cast off the 'old shell' with its wealthy upper-middle-class assumptions. She was well aware that 'I shall in the first instance suffer—even in my work—for my step downwards in the social scale', but it would be a worthwhile sacrifice for a happy marriage.[23]

Another socialist, Margaret Gladstone, further down the social ladder than Beatrice Potter, took a similar step in marrying Ramsay MacDonald. She came from a professional middle-class family with substantial means, while he was the illegitimate son of a semi-illiterate, working-class mother. MacDonald himself was so 'painfully conscious of the social gulf between them, and nervous about facing her relatives', that Margaret chided him for his narrow-minded concern about social convention.[24] But few other women of their class had the courage, the opportunity, or the inclination to take a step which daunted even Beatrice Potter. Margaret Gladstone and Beatrice Potter were exceptional women, able to move down the social ladder partly because of their own commitment to the socialist cause and partly because Society could not wholly deny the merits of their chosen partners.

MONEY AS A PREREQUISITE FOR MARRIAGE

It was generally agreed that a good marriage required good money. Economic interest may not have been the overwhelming criterion for matrimony that it was in the sixteenth century, but it still consumed more time and passion in negotiating matches than all of the other considerations combined. To some extent of course, it is impossible to separate social status and economic advantage, so that discussion of marital finances often related to the social status associated with various degrees of wealth. There was also a very practical reason for the emphasis on the financial aspects of marriage in the second half of the nineteenth century. Lady Jeune argued in 1898 that the 'modern mother' must naturally reject a prospective son-in-law who 'cannot at least provide her [daughter] with the necessaries of life' because of 'the higher standard of comfort which modern society requires'.[25] In the last two decades of the century the upper class was concerned about declining land values and the rising cost of living. It was assumed that a couple should marry only when the male was able to support his wife in her accustomed manner.

Wealth was even more important to political families, because brides with money could help to support an expensive career. Charles Dilke's second wife, Emilia, pointed out before their marriage in 1885: 'outsiders may quite naturally argue that for a man "eaten up . . . by political ambition" a woman who didn't bring great connection or great fortune is an impossibly bad match'.[26] Money was essential for younger political aspirants. Hugh Bell, the millionaire ironmaster, opposed the suggestion that his daughter Molly might marry Geoffrey Howard, the second son of the Earl of Carlisle. Molly noted in her diary: 'we should have been very happy but there was always the insuperable parent difficulty', as well as their lack of money. Molly informed Geoffrey in 1903 that marriage 'would need far greater affection on his side than on mine, as marriage for him means giving up his politics. On £1,500 you cannot keep a seat and a wife.'[27] Even Geoffrey Howard generously admitted that Molly's subsequent engagement to Charles Trevelyan was 'such a good match'. Charles was a wealthy elder son and heir; his father, G. O. Trevelyan, was prepared to pay his political expenses in addition to a substantial allowance.

Money was undoubtedly a vital prerequisite for marriage in most cases. Even if money was not necessary for its own sake (which was rare), the possession of means was thought to say something about the character of the man concerned. Hugh Childers was well aware of this when in 1885 he asked his solicitor to investigate the financial position of Stephen Simeon, who wished to marry his daughter, Louise. The lawyer discovered that Simeon's fortune had gradually disappeared since he came of age, because an older acquaintance had led him into speculation resulting in heavy losses. Simeon, however, had paid off all but £3,000 of the whole debt, and the lawyer concluded that the affair did not 'at all affect his character'. But Childers insisted that Simeon try to recover the money still owing to him and also establish a life insurance policy for £3,900, with a most reluctant elderly uncle acting as security. It was not surprising that Childers emphasized the need for a settlement clause to ensure that any money Louise received after marriage was reserved for her and her children, 'so that Stephen could not touch the capital'.[28]

It was generally assumed that if the financial circumstances were inadequate then the couple must wait until they became more prosperous before marrying. Of course, the assessment of 'adequate means' was directly related to the parents' current standard of living. The aim was to ensure that their daughter's marital establishment corresponded closely to the level of comfort she had become accustomed to in her parents' home. 'Adequate means' bore little relation to the parents' own standard of living when they married a generation earlier, and still less to realistic financial assessments of current living expenses. It related far more closely to the concept of maintaining social status, and rising expectations over succeeding generations.

This state of affairs was taken for granted in the second half of the century, and is well illustrated by the case of Evelyn Baring, Lord Cromer. In 1862 he fell in love with Ethel Errington, but:

[his] means were slender; his private resources, with the addition of his army pay, gave him an income of £400 a year. Marriage on this pittance was clearly out of the question; what, then, was he to do? Neither of them doubted; he would work and she would wait. With the attachment came the faith which is capable of moving mountains.

After fourteen years of patient waiting, all the more trying while Baring was in India, the deaths of Baring's mother and his fiancée's father provided 'small incomes' enabling the lovers at last to marry in 1876.[29] A decade later, Mary Bryce reported that Olive Brooks was engaged to a curate with no money, 'so they must wait for some years'.[30] This practice of lengthy marital postponement continued even up to the First World War. H. H. Asquith's son, Raymond, waited several years to marry. His fidelity to his chosen bride, through the long engagement imposed upon them by his lack of money, was exemplary.[31] When Arnold Ward was about to propose in 1907, his formidable mother, Mrs Humphry Ward, was afraid lest 'the very natural demands put forward might be more than could be possibly met—Then you would have to wait'.[32] Edward Cadogan, sixth son of Earl Cadogan, a barrister and aspiring politician, contemplated and rejected marriage in the same period: 'I felt that until my position in the world was more assured, and until I could make humanly sure of a successful career, I did not want to marry.' Cadogan also blamed strict primogeniture within the old landed aristocracy for his failure to marry, since the eldest sons inherited estates, income and title:

younger sons, who had been brought up in the same extravagance and luxury as the eldest, found themselves with only a few hundreds a year to marry, to make a home and to rear children. It is not surprising that they hesitated to take the plunge. It was only natural too that the daughters of these ruling families gave their preference to the inheritors of a proud title and wide acres, rather than to younger sons who lacked these advantages.[33]

The Acland family scrupulously obeyed the unwritten rules regarding the financial prerequisites for respectable marriage. In the summer of 1875, when Henry Acland of the Oxford branch of the family pressed his suit on Margaret Rogers, he met with a lukewarm reception from her family. Mrs Rogers told Mrs Acland that they could not marry at once, though the Rogers would be pleased 'when there are means'.[34] Henry's father wrote on his betrothal three months' later: 'With the uncertainty of your future work it must remain perhaps for some years, very doubtful where or when you may hope to unite your lives into one Home—that is in God's hands.' His mother was no more optimistic. She fervently hoped that Henry would soon have the means to render marriage prudent, but 'I fear you may still have a great trial of patience, and you must face it boldly and bravely now and be like Jacob when he had to serve his 7 years.' Fortunately for all concerned the sentence was unexpectedly reduced to three years, by which time Henry's hard work had secured the vital financial resources.[35]

The Devon branch of the family took an equally strict view when financial misfortune obliged Agnes Acland and Fred Anson in 1883 to delay their marriage for what initially was an indefinite period. Fred had sunk £6,500 capital in a firm from which he was subsequently 'expelled' for his views on sugar trading. He then spent years recovering his good name, his money and his self-respect, by starting up his own business. Sir Thomas and Lady Acland laid conditions upon Fred to establish his new career on a firm foundation before marrying their daughter. A year later, Fred's father urged Agnes: 'don't put it off too long', and Agnes was proud that Fred had started his new business, so that 'our happy future is getting to look more possible'. She asked Fred if she might tell her parents 'in perfectly general terms that you are making a fresh start?'[36] By June 1885, Fred's aunt, Lucy Anson, was glad that he was more hopeful about his business and able to fix the date for the wedding earlier than expected: 'after having waited so long you and Agnes will be rewarded for your patience'.[37]

MARRIAGE SETTLEMENTS

There is little information in marriage manuals or elsewhere about marriage settlements and the precise financial requirements of a suitable marriage. The *Etiquette of Good Society* was not very specific in 1893:

> In cases where the lady possesses a large fortune, or where the gentleman has little besides love to offer, it is considered the more honourable course for him to seek the parent's consent before the daughter's . . . It is a father's duty to go thoroughly into the subject—to examine future prospects, to weigh the purse, to speak of deeds—not 'doughty deeds', but parchment ones—and settlements, and dower.[38]

Mary Scharlieb merely commented in *The Seven Ages of Woman* that some knowledge of the prospective husband's financial position had always been customary, and the bride's father was usually expected to state what he could do for his daughter.[39] Vague comments of this nature assisted parents little and help historians even less.

Three important points need to be underlined about marriage settlements. First, the earned income of the bridegroom was not taken into account in matrimonial negotiations. Parents were expected to provide the financial support for their sons and daughters who were about to be married, and to ensure that they could continue to live at their existing level. Second, there is a widespread assumption that the major contributor to a marriage settlement was the bride's father, who provided the 'dowry'. In practice, both sets of parents were expected to contribute as much as they could reasonably afford, and, ideally, equal amounts.

Third, while the legal situation concerning the property rights of married women was reformed during this period, in fact this had little impact on upper- and upper-middle-class families. The reform was more symbolic than real. The wife had no independent legal rights, since 'by marriage the very being or legal existence of woman is suspended', as Blackstone put it in 1765. Before the Married Women's Property Act of 1870, under common law the wife's personal property (including money, stocks and shares and personal belongings) went to her husband. But there was one law for the rich and another for the poor. Approximately one wife in ten had the benefit of a marriage settlement, by which the wealthy could secure the wife's property through a trust under the law of equity. Such trusts enabled a woman's family to designate certain property as her 'separate estate', free from her husband's common-law rights, to be held for her benefit by a trustee. In the 1868 debate on the Married Women's Property Bill, Robert Lowe protested that 'every marriage settlement that is made is a tacit protest' against the common law. Russell Gurney commented: 'There is probably not a Member of this House who, upon the marriage of a daughter, does not pronounce his condemnation of the principle of our common law by securing to her, by means of a settlement, the enjoyment of her property.' The 1870 Act permitted wives to retain property or earnings acquired after marriage, and subsequent legislation in 1882 allowed them to keep property owned at the time of their marriage.[40]

Women in the political families in this study were among the ten per cent protected by marriage settlements, so that the reforming legislation of the 1870s and 1880s had little direct effect upon them. Evidence has survived about the negotiations over marriage settlements for more than twenty-five marriages in these families (see Table 1, pp. 66–67). This material is sufficient to allow a reconstruction of the customs relating to such settlements in the period 1860–1914. The formal marriage settlement involving a written contract was originally one part of the complex law of entail by which substantial landed properties were protected from subdivision. The daughter's 'portion' or dowry in the richer families would often include her share of her mother's marriage portion, together with an additional sum granted by her father. In most wealthy families, by the second half of the nineteenth century, the daughter's marriage portion was considered the equivalent of the annual allowance granted to sons at the age of twenty-one. It was customary for a certain sum to be granted to the daughter on marriage, according to the father's means and number of children, and then a larger sum would be inherited at the father's death. Usually the woman's portion, the capital sum in the trust fund settlement, could not be touched. She obtained only the annual interest on that capital sum, which was paid to her for life by the trustees for her 'sole and separate use', to be spent as she wished. The husband would have use of the interest for life if he survived his wife and if he provided for the children's maintenance and education. The income would subsequently go to their children in equal portions regardless of sex, unless the parents divided it among them otherwise by deed. If a woman's parents died intestate, she gained an equal share of the personal property with her brothers and sisters. Under the law of primogeniture, the eldest brother and his heirs inherited the real property. If there were no brothers, the sisters shared the property equally, and an only female child would inherit all the intestate real and personal property. Some marriage settlements also included details about houses. The settlement of Gertrude Walrond and Charles Acland in 1879 stated that if Charles died, Gertrude would be entitled to live at their marital home. If they had children and Gertrude was obliged to leave her home, she could live at Killerton, the Acland family mansion.[41] The nature of these settlements and even the amounts involved altered little in the years between 1870 and 1914.

The common rate of interest on the capital sum in the trust fund was 4 per cent, and much of the discussion between fathers and lawyers concerned the safest forms of investment in a century of low inflation. The only example of a 3 per cent interest rate was Margaret MacDonald's settlement. Margaret was anxious that her money should be invested in 'respectable sort of things' and her father, a professor of chemistry with little flair for business, evidently put safety before profit. Not surprisingly, the best interest rates were secured by the two millionaires, Mr Leiter at 4½ per cent and Hugh Bell at 5 per cent. In 1884, £10,000 of Lady Maud Cecil's fortune was invested at 4½ per cent, and the remainder at a safer 4 per cent. Settlements usually included details of a life insurance policy taken out by the husband on his own life for the benefit of his wife.

All negotiations over these marriage settlements underline their primary purpose in providing protection for the wife's money and property. In 1888 William Rathbone pointed out to his cousin the need to settle the wife's trust fund more firmly on her 'as even now our laws are not equal in these matters'. He was determined that the terms of the settlement should ensure that 'the woman's power over her property in settlement and its destination should be equal to the man's'.[42] Occasionally, the parents specifically indicated that their daughter's money needed protection against her fiancé's weakness. Lady Selborne's daughter, Mabel, was engaged to Viscount Howick, eldest son of Earl Grey, in 1906. Lady Selborne was anxious about Charlie Grey's idea of:

getting 'something in the city' in order to have a little more money . . . as I never saw anyone more certain to fall a victim to the first designing Jew he tries to do business with . . . The only thing to do is to tie up all the money we can as tightly as the law will allow us, so he won't be able to completely ruin himself.[43]

The marriage settlement of W. E. Gladstone's eldest son, William, and Lord Blantyre's daughter, Gertrude, in 1875, also emphasized the need to 'ensure that Ladies' fortunes are much more tied up—(secured upon themselves) than was at one time the practice.' Lord Blantyre placed £20,000 in trust for his daughter, specifying that the interest was to be paid, as was usual, 'for her own use always'. Lord Blantyre explained to Gladstone that there were two unusual features in the settlement. First, the capital and interest were to be paid 'as she may Will, at her death', instead of passing automatically to her children equally. Second, Blantyre chose to give Gertrude the larger sum of £20,000 on marriage, leaving a smaller sum of £6,250 until his death, rather than the reverse.[44]

Two years earlier, in 1873, Gladstone had been instructed about the protection of daughters' property rights by his own solicitor, who explained the issue of the woman's 'after-acquired property'. The settlement established conditions for any property Agnes Gladstone acquired after her marriage with Edward Wickham. Half would go to Agnes on the same terms as the £6,000 in her marriage settlement, 'for sole and separate use—and for E C W surviving her'. This money would then pass to their children, but in default of issue it would return to the Gladstone family as if Agnes died intestate. The other half would go to Agnes for life, then to Edward Wickham for life if he survived her, and 'then as A G shall appoint'. W. E. Gladstone objected to securing 'to the husband the life interest in the whole of the after-acquired property' which would come from the wife's family. The solicitor's response throws some light on the use of these settlements for protection of the wife's financial rights, even after the 1870 Act:

Without such a provision any money which she might at any time acquire after her marriage would become the absolute property of her husband and she would have no power whatever over it. But by the proposed clause . . . instead of depriving her of all free action over after acquired property, it is the only mode of giving her any control over it. It is a provision generally made in marriage settlements.

This explanation satisfied Gladstone, 'so far as it is a liberating or enabling effect'. He continued to object to the absolute settlement of after-acquired property on the children, 'because in my opinion children ought to be left far more dependent on their parents than they are now'. But he reluctantly agreed, rather than force 'a sharp departure from common usage'.[45] Similar conditions had been attached to Lord Blantyre's marriage settlement a generation earlier:

Two years after our marriage—the Duke gave to my Wife a small landed Property—for her exclusive use—so I suppose my Rights as Husband had been barred in the Settlements. I have the use of it now—and then the Children—but failing Children by *her* it goes back to the Duke's Family.[46]

The various marriage settlements in the Rathbone family also stated that the wife's future acquired property should be added to the wife's trust fund.

The woman's father and his solicitor were primarily responsible for settlement negotiations. Most wealthy families in this period preferred a contract negotiated through a lawyer if more than £500 per annum was involved. Usually one contract was arranged by the lawyer of the woman's family, setting out the terms agreed for both parties. Where little or no money was involved, the business was often settled informally by correspondence between the two fathers. A number of families retained the correspondence about the settlement, but in most cases the actual contract seems to have been kept by the lawyer. Aristocratic families were obviously more accustomed to the requirements of such settlements than were more recently established upper-middle-class families. This explains why Lord Blantyre was able to instruct W. E. Gladstone on the niceties of property law in 1875. Frequently fathers were obliged to accept their solicitor's advice on unfamiliar aspects of customary practice in marriage settlements. Margaret Gladstone told Ramsay MacDonald that her father 'says I may as well have a marriage settlement, but that won't be any bother—our solicitor can see to it.'[47] Hugh Bell enquired in 1903 whether G. O. Trevelyan intended to formalize his intentions for their children in a legal document, adding that he would certainly send his own proposals in a formal manner.[48]

There was an implicit if irrational assumption that women only married for love, leaving the two fathers and prospective husband to worry about such practical considerations as finance. It was considered commendable in a man to be concerned about the financial aspects of marriage, but reprehensible in a woman. Even the most intelligent of women generally adopted the requisite attitude of ignorance. Maud Cecil told her fiancé, Willy Palmer, in 1883 that 'I do not know much about money or what is usual in settlements.'[49] Mary Gladstone in 1873 doubted if her sister Agnes minded much about money, though she was glad to learn 'something definite about means'.[50] Laura Tennant was alarmed in 1885 that her father was visiting her fiancé, Alfred Lyttelton, to discuss settlements:

Settle all your heart on me and I dont want anything less and there is nothing more. He is very sweet about you and says if you have any 'private fortune' (I might be a clerk in an Insurance Office) you will settle it on me and the whole thing is so vile I can't bear to think of it.[51]

However, there were some more practical women. Ramsay MacDonald's fiancée, Margaret Gladstone, initially admitted that she was 'hazy' about her financial prospects but subsequently took considerable pride in working through all the details with her father in 1896.[52]

If the bride was not usually expected to concern herself with mere money, the two sets of parents often engaged in interminable debate on this aspect of matrimony which consumed their time and energy far more than any other. Lady Stanhope echoed many parents when she told her son, Dick, in 1914 that his fiancée's lawyers 'have no business to ask for pin-money till they say what is coming from their side.'[53] At a more serious level, the fifth Earl of Onslow noted that in 1905 quite 'absurd wranglings' took place over his engagement to Miss Violet Bampfylde, though there could be no genuine objection and there was 'no real lack of money'. He believed that 'every sort of difficulty was made over settlements', because 'to get the full fun out of it everyone had to raise objections'. The participants in the battle seemed to enjoy the row over money, but the whole business caused the unhappy couple considerable trouble in later years: 'Had it not been for the quarrels over our unfortunate affairs we should undoubtedly have been far better off than we are.'[54]

Another interesting example of parental wrangling over matrimonial finance is provided by the marriage in 1886 of Joseph Albert Pease, later Lord Gainford, to Ethel Havelock-Allan. The negotiations were conducted by the formidable mother of the prospective bride, Lady Alice, wife of Lt. Gen. Sir Henry Havelock-Allan. She sought the most lucrative match for her daughter in the best Jane Austen manner; and when a millionaire's son was available she fought for the highest terms. She wrote to Sir Joseph Pease in February 1886 asking him to settle on his son, Jack, £3,000 per annum, representing a capital sum of £70,000. Pease wrote back sharply, reminding Lady Alice that 'you will not find such settlements very common nowadays', though he was prepared to settle £2,000 a year on Jack. This would enable Jack and Ethel to 'marry on more than I did when I lived most comfortably', and Jack would have nearly as large an income as his elder brother. The Pease family considered that Lady Alice 'had her eye to the main chance' and was being too grasping. After three months of further demands, Jack wrote to Ethel in desperation:

I don't know what position your mother wishes to put us in. She has written to me a letter saying she is not satisfied with my financial position . . . As far as I can see ahead my pecuniary position is likely to improve rather than the reverse . . . But as Father has already told your Mother, [that] if you are to marry me for money it is not reasonable that [in] these times he can make me a millionaire . . . Of course I'm in your hands, if you by Mummie's advice like to chuck me over, I've no remedy . . . I can't make myself wealthy in a day. I've offered you all I've got.[55]

In her efforts to raise the price Lady Alice threatened to break off the engagement or at best postpone it indefinitely, but the marriage took place in October. Unfortunately there is no information on Ethel's own marriage portion. If that was greater than £2,000 per annum, then Lady Alice's behaviour would appear less mercenary, but it seems unlikely. Certainly the Havelock-

Allan portion must have been substantial to justify Lady Alice's fuss over the Pease portion.

Sufficient evidence has survived to reconstruct some of the main financial terms of the settlements in more than twenty-five marriages (see Table 1). In most cases, some or all of the correspondence relating to the settlement is available, though the actual contracts seem to have been retained by solicitors. In eleven cases, information is available about the contributions from both partners' families, while in the remaining cases the extant material reveals details of the contribution of one side only. It can usually be safely assumed that the other side paid their share, as in the case of Ethel Havelock-Allan, William Waldegrave Palmer (later Lord Selborne) and the husbands of W. H. Smith's four wealthy daughters.

As the table indicates, the money settled on the marital partners varied quite considerably. A useful starting-point is provided by Sir Joseph Pease's comment that a settlement of £70,000 (or £3,000 per annum at 4.2 per cent) was extremely unusual. Mary Leiter's settlement of £140,000 was extraordinary by any standards. Ashton Dilke and Maye Smith were also quite atypical in acquiring a joint annual income of about £4,500 on marriage.[56] The more typical upper limit of substantial marriage settlements made by wealthy industrialists and rich aristocrats was a capital sum of £50,000 yielding £2,000 annual income—the amount finally agreed in the marriage between Joseph Pease and Ethel Havelock-Allan. Only two other settlements in this sample came at all close to Pease's figure. The first was the equal contributions of Ivor Maxse and Mary Wyndham of £1,000 per annum each. The second was the settlement made by the wealthy iron-master, Hugh Bell, with Sir George Trevelyan, on the marriage of their children, Mary Bell and Charles Trevelyan. G. O. Trevelyan gave his son £1,600 per annum, together with a charming house in Northumberland rent free, and the payment of his election expenses. Charles would also inherit the baronetcy and 'ample means to keep up his position' on his father's death. The current income of £1,600 represented the maximum Sir George could afford in 1903. Although Sir Hugh Bell would ultimately have 'upwards of a million', he could only provide, initially, a marriage portion of about £10,000 in securities, to yield an annual income of £500. As Charles commented, a joint income of £2,100 was 'as

TABLE I. MARRIAGE SETTLEMENTS

	Settlement by wife's family	
	Annual interest (£) (usually at 4%)	Capital—(£)
Mary Leiter m. George Curzon 1895	6,300[a]	140,000
Maye Smith m. Ashton Dilke 1876	?	?
Ethel Havelock-Allan m. Joseph Pease 1886	?	?
Mary Wyndham m. Ivor Maxse 1899	1,000	25,000
Mary Bell m. Charles Trevelyan 1903	500 (5%)	10,000 + +
Maud Cecil m. William Palmer 1884	1,040	26,000
Violet Maxse m. Edward Cecil 1894	400	10,000
Margaret Mackay m. Alexander Shaw 1913	1,000	25,000
W. H. Smith's four daughters	c.1,200 each	28,000–32,000 each
May Balfour m. John Talbot 1898	1,000	25,000
Margaret Gladstone m. Ramsay MacDonald 1896	750 (3%)	25,000[f]
Gertrude Walrond m. Charles Acland 1879	?	?
Gertrude Stuart m. William Gladstone 1875	800 [+ 250]	20,000[g]
Frances Roberts m. Richard Rathbone 1859	400	10,000
Emily Rathbone m. Hugh Rathbone 1888	400	10,000
Katherine McKim m. Henry Rathbone 1894	?	?
Matilda F. Leslie m. Spencer Childers 1883	336	8,400
May Acland m. R. Hart-Davis 1872	?	?
Dorothy Drew m. Francis Parish 1911	440	11,000
Agnes Gladstone m. Edward Wickham 1873	264	6,600
Margaret King m. Dr John H. Gladstone 1869	150 (3%)	5,000
Richard Potter's eight daughters	200 each	5,000 each

[a] Up to £30,000 on father's death.   [b] Rising to £450,000 on father's death.
[c] Plus house.   [d] Also to inherit title and estate.
[e] Probable sum; also to inherit title and estate.   [f] Utimately.

much as two people like us can want with a free country house and no election expenses'.[57]

Below this exceptionally wealthy élite, two levels of marriage portion appear most common. The very rich tried to give their children an annual income of £1,000 each. W. H. Smith, the millionaire and wholesale newsagent, managed to achieve this for all four daughters, providing them with capital sums which varied between £28,000 and £32,000, costing him nearly £120,000.[58] Margaret Mackay, Ivor Maxse, Mary Wyndham, May Balfour

Settlement by husband's family		Total joint settlement (approx.)	
Annual interest (£) (usually at 4%)	Capital (£)	Annual interest (£)	Capital (£)
1,000	25,000[b]	7,300 ++	165,000 +++
?	?	c.4,500 +	c.112,500 +
2,000	50,000	2,000 +	50,000 ++
1,000	25,000	2,000	50,000
1,600[c]	40,000[d]	2,100 + house	50,000 +
?	25,000[e]	1,040 ++	51,000 ++
1,000	25,000	1,400	c.35,000
300	7,500	1,300	32,500
?	?	?	c.30,000 ++
–	–	1,000	25,000
–	–	750 (3%)	25,000
?	?	1,000	25,000
?	*Hawarden estate*	1,050	26,250[h]
?	[10,000?]	?	[20,000?]
400	10,000	800	20,000
800	20,000	800	20,000
300[i]	7,500[j]	636[k]	15,900[l]
?	?	600	15,000
–	–	440	11,000
160	4,000	424	10,500
?	?	?	5,500 +
–	–	–	–

[g] Plus £6,250 on father's death.
[i] Plus £300.
[k] Plus £300.
[h] Plus estate.
[j] Plus £7,500 on father's death.
[l] Plus £7,500.

and Maud Cecil all had settlements of about £1,000 per annum. Those who were not quite so wealthy, or had huge families to provide for, tried to contribute a capital sum of £10,000. The Rathbone family of Liverpool believed that each partner to a marriage should contribute £10,000 where possible, yielding a joint average annual income of about £800. When she married Spencer Childers in 1883, Matilda Florence Leslie learned that her three sisters had each received a capital sum of £10,000, but her own portion would have to be £8,400, because of the decline in

value of her father's estate.[59] Any settlements below these figures
were considered relatively small. W. E. Gladstone settled £6,600
on his daughter Agnes in 1873, and felt that he was on weak
ground for pressing any changes in the agreement, 'my daughter's
portion being small'.[60] Since he had eight daughters, Richard
Potter was only able to afford £5,000 each, yielding about £200
annually.

Victorian fiction seems to have created a myth that the main
contributor to the settlement was the girl's father who provided
the dowry. In practice, both partners brought into the marriage as
much money as their parents could afford or were willing to give
them. When William Rathbone's daughter married her cousin in
1886, Rathbone explained that where both parties enjoyed similar
financial circumstances, usually 'the man provides at least an equal
amount to the woman to the joint settlement'. Accordingly,
William and Richard Rathbone agreed to settle £10,000 on each
partner, making no distinction between the sexes in determining
the amount to be settled on their children at marriage.[61] When the
eldest son of Lord Folkestone was married in 1866, both partners
brought an income of £1,000 per annum to the match.[62] Olive
Maxse wrote to her sister, Violet Cecil, about the prospective
marriage of their brother, Ivor Maxse,with Mary Wyndham,
daughter of Lord Leconfield:

You know what Papa always is about settlements, and Lord Leconfield is
very business like and careful about all money investments—so I do not
quite know how it will all work out. Lord Leconfield is willing to settle
£1,000 a year on her if Papa will do ditto, but of course he won't, and what
is more, I do not think he *can*.[63]

But apparently he did, and other parents did likewise when they
could actually afford to contribute.

Obviously it was not always possible for both families to
contribute equally. Where there was economic inequality, it was
more common in these political families for the woman to be the
richer partner. Bridegrooms were aware of the financial demands
of a political career, and could not often afford a poor wife. There
was plenty of gossip about male fortune-hunters but envy was
mixed with the contempt. It was widely assumed that Disraeli
married Mrs Wyndham Lewis only for her money, since he was an
ambitious, bankrupt young politician, and she a rich middle-aged

widow. Evelyn Stanhope was sorry to hear in 1873 of 'Lord Eliot's marriage to a Miss Heathcote with money which I suppose means Lord Willoughby's plain and middle-aged daughter.'[64] Lady Londonderry in 1895 was scathing about a bridegroom who 'married the £10,000 a year as well as the Lady'.[65] When Edith Balfour was courted by George Curzon, she did not imagine he was serious: 'He knew I had no fortune, and I knew he needed money.' She was not surprised when he subsequently married Mary Leiter, the rich American heiress, who provided Curzon with the wealth to become Viceroy of India. Mary acquired the capital investment of £140,000 on marriage, producing an annual income of £6,300, which rose to £30,000 on her father's death. But then Curzon himself was scarcely poor, with his annual allowance of £1,000, even though he had to await his father's death to inherit his own half million pounds.[66] At a lower financial level, May Balfour received an annual income of £1,000 for her marriage in 1898 to Jack Talbot, who had 'hardly any money'. May's sister, Edith Lyttelton, initially feared that their father would oppose the marriage so fiercely that they might have to run away.[67]

Ramsay MacDonald moved into a different class as well as acquiring financial means through his engagement to Margaret Gladstone in 1896. Margaret told him: 'My financial prospects I am hazy about, but I know I shall have a comfortable income.' She thought her married half-sister received about £500 per year, and they would each gain their 'full share' when her father died. Margaret's mother died when she was born, and as the only surviving child she inherited all her mother's marriage settlement of £5,000, producing about £160 per year. Her father gave her a further £300 annual income at marriage, but stated his intention of leaving her at least £10,000 in his will. The capital sum in her trust fund was eventually over £25,000, providing for Ramsay Mac-Donald 'a degree of economic security unique in his generation of Labour leaders'. Margaret teased Ramsay that people would gossip: 'Your Social Democrats will I suppose say you've married a fine miss or that it's convenient for you to have a little money coming in.' She subsequently reassured him that 'nobody imagines that you marry me for the filthy lucre'.[68]

The 1913 marriage between Margaret Mackay and Alex Shaw, Lord Craigmyle's son, was unusual in several respects. Since her fiancé hated such 'mercenary subjects' she worked out a detailed

statement of their income, savings and expenditure. She also
sympathized with his desire not to live off her allowance and
attempted to organize their funds so that his feelings would not be
hurt. Her marriage settlement yielded £1,000 per annum, while he
only had £300 from his father's allowance, supplemented by about
£500 from his own income. Margaret told her fiancé that 'I used to
think I would like my husband to be quite independent of my
allowance, because I used to think and still do that it is a good
thing to be independent of one's father when married.' But now
her love took precedence over her principles and she was
'prepared to marry you at once and wait for the independence'.
She suggested a compromise whereby they should each contribute
£500 'to our joint exchequer, I will be saving half my allowance
and you your father's contribution'. Any savings from their yearly
income 'must please be considered our *mutual* savings,and be
added to our next year's income', though she feared they would be
unable to live on less than £1,000 per year. She further reassured
her fiancé that her father's business was on a most secure
foundation, so she was most unlikely 'to be left penniless even if
you could not make sufficient provision for me'.[69] It is impossible
to know whether this lengthy letter improved Alex Shaw's morale,
but it is an interesting indication of the proud male's desire to
contribute at least as much as his wife and the female's wish for
financial responsibility to shift from father to husband.

Conversely, there are fewer examples of males from these
political families marrying females poorer than themselves.
Pamela Plowden's 'total absence of means' caused comment about
her forthcoming marriage in 1902.[70] There were fears that Betty
Lytton's 'income would be small' in her marriage to Gerald
Balfour in 1887.[71] When Ivy Dundas married Austen Chamberlain
in 1906, her father informed Chamberlain that he had 'nothing to
give her', but she had been trained to know the value of money and
to be satisfied with little. Edith Balfour told Alfred Lyttelton
before their marriage in 1892 that 'I haven't a farthing', and her
father feared 'that when Alfred found I had no fortune he would
cry off'.[72] It was assumed that a wealthy man should have little
difficulty attracting a wife. In 1875 Dolly Herbert wrote to thank
her brother, Lord Cowper, for the gift of a pleasant family home
and substantial income to their bachelor brother Henry: 'I think it
must bring a wife soon. Do you see or hear of anything?'[73]

In the second half of the nineteenth century, money was thus still considered a crucial ingredient in any socially acceptable marriage. Even when the bridegroom was only a land agent with a big nose, a Yorkshire accent and 'rather a bounder', Olive Maxse considered that his money compensated for his defects: 'they will have £2,000 a year to live on which is very comfortable and covers a multitude of deficiencies.'[74] The lady in question, Beatrice Duff, had few expectations, so wealth in a mate was an unexpected bonus and lack of other desirable features a matter of little moment. When Lady Abercromby heard of William Haldane's engagement to Edith Nelson in 1891, her immediate response was to express the hope that she would have considerable fortune: 'that is always a comfort, it is such a rest from anxiety and small cares in everyday life.' May Harcourt in 1909 was delighted to learn that:

Mr Cunard has at last consented to his daughter's marriage to Bobby on conditions that make it possible . . . I suppose they, the young people themselves, will be the ones to settle what they will be content to marry on although one can strongly object to their doing so under a certain sum. They are both of an age to take the matter into their own hands but I do hope and trust a requisite amount may be forthcoming for their happiness.[75]

Money was vital but the amount of money deemed adequate was relative to the parents' means and social aspirations. The usual aim was for the newly married couple to begin their joint life at the material level which the richer set of parents had only achieved after a generation of living together. This was much harder to attain for a small landowner with eight children, hard hit by the depression of the 1880s, than for a successful railway or shipping magnate with fewer children. Lady Salisbury told her son Edward Cecil in 1894 that she hoped he was prepared for 'love in a cottage', but Edward's marriage to Violet Maxse scarcely involved great poverty since their joint annual income was £1,600.[76] The Cecil concept of poverty would have seemed comfortable to Fred Anson or Henry Acland. Both Agnes and Mary Gladstone married on approximately that £400 a year considered an impossible 'pittance' by Evelyn Baring. Yet Mary Gladstone stated several years before her marriage that £1,200 per year 'would be ample for any couple who didn't mind living rather

humbly—going 2nd class and in a bus and inhabiting an un-
fashionable part of London and not going in for smart cooking'.[77]

It is perhaps surprising that the conventional view of the
importance of inherited family wealth in marriage was so readily
accepted. Many of the men in this study were highly educated and
might have been expected to provide reasonably well for their
prospective brides. Yet the bridegroom's own occupational income and expectations were usually almost entirely ignored in
calculating marriage settlements. Men in their twenties and thirties
assessed their economic eligibility for marriage in terms of the
allowance received from their parents. The strength of the
conventional attitude to the financial factor in marriage is attested
by the unquestioning acceptance of parental veto or postponement
by such people as Geoffrey Howard, Molly and Gertrude Bell, the
Aclands and Raymond Asquith.

3

Love and Other Complications

LOVE AND MARRIAGE

MOST Victorians liked to think that they married for love and would have shared Constance Wilde's assumption that people could not 'be happy unless they do marry for love'.[1] Precisely what they meant by love is difficult to determine. The ideal of love held by these men and women was obviously related to the love-ideal in the fiction of the period, especially in the pre-marital courtship phase, when absence and abstinence encouraged sentimental dreams. Protestant religious beliefs seem to be the more important source of the ideal of married love, based for women on such values as patience, duty, forbearance and obedience. The religious and literary sources of inspiration often overlapped, as they did for the adolescent Laura Tennant whose ideas of love crew as much on biblical imagery as on gothic romance. The individual experiences of courtship and marriage analysed in the next chapter will also underline the point that Victorians varied widely in their ideas on love, which were derived from observation and family experience, as well as from literary and biblical models.

Some Victorian upper- and upper-middle-class men and women married primarily for love. Mary Gladstone certainly married her handsome vicar for love in 1886, since Harry Drew had few of the more conventional advantages to recommend him. Her views on this subject four years before her own unworldly marriage are worth considering, as they are based on the observations of a well-balanced woman of thirty-five, as well as on her own experience of unrequited love for A. J. Balfour. The Gladstone and Lyttelton families were debating the merits of a match between Neville Lyttelton and his second cousin, Katherine Wortley, late in 1881. Mary Gladstone believed that

nothing matters when the love and trust are perfect . . . Heaven sometimes takes much of the responsibility by allowing the two to fall so gloriously in love with each other that it will float them over the roughest sea . . . And oh the power and in a way the glory of that headlong thing when it does come in a dazzling flash, the awakening transfiguring effect it has.

But in this case Katherine was not in love with Neville, yet she was hesitating: 'very few girls have the strength of mind to shut the door of hope absolutely while they feel that if nobody better turns up, there may be a chance of their falling back on it.' Moreover, Neville's financial prospects were not yet good enough to satisfy Katherine, who 'sometimes fished as to Nevy's prospects, and what his present income amounted to'. Since Mary also had her doubts about Katherine's health, she believed this match involved 'fearful risk':

When people *walk* into love, not trotting or galloping, let alone being run away with, there is no excuse for ignoring drawbacks such as poverty and ill health. Both these drawbacks are as all experience shows, a terrible strain on the affections, after the first halo and novelty have passed off—a strain that can only be borne by the most perfect devotion between the two—the uniting of two lives is an awful solemn thing.[2]

Mary Gladstone firmly believed that a great love conquered all, whilst moderate affection required material comforts and social status.

Others besides Mary Gladstone experienced that 'headlong flash of lightning'. A generation later Mary's own daughter, Dorothy, married 'a subaltern with no prospects' and only £360 a year. Despite her own doubts about the match, Mary was forced to agree with her sister Helen that 'if it is the real thing [poverty] won't choke it off'.[3] Whenever a major obstacle to matrimony was overcome, particularly lack of money, then it was assumed that it was a love match. When Winston Churchill married Lady Blanche Hosier's daughter in 1908, Lady Selborne remarked that 'the girl literally hasn't a half penny, so it may be regarded as a genuine love match.'[4] In general, it was easier for partners of similar background in class, wealth and age to emphasize affection as their sole motivation for matrimony. Mary Curzon warned her sister, Nancy Leiter, in 1895: 'No one can be content with a little affection, it must be love', the right man should send thrills 'running up and down your back with pure joy . . . Don't give your heart away till you feel all this, which I feel when George appears.'[5] It was easier to be uncompromising and highly selective when you were a beautiful American heiress.

For most couples, mutual affection seems to have been more common than the 'headlong flash of lightning' described by Mary Gladstone. The existence of affection between the marriage partners tended to be taken for granted, like equality in social status. Any serious lack of affection excited adverse comment, and often led to the courtship being broken off. There are countless expressions among these family papers of the love and happiness experienced by couples who agreed to marry. The usual nature of this love was described by Lady Selborne, in a letter of advice to her son, Roundell, in 1909. She told him to 'fall in love with your head as well as with your heart':

As the choice of a wife is a very important thing, it ought to be submitted to your *judgement* before you give free rein to your affections. People of our race very seldom fall in love all of a sudden, and it is in the intermediate period, when you are still sane, that you should decide whether a girl will make you the kind of wife you desire or not, and if your judgement gives a negative answer, withdraw from the acquaintance while there is yet time. Does this seem very coldblooded advice? It is not really, because the affection that is inspired by the judgement is a much higher and more lasting affection than that which depends merely on the passions.[6]

Most of the marriages in these families involved love inspired by judgement rather than passion. There is often evidence that couples, like Charles Trevelyan and Molly Bell, 'fell in love' only after other partners, who were equally lovable but less suitable, were considered and set aside. Even where the primary emphasis was placed on love between the partners, it was generally felt that love would only last if compatibility existed in other respects also. Lady Cowper wrote to her newly married son, Francis, Lord Cowper, on his honeymoon, expressing her delight that he had married for love, as she had herself:

It is the only marriage that reminds me of my own. Perfect love, and perfect trust, and confidence, perfect suiting in all ways which lasted to the end . . . So many people love but don't suit, and tho' they love on to the end in a way, the wedge widens, and they end by loving still, but going different ways—like Shaftesburys, Jocelyns and many others.[7]

It was generally assumed that where social and economic interests coincided, affection would normally increase with time—and it often did. When Henry Acland pressed his suit on Margaret Rogers in 1875, Mrs Acland reported back to Henry on her discussion with Mrs Rogers:

She said that if her daughter were pressed for an immediate definite answer it would be a negative, as she did not know enough of you to give the contrary reply. I said, that if she knew that there would be no Chance for you ultimately it would be kind to say so at once. To which she answered that she did not know any reason why it should not ultimately be . . . My impression was that the Parents would be glad of it, when there are means, and if the person most interested were so inclined, but that at present she is not so, having never thought of you in that light, and that the inclination has to be originated.[8]

Within three months of this conversation, Margaret admitted that Henry had secured her affections: 'Every day I grow to love Harry more and more as we learn to know each other better through our letters; he had been so good and patient with me all this year that I have kept him waiting for an answer, and now we are happy.'[9]

Most of the unsuccessful courtships ended supposedly because one party or the other decided that feelings were 'insufficiently engaged', but that was often the acceptable excuse which covered more complex explanations. The crucial period of courtship was usually Lady Selborne's 'intermediate stage' and rejection was determined by rational judgement quite as much as limited affection. Since the male initiated proceedings, it was more often the man whose overtures were rejected and whose feelings and pride were wounded. This happened twice to the rather forbidding young William Ewart Gladstone, who frightened off two young women even though he might have been considered a good match on other grounds. A generation later his own son, the Revd Stephen Gladstone, had a similar experience at the advanced age of thirty-seven, when he 'fell in love at first sight' with Constance West in 1881. Stephen behaved like a love-sick hero in a classic Victorian melodrama, 'perfectly happy in the mere act of pouring out his love' to anybody who would listen. The families on both sides were heavily involved in the negotiations concerning this ill-fated courtship. Since Constance at nineteen was only half Stephen's age, her parents 'put the drag on' and refused to let Stephen show his feelings for her. Consequently, when she visited

the Gladstones at Hawarden, she appeared unconscious of poor
Stephen's ardour and 'thinks only of the prime minister'. Stephen's
expressions of his affection had to be sent instead in writing to her
parents. This was a poor substitute since they refused to show the
letters to Constance, telling Stephen only that she did not share his
feelings. Mary Gladstone was deeply committed on her brother's
behalf: 'Is she cold and shallow I keep wondering or has she not
realised what it is to win the heart of one like Stephy? Is she too
young to know what deep strong love is? or does she already care
for somebody else?' But Stephen was determined not to give up
hope until he 'had it out with her face to face', and the Gladstones
allowed him to hope till the end of the 1882 Season. Then he had to
be 'weaned from the great uncertainty', but remained very sensible
about sleeping and eating' despite his disappointment.[10] Stephen
finally married Annie Wilson in 1884, when she was twenty-one
and he forty-one—on this occasion the difference in age proving
no obstacle to love. But Constance West may very well have
shared her parents' repugnance for marriage with a man twice her
age, so that the decisive obstacle may have been age rather than
affection.

Richard Burdon Haldane failed on two occasions to marry for
love. In 1881 Miss 'A K.' rejected his proposal, clearly made from
love since other considerations were not as his own family would
have wished. Not only was she considerably older than Richard,
but his aunt Jane Sanderson opposed the match on practical
grounds: '*Advantageous*, for his professional, or at least his
general prospects of success in life, I suppose so early a marriage
could hardly be considered.' As his aunt expected, he was 'terribly
cast down' when the verdict of the lady went against him.[11] Nearly
ten years later Haldane was far more deeply distressed when Miss
V. Munro-Ferguson broke off their engagement after five weeks,
'allegedly on the grounds that she was romantically involved with
another woman'.[12] A post-mortem on the relationship took place
at some length between Haldane's mother, aunt and sister,
together with Lady Grey, Lady Abercromby and Lady Helen
Munro-Ferguson. Lady Grey had thought the relationship ideal
and feared 'some demon must have got loose to destroy all that
seemed so good'. Elizabeth Haldane, however, had the strange
feeling that even while the courtship was in full flight 'the two
turtle doves' were 'pretending'. This was reinforced by Lady

Abercromby's information that Miss Munro-Ferguson felt 'an intellectual friendship' for Richard which she mistakenly believed would grow into a warmer feeling. Lady Helen Munro-Ferguson believed Richard 'had intellectual power over V. that carried her away while she was with him and that afterwards this passed and finally a sort of revulsion occurred. She blames herself more than is reasonable.' The Munro-Ferguson family had urged on the engagement, putting her under considerable pressure to maintain it. Lady Abercromby argued that greater misery had been prevented and Richard would find a gentler and 'more pleasing' wife. Elizabeth stayed with her brother throughout the crisis over this broken engagement, minimizing the humiliation and embarrassment which it caused him as a public figure. She had to return 'a cargo of presents' and found it 'all so painful getting the presents together and all the rest'.[13] Haldane never married and nursed the vain hope for the next seven years that Miss Munro-Ferguson would reconsider. Instead she wrote three romantic novels, and when she died tragically young in 1897, Haldane confided in Rosebery that his old love remained and 'will end, not in her grave, but in mine'.[14]

George Macaulay Trevelyan had a similar experience of un-requited love in his courtship of Hester Lyttelton in 1899, when again other circumstances were also unfavourable. Lady Tre-velyan wrote to tell Lady Lyttelton that 'George has begun to entertain a very warm feeling for your Hester'. Lady Lyttelton was surprised and deeply distressed: 'I do not think Hester would ever be able to return his affection in the degree in which he gives it.' She felt partly to blame for allowing Hester and George to walk and cycle together for two days, alone and unchaperoned. Since George was younger than Hester, and at the outset of a brilliant career, 'the thought of his contemplating marriage never struck either of us'. The Trevelyans 'felt bound to tell George that we could not consent to his marrying for some time, and he quite sees that it would be out of the question at present'. He was only twenty-three and would have to concentrate his efforts on making a career for himself. The difficulties of age, finance and parental opposition presumably had some influence on Hester's feelings. Two months later Lady Lyttelton decided that further meetings between the two young people would be painful and fruitless.[15] George renewed his suit after Lady Lyttelton's death, but Hester gave the final refusal two years after their initial meeting: 'I can't give him the big return of love that his love would demand.'[16]

THE PROPER AGE FOR MARRIAGE

Money and love were usually the most significant considerations, but decisions about marriage partners could be complicated further by questions of age, health, religion or politics. The proper age for marriage often excited considerable controversy. The ideal age for marriage was considered by marriage manuals to be about twenty to twenty-five for women and twenty-three to twenty-eight for men. In reality, William Farr calculated that the mean age at marriage was rather higher than this; in 1872 it was 25.7 years for women and 27.9 years for men in all those registered marriages where age was specified. The husband was expected to be older than the wife, ideally by three to seven years, since women were supposed to age faster than men.[17]

There was considerable pressure on young girls to marry very young if a suitable opportunity offered itself, rather than risk the humiliation of spinsterhood. In the 1860s and 1870s, as Mary Paley Marshall noted, 'the notion was common that if a girl did not marry or at any rate become engaged by twenty she was not likely to marry at all'.[18] Most families, especially those with large numbers of children, were only too happy if their daughters married around the age of twenty. Maye and Olive Eustace Smith each married at the age of eighteen in the 1870s, to the evident delight of their family. Lady Angela Forbes described her sister Millie's unexpected engagement at the age of sixteen to Lord Stafford in the 1880s. Millie had been allowed to stay at Dunrobin as a companion for the Duchess of Sutherland's daughter on the clear condition that 'she was not to be treated as a grown up'. Lady Angela doubted whether Millie was old enough to be engaged, but 'everyone else was hugely excited about it all', though Millie was obliged to continue her lessons.[19] On the very rare occasions when mothers deeply regretted their daughters' early marriages, other considerations came into play. Mary Drew's unhappiness about the marriage of her daughter Dorothy at the age of twenty is readily explained by the two facts that Dorothy was an only child and Mary recently widowed. Mary felt 'horribly and desperately lonely and anxious and regretting they should have settled it all while she was so young and inexperienced and had met so few people'. Her friend, Maggie Cowell-Stepney, had to remind her that 'though it's very sad having a daughter who insists on marrying at 20, there is also a sadness if she refuses to marry at all—!'[20]

Moreover, it was often impossible to separate the question of age from that of financial means. There was generally far more concern about a son marrying too young, because a male child was considered more precious and less of a liability. Cecilia Maxse's reaction to the news of her son Leo's engagement in 1889 was typical: 'Of course I regret intensely his youth—his not having as yet any profession—or any means!!—if this could only have taken place 5 years later.'[21] This was similar to Lady Trevelyan's feelings about George's first courtship of Hester Lyttelton. Years earlier, in 1864, Lady John Russell was unusual in expressing great joy at the engagement of her son, Lord Amberley, to Kate Stanley of Alderley. At twenty-one, 'we might have wished him to marry a little later, to have him a little longer at home. But on the other hand, there is something to me very delightful in his marrying while heart and mind are fresh and innocent, and unworldly.'[22]

Since the popular ideal was for a girl to marry in her early twenties while the census statistics indicate the most common age of marriage for females was later, large numbers of women spent many anxious years worrying about spinsterhood. Many women did marry in their thirties and even their forties, novels and popular images notwithstanding. Beatrice and Kate Potter married at thirty-four and thirty-six respectively, and Mary Gladstone at thirty-nine; they were resigned to impending spinsterhood but delighted by salvation through later marriage. Thomas Dyke Acland's second wife, Mary Erskine, was fifty when she married and her husband three years younger. The Duke of Atholl's daughter, Helen, married at forty-nine, Marion Ashton married James Bryce when she was thirty-six, and Grace Duggan married Lord Curzon at the age of forty, when he was fifty-eight. The list could easily be extended. It is scarcely surprising when one considers that so many upper-class marriages were postponed for financial reasons. Lord Stanhope would not have been astonished by the delighted letter from his niece, Mary Lygon, in 1905, saying she was to marry Harry Trefusis: 'I have known him for 15 years: but I had not seen him for 7 years until that dinner at Susie's last

Wednesday. I had long made up my mind not to marry—but there it is!'[23] What is surprising is the persistence of the myth of youthful marriages which flew in the face of the evidence and tortured many women in their later twenties and thirties with their perceived inadequacies.

Disparity of age between the two partners was both common and at the same time controversial. Marriage manuals sternly opposed unions between an older wife and younger husband since the childbearing woman aged faster: 'until some day she is aroused to the fact that she is an old woman, while her husband is still comparatively a young man'. This view was widely accepted by many such as Jane Sanderson, R. B. Haldane's aunt, who argued that a woman 'should shrink from the idea of a husband younger than herself and certainly it is better for the wife to be the younger for women age soonest.'[24] Consequently, the marriage of the younger man with the older woman could provoke Society's scorn, as was indicated by the remark of Louisa, Lady Antrim in 1901: 'Victoria Lothian *married* Bertram Talbot last week—it is beyond words—revolting I think—she 59—he 37!—22 years between them.' Her sister, Victoria Dawnay, shared her feelings: 'I hear Seymour's youngest son—a boy of 21 at Oxford—has been married by a widow of 45 and carried off to Canada. What dangers these poor young men run!'[25] Lady Randolph Churchill shocked Society in 1900 when she married the much younger George Cornwallis-West. Undaunted, eighteen years later she married Montagu Porch, when she was sixty-four and he forty-one. Occasionally a woman could escape unpleasant gossip in this situation, but she had to be beautiful and still much sought after, as was Sibell, Lady Grosvenor, who was thirty-two when she married the twenty-four-year-old George Wyndham in 1887.

The most common age difference was that between a younger woman and a man ten or twenty years older, often a widower with children. In general, such marriages excited little adverse comment, unlike those where the woman was the elder. Catherine Gladstone was delighted to learn in 1884 that her son Stephen, at the mature age of forty-one, was to marry Annie Wilson: 'a little young, not quite 21 but all we could desire—pretty, nice figure . . . intelligent, nicely and very carefully brought up'.[26] Another such match was that of the forty-seven year old Lord Carnarvon in 1878 to his twenty-two-year-old cousin, Elsie Howard. Eveline,

Lady Portsmouth did not seem too concerned in 1876 that her daughter was marrying a man fourteen years older than herself. It was more important that he was rich, honourable, of good character, and anxious to make her happy.[27] Kate Potter met a trifle more family criticism when she married Leonard Courtney, fifteen years her senior. Beatrice commented in her diary that 'marriage at their ages is rather a leap in the dark—curious to see how it turns out'. Kate preferred to avoid 'all the family criticism', allowing time to justify her position.[28]

Extreme differences in age between spouses could arouse great abhorrence, even when the woman was the younger partner. One marriage manual found 'something utterly repugnant to good morality and good taste in such a union'. Lady Constance Malleson wrote of her own parents: 'He was thirty five years older than she—and they had not a taste in common . . . Why my father married my mother God alone knows.'[29] In 1894 the Campbell clan was greatly agitated by rumours in the newspaper that the head of their family, the fearsome Duke of Argyll, at the age of seventy-one intended to marry a twenty-five-year-old girl. Lady Victoria Campbell raved to her sister, Frances Balfour, about the 'horror' and the 'dirt' of it, while Frances despaired of instilling sense into her 'cracked' family. The old Duke poured scorn on the idea that he would marry that particular girl, but no doubt he saw the humour of marrying a different younger woman the following year.[30] The Tennant daughters experienced the same uncomfortable reaction when their father, Sir Charles Tennant, at the age of seventy-five, decided to marry a woman of thirty-three. Charty was horrified, partly because Miss Miles was the ugliest woman she had ever seen: 'an enormous shapeless body like a chest of drawers with hardly any curves'. But her more serious fault 'besides her ugliness is her youth. She is almost young enough to be his granddaughter'. However, the daughters suppressed their instinctive revulsion since 'she will cherish my dear Father and will I think make him happier'.[31]

Such a match could indeed work remarkably well in some cases, as with the marriage between Baron Beauvale and Countess Alexandrine de Maltzahn. They married when she was twenty-two and he sixty, and she was grief-stricken at his death ten years later in 1853, as Henry Greville recorded:

it is really a singular and extraordinary case. Here is a woman thirty-two years old, and therefore in the prime of life, who has lost a husband of 71 deprived of the use of his limbs, and whom she has nursed for ten years, the period of their union . . . she is in fact broken-hearted; and that for a man old enough to be her grandfather and a martyr to disease and infirmity; but to her he was everything; she had consecrated her life to the preservation of his.[32]

In many cases the marriage of a younger woman to a much older man also involved the responsibility of stepchildren. It was socially accepted that unfortunate husbands who had lost their first wives in childbirth would seek a second wife to care for their children, after a suitable time had elapsed. Joseph Chamberlain lost his first two wives in childbirth in 1863 and 1875. His third wife, Mary Endicott, was only just born in the year of his first wife's death, but the partnership seems to have worked well for them and also for Mary's stepchildren. Mildred Buxton also took on the responsibility for two children when she married Sydney in 1896. Evelyn Talbot remarked: 'He is rather old, isn't he and a widower, but I still think it is a splendid thing.' Mildred read the diaries of Sydney's first wife, Connie: 'to find ou for oneself is such an immense assistance to one's efforts to follow her steps'. Two years later she told her family of her 'extraordinary happiness ever since my engagement'.[33]

The experience of Lady Fanny Elliot is particularly interesting, since she married a man twenty-four years older, became stepmother to six children, and also moved into the national limelight as the wife of the Liberal leader. Lord John Russell fell in love with Fanny in 1840, when he was forty-eight and she twenty-four, but she had a long struggle with her instinctive repugnance at the thought of a physical relationship with a man twice her age. In the course of three months Lord John changed from a distant political hero to a family friend Fanny liked and respected. But she was shocked when she understood that 'Lord John's great kindness to us all, but especially to me, meant something more than I wished.' Lady Minto, Fanny's mother, was relieved when Fanny rejected Lord John's proposal in early September 1840, and confessed to her other daughter, Lady Mary Abercromby, that 'I should be too unhappy to be able to look as I ought to do' if Fanny married him. The following year, Lord John persisted in seeing

Fanny whenever possible, despite her protestations that her feelings had not changed. Fanny felt it was a false situation which must stop: 'we had no right to expect the world to see how all advances to intimacy, since we came to town, have been made by him in the face of a refusal'. By mid-March, both Fanny and her mother were increasingly regretting 'the barrier that prevents him from becoming one of us', as Lady Minto reported to her married daughter, Lady Mary Abercromby:

[Fanny] said she was too old to think it necessary to be what is called desperately in love, and without feeling that his age was an objection or that the disparity was too great, yet, she said, if he had been a younger man she would have decided long ago. And that is the truth. It is his age alone that prevents her at once deciding in his favour. It prevents those feelings arising in her mind, without which it would be a struggle to accept him, and this she never will do.

When Fanny's hesitations finally ended in June, Lady Minto was 'now perfectly happy about the marriage', though still anxious about the disparity of age and her daughter's heavy responsibility for six stepchildren. Lady Minto need not have worried. Even twenty-six years later, Lady John Russell was still thanking God for giving her a husband 'so noble, so gentle, so loving, to be my example, my happiness, my stay'.[34]

HEALTH AS A PREREQUISITE FOR MARRIAGE

Health was always an important consideration in matrimonial choice in the nineteenth century and its significance increased towards the end of the century with the influence of eugenicist ideas that the nation's future citizens should come from the best stock. The general view of marriage manuals was that 'it is a mooted question whether those in ill-health have a right to marry, and thus run the risk of entailing their diseases upon children'. Those afflicted with hereditary diseases like consumption 'had certainly best remain unmarried'. Doctors were urged to dissuade from marriage any women with chronic heart disease. Women were advised not to marry confirmed invalids, since the woman could not be housekeeper, nurse and provider for the family. Likewise no confirmed invalid woman should consent to marry: 'The man will naturally tire of being tied to a sickly and no doubt fretful life-companion', while she would suffer from neglect and was liable to leave her young children motherless.[35] There was some medical controversy about marriage by 'neurotic subjects', since marriage was thought to cure some nervous problems while it was positively harmful in other cases.[36] By the last quarter of the century, Dr H. A. Allbutt's handbook, which ran to many editions, warned women against marriage to men with venereal disease:

Before giving her consent to marry . . . she should also be sure that he is free from any contagious disease which can be communicated through sexual relations . . . A young woman may be ruined in health for life, and have her innocent offspring diseased, if she is allied to a man who has disease lurking in his system. I refer to what is called syphilis. I should like to see it the custom for women or their parents to demand a recent certificate of freedom from syphilis from all men proposing marriage. In this matter false delicacy should be dropped.[37]

There is ample evidence throughout the years 1860 to 1914 that the state of each partner's health was very seriously considered by the families before agreement was given to marriage. Delight was often expressed in letters of congratulation on engagement that 'our new daughter is strong in health and active too'.[38] In the late 1870s, W. H. Smith's niece, Edith Beal, wished to marry a clergyman named Mr Bleadon. But Edith's sister was' most concerned that 'Edith's health must, of course, be quite re-established before she marries', and they should wait a whole year until she was 'quite strong again'. Moreover, a long and happy engagement was 'sure to make her very prudent and careful', while happiness was a tonic in itself.[39] Mary Gladstone felt that poor health was one of several obstacles impeding a possible match between Neville Lyttelton and Katherine Wortley: 'she looks very weak and the Wortley health has never been a strong point'.[40] In 1890, Edith Balfour was anxious about the effects of her recent illness on her matrimonial prospects, especially since she had now reached the advanced age of twenty-five. Recurring illness led to medical advice to rest almost totally and go abroad in the winter, severely curtailing her social life. She became sufficiently depressed at times to consider abandoning the hope of marriage entirely, but her story ended happily with marriage to Alfred Lyttelton in 1892.[41] Maud Selborne argued in 1906 that a

Miss Pratt Barlow 'would have been wiser to postpone her marriage until the doctors could call her well', since some said she was foolish to marry at all in her state of health.[42]

In 1889 there was intense concern in the Balfour family as to whether Gerald's health was strong enough to allow his marriage to Betty Lytton, daughter of Lord Lytton. Kidney trouble had previously caused the doctors to forbid marriage for Gerald. Frances Balfour wrote to her brother-in-law, Arthur Balfour, that she had never been reassured about Gerald's health, knowing how ill he was the previous summer. In October he caught another severe chill, with the same symptoms of chest pain, breathlessness and great weakness, and the danger of pleurisy. Frances felt that although Gerald's kidney was apparently now sound, if he did get pleurisy he would not recover, and they were still 'sitting on the edge of a volcano'. She was also 'haunted by Uncle Robert's cheerful prophecy that Betty would be a widow in less than two years'. One of the doctors consulted advised against marriage 'on the ground of Gerald not being strong eno' to live a married life'. But this doctor's advice was rather confusing, for when Gerald suggested that he and Betty might live apart for some time, that course of action was also vetoed. In the end the doctors recommended postponing the wedding, but the two families allowed the couple to go ahead with their marriage regardless.[43] Despite all the fears and the fuss, Gerald lived to be ninety-two and fathered six children.

William Rathbone had a similar anxiety in 1894 about the marriage of his son Henry to an American girl, Katherine McKim. Rathbone put the question honestly before Randolph McKim, explaining that Henry's health was not strong since his mother died of consumption, though he had not shown 'more than general want of strength'. Rathbone asked whether McKim and his daughter 'were quite satisfied of the prudence of her undertaking a marriage with a delicate man like my son' with all its potential 'cares and anxieties'. McKim replied that he had never even considered withdrawing his consent on account of Henry's health, since he believed Henry was unlikely to develop consumption after the age of thirty-two. Physical health was always uncertain and must be left in God's hands. 'In my view the most important elements of happiness in married life are mental and spiritual sympathy, and mutual confidence and affection.'[44] Not all the barriers of health were overcome so readily. A few years later, Wentworth Dilke, son of Sir Charles Dilke, set his heart on a marriage 'which was rendered impossible by the fact that the girl had heart disease of so advanced a description that the parents refused their consent'. Wentworth returned home 'half crazy' at the tragedy.[45] Another example was that of Anna Maria Philips, unmarried half-sister of Caroline, Lady Trevelyan. The family believed she remained a spinster 'because her mother had been slightly defective in mind, and the daughter's strong moral sense forbade her to run any risks of carrying on this failing into another generation.'[46]

Dr Mary Scharlieb's advice manual for women in 1915 was heavily influenced by eugenicist aspirations. She argued that 'formerly' it was not usual to enquire into the vital question of health. While parents rejected marriage for their daughters with poor men, they 'cheerfully contemplated' their union with diseased men, suffering from tuberculosis or alcoholism. The above evidence suggests that Dr Scharlieb was wrong. However, she was justified in stating that 'formerly it would have been considered indelicate and most extraordinary' for a girl to visit a doctor before her marriage to request a general examination and special assurance of fitness. None of the girls in these political families made such a visit, though Scharlieb asserted that such requests were becoming fairly frequent by 1915: 'and women doctors are often asked to certify not only to the condition of the lungs, the heart, and digestive apparatus, but also as to whether the organs of generation are normal.' Her book included an appeal for both parties to the marriage to undergo careful medical examination to ensure that they were physically fit 'for their new and onerous duties'.[47]

RELIGION AND MARITAL CHOICE

Differences in religious faith between marriage partners were frowned upon, but did not usually provide an insuperable obstacle to the match. As with social and economic considerations, matters were generally so carefully arranged that the question did not arise, since the vast majority of these families were Protestant and usually Anglican. All parties were generally happier when 'their

Church principles are the same'.[48] In a few cases marriage was vetoed on grounds of religion. In 1846, R. B. Haldane's mother, at the age of twenty, was obliged to reject a suitor because her parents did not consider him sufficiently religious, and she herself was not 'sure of his being a Child of God'.[49] Wentworth Dilke asked his father's advice in 1896 about Miss Cohen, who was half Jewish: 'I know it would be a bad match and I fear it would cause you pain.' He believed he loved her, but would not marry her if his father advised against it.[50] The same fate befell Robert Brand in 1909, as Lady Selborne explained to her husband:

Poor Brand has fallen in love with Philip [Kerr]'s prettiest sister, who won't marry him, because he is not a Christian . . . He is very nearly a Christian, much more religious than I thought him . . . But I don't see there is any hope of his becoming a Roman Catholic, and I don't suppose Miss Kerr would acknowledge anything short of the Council of Trent.[51]

Religious differences caused some concern for George Macaulay Trevelyan in two courtships. The first, with Hester Lyttelton, ended unhappily, but he married his second love, Janet Ward. Janet's mother, the popular novelist Mrs Humphry Ward, described the nature of the problem:

. . . he is so wholly non-Christian . . . Certainly Hester Lyttelton could never have married him with any prospect of happiness, and I doubt whether even Janet realises how different his ways of thought are from those in which she has been brought up. It is the absence of any English-church tradition *whatever*, combined with the Unitarian provenance of Lady Trevelyan, and the scepticism of Sir George that seem to have produced the result.[52]

The relationship with Janet Ward in 1903 was harmonious in all other respects, and their mutual love was great enough to surmount the religious hurdle.

There seem to be as many cases where religious differences were overlooked as where they provoked a family veto. The strength of family religious belief and tradition had to be weighed in the balance against the power of love. If affection was reinforced by economic and social compatibility, then religious differences were often overcome, if with some reluctance. The Duchess of Cleveland was dismayed in 1878 at the engagement of her son, Lord Rosebery, to the Jewish heiress, Miss Hannah Rothschild:

. . . this marriage is, from religious grounds, very far from being acceptable to me. I feel it is a *sore trouble* that my son should choose as his wife, and the mother of his children, a woman who is not a Christian. My only comfort is that he seems very happy.[53]

Helen Gladstone was 'rather disgusted' at the news: 'marrying a Jewess isn't very nice. She's perfectly gigantically rich—about 3 million I believe.' The Rothschild family was also concerned about the match since Hannah was 'devoutly attached to her faith and for her such an alliance necessarily meant a severe moral wrench'.[54] Previously the Rothschild family had intermarried, but this was one of a series of alliances between Rothschild women and aristocratic Christians, which increased the family's social prestige. The marriage was made more acceptable by Rosebery's established friendship with the Rothschild cousins and by strong political affinities, while her great wealth could have been no disadvantage.

A number of people coped with mixed religious marriages with equanimity. Evelyn Baring, Lord Cromer, married a Catholic, Ethel Errington, in 1876. They both strongly opposed the Vatican ruling that children of a mixed marriage should be brought up as Catholics, so they married in a Protestant church and their two boys became Protestants.[55] Joseph Chamberlain's third wife, Mary Endicott, in 1889 approved her brother's engagement to a Catholic: 'if people care for each other truly then any difference of religion can be settled so that it does not come between them for evil'; moreover, William would not take an 'intolerant view' of the observances of the Roman Church.[56] Herbert Samuel's cousin, Walter Yates, married a Protestant 'for herself alone and not from any worldly or mercenary views'. He asked Samuel to tell their family, expecting to be cut off from the 'narrowminded and prejudiced amongst present Jewish friends'. The family did indeed try to stop the wedding, but Yates persisted and was married 'quietly in the country'.[57] Lady Desborough remarked on the engagement between Venetia Stanley and Edwin Montagu: 'She will have to become a Jewess, or anyhow renounce being a Christian, or else he loses *all* his immense fortune.'[58] In 1910, Lady Ribblesdale was 'large and unprejudiced' in her response to the marriage of her grand-daughter, Laura Lister, to the Catholic Lord Lovat. Though Lady Ribblesdale felt deeply on matters of religion, she accepted that Laura must be received into the

Catholic church: 'It is difficult to realize she is no longer in our Church . . . surely the difference is not sufficient to separate her from us.'[59]

There was almost no discussion or controversy in these political families about problems created by conflicting political opinions between the marriage partners. This was partly due to the natural tendency for families to mix with other families of similar political sympathies. Where political families intermarried, they were often from the same party, well illustrated by the alliances between the Melbourne, Cowper and Palmerston families, or the match between Gerald Balfour and Betty Lytton. It also perhaps reflected the situation which existed throughout most of this period, whereby political differences did not prohibit social friendships. Therefore marriage alliances between families of opposing parties could usually be countenanced, except at times of acute political controversy. In any case, it was assumed that the wife could change her politics to suit her husband's party rather more easily than she could change her religion, her beauty or her money.

Sir William Harcourt's second marriage to Elizabeth Cabot Ives was considered ideal from the political perspective: '[she is] a good Liberal, and I hope will do her duty to the party and its leaders.'[60] At the very highest levels of politics and the aristocracy, political considerations occasionally seem to have played a more than usually important part in the marriage. The dynastic union in 1892 between Lady Evelyn Fitzmaurice, Lord Lansdowne's daughter, and Victor Cavendish, the Duke of Devonshire's heir, meant a closer political bond between these two great Liberal Unionist and Conservative families.[61] To a lesser extent the marriage of Lucy Lyttelton, W. E. Gladstone's niece, and Lord Frederick Cavendish, brother of Lord Hartington, improved strained relations between Gladstone and Hartington. Sometimes good sense overcame political differences, as in the 1867 marriage of Lady Georgiana Peel, daughter of Lord John Russell:

My father was very well pleased with the alliance—through my marriage to Archibald Peel—with the Peel family, for, although Sir Robert Peel was his bitterest and most powerful opponent in affairs of State, he had a great admiration and sympathy for his high-minded and disinterested policy. They also had a common enemy in Disraeli.[62]

Rarely did a marriage appear to depend on the politics of the day. Most exceptional was the experience of Cynthia Charteris who married Herbert Asquith in July 1910, in the middle of the political tempest caused by the constitutional crisis over Lloyd George's 1909 budget and the Parliament Bill. Although Herbert Asquith was the Prime Minister's son and a 'budding barrister', the forbidding Lord Elcho did not consider him a desirable match in terms of money or prospects, and warned his daughter of the privations she would incur by her folly. But Cynthia's worst sin was to seek to marry the son of the Liberal Prime Minister, and her father's opposition to the match was well known. Hostesses no longer asked the loving couple to the same parties and their 'underground movement' was reduced to secret meetings. Cynthia was even 'extradited' to Canada for a whole winter in a futile attempt to cool her ardour. Her father at last surrendered to the inevitable after a lengthy engagement, when Herbert formally presented himself at Cadogan Square to ask Lord Elcho for his daughter's hand:

So much indeed was a kind of Montagu and Capulet feeling abroad, that one of my friends was actually forbidden by her father to be my bridesmaid! . . . So crackling with party politics was the atmosphere of July 1910 that I told the ushers to substitute for the usual query 'Bride or Bridegroom?' the words, 'Conservative or Liberal?'[63]

Finally, political power in itself appealed to some women in choosing their marriage partner. The chief consideration for a few young brides may well have been the vicarious power and glamour which accompanied a bridegroom who was already a prominent politician. However, such motivation in a woman was not freely acknowledged and the attraction of political power is usually impossible to disentangle from accompanying social, economic and sentimental considerations. One can only speculate that Fanny Elliot, Mary Leiter, and Mary Endicott, for example, were not oblivious of the political power of their mates in marrying Lord John Russell, Lord Curzon and Joseph Chamberlain respectively. Margot Tennant, however, provides us with far more evidence about the mixed motivations governing her marriage to H. H.

Asquith, a man already marked out by many as a future Liberal prime minister. Like Fanny Elliot and Mary Endicott, Margot Tennant married a widower older than herself with a number of children. A. G. Gardiner described H. H. Asquith's marriage to Margot:

His second marriage was an adventure for both. He was approaching middle age, immersed in law, politics and serious affairs, bred in an austere and Puritan tradition and with five young motherless children to care for. She was the darling of society, the most be-photographed young lady of the time, whose name suggested all the gaieties and irresponsibilities of life. No wonder the friends of both looked askance at the union of such opposites. Rosebery and Randolph Churchill issued them warnings from one side, Jowett of Balliol from the other. These pleaders saw [that] his career would be ruined: those that her bright light would be extinguished by the burden of a family not her own.[64]

Margot Tennant had previously considered marrying a hunting friend, Peter Flower, who had been devoted to her for eight years 'with a short interruption of Lady Randolph'. She and Peter shared similar sporting interests and considerable mutual physical attraction and affection. Margot discussed the merits of marriage to Peter with A. J. Balfour in 1891, chiefly concerned that he lacked occupation and 'honourable ambition' and had only '£1,000 a year and some debts'. Margot could imagine 'more suitable and better marriages from every point of view but the perfect unions that might have been do not come to pass'. At the end of this debate on Peter Flower, Margot added significantly:

. . . the duty marriage of union with character of a high type: and intellect and education and career may be better—a marriage of deliberation with a man like Milner or Asquith may be the best but it wants pluck and may be undertaking more than one can quite manage.[65]

At the same time, contact with Asquith was causing her to doubt the sufficiency of the 'heedless life' she was living. A letter to Edith Lyttelton reinforces the sense that she was moving in a cold-blooded manner towards the 'duty marriage of deliberation':

If I marry Asquith it will be for one reason and one only—because I admire his character—I have not much sympathy with his politics . . . He has *none* with my artistic or country tastes and life—I lean towards him by strong approval more than by love . . . .

She was not convincing when she claimed that she was not

ambitious enough to be 'tempted by ambition', and that she cared for Asquith more when he was a less great man.[66]

But Margot hesitated for some time, perhaps waiting for affection to grow, while removing her remaining emotional ties with Peter Flower. She also had considerable misgivings about her abilities as a stepmother to five children. Asquith himself, on the other hand, had no doubts: 'he would marry Margot or no one and he pressed his suit with a fervour nonetheless passionate because it was always couched in exquisite English.'[67] After her marriage to Asquith, Margot told Mary Drew that 'no two lives could feel more different than my Margot and my Asquith one. Five children and governess at meals and other times seemed a kind of dream.'[68] Margot confessed to A. J. Balfour that 'children are so fatiguing and *between ourselves* I marvel at the life I have selected for myself . . . They are nice children, all clever but with ugly voices and ways, the 2 small ones are quite uninteresting.'[69] Even so, despite its limitations, 'My life with Henry is happier than I can describe: constant interest and company—endless discussion and a sort of easy 3 and 4 to dinner.'[70]

Thus love was by no means the only consideration in these Victorian and Edwardian relationships. In practice, social and economic interests were often as influential in marital selection as in earlier centuries. Powerful forces restricted the possible field of personal choice, so that many factors operated before individual selection could be exercised. Society had become sufficiently sophisticated and highly organized in its marriage market to ensure that the coincidence of economic, social and personal interests was generally assured. The young could aspire to have affection as well as money and social class. Love between the partners could safely be emphasized as a prime requirement of a good marriage when the other major factors were considered satisfactory. These couples expected to feel a certain degree of affection before they would finally consent to matrimony. But there were few cases of love being so blind that major inequalities in class, wealth or background were entirely ignored. Compatibility in age, health, religion and politics was preferred, but not absolutely vital if class, money and affection were all assured. It is a tribute to the adaptability of human beings that so many secured apparently contented marriages in a restricted and manipulated market.

4

Experiences of Love, Courtship
and Early Marriage

VICTORIAN and Edwardian behaviour did not always conform to
the prevailing social norms, to the ideal, or the prescriptive.
Individuals responded to the elaborate rules established by Society
in many ways. There were variations related to class, wealth and
location, and to the special features of particular groups such as
the Quakers, the Unitarians, the intellectual aristocracy, or even a
small self-appointed élite such as the Souls. The only way to
understand the varieties of courtship behaviour is to reconstruct
and examine a number of case studies.

THE PERFECT ARISTOCRATIC MATCH: CECILIA HARBORD

A useful starting point is provided by an aristocratic courtship
which followed Society's rule-book to the letter. The Hon. Cecilia
Harbord, born in 1856, was the eldest of a close family of seven
daughters of the fifth Baron Suffield. Cecilia enjoyed her Seasons
to the full, delighting in the two or three balls she attended each
week and noting in her diary the finer details of ladies' dresses and
gentlemen's behaviour. She was frequently invited to dinner
parties and country house weekends where the guests were socially
distinguished or politically prominent or both. Her favourite
pastimes included the theatre, opera and concerts in town, and
hunting and riding in the country. Involved in all the major events
in the social calendar, she epitomized the archetypal aristocratic
young lady with every social advantage. Cecilia's 1877 diary
recorded the tribulations of coping with unwanted admirers at the
age of twenty:

[14 March] I received a lovely white bouquet of lilies and roses from
Ld. Grimston! Hum! I am afraid I wasn't half as grateful as I ought to
have been.

[11 April] Ld. G. paid Motherkins a visit!! and they had a talk together—Poor little Mother. I am dreadfully sorry for her but it is a great relief to me!

[13 April] Mother dear had another interview with Lord G. and then I had to go down. It was *very dreadful* but I am thankful it is over.[1]

The tiresome Lord Grimston was soon forgotten when Cecilia was invited with her sister and parents to dine at Marlborough House on 8 April 1878. Her diary noted cryptically that they were the only girls there and '*somebody* took me in' to supper. Her whirlwind romance with the third Baron Carrington moved rapidly to betrothal at a ball on 28 May 1878:

. . . after a short time Lord Carrington arrived, danced with me, and then something took place which has made me *very very* happy. I went to Mother and whispered to her ear 'I have won the jacket' (one that Mother worked and put aside for the first one of her girls who married). I ought indeed to be grateful for this great happiness, and I *am*. There is no one like him in all England and Father and Mother are *very* fond of him.

This rapid three-month courtship was possible because there were no conceivable objections to the highly eligible Lord Carrington. The social match was perfect since both families gained their baronies in the late eighteenth century, and nobody was the least concerned about the fifteen-year age-gap, especially when the couple were so obviously in love. Both families were extensive landowners and it was all the more of a success for Cecilia that her fiancé owned twice as much land as her father. Carrington had already entered politics as Liberal MP for High Wycombe from 1865 to 1868, before succeeding his father to the peerage.

Cecilia described the engagement celebrations on 29 May 1878:

I had all my sisters in my room . . . at a very early hour. It makes me choky even to write about it—my own sweet sisters; if possible I love them more than ever— . . .Charlie! (a very nice name) took me out walking in the morning, and we saw all the coaches pass on the way to Alexandra Palace—Felt shy seeing so many friends. He gave me a beautiful diamond ring. We then went to see dear Lady Carrington, who was so kind to me—for Charlie's sake of course—that I shall never forget it . . . I am more and more happy every moment.[2]

In the course of one day Cecilia went through the ritual of taking leave of her own family and being formally accepted into her new family. This was inevitably an emotional experience for a girl of twenty-one who was the first daughter to leave the parental home. After the official engagement the couple spent the days up to their wedding in July in a social whirl, never alone except for occasional drives. Cecilia had only three months of hectic social activity in which to adjust to the prospect of a lifetime of marriage.

Lord and Lady Carrington spent their honeymoon at Barley-thorpe, their married home. The next few months were dominated by visits to various country homes for shooting, and a succession of dinner parties and balls. Cecilia missed her family, especially on Christmas day: 'It was rather dreadful not seeing dear little Mother or the others but I had Betty [her sister] and my first Xmas with all my new relations has been a very happy one.'[3] But she seems to have been contented in her married life. She and Carrington shared a bedroom—not the normal practice, by any means, and she noted her wedding anniversaries each year with pleasure. Her life became increasingly involved with politics and babies, though hunting, riding, tennis, dinner parties and balls continued at a slower pace. Judged by conventional standards, her marriage was a success, even though she had five daughters before the longed-for heir arrived. Her husband prospered, becoming Governor of New South Wales from 1885 to 1890 and winning a position in Asquith's Liberal Cabinet from 1905 to 1911. His services were recognized by an earldom in 1895 and a marquisate in 1912.

A generation later, the ritual of courtship was repeated when Lady Carrington supervised the 'coming out' of her own daughters. In 1898 her eldest daughter, Marjorie, appeared for the first time in Society at a Devonshire House party, and was presented to the Queen at a Drawing Room. The Seasons had their desired effect, for Marjorie was married by 1901 to Charles Wilson, a shipowner, who became the second Baron Nunburn-holme in 1907. During the next few years Lady Carrington acted as chaperone for her other daughters, noting in her diary in 1907: 'Ball Stafford House. All the 3 daughters there. The Queen was kind to Rupy.' Ruperta married Viscount Lewisham, eldest son of the Earl of Dartmouth; in 1910 Alexandra became engaged, seven years after coming out, and Victoria had her 'first dinner in a low gown' seated next to the King.

THE BELATED TRIUMPH OF TRUE LOVE: MARY GLADSTONE

Mary Gladstone's story is unusual for several reasons. She was not only the Prime Minister's daughter, but also his private secretary from 1880 to 1885. Born in 1847, Mary had a sheltered childhood in a large, happy family, which often included the twelve Lyttelton cousins as well as the seven Gladstone children. The lives of the Gladstone children were dominated by their famous father. Six of the seven found it almost impossible to leave the parental home at Hawarden. Helen remained a spinster, Henry married at thirty-eight, Stephen at forty-one and Herbert at forty-seven—all in their parents' last years or after their death. The third daughter, Agnes, who married at the age of thirty-one, made the revealing comment in 1891 that 'I am the only one of the seven with a separate home and life apart.'[4]

Mary was over-protected and given little independence until her later twenties. Although she officially 'came out' at seventeen, she was far more interested in music, religion and her father's career than in the few balls she attended. Her mother, Catherine, had the beauty to shine without much help from others, and the personality and political status to be indifferent to the niceties of social etiquette. Unlike Lady Carrington, she did little to push her daughters forward in Society and encourage them to marry. Mary's sense of inferiority and her lack of conventional beauty probably increased her antipathy to the Season. During a visit to Ashridge in 1870 Mary was tormented by comparisons with the three lovely Talbot sisters, and her own assumption that 'the gentlemen here think me a very staid young woman only perhaps rather dull'.[5]

Mary Gladstone's emotional development was retarded by her family life. Her hero-worship of her father probably limited her ability to develop close relationships with other men for many years. In their different ways both brilliant parents unintentionally made her feel inadequate. Throughout her early years Mary suffered quietly from an inferiority complex and a 'terrific feeling of shyness'. She threw herself into the social activities of the extended family and was intensely involved in religion and music, but increasingly lacked a sense of purpose in her later twenties.

A milestone in her emotional life in the 1870s was her struggle to

come to terms with her unrequited love for A. J. Balfour—the first
and perhaps the greatest love of Mary's life. She had few suitors
after 'coming out', in part because her formidable father was a
deterrent to most young men. Balfour was one of the few men who
could equal her father in Mary's eyes, and he spent considerable
time with the Gladstone and Lyttelton girls from 1870 to 1874. In
July 1870, Mary visited Hatfield while Balfour was there, and a
month later she was invited to spend a week at the Balfour home
at Whittingehame. Balfour visited the Gladstones at Hawarden in
November, and the Gladstone family scented romance when
similar visits followed during the next year. Mary felt deeply hurt
and shocked when she discovered that it was her beloved cousin,
May Lyttelton, who had captivated Balfour, and not herself. Mary
sent a long, sad letter of 'confession' to her mother in 1871,
explaining that she had sought in vain to prevent her love
developing, even though she knew society viewed such a one-sided
love on a woman's part as wrong and unnatural:

it is dreadful to have to speak of it and you will understand me when I ask
you to lock it up in your own mind . . . Any question you wish to ask me I
will answer by letter, but I cant *bear* to *talk* about it . . . Though it is
utterly impossible to some people to be able to understand the feeling
being awakened when there is not the shadow of grounds for hope, still I
think you will be able to enter into it when you think of what he is. I never
allow myself to think of the future unless to try and face the reality of his
not caring . . . for *anybody* to know is like taking the bandages off a
wound.

Even in 1885, the love and the hurt remained: 'how shall I be able
to help loving him always but I can think *now* quite calmly of all
that is past, and see that it must have been good for me'. This
emotional trauma helps to explain the fourteen year gap before
Mary fell in love again. The experience increased her maturity and
also her resignation to the role of spinster.[6]

On her thirtieth birthday in 1876 Mary Gladstone lamented: 'I
can't say there is much that is satisfactory to look back on.' Two
years later she considered life 'a great failure on the whole', as she
contemplated her lonely fate as spinster with trepidation.[7] But her
life was transformed after 1879 because of her increasing involvement in her father's political career. Her total absorption in
politics from 1880 to 1885 as her father's private secretary

probably also involved a degree of emotional sublimation after her experience with Balfour. Mary flourished at the centre of the political world and fully appreciated the advantages she derived from her privileged position at 10 Downing Street. She delighted in regular visits to the theatre, concerts and art galleries, while frequent trips to Oxford and Cambridge gave her easy access to the intellectual world.

Mary Gladstone's political involvement also caused a dramatic change in her personal life. A circle of eminent and talented male friends replaced the diminishing group of unmarried female friends of her youth. The glittering new coterie included Lord Rosebery, Sir Arthur Gordon, Professor James Stuart, George Russell, Burne-Jones and Henry Holland. Mary commented: 'Very odd how my greatest friends are all about fifty . . . But it's a pleasant footing because so delightfully safe.'[8] The close friendship and esteem of Lord Acton, in particular, worked wonders for Mary's self-confidence. During a successful visit to Walmer Castle in 1881, she noted: 'altogether it was a very different thing to the snubbed Mary Gladstone of 1870'. She commented in 1885 that 'there are about six who each think I am specially dedicated to them in a sort of sacramental friendship'.[9]

Mary's self-esteem benefited further from a number of marriage proposals from younger admirers. Clearly she blossomed in her thirties. She rather regretfully turned down Edward Ottley, the curate of Hawarden and a man of 'great personal beauty' in 1879: 'just one or two differences and it might have been perfect. As it is I have had no kind of repentance though I do love him really in a way—but not the real way.' Mary's susceptibility to male physical beauty was not surprising, given her conviction of her own inadequacies. Edward Ottley boosted her female ego at a critical time, and she noted in her will, years later: 'I owe much more to him than he knows.' Hallam Tennyson also suffered a broken heart on Mary's account from 1879 to 1883, though the relationship was gradually restored to a comfortable friendship. One evening in 1883 when Hallam was feeling especially depressed, he told Mary that she must marry sometime, only to receive the reply, 'I thought very likely not.'[10] By this time Mary was more happily resigned to the likely prospect of spinsterhood, because she was finding considerable fulfilment in her political life.

To the surprise of her family and friends, Mary Gladstone

eventually achieved the goals of marriage and motherhood, which her father clearly saw as the feminine ideal. When she fell in love with Harry Drew at the advanced age of thirty-nine, her parents were shocked, not least because he was yet another poor curate at Hawarden and nine years her junior. Mr Drew's appeal lay in his intelligence, sensitivity and 'great personal beauty'. The fact that he was a clergyman living in a world so far removed from politics no doubt also contributed. There was no question of competition with Mary's formidable father, as in the case of political suitors. A clergyman had the additional advantage of a vocation which assured Gladstone's supreme respect. Mary gained personal happiness through marriage by retreating entirely from her father's world. Their courtship was unusual in Mary's social circle. In July 1883 Harry Drew became the new curate at Hawarden, working under Mary's brother, Stephen Gladstone. In the months that followed he dined frequently at the Castle, while Mary went to church nearly every day. She noted in her diary for 29 December 'a most tremendous anxious day', when she evidently fell in love. Two years later Mary 'kicked away the only barrier that remained' and became engaged.[11] She explained the situation in a farewell letter to Rosebery on 29 December 1885:

The person I am going to marry is a curate here, and it means a complete change of life to me. I do not shrink from this and I think I have realised in my soul all it means—But he is the first who has loved me whom I have loved, and so though he has none of the things which would recommend him to the world, and is most shy and humble and quiet and penniless, everything else must go to the winds . . . I don't expect my friends to understand it. They will think it giving up *the* most interesting and unique kind of life in the world, for one which is quite the ordinary lot of ordinary mortals. I want you to send me your blessing and to try and sympathise with me a little, for your friendship has certainly been one of the best things in my past life.[12]

This 'farewell letter' illustrates the Victorian view of the finality of marriage and the woman's inevitable movement away from her former family and friends.

The Gladstone and Lyttelton families made relatively little fuss about Harry Drew's poverty and general unsuitability because of Mary's 'advanced age'. They had assumed she was a confirmed spinster for so long that they had no high expectations of a match for her. Instead they tended to emphasize the loss to the 'Grand

Old People' rather than the gain for Mary. Mary had made herself indispensable at home and her marriage would automatically disrupt her parents' self-centred routine. The inconvenience her marriage would cause the Prime Minister was inevitably a powerful factor in her family's response. She was made all too painfully aware that she must view her engagement through the critical eyes of 'brothers and sisters and mothers and fathers and cousins and aunts'. Her sister Agnes thought it pathetic to think of their mother so late in life 'without her front tooth'.[13] Catherine Gladstone's stunned response reflected a rather ungenerous attitude to the spinster daughter she had so long taken for granted: 'the difference of age is a bore but then she is so very young for her age . . . I have been *immensely taken by surprise*—another drawback is poverty . . . as to London, I dare not think of that—and the gap . . .'[14]

For Mary herself there was another personal crisis to confront. She was fully aware of the major break in her life that this marriage involved, and more than a little afraid that she would lose her hard-won sense of personal identity. Marriage involved a dramatic change in life-style for most Victorian women, but for Mary it meant a greater break with her social and political past. During December 1885 Mary suffered 'the great crisis of my life', as she fought the doubts and fears that marriage would mean a 'White Burial' of 'awful overwhelming change'. She could neither eat nor sleep properly for a few weeks and 'worked myself up into a fright'. Alice Balfour tried to reassure her: 'I don't see why your new life should be so absolute a goodbye to the me-in-the-world parts of the old. Don't go and resolve beforehand that the break will be complete.'[15] Now established as a capable woman in her own right, she was afraid that her identity would be submerged in marriage, just as it had been in her earlier family life. But by January 1886 the 'nightmare of uncertainty' was over and the wedding day brought complete relief: 'still the great wonder was to feel it all so natural, to feel I was I when I thought I was going to be somebody else'. They were married at St Margaret's, West-minster, the bride and bridesmaids wearing the plain white muslin deemed appropriate for a poor clergyman's wife. They honey-mooned in a 'dear little snug nest' at Berkhamstead House, lent by Lord Brownlow: 'quite happy from the first to the last, and never felt bored for one minute'. They talked, wrote letters, drove out in the pony carriage, read four chapters of 'Job' and other books. Mary's mother, sister and friend visited them at intervals and afterwards they toured Harry's relations.[16]

Mary Gladstone's fears were never realized because she had chosen her husband and future life wisely. She exchanged her father's full and satisfying world of politics for the equally demanding and all-embracing life of a clergyman's wife. Politics and religion had always been her supreme passions and she was able to satisfy them both at different stages. She would have been bored as the leisured society wife of an upper-class politician, but found fulfilment in sharing the burden 'of a young clergyman's life, the perpetual contact with sickness and suffering, Sin and Death and every form of sorrow and poverty'. Six weeks after the wedding Mary wrote: 'I have never [missed for] five minutes the old life and excitement one bit, and feel increasingly the wonderful snugness and serenity, "quietness and assurance" of married life.' She assured her mother that Harry was the ideal husband: 'He is a most wonderful person for fitting in to all my nooks and crannies, and yet at the same time keeping his own individuality, letting me propose and plan and initiate, and yet like a firm rock for me to lean upon.'[17] Harry Drew was also the right man to deal with her father. For twelve years the Drews lived with the elder Gladstones at Hawarden Castle, a difficult arrangement made practicable by Harry's busy, independent life and quiet strength of character, combined with William Gladstone's respect for clergymen. During these years Mary had two miscarriages, but was overjoyed at the birth of a daughter in 1890.

FLIRTATION AND CALCULATION: LAURA TENNANT

Laura Tennant was born sixteen years after Mary Gladstone, in 1862, and they were too dissimilar to be close friends. Laura was one of eight children born to Sir Charles Tennant, the illegitimate son of a Glasgow merchant. Sir Charles made a fortune out of railway development and rapidly trebled his father's capital. This large, happy family lived in a baronial style modern castle called 'Glen', amid wild moors thirty miles from Edinburgh. Laura and her closest sister, Margot, saw little of their parents: 'we were wild children, and, left to ourselves, had the time of our lives', despite the succession of helpless governesses.[18] In 1882 Mary Gladstone described the Tennant circle at Glen as 'the maddest, merriest whirl from morn till night—wonderful quickness, brightness, wit, cleverness'. Laura at twenty fascinated her most—small, sharp, delicate, talented, full of life and high aspirations. Laura was already determined to take warning from her sisters' early marriages and 'keep her own freedom'.[19] Her complex nature also included elements of mysticism, a profound sense of sin, and a deep religious devotion, illustrated in a journal she kept at the age of thirteen: 'one long wrestling in prayer . . . such a relentless searching out of her own short comings'.[20] Adolphus Liddell, one of her many devoted admirers, saw Laura as 'a mixture of innocence and mischief', combining the gaiety of a child with the tact and aplomb of a mature, radiant woman:

In the deeper parts of her nature was a fund of earnestness and a sympathy which enabled her to throw herself into the lives of other people in a quite unusual way, and was one of the great secrets of the general affection she inspired . . . But there was something more than all this, an extra dose of life, which caused a kind of electricity to flash about her wherever she went, lighting up all with whom she came in contact.[21]

The courtship experience of Laura Tennant can only be understood in the context of the exclusive 'elective affinity' known as 'the Souls'. Membership was confined to a charmed circle of 'personages distinguished for their breeding, beauty, delicacy and discrimination of mind'.[22] They consisted of about three dozen members of the Wyndham, Talbot, Charteris, Curzon, Brodrick and Lyttelton families, with George Curzon, Alfred Lyttelton, A. J. Balfour and St John Brodrick at their centre. Elizabeth Haldane defined them as 'men and women of the world who helped to break down many stupid social shibboleths . . . conversation was at a high level, without the priggishness of the blue-stocking or the solemnity of the salons'. Balfour stressed that the group had no organization or purpose, but was rather a spontaneous circle born of natural friendship and sympathy.[23] The male Souls mainly came from older landed families, with close public school and Oxbridge ties, but the group provided a means of entry into aristocratic society for women like the Tennants and Edith Balfour. The Souls allowed their female members to seek a more advanced role for themselves without being categorized either as bluestockings or political hostesses. They were able to ignore some of the social conventions because of their celebrity status as Souls.

The Tennant girls were a great success when they 'came out', and the family became linked with the Souls when Charty Tennant married Lord Ribblesdale in 1877. Edith Lyttelton later recalled that Laura had 'several lovers' by the time she was twenty-one; 'and I have no doubt that with some of them she had expressed affection and pity with caresses and kisses'.[24] Mary Gladstone was shocked by the unorthodox behaviour of the Tennant girls and afraid to leave her brother, Herbert, with them at Glen in 1882: 'I don't want him to fall in love, as everybody does who goes there, those sort of girls get proposals everyday, and they get so used to refusing it costs them nothing.' Mary considered both Margot and Laura 'a little doubtful as a wife'; there was always a danger of them doing 'something just a little too wild and unmaidenly'.[25] Mary disapproved of the Tennant household, in true Victorian manner:

There was a kind of Star and Garter freedom and recklessness of manners and talk, there was no reserve, no restraint, no holy places kept sacred . . . It must do harm to some who came there, seeing every barrier knocked down, some it must inflame to flirtation and waste of emotion, some bloom it must surely knock off a girl. Was maiden reserve a passed-away dream, a blown-up delusion? Ought there to be no sanctuaries?[26]

Mary later blamed the Tennant parents for gross dereliction of duty in bringing their daughters up so irresponsibly, 'never dreaming any kind of protection or guard was necessary, expecting them to run about London all by themselves, no matter what house or what quarter'.[27]

By the 1884 Season, Laura began to become involved with three members of the Souls—Adolphus (Doll) Liddell, Gerald Balfour and Alfred Lyttelton. She first met 'Doll' Liddell, a barrister, in January 1884 when she was twenty-two and he was almost twice her age, with considerable experience of women. Liddell combined good looks with powerful physical sensuality and refinement of taste. Doll noticed Laura as 'an able little animal, very smart and flirty' and was unable to resist 'her wonderful charm, her wit and gaiety, her sudden storms of emotion, her sparkling mind'. They were soon holding hands and indulging in long, passionate kisses, regardless of the convention that a kiss signified engagement. Laura wrote to Doll that many men had wanted to marry her, but none was like Doll and she had never before 'got to know a man as quickly'. Edith Lyttelton later explained that Laura had not previously experienced 'the surge of physical passion, and when it touched her she was overwhelmed by it'. But Laura's unrestrained manners, her affectionate gestures and caresses led Doll to misjudge her at first, assuming 'she was light and of an easy virtue'.[28]

In late September 1884, Laura invited Doll to her beloved home, the Glen, where they had long talks and 'occasional fondlings' in an atmosphere untroubled by chaperones. Laura's penchant for gothic romance was demonstrated by an incident described in Doll's diary when she 'dragged' him one evening up to a high tower, clutching him in a frenzy, then 'threw herself back into my arms'. They met again in Newcastle in mid-October, supposedly chaperoned by her brother, who was 'most obliging and stayed away for a long time'. In December 1884, Doll entered Laura's bedroom at Mells (Frances Horner's house), remaining 'about an hour with her in my arms'. Laura's love-letters were just as provocative as her physical presence, with their curious mixture of whimsical sentimentality, childish exuberance and biblical imagery. She could be tantalizing, coy and flirtatious. Laura described to Doll how she used to stand almost naked in her nightgown on her balcony: 'the wind is my dearest lover . . . his strong arms are round me and I seem to be one with him and sometimes when he is almost savage he bears me away'.[29]

Laura's behaviour was unbearably frustrating for Liddell. In November 1884 he noted: 'She won't marry me, she says I am too near herself—odd things females that she should like all this caressing and not be able to go beyond.' She teased him physically and mentally, but refused to advance towards matrimony or greater physical satisfaction. She wrote to him on 3 December:

Yes. I quite see the impossibility of understanding how I can go *so* far and no further . . . Anyhow you must forgive her—She never gave way before and think *how* many times [Doll] has—bless him—and she has given him *so* much of herself.[30]

Doll justifiably wrote 'horrid things about her looking at life from the footlights of her own egoism'. Laura argued that she had hoped they could just be natural and not worry about self-control in friendship. Bacon was cited in defence of ideal friendship: 'Nuptial love maketh mankind, friendly love perfecteth it.' She would descend into the 'cellars of life' with a husband but into heaven with a friend. While she supposed she would one day have 'a grown up man in her life', meanwhile she liked being 'a little Bambina' with her Doll.[31] To place the most favourable interpretation on her behaviour, she was deceiving herself about the nature of the friendship Bacon had in mind. The spiritual friendship of her fantasies was scarcely compatible with her passionate response to the pleasure of sexual caresses. While Laura indulged her physical senses, her brain cautioned her against marriage to Doll.

Doll's torment was not over when Laura agreed to marry Alfred Lyttelton in January 1885. On the day of her engagement, she admitted to Doll that she had kissed Alfred but not that she was engaged: 'there was more of the old thing', and the night ended as they sat together 'clasped and fondling, poor Bina crying hard'. They continued to meet almost every day until Laura went abroad in March and married in May. One evening in February they sat alone in her London bedroom, holding hands and talking until midnight. In May, Frances Horner protested about their 'lover-like behaviour' in a train, saying that there had been 'rows about Laura's goings on'. Laura certainly married Alfred while still under Doll's sensual spell, and Frances Horner believed that Alfred must have suffered considerably. Edith Lyttelton commented: 'I should never have allowed the scenes and episodes which she did—after engagement—after marriage. But I was brought up differently.'[32] It is a tribute to Laura's spell over Society that her unorthodox behaviour was so readily overlooked.

While Laura was tormenting Doll, late in 1884 she was making yet another conquest in Gerald Balfour, Arthur's youngest brother and nephew of Lord Salisbury. Laura was never serious about Gerald. She apparently wanted to prove to herself she could captivate even the Balfour family, particularly as Arthur seemed immune to her charm. Laura boasted to Doll in October 1884 that she had made a convert in Gerald Balfour: 'I am very proud of him because he was *such* a heretic—and vowed he never would like the Bina—and now he likes her very much.'[33] Laura took the unusual step of calling on Gerald's sister-in-law, Frances Balfour, in London late in November. Frances wrote immediately to Arthur expressing her concern about the motivation of 'that extraordinary creature' who 'fairly stumped me' at first meeting. Her reaction to Laura was akin to Mary Gladstone's. Both women saw the need to protect their menfolk from this bird of prey. Frances considered Laura entirely lacking in refinement, while not exactly vulgar: 'as for him, the sooner it is over the better . . . it will be a mystery how he can *see* such a lack of refinement, and yet care as he does'.[34]

Two weeks later Laura announced triumphantly to Doll that Gerald 'had proposed to her on the doorstep' at Grosvenor Square.[35] Laura then wrote to Frances of the 'infinite pathos of life', protesting that she could not think how it all happened. Gerald received an unsatisfactory letter from her and went to see her at the Glen, insisting on a better explanation of her behaviour. Frances was infuriated that Laura gave no reason for her conduct, though she 'steadily encouraged Gerald *until* he proposed'. Even the infatuated Gerald said that Laura had 'not behaved well to let it come to the point it did'. Frances told Arthur that Gerald was left unutterably miserable: 'it is *the* misfortune of the whole thing that it takes away for some time at least the chance of his marrying which is what he wanted and really intended to do, if I can find the right woman!'[36] But Gerald was still young (for a Victorian male) at thirty-one and Frances must have considered his marriage in 1887 to Lady Betty Lytton vastly more suitable in every respect, not least in refinement.

Whereas Laura ignored many of the social conventions with Liddell, her courtship with Alfred Lyttelton was decidedly proper. This probably reflected Alfred's superior social status as the son of Lord Lyttelton as well as Laura's marital intentions. She determined in advance the type of husband she sought, as Margot explained later: '[Laura] wanted to marry a serious, manly fellow, but, as she was a great flirt, other types of a more brilliant kind obscured this vision.' Just as Margot later selected Asquith on rational grounds, Laura picked out Alfred Lyttelton, Gerald Balfour's close friend, as a suitable candidate and prompted Margot to invite him to Glen late in 1884. Laura's confusion over her love affairs had 'worked so much upon her nerves' that she was in bed with acute neuralgia during Alfred's first visit, no doubt enhancing his impression that she was pale and delicate. She recovered sufficiently to prolong his visit and announce to Margot that she intended to marry him. Alfred was the youngest son of Lord Lyttelton, aged twenty-eight and a Liberal. Laura was

attracted by his 'manliness', his extraordinary personal charm and
good looks, his immense popularity and superb athletic ability. He
had had a brilliant cricket career at Eton and Cambridge and a
worthy academic record, before being called to the Bar in 1881.[37]

The transition from the vivacious darling of the Souls to the
betrothed maiden resulted in considerable mental conflict for
Laura. Alfred was very busy during their brief engagement of five
months, leaving her ample time to indulge her feelings in
correspondence. On the one hand Laura professed to be the new
independent woman for whom marriage was a defeat. She told
Doll:

I am so sick of being told I shall have a rock and a shield and a hiding
place—all twaddle. It is odious being engaged because it is so false . . . the
fact is marriage is a lower form of life—a happier I am sure, but a more
egotistical.[38]

Laura told Alfred that some women mistakenly made marriage the
'chief end of their being—and think to have a house and a husband
in it is the highest ideal of life'. Had she not married Alfred, Laura
thought she might have done something more important with her
life. Marriage in the abstract had few attractions, while the
celibate life had 'more nobility'. She warned Alfred that she was
'not a bit a good domestic woman . . . You won't mind my not
marking the towels well or ordering the dinner different every
day.' She insisted that she and Alfred must 'glorify marriage and
never sink below the thrill and never grow stuffy', and not allow
marriage to alter their relationships with old friends.[39] Frances
Balfour was perceptive: 'Some girls marry to get liberty but in this
case everyone fears that Laura Tennant should think people want
her to lose hers!!'[40]

Yet another side of Laura's character delighted in the role of the
passive, delicate virgin bride, enjoying her 'engaged feebleness'.
She called Alfred 'my true Knight' and 'my King', and referred to
herself as 'your little babe clad in white'. Laura sent an odd letter
to her prospective brother-in-law, Arthur Lyttelton: 'after the first
fearful sense of humiliation at being so completely conquered I
feel perfectly happy in my slavery'.[41] She assured Alfred that she
liked being commanded and would work for the glory of the 'Best
Beloved'. Throughout her engagement Laura emphasized her

frailty and her delicate constitution, encouraged by Alfred's solicitude:

I saw the doctor today . . . He said I was tremendously below par—a thing doctors always say . . . and that I had no blood in my body and no pulse and no vitality—He said I had an ulcerated sore throat and that I was to drink port and tonic and put salt into my bath and never to get tired so that when I marry you may not have a little washed out bride whiter than a tablecloth.[42]

Alfred responded protectively that 'it is so easy to see that in many things you are not as others are'.[43] Perhaps Laura over-reacted in her evident anxiety to assure Alfred that despite her reputation, she could indeed 'sit still and rest and be a woman, instead of a cracker or a penny pop gun'.[44] Her love letters to Alfred contrasted strongly with the passionate epistles to Doll. They were rather formal, passive and childish in tone, even hinting at fear of a full sexual relationship now that it was a definite prospect: 'you will be very tender to me 'cos it makes me better than the other thing and you will forgive me—and understand—I feel you are so strong and big and wonderful that I have nothing to do but to rest'.[45]

They were obviously deeply in love (as even Doll admitted), but Laura's emphasis was on the spiritual love of the soul. They were married in May 1885 at the fashionable St George's church, Hanover Square, before a huge crowd of friends. Their honeymoon was spent at Lady Ashburton's house, Melchet, and seems to have been unusually idyllic. They spent the first few months of married life at 21 Carlton House Terrace, lent to them by Lady Frederick Cavendish, Alfred's sister, before moving into a house given by Laura's father. Soon after the wedding, Laura wrote to Alfred: 'How wonderful it is that 5 weeks should graft our souls so close to each other', and Alfred replied, 'I never expected to be so happy as I have been since our marriage.'[46] Society saw them as the perfect married couple. Eleven months after the wedding Laura died after childbirth and her legend began.

TEMPTATION, REMORSE AND AN HONOURABLE CONCLUSION: EDITH BALFOUR

Edith Balfour was the second Soul to marry Alfred Lyttelton after a stormy relationship with Adolphus Liddell. Edith (known as

DD) was the eldest of seven children of Archibald Balfour, a London businessman. Through Spencer Lyttelton, Edith was introduced to the Souls, and her intelligence, wit and charm gave her entrée to 'the most attractive and brilliant life possible'. The Balfours had not lived in London very long and DD admitted later that she was very immature, ignorant and inexperienced for her age: 'though I was 23 I had never been moved by any man, or ever been kissed', though one or two had proposed and several others turned 'spoony'. But in June 1888 she became involved with Doll Liddell and for the first time experienced an overwhelming physical attraction. At the time, Doll was also engaging in 'petting episodes' with Laura's two sisters, Margot Tennant and Lucy Smith. He was twenty years older, the gap in experience between them was very wide, and DD allowed him to treat her as a child. Despite her powerful physical response, she knew that she could never marry him and she was continually beset by moral scruples which had never worried Laura. Edith's retrospective view of her own behaviour is revealing:

In those days kissing and petting was not a pastime among boys and girls of our kind and by disregarding convention in Doll's case I was punished by over three years of struggle against an overmastering influence . . . There is a great deal of wisdom in the convention I was brought up in, and did not adhere strictly enough to, that one should not kiss unless one loved sufficiently not merely to give oneself, but to be ready to pass the rest of life with one's lover. That was what damned me. I wanted to eat my cake of sensation and thrill and have it also intact . . . My advice to any girl is to avoid allowing her physical passions to be stimulated by anyone but the man she profoundly honours and admires.[47]

Edith Balfour felt even greater remorse because she briefly considered marriage to Doll as an escape from the consequences of threatened family financial ruin. She was appalled by the prospect of 'the sordid effort to make a living' as a governess, but was quickly shamed out of her temptation to accept Doll's proposal, and the family fortunes were happily retrieved.[48] Yet she disregarded the convention that a rejected proposal should end the relationship, causing distress on both sides. Edith's mother finally intervened, after Doll had stayed with their family party at the Tyrol for three weeks in September 1889. Edith warned Doll

that he could join them only on strict terms of friendship, but Mrs
Balfour was understandably confused and her patience exhausted:

my mother took me out for a walk and then reproached me bitterly for not
telling her that I was engaged to Doll and when I said I was not she
became very angry and said I ought to be. She declared my reputation was
being ruined and that I was behaving abominably. I told her that Doll was
behaving like a friend only, but that though I loved him very much I could
not and would not marry him. She begged me to for she said people were
talking about me—that awful Victorian threat. I cried and she cried and
altogether it was a terrible interview and the end of it was that she said I
must tell him that he was to go and that we were not to meet.

Edith found the parting agonizing, but the pain was followed by a
sense of 'relief—almost peace—an obsession lifted'.[49] They did
not meet again for about five months, but eventually, after Edith's
marriage, Doll proved that 'a lover may be turned into a friend'.

From 1886, Edith had viewed Alfred Lyttelton as a man set
apart, sanctified by the loss of both wife and child. 'I did not think
he could or would ever love again—not realising that love of the
dead need not be lost in love of the living.' She first became
friendly with Alfred during a week's visit to Mary Gladstone at
Hawarden in September 1888. His 'strong vigorous personality,
his lovely sympathy, his intuitive understanding of all my gropings
were in such glaring contrast to Doll's exotic and poetic influence'.
During the struggle with Doll in 1889, Edith gradually fell in love
with Alfred. She did not expect love in return, 'only that it would
fall to me to give him back a home and some happiness'.[50]

Edith sensed that Alfred was about to propose on 21 February
1892, but he was too nervous to say the words and held out his
arms to kiss her instead. Alfred's formal proposal arrived by letter
next day, correctly assuming that her kiss signified acceptance. He
used conventional masculine and feminine images: 'I felt your
gracious tender soft figure bend within my great rough arms.'[51]
Having expected only warm affection, Edith was surprised and
delighted at his ardent tone, and all her repressed feelings 'burst
their banks'. Alfred's formal interview with her father took place
three days later; as was normally the case, it came after the woman
had accepted the proposal and its main purpose was to discuss
financial arrangements. Edith's father feared that Alfred, as a
youngest son, would change his mind when he discovered the

parlous state of the family fortunes, but all was well. In any case, Mr Balfour's business interests recovered sufficiently to allow Edith's sister, May, an annual income of £1,000 by 1898, and Edith presumably received the same.[52]

The only serious problem affecting their marriage was of quite a different order. Laura's two sisters, Margot Tennant and Charty, Lady Ribblesdale, deeply resented Alfred's second marriage 'and in many trivial ways did what they could to prevent it'. Margot instinctively felt that a second marriage involved disloyalty to her beloved Laura, as she explained to Mary Drew: 'Alfred's engagement is a wrench at the old ties, and I am bound to say from my point of view they are broken in two.'[53] Margot's resentment was intensified because of Charty's love for Alfred, which developed when Charty's 'constant companionship' helped him through the first years of loneliness after Laura's death. Charty had married the handsome, sports-loving Lord Ribblesdale when she was nineteen, but Alfred 'was the love of her life, and the fact that he was her brother-in-law had made constant intercourse possible'. The law against marriage to a deceased wife's sister was designed to discourage precisely this sort of situation, which must have been fairly common after the death of a first wife in childbirth. Alfred later confessed to Edith that he had once been afraid of his feelings for Charty developing into a stronger love, but instead he felt 'devoted affection mixed with gratitude and sympathy'. Charty suffered greatly, having dreaded a second marriage for years, but she behaved well. Margot was the 'bludgeoner' who informed Edith that Alfred had loved Charty for years and that he ought never to marry again considering all Charty had done for him. Alfred, in turn, had to listen to criticisms of Edith's looks, her intelligence and her health.[54] Margot's behaviour caused considerable distress but failed to stop the marriage.

Edith and Alfred were engaged for only three months before their Easter wedding in 1892. The first month was devoted to 'new relations, friends, presents, trousseau'. Edith then followed Laura's example by travelling to Bordighera, where she usually spent the early months of each year on a doctor's advice, as a cure for incessant headaches. Alfred was left in England to organize a wedding abroad, since this was better for DD's health and they wished to avoid a London Society wedding. They decided to live outside London for the following summer and Alfred found a house in Wimbledon which would give her peace and quiet. Edith admitted later that she was far too romantic to worry about the 'possible strain on our relations if we were to be alone together evening after evening'. But their three months in Wimbledon were a 'great success: 'we got much closer to each other than if we had spent the usual "Season" months in London in a ceaseless round of parties and visits.' This was an intelligent move on Edith's part, since she confessed later that year to a jealousy of Alfred's 'extraordinary popularity and the way everyone wanted him.'[55] She gradually came to terms with his sociable nature, and found in their relationship 'a passion of the spirit as well as of the body'—a rare combination which lasted a lifetime. Three years after their wedding, she recalled for Alfred their joys in married life:

. . . the education of one's mind, the training of children, the ordering of one's house, the talk, the books, the pictures—and oh best and worst of all—the merging of all interests and aspirations with the interests and aspirations of only one man! . . . I can never complain of life for lacking interest and fulness.[56]

SELECTING THE ELIGIBLE CANDIDATE: MOLLY BELL

A generation later, moving far up the financial scale, though not so far up the social scale, Mary (Molly) Bell's experience of courtship was a good deal more conventional. Molly was the granddaughter of a millionaire iron-master from Durham, Sir Isaac Lowthian Bell, Fellow of the Royal Society and Liberal MP. In 1904, her father, Hugh Bell, inherited the baronetcy together with three-quarters of a million pounds.[57] Hugh Bell's first wife died of pneumonia after childbirth and he later married Florence Olliffe, daughter of a distinguished Irish physician. The three children of the second marriage, Hugo, Elsa, and Molly, grew up in a happy, devoted family circle at Redcar. Despite, or perhaps because of, their privileged background, Molly and Elsa received a poor education from an ill-equipped governess, with an emphasis on ladylike accomplishments.[58]

Molly and Elsa were launched into the national marriage market at the age of seventeen. They had already learned to mix with young people of both sexes through their relationships with the Bell and Stanley 'cousinry'. The Bell family took a house in

London for the Season every year until they acquired 95 Sloane
Street on the death of Lady Olliffe. The two girls had enormous
social advantages before 'Coming Out' as their mother, Florence
Bell, was an excellent hostess who gave frequent parties and one
large dinner party each week. Every Friday from 4 p.m. she gave
'At Homes' where her two daughters poured tea and helped to
entertain the guests. In February 1899 Molly's aunt, Mrs Lyulph
Stanley, gave a Coming Out Ball for her daughter Sylvia and for
Molly. A month later Molly was presented at Court, like her two
sisters before her: 'To those who had any pretensions to be in
Society, with a big S, it was essential to be presented, at Court. My
parents were not in the highest circles', but all their friends'
daughters had been presented, so the Bell girls followed suit.[59]

Molly believed that the three Seasons of 1901–3 were crucial for
her future life, and they were fully documented in her daily diary.
As the months passed she experienced increasing pressure to reach
the all-important decision about her marriage partner, especially
since the oldest girls on the Season's circuit were only twenty-three
or twenty-four. Molly was quick-witted, vivacious and very
attractive, with a constant string of admirers and a steady flow of
invitations. During her three Seasons she went to dances three or
four times each week, chaperoned by her mother or an aunt: 'In
our social circle no self-respecting girl would be seen at a dance
without her chaperone.' At the end of each dance there was a
break of five to ten minutes when the ballroom emptied and the
partners sat out without their chaperones in the library, the
smoking room or on the stairs.[60]

Molly's vital three Seasons were dominated by the Hon.
Geoffrey Howard, second son of the Earl of Carlisle, amongst a
host of other admirers. Geoffrey was a handsome Liberal, four
years older than Molly, educated at Cambridge and harbouring
keen parliamentary ambitions after an unsuccessful candidature in
1900. They had known each other since Molly came out in 1899,
but their friendship grew much closer during the 1901 Season. In
July 1901 Molly rather reluctantly allowed Geoffrey to kiss her on
the mouth at a dance interval, causing a day of torment
afterwards: 'I think I've never spent a more absolutely beastly
day', thinking of nothing else and blaming herself entirely for the
shameful indiscretion.[61] During the next two years they analysed
their feelings at frequent intervals to decide whether they loved

each other sufficiently well to overcome the obstacles. Hugh Bell did not need to exercise any direct veto because the two young people were fully aware of the problems involved, and not apparently resentful of family disapproval. Geoffrey confessed that he could not make up his mind whether he wanted to marry Molly, as 'it was not a consuming passion'. He had nearly proposed on several occasions but 'had always feared the abyss', while Molly's parents 'had of course been an obstacle, and our lack of money'.[62] Geoffrey's political ambitions appeared to be nearer fulfilment in February 1903 when he was offered the safe seat of North Cumberland at the next general election. Molly recognized that marriage for him would mean sacrificing his political ambitions. 'On £1500 [a year] you cannot keep a seat and a wife.' The decision to break off their relationship was taken by Geoffrey in mid-1903 when he admitted that he could not risk marrying her: 'I am not going to marry until it becomes absolutely necessary, and as yet it isn't.'[63]

Throughout these two years of soul-searching Molly and Geoffrey met frequently. During the 1902 Season, Molly flirted with 'my three' as she labelled Jack Pollock, Geoffrey Howard and Charles Trevelyan, uncertain which, if any, to marry, though with a strong preference for Geoffrey. She was initially relieved that the immediate decision lay largely out of her power since it was the man's prerogative to propose, but increasingly she recognized her responsibility to make up her own mind. Her discussions with Geoffrey usually took place at balls, while they sat out dances together on the stairs. But she took the initiative for an important conversation in February 1903, when she sent a messenger to ask Geoffrey to visit her at home for an hour at midday, while her mother was out. She was also far more than a passive partner in their final meetings. On 15 June 1903, Molly persuaded Geoffrey to join their party at a ball, where they sat out a number of dances on the stairs. When they lost the coveted top stair to another couple, Molly daringly suggested they climb up to the attic stairs: 'the game was up, then, obviously, and we behaved more ill than I could have believed of either of us.' Molly knew that 'he was being tempted by the same physical attraction' which prompted him to kiss her two years earlier. For some time they discussed 'if we ought to [kiss] without ever calling it by its name' and weighed the remorse to follow if they sinned. Geoffrey argued that 'if I did now, I should degrade your standard, both of a girl, and of a man'. But Molly put her arm round his neck and kissed him twice. After much agonizing, Geoffrey insisted they break off their relationship entirely since they did not intend to marry, and they agreed not to see each other at parties or balls.[64] Molly concluded in her diary:

No. I am not now in love with him. Passion seized me that night at the Ross Winians, but it was nothing more than insuperable physical attraction, to the strong man who is my best friend, and whose mere bodily presence is so much to me. That was all that he felt too—the desire to have and to hold my life and youth and radiance. Was I wrong to give it to him as much as I did? Maybe—but oh it was pleasant![65]

Their resolution weakened when they met at another dance a week later, but Molly's cousin, Sylvia Stanley, prompted Geoffrey to write to Molly, insisting on a complete break. He should not come to call and they must not dance together, if they were to restore their relationship to a reasonable basis of good friendship: 'It is only because I like you so that I do this. If I cared less, I should not trouble. If I cared more—well, things would be otherwise.'[66]

Three months later, when Molly was safely engaged to Charles Trevelyan, she met her first love again only to find that Geoffrey had at last decided he was 'more or less in love with me now'. Molly experienced a wave of bitterness that 'it had come too late for either of us'.[67] Eight years later they held a post-mortem on their relationship. Molly charged that Geoffrey 'cast matrimony in my teeth . . . he had behaved ill towards me—he had made me fall in love with him, and then had retreated'. He responded that Molly's mother 'had choked it off as much as anyone could, by showing how much she disliked it'.[68] The ambivalent nature of their relationship seems to have been largely a product of the practical barriers. He felt free to love her only when she was engaged to another, because he was still very young and was not prepared to sacrifice a political career for an expensive wife. Howard did not marry until 1915, when he was thirty-eight, but neither did he attain a political career of the first rank. Molly's feelings were more deeply engaged, but her pride was hurt; besides, her parents disapproved strongly and she probably felt she could make a more suitable match.

Charles Trevelyan courted Molly Bell in two stages, enabling her to mature and to learn from experiences with other suitors. Molly did not meet Charles through the Season's festivities, but at one of her mother's parties, to which her half-sister, Gertrude Bell, had invited him. Charles was the eldest son of Sir George Otto Trevelyan, politician, historian and third largest landowner in Northumberland. After Harrow and Cambridge, Charles won a by-election as Liberal member for Elland in 1899. As a young man he had fallen deeply in love with a beautiful girl of his own age, probably Angela Kay-Shuttleworth. He persisted in his suit for many years in the face of refusal, and suffered acutely as a result, conducting later love affairs 'with a view to marriage and not because passion had swept him off his feet'.[69] Charles was eleven years Molly's senior and she felt quite 'unprepared to talk seriously with one so far above myself in experience and achievement'. She was attracted by his striking good looks, impressed by his lively intelligence, and awed by his political career, particularly as she knew nothing of politics.

They saw a good deal of each other through the summer of 1902, despite Molly's preference for Geoffrey Howard. Charles attended the Bell parties, they met at the houses of mutual friends and went on occasional group walking and cycling expeditions. He was a poor dancer and sought quiet corners at dances where they could talk. Charles was idealistic, intense and deeply serious, utterly unlike any other young man of Molly's acquaintance. He sought to educate and mould Molly's 'untutored mind into a more reasonable shape', lecturing her on ethics, politics, tariff reform and Irish home rule. Her ignorance was criticized and her frivolous behaviour condemned. When he praised her beauty he did so in the 'earnest hope' that its power would be '*unceasingly* used for high ends and not frittered away in unpurposeful pleasantness'.[70] Molly wavered between boredom and fascination at this unusual education, grateful to have for a friend a man 'so infinitely my superior in nearly all things'. But Geoffrey Howard was still her 'dearest friend', while she considered Charles too opinionated, rather selfish and too engrossed in his own aspirations.[71]

By June 1902, Molly felt confused, overwhelmed and 'rather in a dark hole'. She acknowledged later that she had played her three 1902 suitors off against each other and 'behaved disgracefully to all of them'. She was already twenty-one and fully aware of Society's expectation that she must make a good match very soon. Family pressure to marry Charles intensified and they discussed her matrimonial intentions with enthusiasm. The end of the Season in itself added to the tensions, since the prospect of many months' separation encouraged a suitor to propose or risk losing the lady. Molly was mortified at a dance on 30 June 1902 because she had to refuse both Charles Trevelyan and her old suitor, Jack Pollock, on the same occasion: 'it was almost more than I could bear; I nearly cried. I was so sick of refusing people by then.' She felt wretched over the next few months, knowing she had hurt Pollock badly, lost two good friends, and failed to find a man she could marry.[72]

Trevelyan withdrew completely from Molly's social circle for a year. Meanwhile he again fell in love with a lady who failed to reciprocate, and at the age of thirty-two began to dread 'the long loneliness of life'. Society's matrimonial organization favoured men in two respects well illustrated here. Charles only became anxious about his choice of marriage partner in his early thirties, whereas the pressure affected Molly ten years earlier. Moreover, an eligible male could move in and out of the Seasons' events for two decades, whilst a woman's prospects were made or marred by her performance over two or three brief years. Late in the 1903 Season Charles met Molly again by chance and they were both glad to resume their friendship 'on a Platonic basis', with an agreement not to fall in love. They had both matured in the intervening year. Charles was 'less domineering' and Molly no longer such a 'silly flirtatious creature'—more amenable to becoming the serious-minded woman of Charles's dreams. This time Charles supervised her political and literary education more systematically, starting with Morley's *Cobden* and a 'course of philosophy'. Molly rapidly recognized that 'mine will generally be the under side in a discussion, and you will ride triumphantly over my flattened corpse'.[73]

Mrs Bell was thrilled by Lady Trevelyan's formal invitation for Molly to visit the Trevelyan family home in August 1903. All parties involved were aware that Molly was 'on approval' on this first visit to Wallington. There were many opportunities for long walks together, evading other guests and the inevitable chaperone. They kissed for the first time and agreed that they were not yet in love, though Molly confessed her mother's enthusiasm for their marriage. Charles expounded on 'the sort of love I must expect to get, which is not merely the romantic passion'. During one walk 'he talked nearly all the time, telling me his views on marriage, and the bringing up of children, and what my part would be'.[74] Years later Molly claimed that she never thought about Charles's wealth and prospects during that visit, though her mother had made it abundantly clear that he was an excellent match. The questions which concerned her related to Charles as an individual—their differences in temperament and education, and the eleven-year age gap.[75] Yet she was naturally receptive to a brilliant marriage which carried obvious social and economic advantages, combined with powerful parental approval. Even Charles's authoritarian nature was counterbalanced for Molly by respect for his knowledge, talents and experience. She viewed the wife's role as subordinate and believed Charles was 'a better example to take than Geoffrey'. Her definition of a beloved husband was 'the person to whom you wanted to refer everything, who was the standard by which you measured things.'[76]

Molly was alarmed by the daily love letters which descended on her after the Wallington visit. The first letter was 'so full of passion that it frightened me, and I longed to be quit of him for ever. However he calmed down and I got to like his letters more and more.' Molly asked Charles to confine himself to 'sensible letters': 'at my age, when I am only just growing out of the romantic idea of falling in love, I cannot leap into the real passion as you have done.' Moreover, he had no right to send love letters since they were not engaged. Charles was certain of his love for Molly, but she sometimes felt averse to being 'tied down to Life in any way'. Mrs Humphry Ward's daughter, Janet, who was engaged to Charles's brother George, told Molly firmly that Charles was too good a man to lose. Janet also admonished Molly for her uncertainty and 'for having gone as far as I had if I didn't mean to marry him.'[77]

When they met again on 15 September Molly told him to kiss her, because she had made up her mind: 'Confident of our love for each other, with the gates of Paradise opening before us, it needed nothing but that he should be assured of my complete understanding of his views on religion, and on the possession of money and its use.' It was important that they agreed on religion since they were both agnostics, though Molly retained a belief 'in some ruling Spirit'. Her parents were overjoyed after their fears that she would choose 'the wrong man'.[78]

They were engaged for only three months, though there was some debate about an Easter rather than a January wedding. But Molly contended that she loved Charles too much to wait two months longer than necessary: 'to have you absolutely my own: soul and body, in as much greater degree as marriage means'.[79] The formal engagement seemed suddenly to release the floodgates of 'the real passion' in Molly, and her letters show how far she had come to appreciate 'the physical joy of love'. By October she lived for 'nothing but your love and our happiness'.[80] She was frustrated even at such a short engagement: 'I long for you more strongly and passionately than any words can tell you . . . How much we are still animals! This is far more physical than mental, my desire to be with you.' By Christmas Molly admitted that 'as *you* put on self-restraint, *I* took it off. I think we *have* used our opportunities with moderation—and it is only because we know how near our marriage is, that we dare to look forward to the greater intimacy that comes with it.'[81]

During their brief engagement Charles was away for much of the time keeping prior appointments for a series of constituency meetings. Molly made supportive comments about his speeches in her letters, regretting that she knew so little of his political views and that she had not considered his 'great public life' more fully. However, her own political début was a great success when she was presented to his constituents in Elland: 'Once on my feet, the spirit moved me to say something, and without any forethought I made my maiden speech—the first of many hundreds.' Molly experienced the usual engagement ritual of being introduced to his friends and family, but it was not too arduous as their parents liked each other and their social circles intersected.[82]

They had a 'thoroughly conventional society wedding' on 6 January 1904 at Holy Trinity Church, Sloane Street—'bride in white satin, bridegroom in a frock coat, five bridesmaids'. Charles would have preferred a registry office, but Mrs Bell insisted on a smart church wedding followed by a reception at 95 Sloane Street. The first few days of the honeymoon were spent at Merevale in Warwickshire, the seat of Frank Dugdale, Charles's cousin. The remaining three weeks were a typical Trevelyan holiday in Cornwall—talking, reading, and walking over a hundred miles.[83] Molly Trevelyan later recalled the joy of her wedding night when she discovered with delight 'what a man's love was'. Her new husband's sensitivity and their mutual love overcame her shyness and her ignorance of sex, while Charles reassured her that the act of love did not necessarily mean having a child.[84] Their happiness in married love continued, with frequent references in Molly's diary to nights of 'wonderful love'. Their mutual delight in a passionate sexual relationship shone through their correspondence during frequent separations and despite the births of five children. Five years after their marriage, Molly considered it 'a very perfect state of things that we are not ashamed of our love and of our desire'.[85]

TWO MIDDLE-CLASS MARITAL STRATEGIES

(i) ESCAPE FROM HOME: MARGARET KING

The last two case studies move down the social ladder to the professional middle-class families below the level of Society's prime marriage market. Ramsay MacDonald, Labour leader and first Labour prime minister, was the illegitimate son of a servant girl, but he married Margaret Gladstone, daughter of a professor of chemistry. This last section examines the courtships of Margaret Gladstone and her mother, Margaret King, twenty-five years earlier.

Margaret King was born in 1844, the eldest of five, with two sisters and two brothers. Their father, the Revd David King, was a Scottish Presbyterian minister, while their mother came from a gifted Scottish academic family. The parents were authoritarian and possessive, resenting independent behaviour in their children, which they interpreted as lack of love for themselves. The children were brought up on a strict regime of earnest piety and rigidly observed social conventions. Margaret was always far more independent than her two younger sisters, who never escaped their mother's control. Though deeply religious, she was also gregarious, emotional and impulsive—inevitably frustrated by the claustrophobic constraints of her family life.

Even in her early twenties Margaret's emotional life was still at the immature level of passionate fantasies in her diary. When her imaginary love life left her sleepless she soothed her nerves by reading sermons. Evidently she was not short of admirers; her diary hints at several disappointed suitors, and her mother had

plans for a suitable marriage with a certain Mr C.E.   Margaret
noted that 'Mama is making a heavy cross for herself, and one for
me too about Mr C. E.' Through her voluntary work as a bible
class teacher, in 1869 Margaret met Dr John H. Gladstone,
seventeen years older than herself and a widower with four
daughters. Within a few weeks he figured prominently in her
fantasies, and this time she took practical steps to turn dreams into
reality, since her opportunities for meeting suitable marriage
partners were so limited.[86] Well aware that it was not socially
acceptable for the woman to take the initiative, she recognized
that careful manoeuvres were necessary to circumvent family and
social constraints. Her efforts to further her acquaintance with
Dr Gladstone were frustrated even by the etiquette of paying calls.
On 6 March 1869 she noted: 'After dinner the drawing room was
bright with cheerfulness and sweet with flowers and I was ready,
but no-one came . . . not Dr Gladstone. Afterwards it occurred to
me he could not well till Papa had called [first on him] as he said he
would.' This must have been a familiar situation for many middle-
class girls who were excluded from the balls and parties of the
Season, since social rules were often applied more rigidly at lower
levels. By 26 April, however, Margaret grew tired of waiting for
the good Lord to overcome the hurdles of social convention. She
wangled an invitation to Dr Gladstone's home with the help of
mutual acquaintances. Margaret tried to persuade herself that
'God had arranged it all. I was free from blame or forwardness in
this matter.' Yet she felt deeply guilty about deceiving her mother:
'I was so frightened and ashamed when Mamma questioned me
about when and where I had last seen him.' That particular ploy
was successful, but her plans seemed to be shattered by her
family's move from London to Edinburgh in May. Margaret
treasured 'the clasp of his hand and words of blessing', but feared
that 'he may not do anything himself now I am away'.[87]

   Her prayers were answered on her twenty-fifth birthday on 19
May 1869, ten days after they parted. Dr Gladstone's proposal
took the unusual form of an initial letter to Margaret's mother
intimating his intentions. His formal letter to Margaret followed
and it was handed to her after morning prayers, with instructions
to read it alone upstairs:

Since we parted ten days ago I have felt more and more strongly that there ought to be no longer any reserve between us, but that I ought frankly to tell you the great affection I have for you, and so to leave you free to express whatever sentiments you may entertain. I have hesitated to ask you to become my wife—and I still pause—for there seem to me peculiar circumstances which in justice both to you and myself we ought calmly to discuss.

He suggested that he might call on her family in Edinburgh to discuss the matter further, knowing that God would direct their decision.[88] Margaret thought her parents were pleased, though Mrs King privately told her other daughter, Elizabeth, that it was not what she would have chosen. When Dr Gladstone arrived from London, 'we had a long talk and our troth was plighted'. The 'peculiar circumstances' mentioned in his letter were presumably the seventeen-year age difference and the four stepchildren, but these evidently caused no anxiety for Margaret, though they may explain her mother's reservations. Dr Gladstone talked to each of Margaret's parents in turn, and the newly engaged couple ended the day with 'a happy talk in cosy schoolroom by firelight'.[89] After John Gladstone returned to London, Margaret confessed in her diary her fear that she might have made a mistake: 'it seemed as if I did not love him and were not happy'. But, like Mary Gladstone, she recovered from this natural fit of nerves and her loving letters to her fiancé gave no hint of anything but devotion: 'I hope God will help me to be only a joy and comfort and help to you in your home, and in all the work of your beautiful earnest life.'[90]

Margaret's major problem on marriage was not the transition to stepmotherhood, but rather her mother's abnormal resentment. Mrs King's early show of pride that her eldest child was to be married soon changed to bitterness at the loss of a daughter. During her ten-day honeymoon in the Perthshire highlands Margaret wrote three times to her mother, who still protested that she was being forgotten, even though the newly-weds stayed with the King family immediately afterwards. Margaret felt obliged to warn her mother that she could not write so often in future: 'You know I have a much larger household than yours, in this much busier place, and far more people coming and going.' Mrs King alternated between passionate endearments and harsh recriminations.[91] It was perhaps inevitable that her bitter sense of loss should eventually be turned against the man responsible. Two months after the wedding she sent a savage letter to Margaret:

[John] has not once written to me since he took you away and I have felt as if I had lost a daughter without gaining one single thing. He seems nothing to me sometimes. I look upon him as a robber who has carried off a treasure without making any compensation—and I feel bereaved and cold and hard and unkind and miserable.[92]

The sense of loss was natural, but in Mrs King it took on obsessive proportions. Margaret asked John to 'pity the pained feelings and not be vexed', for she understood that her mother's behaviour partly reflected jealousy of Margaret's marital happiness when 'the blossom time of [her own] life seems gone'. The saga continued during Margaret's one brief year of marriage, since her loving letters of reassurance could never plumb the depths of her mother's bitterness. Margaret wrote in May 1870 that she hoped the coming grandchild would help to compensate for the loss of her mother's 'first baby'.[93] Margaret's enthusiastic response to marriage and stepmotherhood may have increased her mother's sense of betrayal.

Margaret's only doubts about her marriage came understandably at the start of their honeymoon, when tension and uneasiness were high, as she recorded in her diary:

the loneliness and pain grew, and more and more as we walked to the Falls of Bracklinn. He was speaking of the Presidentship of the Royal Society, we were looking at the view, but my heart was aching sorely. I was thinking too of the going to Pembridge Square so soon, and fearing the mistress's duties, when we sat down on a large stone at the falls. I told John a little and some tears fell, but I felt still as if he did not understand me and oh so sad that it was possible to be lonely walking by his side, and wondering if it must be often thus through life, till half before tea half after sitting at his feet I told him all, and was comforted 'as one whom her husband comforteth' and understood his love better and was understood and not thought foolish, and the sorrow and loneliness were gone, replaced by utter rest and peace.

Two days later they had a happy talk in their bedroom about Margaret's willingness to leave her old home, 'of John's being father, mother, brother, sister all to me'.[94] By 7 August Margaret wrote to her mother: 'I am more and more happy as John's wife, daily finding in him more to love and honour, and nothing to need to get used to.' Margaret's journal records a delightfully relaxed intimacy between husband and wife, founded on a powerful love mixed with pride in 'my noble and bright and beautiful husband'. A typical October entry suggests a happy companionship:

After dinner John and I had a merry romp like two wild children chasing one another round the room. He finally caught me by jumping over the table. Later came the serious grateful talk and prayer, and I thought ere going to sleep with thankful wonder how every part of my manifold life, wild fun and mischief, deepest thoughts and highest longings are met and responded to in John.[95]

They also talked freely about John's first wife, May, 'and how past things make us nearer and dearer to one another rather than less so'. John told Margaret that she resembled May, but Margaret had no more fear of living in the first wife's shadow than had Edith Lyttelton.[96] These women came to terms with the memory of the first wife through frequent honest discussions.

Margaret took her four stepdaughters in her stride, as so many Victorian stepmothers seem to have done, and she rapidly became an efficient housekeeper. After the ten days' honeymoon in Perthshire and the brief visit to Margaret's family, they returned to John's London home for five days, 'during which I made a great dive into the housekeeping and took full possession of my new dominions . . . and the necessity of taking at once a good deal upon myself made me quite brave'. Margaret's pride and possessiveness about her female domestic sphere are worth noting. Then the second stage of the honeymoon began, when the four children and their nurse were included in a month's holiday in the west country. On returning to London, Margaret organized the children's lessons, established a regular routine for the housekeeping and accounts, and began receiving calls. Two months after their wedding she reviewed her achievement with considerable satisfaction:

Few new mothers and mistresses find things so smooth and bright as all is for me. The servants one and all are good and thorough and obliging, and not only allow, but like me to look into everything, and take my own way, which is wonderfully little different from previous arrangements. The children have all accepted me warmly and lovingly; they fully expect me to arrange and decide everything about their lessons, dress, and all that they may or may not have; and are always happy and satisfied . . . I am very happy and thankful.[97]

She was fully aware how fortunate and privileged she was: 'God seems to have given me the cream of all things. I can have all the uninteresting troublesome parts of work done for me' by the servants, while she had the 'pleasant superintendence'. Margaret enjoyed the 'happy duty' of sharing John's studies, the daily reading with the children, 'and winning all loving influence over them, watching to help and guide and make them happy day by day. This too with my servants.'[98] But 'this whole perfect lot' came to a premature end for Margaret with death in childbirth, only a year after her wedding.

(ii) THE SEARCH FOR A SOUL-MATE:
MARGARET GLADSTONE

A generation later the cycle of courtship and marriage was repeated by Margaret's daughter, a second Margaret Gladstone. Dr John Gladstone brought up Margaret and her four stepsisters, and his sister-in-law, Caroline, 'was the nearest approach we ever had to a mother'. Like her mother, Margaret's late adolescent years were dominated by her religious faith, which led in turn to infatuation with her parish vicar, Mr Glyn, for three years after she was nineteen. During her early twenties Margaret's chief emotional involvement seems to have been with three male cousins, all of whom came close to proposing to her. The one she cared most about was Andrew Henderson, a worthy businessman twenty years older than Margaret. For eight years his devoted unselfish affection made him a closer friend than any of her immediate stepfamily. Consequently, when Henderson's sentiments became romantic, Margaret blamed herself for having innocently encouraged him, though she never remotely contemplated marriage. She felt it was the worst mistake she ever made, since she nearly wrecked a rare friendship which meant much to her: 'The only things on my side are that for all these years he has never dared to propose to me . . . I don't think I ever sent him a letter or met him anywhere without asking God not to let me go further than I ought.'[99]

Margaret was in no hurry to marry before she found the right man. As she tried to relate her Christianity to 'present-day needs' she gradually moved in the direction of socialism from 1892. Like Margot and Laura Tennant she quite deliberately sought out 'a suitable mate', and like them and her own mother she was not

afraid to take the initiative. Margaret subsequently confessed to
Ramsay MacDonald that she heard a great deal about him from
the Montagu girls when she became committed to socialism, 'and
thought you were the sort of person I should like to marry'. It was
not difficult to arrange for Lily Montagu to introduce her to
MacDonald in 1895. At the same time she sent a donation for his
electoral support to Herbert Samuel, whose reply strengthened
her confidence in her hero's -character and political prospects.
They were engaged within a year. Margaret's first love letter after
Ramsay's proposal was written on 25 June 1896, rejoicing
contentedly in this 'new good gift' of his love.[100]

The double commitment to MacDonald and to the socialist
cause was vital to Margaret. Before their engagement, both
MacDonald and Ben Tillett warned her strongly about 'all the
hard and dreary and bedraggling side of the work in the Labour
movement', and the immense change that it would mean in her
life. She replied briskly to Ramsay: 'From the practical point of
view the advantage seems to be all on my side—I want to be more
free to do works for the Socialist movement and at the same time I
don't think it right to cut off family ties. If I can combine the two
by marriage so much the better.'[101] Margaret's half-sister, Bessie,
was sceptical about this motivation for marriage: 'It seems to me
that you and Mr MacDonald have sympathy on only half the
points necessary—and the political basis is not enough for life-long
happiness.' Margaret quietly assured Bessie that 'we weren't
marrying on a political basis but for something rather better' and
were indeed well-suited to each other.[102]

MacDonald was far more concerned than Margaret about the
gulf between them in terms of social class and finance. She tried
to reassure him that their class differences could be an advantage: .
'the contrast between our upbringing is encouraging, not despair-
ing; we have come by different paths to the same beliefs and aims.'
The matter of her private income of about £450 per annum
required more consideration, in view of his lack of money and
their socialist ideas. Her ideal was 'a simple life right among the
working people', giving up her private income to the socialist
cause, and doing 'my share of potboiling'. But they decided to
keep her income to allow them more freedom 'to do the work we
thought right'. Margaret dispelled Ramsay's concern about their
religious differences equally forcefully. She sent him her private

128   *Courtship and Marriage*

journal to help him understand how her religious views had
changed as her socialism developed. She was convinced that now
they shared 'broad religious views' and a 'practical working faith'
which transcended denominational differences of dogma.[103]

Margaret and Ramsay were afraid that their engagement might
give 'pain or offence' to Margaret's family, especially since none of
them shared her interest in the socialist movement. Margaret
knew it would be 'a very great blow to them if they disliked
my marriage', though she would survive 'if they cut me off
unpleasantly from some of my old surroundings'. But she need not
have worried. She took her father into her confidence soon after
Ramsay proposed, 'told him a good deal' about Ramsay,
concealing only the details of his illegitimate birth, and even
provided a prospectus of Ramsay's lectures. Dr Gladstone's
favourable response was echoed by the rest of the family: 'when I
said you were a Socialist and I was afraid they wouldn't like it they
only smiled'. The family arranged a dinner on 23 July to welcome
Ramsay, despite the death of Margaret's grandmother. He was
urged to come as originally planned: 'they are all anxious to
welcome you as one of the family . . . Don't feel an intruder even
in this sadness'.[104]

The wedding took place on 23 November 1896, but Margaret's
journal and correspondence are most unusual in making little
reference to wedding preparations, except for the discussions
about the marriage settlement. Her wedding day journal entry
merely noted: 'My aunts came. Wedding. Down to Exeter.'[105] The
only direct references to the marriage in the correspondence were
highly practical. Margaret received an abrupt note from the
London School Board, informing her that marriage 'involves the
loss of your services as a Manager' at the Portobello Road
School.[106] The other communication was a most unusual piece of
written advice relating to sexual activity on honeymoon from her
married half-sister Bella:

There is just one hint I should like to give you before you are
married—Auntie Carey gave it me . . . Be sure to provide yourself *at first*
with a diaper or something of the kind—*that* is best—for your own
personal use—to save soiling the bed clothes. You can pop it under the
pillow till required. And do not overdo yourself at first—don't take long
walks etc, but behave as if you were not quite well [i.e. menstruating]—
which will be the case.[107]

Margaret's happiness in marriage was clear to all. Six months after the wedding she told her aunt, Elizabeth King, that she was blessed by 'a growing happiness as all true love ought to be'. Six years later, a fellow socialist expressed the hope that Margaret's face would always reveal such 'clear unmistakeable happiness and content'.[108] An added benefit for Margaret was that she found the mother she had always sought in Ramsay's semi-literate mother, Annie Ramsay. She welcomed Margaret generously, showing no hint of jealousy at losing her only child. She told Margaret: 'i feel i have left charge of him now as i now you will be nearer to him than ever I have sinse he left home.' The two women were delighted with each other when they met and Annie Ramsay was determined to 'do all in my power to make you bothe happy'. Annie Ramsay became an indispensable part of the MacDonald family in subsequent years, frequently taking care of the six children while their parents engaged in socialist activities.[109]

Affection was an important factor in all these experiences of courtship, but it was an overwhelming force only in the case of Mary Gladstone, whose primary motive for marrying Harry Drew was romantic and physical love. It could be argued that Margaret Gladstone and her mother, Margaret King, also married chiefly for love, but other forces may have been operating in both cases. Marriage to Dr John Gladstone offered Margaret King a number of advantages—higher social status, escape from a claustrophobic family life, and the transition from aimless daughter to wife and stepmother. Her daughter, Margaret Gladstone, actually selected Ramsay MacDonald as a 'suitable socialist' and the type of man she wanted as a mate. If Laura Tennant and Edith Balfour had married for sexual passion and romantic love, presumably they would have chosen Doll Liddell. While they emphasized their bond of 'spiritual love' with Alfred Lyttelton, both women were aware of his elevated social status and his immense personal popularity, not to mention his handsome appearance and charming personality. Alfred Lyttelton was an eminently suitable man for Souls to marry. Similarly, if Molly Bell had married for love alone, she might have chosen the unsuitable younger son with little money rather than the highly eligible heir to a baronetcy.

These case studies provide valuable evidence about courtship behaviour and the initial experience of marriage, to compare with the stereotypes derived from fiction and elsewhere. Victorian marriages have often been portrayed as formal and distant, with partners unable to develop close physical and emotional relationships. Peter Gay has rejected such prevailing stereotypes: 'The bourgeois experience was far richer than its expression, rich as that was; and it included a substantial measure of sensuality for both sexes, and of candor—in sheltered surroundings.'[110] My own study justifies a similar conclusion. With one exception, the women in these case studies observed Society's rules regarding courtship behaviour with considerable care. Even the inimitable Laura Tennant did not throw discretion entirely to the winds. The degree of continuity throughout the period from 1860 to 1914 is remarkable—Molly Bell was still firmly bound by Victorian courtship conventions in the Edwardian years. However, despite the stress on pre-marital chastity and ignorance, combined with the lack of opportunity for pre-marital sexual experiment, most of these women established loving, close and fulfilling relationships with their husbands.

Sexual and emotional behaviour within the privacy of the pre-marital and marriage partnership is always difficult, if not impossible, to reconstruct. Victorians and Edwardians make it even more difficult for us because their public use of written language has proved a misleading guide to their behaviour. The formal styles and prudery of language, with their irritating euphemisms, have been interpreted as evidence of repressed and inhibited behaviour. Prescriptive manuals, religious writing and novels of the period strengthened this image. But the relationships explored in this chapter suggest that the Victorians and Edwardians talked and wrote much more freely in private than in public and their actual behaviour was far richer and more rewarding still. As Jane Hardy wrote to her husband in 1857: 'It is better, perhaps easier, to shew love in deeds than in words.'[111] This perception was expressed innumerable times by Victorian and Edwardian wives, within the world of domestic privacy.

PART TWO

CHILDBIRTH

5

The Joys of Childbirth

THE history of childbirth in Victorian and Edwardian Britain has been neglected for a number of reasons. It has been argued that childbirth is beyond the scope of distinctive historical analysis because the essential female experience of birth has remained more or less the same over time. Yet attitudes and rituals have changed and the problems experienced in pregnancy and labour have varied with the advance of medical knowledge. Moreover, as one French historian has recently pointed out, 'the greatest difficulty for anyone who tries to understand [childbirth in history] is the total lack of firsthand testimony'.[1] Until now the major sources for the history of childbirth have been contemporary literature, medical texts, and health manuals written largely by doctors.[2] The correspondence and diaries of the women in these political families provide a significant new source of evidence about women's personal experience, which complements and questions the more prescriptive and literary material.

WOMEN, HEALTH AND DOCTORS

The history of childbirth has recently become involved in a wider debate about women's health, arising chiefly from research into American sources. For example, Ehrenreich and English have argued that from about 1850 to 1910 'the boredom and confinement of affluent women [in the United States] fostered a morbid cult of hypochondria'.[3] This view has since been transferred to Britain, with the claim that 'sickness . . . came to pervade middle class female culture . . . their main role was that of sickness.'[4] More research is needed before this argument can be validated for Victorian Britain, especially as the wider social and cultural history of Britain and America was significantly different. Many British medical texts certainly expressed sexist views of women's reproductive functions, with arguments about the governing role of the uterus in women's lives, and the debilitating effects of menstruation and menopause. But this chapter is concerned with the experience and the response of the women themselves. It is not enough to state that women were an inarticulate group whose views were unrecorded. There is a tendency to patronize women of the past by assuming that they all blindly accepted medical authority in all forms, and to trivialize real pain and suffering by labelling it psychosomatic.

Only a few observations will be offered here on this general thesis about women's health, since this chapter is chiefly concerned with childbirth. There were certainly some female hypochondriacs among the families in this study, but they were in a decided minority. For example, there was a female relative of Lady Emily Hankey and her daughter, Lady Stanhope, mentioned in their correspondence simply as 'Cecil', who subscribed to the cult of sickness. In 1882 Cecil 'feels her nerves very irritable . . . and the swimming in her head hums', so she constantly visited different doctors and hydropathic establishments. But Cecil's relatives considered her health excellent; she looked 'uncommonly well' and was excessively 'fanciful about her health'.[5] This critical judgement could be reproduced a number of times, showing that most women regarded hypochondriacal behaviour as abnormal. The most extreme cases of female invalidism in these families were a tiny minority of rather desperate spinsters, who will be examined in detail in a later chapter. Women like Gladstone's sister, Helen, and Evelyn Murray turned to psychosomatic illness as the only way to gain attention, given their lack of any acceptable role. Some adolescent girls showed tendencies to hypochondria for similar reasons, in a phase of their lives often marked by boredom and aimlessness. But the majority of the married women in these families seem to have had little time or need for imaginary ailments. Most of them led busy lives, bearing and rearing children, organizing large households, participating in social and philanthropic activities, and fulfilling the role of politician's wife.

It is surprising that there were not more genuine invalids, in view of the serious threats to life posed by disease and medical ignorance. When they did suffer from severe pain or a fatal disease, most of them did so stoically. No doubt the image of the valetudinarian derived in part from the very real suffering caused by miscarriages and birth-induced complaints like prolapse. Women often used the euphemism 'unwell' in attempting the discreet concealment of 'undignified' maladies of a gynaecological nature. Both men and women seem to have endured intense and prolonged pain with resignation and little complaint. Family correspondence frequently attests to serious illnesses and painful medical treatment borne with courage. Margaret Gladstone died painfully from puerperal fever in 1870, with pyelitis and pelvic cellulitis. But she never complained, merely accepted that 'I must suffer now', and 'wished the doctors to learn what they could from her case'.[6] In 1888 Margot Tennant submitted stoically to 'deep burning' of the throat four times in four weeks, as treatment for an unspecified throat complaint: 'My head felt as if it were coming off when the little red iron hissed across my throat.'[7] When Mary Playne had a mastectomy for breast cancer in 1907, the operation was 'deeply and radically done' leaving her 'very miserable physically'; yet her family marvelled at her 'calmness and courage and determined cheerfulness, so that her relatives have not been allowed to worry and be miserable. She really is a heroine!'[8] These family records indicate that the Mary Playnes and Margaret Gladstones were more representative of Victorian and Edwardian women than the notorious hypochondriacs.

The general attitudes of the women in these families to their doctors deserves brief consideration since it has some bearing on their experience of childbirth. Most of these women could afford the best doctors available, who were often the authors of the influential medical texts of the period. There is no evidence that these women read the popular health and childbirth manuals, but they received the benefit of the verbal advice of the top medical authorities. Such advice sometimes conflicted since the Victorian medical profession was far from monolithic. Overall the women's negative comments about their doctors outweighed the positive, and their dominant tone was sceptical. They exchanged information about doctors, and frequently substituted a second doctor with a different remedy if the treatment of the first seemed inappropriate or ineffective. They were very clear that they were employing the doctors, there was little exaggerated deferential behaviour and they had no qualms about seeking second opinions. The treatment which Lady Frances Balfour and her sister received for hip and leg disorders caused Lady Frances to attack 'the not infrequent absurdities of medical advice' in the 1870s.[9] Lady Constance Stanley was convinced in 1870 that Dr Comberbatch's

remedies 'have most certainly made her [Emily] worse'.[10] Fifteen
years later Elizabeth Haldane described a particular doctor as
'untruthful and quacky'.[11] Katrina Conway in 1900 condemned
her daughter's medical treatment as 'abominably organised,
wretchedly carried out, and tinged with so much that is ugly and
incompetent and revolting'.[12] Lady Evelyn Murray in 1911
condemned doctors on several counts; 'they normally have a way
of fibbing to their patients', they 'only think of their pockets', and
their numerous fatal mistakes were 'covered by the earth'.[13]

These women were unlikely to be manipulated by their doctors
or to become mindlessly dependent on their opinions, nor would
they easily be persuaded that women were congenitally sick. They
had few illusions about the advances of medical science. Lady
Acland summarized their view of doctors very well in 1879: 'I have
always found in anxiety I cared little for medical opinions . . . they
can only say, as to the future it is in God's hands.' But she was
quick to admit that good doctors like her brother-in-law, Professor
Henry Acland, could provide 'help and comfort'.[14] Doctors who
gained an especially bad reputation quickly lost their richer and
more discriminating patients. Mary Drew remarked of her
physician in 1893 that he was 'unnecessarily careless and bungling'
so that now 'none of the gentry employ him'.[15] On the other hand
they were ready to praise and recommend those who did their best
to advise sensible treatment to ease the pain and who offered
comfort when they could not cure. Lady Lyell gave Lady
Campbell-Bannerman the name of 'a very famous "woman's
doctor"', whom she deemed cheerful, helpful and sensible.[16] Mrs
Marion Bryce spoke highly of a particular lady doctor in 1904:
'sometimes a new mind gives a fresh idea and the woman's point of
view is very helpful.'[17] Lady Cowper in 1875 was well informed
about various medical specialities: 'Comberbatch is very attentive
and very clever about Chest. Reed *I* think very clever and very
safe. Burrows is tip top, but more for kidney diseases like
Bright.'[18] These women examined their doctors before allowing
continued medical treatment.

PREGNANCY

It has been claimed that the cult of female invalidism was at its
height during pregnancy. Lorna Duffin has argued that 'a pregnant

woman was ill. The more time she spent lying immobile and inactive in bed, the better. By removing pregnancy and childbirth from the sphere of the normal into the sphere of illness doctors also removed its control and management from the women themselves.'[19] Impressions gained from Victorian literature have led to a similar conclusion that pregnant middle- and upper-class wives 'took to the sofa and a French novel, expected sentimental pampering, and were privileged to go off into frequent hysterics'.[20] Yet this stereotype represents another myth about Victorian society. Even the most popular British manuals written for women by the doctors themselves rejected the view that childbirth was a disease. Dr Thomas Bull's *Hints to Mothers* was the first advice manual solely devoted to antenatal care. First published in 1837, it was extremely popular, reaching its 25th edition forty years later. Attacking common errors, Bull contended:

My principle aim is to convince the nervous and timid woman that pregnancy is not to be looked upon as necessarily a period of deprivation and suffering; but, as it truly is, *a state demanding only a little more than ordinary care and prudence, and compatible with the enjoyment of health and comfort.*[21]

Another popular advice book by Dr John Conquest argued in 1848 that 'pregnancy is a natural alteration in the condition of the animal economy which every female seems originally intended to undergo, and therefore not to be considered as a state of "disease" '.[22] Towards the end of the century Dr Westland's *Wife and Mother: A Medical Guide* stated that parturition was a perfectly natural process, in which the doctor's duties were very limited.[23] Dr Mary Scharlieb assured women as well as doctors and nurses in 1895 that 'pregnancy, parturition, and puerpery are normal processes, and not in any sense diseases'.[24] Specialist medical texts which conveyed a contrary impression were usually dealing with potentially pathological developments in pregnancy and clinical problems in childbirth. Many individual doctors were anti-feminist and medical theories emphasized that female ill-health was often caused by uterine disorders, and by menstruation and menopause. But they took care to exclude the normal states of pregnancy and parturition from their lists of pathological conditions.

The most important evidence must surely come from these women's own perception that pregnancy and parturition were natural processes. They did not usually regard themselves as ill, except in the literal sense when suffering from morning sickness. Meriel Talbot's diaries record the births of ten children with remarkably little fuss, and Evelyn Stanhope treated her four pregnancies as a routine part of her life. Likewise Lady Carrington gave no hint of indisposition in her diary during her seven pregnancies, except for enforced rest to avert two threatened and one actual miscarriage. Despite prolonged sickness day and night for three months in 1869, Margaret Gladstone assured her mother that she was 'on the whole exceedingly well'. In her ninth month of pregnancy she reported that she was 'very well indeed', she suffered 'little inconvenience', and was still running up and down stairs as 'there seems so much to do'.[25] When Mrs Graham Smith was impatiently awaiting an overdue delivery in 1883, she wrote to a friend: 'I thank God that I am so well, just as well as any other person and as active as a cat . . . I expect to have a very easy time, and shall be all right again directly.'[26] Edith Lyttelton, May Harcourt and Margaret MacDonald all considered themselves 'extremely well', despite morning sickness in the early months.[27] Five days before Katherine Lupton's confinement, her mother wrote: 'Katherine continues very well and frisk, and is bright and cheerful too. She walks about still, with ease, and does her household work daily with precision and regularity.'[28]

Pregnancy was only perceived as an illness if there was a serious danger of miscarriage, which threatened the woman with painful death as well as loss of the foetus. Pregnant women who spent days on the sofa or weeks confined to bed usually took this course for excellent reasons which will be examined in the next chapter. Otherwise, activities during pregnancy reflected the women's view that it was a naturally healthy condition. Most followed the advice given by doctors and manuals that regular out-door exercise, such as an hour's walk each day, was necessary during pregnancy, but that violent or jerky activities like horse-riding or lifting weights should be avoided. Mary Drew found London's social life 'a perfect Godsend' at eight months: 'the variety gets me along . . . and I find plays and people the greatest boon'.[29] Mrs Graham Smith joked that she might go into labour 'at some art collection' in 1883.[30] Molly Trevelyan's detailed diary for 1906 gives little indication that she was pregnant. Her busy life continued much as usual, caring for her first child, maintaining a fairly hectic social schedule, participating actively in committee work for the Women's Liberal Federation, and doing many miles of serious walking. The only reference to pregnancy described a threatened miscarriage when she was obliged to spend two days in bed.[31]

When they discovered they were pregnant, most of these women were delighted. Frances Horner thought the condition 'vulgar in other people, and so extraordinary and almost poetic in oneself'. Edith Lyttelton felt as if she had 'a wonderful secret in me', while Margot Asquith experienced 'all the awe and hope of my condition'.[32] Lady Acland in 1874 eulogized the sanctity of motherhood when her stepdaughter, May, was pregnant: 'It is a mysterious dispensation, and seems to bring home the truth of the Fall of Eve and also of God's mercy.'[33]

A minority of women, on the other hand, found pregnancy unwelcome. They were not all uncritical exponents of the Victorian ideal of sacred and dutiful motherhood. Inevitably the timing was often wrong, particularly because so many of these women were either ignorant or ineffectual about contraception. It was fairly common for women to conceive on their honeymoon or shortly afterwards and have their child within the first year of married life. Some would have preferred a longer period in which to adapt to marriage before coping with the additional responsibility of motherhood. Maggie Acland was 'not as happy' about the news in 1879 as she felt she ought to be, largely on economic grounds: 'I would rather have waited a little, as it all adds to the expense of furnishing [the house]; there will be a nursery and a nurse to be provided very soon after we settle into our house.'[34] Refreshing honesty of this sort was not so unusual among Victorians as might be expected, especially when families were already large. Evelyn Stanhope was very sorry to discover in 1872 that an acquaintance was 'in the usual condition and expects an event in the spring, there being already seven children under ten years old'.[35] Katharine Bruce Glasier refused to allow herself to entertain the fear that she was pregnant again in 1894: 'for many sakes we don't want it yet'.[36]

Some women wrote endless letters to mothers and married sisters about their hopes and fears if menstruation was a few days late. Louisa Lady Antrim carried this habit to ludicrous extremes. When her period was one day late in 1884 she wrote to her sister, Lady Minto: 'I am filled with gloom, misery and depression as my relations [menses] have not come!' This performance was repeated three months later when menstruation was six days late: 'I was so certain that twins were due in May and I had written to Mrs Walters [nurse] and my misery can hardly be described.'[37] Twenty years later, Molly Trevelyan suffered similar anxiety but for the opposite reason. She desperately wanted her first child, informing her husband, mother, and sister of her slightest hopes whenever she was a few days' late 'diping' (menstruating). In July 1904 Charles Trevelyan visited their doctor to ask why Molly was not yet pregnant and was exhorted to be patient. Molly 'tried the dodge of not being at all active' for two or three months to avert early miscarriages—all to no avail. But on 26 February 1905 she recorded the good news in her diary that 'I have not been a dipe since Jan. 6th' and was certainly pregnant.[38]

The difficulties in diagnosing pregnancy with any certainty before the fourth month accentuated any fears or hopes when menstruation was overdue. Victorian women could only diagnose themselves according to the obvious symptoms, including amenorrhoea, fullness of the breasts and morning sickness, followed later by 'quickening' of the foetus and enlargement of the uterus. But these symptoms were not always present in early pregnancy and uncertainty could cause months of anxiety. A more certain method of diagnosis had been discovered in the 1830s—namely that the vaginal skin and cervix turned a violet colour in pregnancy due to congestion. However, this was only helpful if a pelvic examination was undertaken in the early months and this seems seldom to have been done until the end of the century.

In 1886 Mary Drew at the age of forty relied on her married sister, Agnes Wickham, for the information that 'the sea sickness comes in with some as early as possible and is usually in the first 3 months'. Years earlier Agnes herself had not quite believed she was pregnant until she had to let out her gowns.[39] In February 1875 Lavinia Talbot consulted her doctor to discover whether her ailments were the result of pregnancy or dysfunction of the menstrual cycle due to the strain of her sister's terminal illness. After a long talk, Dr Freeborn said that pregnancy was likely, but he 'cannot pronounce yet, and we must have patience. He says sickness and malaise would also be the result of "suppression" from causes of anxiety.'[40] Inevitably, many women experienced difficulty in calculating confinement dates because they were so uncertain about conception dates. Lady Constance Stanley thought Lady Newport must have made a grave mistake in her calculations in 1870, since she was 'on the wait' for her baby for ten weeks more than expected.[41] Mary Drew was most uncertain about the 'probable beginning' of her pregnancy in 1889, 'except that when I had antics [menses] last they amounted to so little'. Mary's mother dated it earlier, according to the onset of toothache.[42] Even in 1914 Margaret Shaw was convinced that 'doctors never really know' the expected date of birth.[43]

There is no evidence that the women in these families sought information about pregnancy in popular advice manuals. They usually consulted married sisters and close female friends, but they relied most of all on their mothers for moral support, advice and reassurance. Margaret Gladstone appealed to her mother in 1869: 'I don't know much about these things . . . you can give me some benefit of your experience.'[44] Elizabeth King responded with numerous lengthy letters full of sensible and practical advice. Lady Selborne did the same for her daughter, Lady Howick, as did many other mothers.

Doctors were not much more helpful with general antenatal care than they were in diagnosing pregnancy. Serious antenatal care was a post-1914 development, while women previously only received elementary advice about exercise, diet and constipation. Many women never saw a doctor until their pregnancy was well advanced, when they booked him to attend their confinement.[45] Even as late as 1897, when Mildred Buxton felt 'so very bad' during her pregnancy with twins, her only expectation of the doctor was that he might give her a tonic.[46] Doctors were mainly consulted for reassurance about exercise, diet, and more strenuous activities, especially if there was any fear of miscarriage. The earliest direct reference to an antenatal internal examination in these family papers came in 1895 when Edith Lyttelton saw Dr Hayes: 'We have had such a time with Hayes this morning . . . he measured me with a long iron instrument inside . . . said that everything was going on splendidly.' Far from feeling humiliated or embarrassed at the procedure, Edith fumed at the doctor's ignorance and objected to his advice to take life easily:

[Dr Hayes] has been most aggravating—in the way of never letting me know what he really wants me to do, and even when he gives me a direction he only gives it vaguely. 'You must lead a very careful life for the next few days.' And then when I try to ask him what he means, I have the greatest difficulty in discovering whether stairs matter, or drives or walks or indeed anything.[47]

Louisa Lady Antrim recommended in 1884 that her sister, Lady Minto, have a medical check-up from time to time: 'any pressure is so apt to cause a little disturbance of the kidneys', which was one of the most common problems of pregnancy and 'very easily checked'.[48] This seems to have been unusual advice in the 1880s. Even during the Edwardian period Molly Trevelyan made few references to antenatal care in her diary. The doctor's main visit before the birth of Molly's first child in 1905 was not until eight months: 'She [the doctor] prodded about inside me and said it had turned round and was now head down, and would be perhaps a week early.' During her 1908 pregnancy Molly telephoned the doctor to ask for a check-up at an earlier stage.[49]

Most of these women sought to keep their pregnancy a secret in the early months, until it was too obvious to disguise. This should not be ridiculed as Victorian prudery. As Lucy Stanhope admitted in 1872: 'it must be odious to be talked over by outsiders—and spoils half the pleasure—of a secret of *that kind*.'[50] Margaret Gladstone felt the same way in 1869: 'please don't speak of it yet. Nobody need know for a long time and I had rather not be watched and talked about.'[51] Some women preferred not to publicize their pregnant state because of uncertainty about the diagnosis. Lavinia Talbot had a strong disinclination to talk about her possible pregnancy in 1875 'as it is on the cards it will go off in ginger beer'.[52] A more serious reason for secrecy was the fear that publicity would make a miscarriage even harder to bear. When her 1886 pregnancy became a dangerous miscarriage which nearly killed her, Mary Drew was mortified that so many people knew the real cause of her long illness. For the same reason Margot Asquith kept her pregnancies 'a dead secret', even from her sisters, for as long as possible.[53]

Once secrecy became impossible women had to solve the practical matter of dress. Edith Lyttelton abandoned her secret in August 1892 since 'my clothes are beginning to be let out already—a degrading admission'.[54] Charty Ribblesdale made Mary Drew a 'circs.' tea gown when she began to feel 'fearfully fat' in 1889.[55] Margaret Gladstone sought advice from her mother on the 'inconvenient' dress problem in her fourth month of pregnancy in 1869. Velvet jackets and opera cloaks would help to conceal the extra inches, some dresses could be let out and pieces inserted in others, but perhaps a 'wide and comfortable' gown should be specially made for the occasion.[56] Even when Margot Asquith concealed her pregnancy from her sisters, she had to tell 'a few select people like the dressmaker'. Margot was small and her 'April mountain' in 1895 all too obvious. She abandoned a visit to Chatsworth in 1897 because she did not 'look decorative'. She had some cause to avoid tongues as sharp as her own, like Lady Alice Cecil in 1900, who compared Margot to 'the picture of the frog just before it burst'.[57]

Another practical problem to be solved once pregnancy was confirmed was the search for a suitable 'monthly' nurse for the confinement. The monthly nurse was usually only summoned when labour began, to attend the mother and child for one month from the date of confinement. Most women sought personal recommendations from friends and tried to obtain the same nurse for later confinements if she proved suitable. In 1908 Lady Selborne suggested that her daughter, Lady Howick, should apply to a staffing agency in London for a nurse: '[ask them] to send you several to see, so you can choose one you like, and then take up her character from her last employer and doctor'.[58] It was a process of trial and error. Mary Drew was pleased with Mrs Ballard in 1889: 'She understands and does not worry or fuss me, but is so very quiet and sensible.'[59] Some nurses inevitably turned out to be unsuitable, as Margaret Gladstone discovered in 1870: 'I may however have another nurse than the one you saw, as she does not improve on longer acquaintance and has been rather disagreeable—also tyrannical which would worry me exceedingly if shown to myself or the baby while I lay helpless.'[60] Lady Salisbury complained in the 1870s about the unnecessary worry and suffering caused in confinements by the 'extreme ignorance and folly of the nurses'.[61]

CONFINEMENT

For the majority of women with no complications, labour was just as natural a process as pregnancy. Confinement was treated with as little fuss as possible and integrated into the natural rhythm of family life as far as it could be. Normal labour was certainly not perceived as a serious illness controlled by the medical profession. The experiences of two women illustrate fairly typical attitudes. The births of Meriel Talbot's ten children were mentioned in her diary in a brief and matter of fact manner, as with the fifth in 1886: 'Drove with Johnny [her husband] to Hampstead Heath. Felt more or less pain all day from 11 o'clock. Sat through dinner. Dr Farre came about 9 p.m., and a pretty little girl was born at 10 minutes to twelve.' With the sixth child in 1870, she felt 'symptoms of the baby coming' at 8.30 a.m., but lay on the sofa till 4 p.m., 'thinking nothing imminent. Hardly time to jump into bed, when a nice little boy was born' at 4.30 p.m., without the doctor. When twins were born in 1873 she merely noted: 'quiet and comfortable all day'.[62] On the day her first child was born in 1905, Molly Trevelyan went walking in the afternoon and studied German after the pains began. She read *Martin Chuzzlewit* aloud before dinner, though 'the pains were so bad it was difficult to keep my voice steady'. Molly went driving in Regents Park during the first stage of her next labour in 1906, and then visitors came for afternoon tea. The monthly nurse and doctor arrived at 7.30 p.m. and joined the family for dinner as the birth was very close: 'By the end of dinner I felt very bad . . . and at nine I couldn't bear it any longer and went to bed.' The baby was born forty minutes later.[63]

All births in these families took place in the home, even when complications were anticipated. The most surprising finding is that the husband was present at the birth in almost all cases. This is unexpected since it is often assumed that the husband's participation is a modern development of the natural childbirth movement. Prince Albert's presence during Queen Victoria's confinement in 1841 stimulated considerable discussion in the *Lancet*. It was condemned by 'a country doctor' as a fashionable London practice which offended his notions of delicacy and propriety. Another provincial doctor agreed that it was 'indecent, unbecoming, and unnecessary', and unknown among the lower classes. But several London doctors believed husbands had every right to 'whisper words of comfort and solace' during their wives' suffering. They hoped the example shown by the most exemplary married couple in the realm would encourage the reform to spread to the provinces. A layman who had been present at two of his wife's accouchements felt it was insulting to exclude husbands from their 'proper place at a wife's side, to cheer her in the intervals of pain'.[64]

Whatever the influence of the royal couple, it was common practice for husbands to attend their wives' confinements in these political families from the 1830s onwards. In 1831 Lord Porchester left Parliament during a crucial debate on the Reform Bill to be present at his son's birth.[65] Lady Fanny Russell noted in her diary in 1848 that 'John was with me' for the birth of her child.[66] W. E. Gladstone was present during the painful birth of his first child in 1840. Forty-two years later that same son experienced the birth of his own first child, as his mother related: 'poor Willy had indeed a terrible experience, and he seems to have been nearly *31 hours* by her side!—helpless, as he said, to assuage the agony.'[67] Meriel Talbot's husband was present at most of her confinements. At the birth of the first child in 1861, for example, she noted that she was in labour most of the day and 'Johnny was with me all the time'.[68] William Conway insisted in 1884 that a husband should always be with his wife when she was in labour.[69] Alfred Lyttelton held Laura's hand in 1886 during her 'tremendous ordeal' which ended in her death.[70] Charles Trevelyan was with Molly at most of her confinements a generation later, and his presence was enormously important to her. In 1906 she noted that 'Charles had been there all the time holding my hand', and two years later he came home a week before the birth 'because he wants so to be with me and look after me'.[71] Lord Charles Nairne held his wife's hand in 1910 throughout the 'horribly long business' of thirty-six hours of bad pains.[72] Many of these comments would be seen as indicating a progressive approach to labour today. Two important points emerge. These husbands were present at their wives' confinements to provide emotional support, suggesting a high level of intimacy in close marital relationships. Secondly, some 'progressive' customs during labour have a much longer history than is usually assumed. The more privileged classes led the way in encouraging the attendance of husbands at labour from the 1830s. The process was undoubtedly ended by the hospitalization of middle-class childbirth in the inter-war years of the twentieth century.

In most cases the husband and mother of the labouring woman, and the monthly nurse, were the only participants throughout the labour, while the doctor made a brief appearance towards the end.[73] There is no evidence of women in labour relying on female friends or neighbours for emotional support during the actual confinement, though communal childbirth practices died out more slowly among the poorer classes.[74] The correspondence between Margaret Gladstone and her mother in 1870 contained the only reference to an earlier custom of this sort. Margaret was clearly disturbed that four female friends had volunteered their services for her confinement; Margaret only wanted her mother and husband to be present, in addition to the nurse. Elizabeth King replied to her daughter:

you asked me about whether you should have a lady in the room when you are ill . . . I think much depends on your own feelings—Aunt Eliza was in the room with me every time except when Elizabeth was born and then Aunt Gall was in the house but not in the room. With a good doctor and nurse no one else is needed but a friend at hand is pleasant. I could not have endured anyone with whom I was not absolutely at ease, and who was not very quiet . . .[75]

The Victorian age seems to have been a period of transition among the privileged classes between an earlier communal style of childbirth and the modern medical event.

Doctors, rather than midwives, attended all these confinements, confirming that Victorian obstetrics became the preserve of the medical profession among middle- and upper-class women. However, doctors played only a minor role in normal labour, and sometimes did not appear at all. Meriel Talbot's second child was born in 1862 in the presence only of her husband and her mother-in-law—the latter taking the place of her own mother who was dead. Dr Pyke arrived too late, 'only to be in at the death', as he did again at the sixth confinement. Her main support came from her husband and mother-in-law for all nine confinements, and there was no mention even of a nurse.[76] Lady Carrington, like Meriel Talbot, seemed to send for the doctor only an hour or so before the birth.[77] Margaret MacDonald's mother-in-law, Annie Ramsay, took the place of her own dead mother and may also have performed the function of nurse. Certainly a cousin was amazed to learn that Margaret 'had neither a nurse nor a doctor when this wee girlie arrived' in 1910.[78] There is little evidence of doctors trying to control these births. They seem more often to have arrived on the scene of normal births as late as possible, leaving matters to husbands, mothers and nurses.

These women did not question the value of chloroform in labour. It was first used successfully in childbirth in Britain by Sir James Simpson in 1847. The following year Simpson offered his services free of charge to Lady John Russell: 'With almost all my medical brethren here I use chloroform in all cases. None of us, I believe, could feel justified in *not* relieving pain, when God has bestowed upon us the means of relieving it.'[79] Though a few conservative members of the medical profession opposed chloroform for a decade or more, women themselves welcomed it, and its careful use was gradually accepted for those who could afford it. But it was generally recognized that chloroform should be used only in cases of difficult and exceptionally painful labour. Margaret Gladstone commented in 1870 that a friend 'was always very ill and has chloroform', suggesting that it was by no means a routine procedure. Margaret's husband reported a month later that she herself 'would have suffered more had it not been for the chloroform which I administered carefully in small quantity'.[80] Lady Antrim wrote in 1884 that her sister, Victoria Dawnay, had just given birth: 'luckily she got a lot of chloroform so I hope it was not as bad as usual for her', though it was only administered in the final two hours of a difficult labour. This seems to have been normal procedure. Lady Antrim commiserated with her other sister, Lady Minto, a year later: 'what a mercy you had chloroform at the end'.[81]

There was considerable discussion among the women in these families about the appropriate quantities of chloroform and the correct occasion for its use. Evidently most doctors and patients preferred to keep its use to the absolute minimum, for several reasons. Women were advised by their doctors that less chloroform would reduce the need for instruments. Lady Antrim wrote to Lady Minto in 1889: 'It must have been horrid not having so much chloroform but how also a great comfort to feel tongs will no more be required.'[82] Some women refused chloroform for more personal reasons. Edith Lyttelton knew the birth of her first child in 1892 would be a 'nightmare' for Alfred, since his first wife had died in childbirth. Edith was determined to prevent any extra anxiety 'and I had been told that under chloroform women often screamed. So I was resolute in refusing it in spite of old Williamson begging me two or three times to let them put me under it. I was also naturally curious about the whole process.'[83] Conversely, some women insisted on having more chloroform than the doctor recommended. During a difficult labour in 1908 the doctor advised Molly Trevelyan: 'it won't be born till four if you have so much chloroform. It will be born at two without chloroform'. Molly opted for more chloroform,[84] illustrating that an element of choice existed for women in labour and doctors were not omnipotent.

Instruments seem to have been sparingly used in normal births and the women disliked the use of forceps unless absolutely necessary. References to the use of instruments are rare, suggesting such procedure was only adopted in emergencies. The experience of Edith Adeane in 1882, for example, appears to have been considered unusual: 'it was a very lengthy affair and the child was assisted into the world and had a narrow squeak for its life.'[85] Lady Minto in 1889 was delighted to learn that 'tongs' would not be needed if she had less chloroform which reduced the mother's ability to bear down.[86] Even in 1910 forceps were not used after Lady Violet Nairne had endured thirty-six hours of painful labour: 'Dr Phillips said it was such a· very straightforward case—no instruments, no tearing, nothing wrong.'[87]

Evidence from the end of the century onwards suggests that women were beginning to acknowledge the obstetric skills of some doctors, as knowledge and techniques slowly improved. In the 1890s Helen Acland 'had an easier time than I ever had before thanks to the skill of our good doctor'.[88] Lady Antrim eulogized the skills of the 'modern doctor' at the confinement of her niece, Ruby, in 1908. Doctor Bowland produced the baby

most cleverly for it was a delicate job and he seems to have managed well . . . The Doctor said Ruby is so small that unless he had followed everything by measure and judged his time it could not have been managed—another day and he could not have brought the child's head through. Of course we were anxious—so much seemed to depend on one man's skill—in the old days it would not have been possible—nor do I suppose the child could have been born alive if it had not been done in this way.[89]

As obstetric practice slowly improved, so women compared notes on particular techniques. From the turn of the century doctors seemed less prone to neglect perineal tears. Before 1900 perhaps one woman in fifteen had to suffer the acute discomfort of such tears either badly stitched or neglected altogether.[90] Perineal tears were not mentioned among women in these families before 1900, suggesting that they bore the misery stoically in silence. An Edwardian midwifery text attested to the change in practice, advising immediate repair of perineal lacerations after birth: 'The parts heal better, the patient feels less, and there is less risk of septic infection, if the rent is promptly stitched.'[91] Molly Trevelyan and her female relatives were greatly concerned about perineal tears, precisely because they now expected them to be sutured immediately. In 1906 Molly's sister-in-law, Janet Trevelyan, had a baby which arrived 'somewhat rapidly', causing an extensive tear. Two doctors sewed it up next morning; they recognized that it must be done as fast as possible, but could not operate immediately after the delivery as they dared not give her any more chloroform.[92] Molly's sister, Elsa, Lady Richmond, praised her doctor for his determination to avoid laceration in 1908: 'Parkinson purposefully delayed [labour] so that there shouldn't be any tearing or anything. I think he was very clever altogether and there was *no* tear.'[93] It is worth noting that the deliberate incision to enlarge the vaginal outlet, known as episiotomy, was rarely employed in Britain before 1914, though the technique was explained as early as 1742. Only since the 1930s have episiotomies become routine to allow rapid forceps delivery and protect the child's head from injury in a prolonged second stage of labour.[94]

COMMISERATIONS, LYING-IN AND NURSING

The feelings of many new mothers were beautifully expressed by Molly Trevelyan, writing to her husband a few months after the birth of their first child: 'She is the outcome of our love and of our desire, and she is a constant reminder to me of your delight in me, and of the passion which made her. It is worth all the pain I had—and the next one will be worth all the pain I still have to go through.'[95] Looking back fifty years later Lady Frances Balfour commented:

The woman who does not feel that the greatest event in her life, next to her marriage, is the birth of her first child must indeed be a congenital idiot. That event, which lays the foundation of the family, and brings with it the sense of overshadowing power, came to us with the birth of our first daughter in 1880.[96]

Most women, then as now, seem to have replaced memories of the pain with the happiness which followed, though not all women were so fortunate. Victoria Dawnay was relieved in 1910 that her niece would not dread her next confinement, 'as it does not seem to have given her any great terror which I own I had for a long time after Guy was born'.[97]

The letters of congratulation which poured in to the new parents were revealing. Most women writers generally emphasized thankfulness for the safety of the mother as their primary concern. Mary Drew wrote to Alfred Lyttelton at Easter 1886 when she heard that Laura's child was born, wishing him joy 'on your little darling's safety even more than on the baby's birth. It is impossible at first to think much of the baby otherwise than as a source of peril and pain.'[98] Mary's fears were more than justified by Laura's death a few days later. Lady Mary Beauchamp wrote in 1873: 'How thankful [Evelyn Stanhope] must feel to have it all so well and so happily over I can guess from much experience.'[99] Annie Hicks used a common phrase in 1908 to convey her relief that Margaret MacDonald was 'safely over your trouble'.[100]

· The other main sentiment expressed by both sexes was delight if the child was a boy and commiserations otherwise. Lady Selborne announced after her daughter's confinement: 'the baby made a mistake as to its sex'.[101] On learning that her son-in-law, Percy Wyndham, was a proud father in 1863, Pamela Campbell responded: 'You deserved a boy for having so very graciously received the girl last year!'[102] Alice Balfour noted in 1898 that Betty and Gerald had a child: 'unfortunately another girl (no. 4). Disappointed Betty more so than she owns to.'[103] When Lady Minto produced a girl in 1884, her sister, Lady Antrim, expressed 'disappointment at its being *Miss* Elliot'; the only consolation was the prospect of the 'sensation she will create' at her first Season. Seven years later the family rejoiced that 'at last the little boy has come'.[104] May Harcourt's reaction to the news of two births in 1905 was significant: 'Bridie Starredale is the proud possessor of a son and heir and they are all off their heads with joy. Pauline Clay on the other hand has a girl.'[105] The only difference in response between the sexes was that women tended to give thanks for the mother's safety before commiserating on the baby's gender.

This response seems to have been universal among professional and upper-middle-class families although they had no title or estates to bestow. Like the Chamberlain family they sought a son 'to bear the name and carry on the traditions'.[106] The reaction was all the more powerful among all levels of the aristocracy where a son was needed as heir to the title and land. Lord and Lady Stanhope were besieged by letters of congratulation on the birth of their son in 1880, after two daughters. Lord Derby remarked: 'one thing only was wanting to your posterity, and that one want has been satisfied.' Lord Reay was also delighted at 'this most auspicious event. If the young man just born is like his ancestors he will do much to save the House of Lords from a premature and unhallowed extinction.'[107] The celebrations in the Carrington family in 1895 were even more elaborate, as Lady Carrington had so far produced only five daughters. She noted in her diary that 'letters and telegrams poured in', and she and Charles were overjoyed. It was a markedly different response from the scarcely muted disappointment which had greeted the five girls. The local newspaper summed up the sentiments of all well-wishers in its eulogy on 'The Birth of an Heir to the Carrington Title and Estates': 'On all hands there were expressions of satisfaction, in which all classes and parties joined. The Church bells were rung and flags were displayed.'[108] Unfortunately the long awaited son and heir died in the trenches in 1915, years before either of his parents.

Men and women responded in the same way on this crucial question—the women had long been socialized to accept that only the births of boys merited unreserved congratulations. Many young girls must have grown up feeling unwanted, inadequate and second-best as they observed the behaviour of adults after the births of baby girls. Mary Haldane as an old lady in 1911 knew all about the sorrow which greeted her own birth: 'My advent into this world was a disappointment and my grandfather did not reply to the announcement, as I was to have [been] named after him and been his heir had I been a son.'[109] Lady Constance Malleson wrote that her mother 'was again hoping for a son when *I* arrived: a bitter disappointment'.[110] After the birth of her eldest brother Maud Cecil remembered 'being very much offended' by the admiring remarks that 'it is a good thing it *was* a boy this time'.[111] Most girls kept silent about their hurt response to such open avowals of regret at their sex; it was part of the conditioning process by which they accepted their brothers as superior beings and did not question the differential treatment they received from birth. While letters of congratulation or commiseration poured in, the new mothers were recovering their strength after labour. Advice manuals varied little in half a century in recommending strict rest for at least four weeks or so after confinement for those women who could afford to take it. Even in the Edwardian period 'recumbent' bed rest was advised for ten to fourteen days, followed by an 'easy life' for a month. Medical manuals explained that the uterus required about eight weeks after delivery to contract and return to its normal position, while complete bed rest would also allow the discharge from the placental wound to cease. Carelessness in this 'lying-in period' could result in life-long invalidism; longer bed rest was vital if the uterus was slow to contract or if a recurrence of vaginal bleeding took place.[112]

All the women in these families took advice of this kind very seriously, whether it came from doctors or female relatives and friends. Meriel Talbot's first child was born on 19 June 1861, she sat up in bed for the first time on 3 July, came downstairs on 11 July and drove out three days later. The timetable for her lying-in period was always similar to this and she was normally flat on her back in bed for two weeks after delivery.[113] Mrs Caroline Grey described her post-natal recovery in the 1860s: 'My nurses kept me in the *Dark* almost—two hours sleep from 3 to 5 after luncheon. No one admitted till that afternoon sleep was over! talking to visitors *impossible.*'[114] Lady Carrington's diary shows that she also spent two weeks in bed after each delivery in the 1880s, moved to the sofa after a further two weeks, and dressed formally for the first time when each baby was about four weeks old.[115] In 1895 Lady Salisbury was still firmly recommending the traditional lying-in period for Violet Cecil after the birth of her son: 'Mind that Violet is kept *quite* quiet for a fortnight and do not let her even sit up till then. She will get strong again much the quicker for really great care at first.'[116]

The rules were marginally relaxed in the Edwardian period but only if there were no complications. Betty Balfour complained in 1903:

Apparently my 'uterus' is not going to contract quite so quickly this time as usual—the penalty I believe for my very quick confinement, and I so dread the bother of any womb trouble hereafter that I have consented to stay in bed a fortnight, but bargained that I need not *after* that lead a sofa life, but resume my ordinary ways, only putting up my feet rather more when sitting.[117]

Sylvia Henley was also kept in bed for longer than usual in 1908 as her uterus refused to return to 'its proper place and size'. Elsa Richmond had the same problem in 1910, forcing her to 'wear stays which prop the whole of my lower body up into my waist'.[118] The birth of Molly Trevelyan's third child in 1908 was complicated by a postpartum haemorrhage, so she remained flat in bed with only one pillow for eighteen days.[119]

Mothers were expected to breastfeed their babies in the Victorian and Edwardian period. The practice of wet-nursing by the rich went back to the middle ages, but had been under attack since the eighteenth century. In the Victorian period the rich usually only resorted to wet-nurses if they were unable to breastfeed and if, in addition, their babies were too delicate to risk bottle-feeding. This did not reduce the misery involved for the wet-nurses, who risked the deaths of their own babies, but at least the motive was not female vanity. The very few references to the use of wet-nurses in these families after 1860 illustrate the general dislike of this practice, unless there were extenuating circumstances. Meriel Talbot only resorted to a wet-nurse in 1873 because she was unable to breastfeed twins and the girl weighed only six pounds. Immediately after the unexpected double birth her husband and mother-in-law 'went after a wet nurse' who came the next day, 'by name of Pyle'.[120] Nothing more is said about Pyle's origins, what happened to her own child, or how long she stayed. Lady Minto's cousin left no doubt, in 1885, that wet-nurses were only tolerated for the sake of delicate babies. She was surprised that Lady Minto was unable to breastfeed: 'but I quite agree with you about bringing the little one up by hand [i.e. bottle] as she is strong and healthy and not having a wet nurse. Of course the case is quite different if a child is delicate and one has no choice.'[121]

Apart from Meriel Talbot, the only two other women in these families who used wet-nurses were Betty Balfour and Violet Cecil. Betty Balfour told A. J. Balfour in 1886: 'We have got a wet nurse for he was not getting on well . . . and he is already much improved.'[122] Violet Cecil had a very difficult birth in 1895, followed by weeks of illness, and was unable to nurse. Even so, her mother-in-law, Lady Salisbury, objected forcefully to the use of a wet-nurse:

I am *very* sorry you have agreed to the old fashioned folly of a wet nurse—It is almost always quite unnecessary and in the case of your baby I am certain . . . that it would do perfectly without. Just ask Willie [Lord Selborne] about it? He refused to have one for Top when two doctors tried to insist on it. Have you got a permanent nurse yet? If she is a good one she will soon get rid of the wet nurse. And you will find the expense enormous especially in rooms and food . . . Don't be the least afraid but turn off the wet nurse at once and have the same milk from Hatfield that Alice's baby thrives on—I have ordered it to be sent to you daily till you move the baby to Hatfield but *without* the wet nurse.[123]

Throughout the Victorian and Edwardian eras leading medical authorities, such as Drs Bull, Conquest, Allbutt and Weatherly, agreed on the advantages of breastfeeding and its benefits for the mother.[124] *Lectures to Practising Midwives* was written by a woman physician, Dr Victoria Bennett, in 1909, intended for use by midwives and nurses, and endorsed by Drs Galabin and Scharlieb. Its advice on breastfeeding echoed the great Victorian authorities, with rather more emphasis on the benefits to the child:

The mother's milk is the only perfect food for the infant . . . Breast-fed infants are happier, stronger, have a better hold upon life, and are less liable to infant disease than hand-fed; the death-rate amongst them is also much lower. Breast-feeding makes the mother take a greater interest in her child, and seems to have the effect of increasing maternal affection . . .[125]

The benefits of breastfeeding were generally recognized throughout the period. Even Sir Charles Dilke, scarcely an authority on infant management, commented in 1877: 'when brought up by hand [i.e. bottle] they have a way of suddenly becoming very ill.'[126] The majority of women in these families breastfed their babies if they were able; the remainder bottle-fed them or supplemented the breast with the bottle. Meriel Talbot, for example, breastfed all her ten children in the 1860s and 1870s, except for the twins, and began nursing within one or two days of each birth.[127] Even Lady Carrington breastfed her babies, despite an exceptionally busy social schedule.

Women were well aware of the dangers of bottle-feeding in the mid-Victorian period, when cow's milk could carry disease and feeding bottles were usually unsterilized. Consequently they persisted in trying to breastfeed, even when they experienced difficulties and some risked their own health. In 1868 Lady Cowper was anxious about Adine Fane, who had been ailing for several months after producing two children in two years of marriage: 'Adine has been very poorly since she got to Brighton, all the results of nursing when she is not fit for it.' Adine died a few weeks ·after weaning her child, despite the services of 'a good doctor who understands her case'.[128] In 1868 Charlotte Danvers was most concerned about her daughter's attempt to nurse her new baby, especially since her first child had died in infancy two years earlier: 'I really do hope dear Emily will be better this time and the dear baby will of course benefit too—I only hope she will be careful not to nurse too much *at first*.'[129]

Women felt less pressure to breastfeed in the 1880s and 1890s when the hazards of bottle-feeding slowly diminished, with greater knowledge of infant nutrition and the importance of cleanliness. This improvement was reflected in the relaxed attitude cf Louisa Antrim when she learned that her sister was unable to breastfeed in 1885: 'I am so sorry the nursing does not succeed—if the baby is well and takes kindly to the bottle it will not matter so much.'[130] A generation later in 1904, Margaret MacDonald told her aunts: 'I am having to give up nursing him as it evidently did not satisfy him, and he is much more contented with a bottle, which he takes to without any difficulty.'[131] There is no evidence that bottle-feeding increased for social or vanity reasons when the bottle became safer. But fear of such reactions may have led to the increased propaganda for breastfeeding from the 1890s. A popular medical guide of 1892 warned that 'it is the duty of every mother who can do so to suckle her own infant . . . on its proper fulfilment may depend largely the future health of her child'. A 1909 text warned nurses and midwives that 'every effort should be made to promote breast-feeding'. Bottle-feeding was condemned as 'expensive, troublesome, unsatisfactory' and extremely risky unless carried out with extreme care and cleanliness.[132] Bottle-feeding was taboo in Edwardian manuals, unless justified by the health problems of both mother and child. Olive Ilbert wrote to Molly Trevelyan in 1905: 'I trust Pauline is not a Bottle Babe!'[133]

The medical propaganda from the end of the nineteenth century emphasized that breastfeeding was not only natural but that it should also be scientifically organized. There was less detailed discussion about methods of nursing babies in the Victorian period and many women seemed to nurse on demand. Lavinia Talbot, for example, in 1875 grew 'very much bored at the nursing being quite irregular, as it ties her down so—but the nurse, Mrs Ball, is determined never to wake the baby, and as it sleeps quite endlessly, Lavinia never has an idea when it is coming to her.'[134] But from the turn of the century an obsession with regularity and 'strict punctuality' developed. The medical texts prescribed two-hourly feeds during the first month, followed by regular feeds at longer intervals until the child was weaned at nine months.[135]

The women in these families received this 'scientific' advice from the doctors and nurses who attended them and also from female family members and friends. Most of them followed the rules with great devotion, provided they were able to breastfeed. In 1913 Lady Cowell-Stepney described the nursing routine of her daughter, Alcy, two weeks after parturition: '9 a.m., 11 a.m., 1 p.m., 3 p.m., 5 p.m., 7 p.m., 9 p.m.—and once in the night—a bottle being given for the *other* meal in the night. You would be edified by her absolute devotion and cheerfulness, over her night rest being all broken up!'[136] Lady Cowell-Stepney's surprise at her daughter's regime testified to the more relaxed 'feeding on demand' of the earlier generation. Molly Trevelyan's routine was almost identical and was obviously so important to her that every detail was recorded meticulously in her diary. Pauline, the first baby in 1905, was nursed every two hours from 7 a.m. to 10 p.m., and had a bottle in the middle of the night. George's routine in 1906 was more arduous because the bottle disagreed with him, forcing Molly to nurse him two or three times during the night, 'which I hate'. Even the nurse had to be encouraged to become more methodical to adapt to Molly's strict feeding regime.[137] Babies seem to have been weaned around nine months after birth. In February 1906, for example, the doctor told Molly Trevelyan that she should wean Pauline as the child was not putting on much weight and Molly was 'run-down and anaemic'. After feeding Pauline for the last time she noted in her diary: 'Got to feel very bad and uncomfortable by the evening and very miserable.'[138]

Few formal ceremonies were associated with childbirth. During the mother's confinement and lying-in, friends left cards 'with kind inquiries', but the mother and child were not disturbed until the mother 'announced her reappearance in society by sending her card in return'. The christening of the child was usually fixed to take place as soon as the mother was well enough to go out, when the child was about a month old. Baptism was the rite whereby the child was received into the Church, in its parish of birth.[139] Boys had two godfathers and one godmother, and girls the reverse, and they formally presented the child at the christening ceremony. Charty Ribblesdale defined the role of godparent succinctly when she asked her mother-in-law to be godmother to her baby daughter in 1892: 'I know if anything was ever to happen to me you would be the one person I would trust to take care of her.'[140] Mary Lydia Hart-Davis asked her brother, Charles Acland, to be godfather to her daughter in 1874: 'For love of old days, and for all that we have been to each other I want to think that she will have a special place in your affection and your prayers.'[141] Usually the baby was named after several or even all the godparents—a custom responsible for some of the ugly strings of names which encumbered unfortunate babies. Most godparents expressed delight at the prospect of 'standing sponsor', though a few, like Eleanor Cecil, privately admitted to boredom: 'lucky Alice to be in bed and escape the christening!'[142] Some couples liked to have the christening in the same church with the same clergy as at their wedding: 'just the wedding over again'.[143] Sentimental grand-mothers enjoyed fussing over the christening robes, using clothes worn by innumerable family babies previously. Catherine Glad-stone took this custom to unusual lengths in 1885: 'baby had the dear vest which I wore when married, and which all my children were baptised in—and Annie married in and *her* children christened in'.[144]

The final rite attached to childbirth was the ancient and brief ritual of 'churching' the mother, which usually took place immediately before the christening. 'Churching' was originally a purification rite after the supposedly unclean business of pregnancy and parturition. There is no evidence that any of these women saw the brief ceremony in such terms, but rather as a traditional form of thanksgiving. Lavinia Talbot, Ivy Chamberlain, Mary Gladstone and others all mentioned being churched before the baptism; but they referred to it only in passing, as if it held little meaning for them except to mark the end of their confinement. The only vestige of the old idea of uncleanliness was to be found in the custom that a newly delivered mother could not attend a wedding before she was churched and hence purified. Lady Carrington, for example, in 1880, regretted that she could not attend her sister's wedding as it was only two weeks since the birth: 'it was very sad not being actually in the church.'[145] The exclusion was not simply due to practical consideration for the new mother's health.

For the majority of Victorian and Edwardian middle- and upper-class women the experience of normal childbirth followed a pattern which might have been applauded by the modern movement for natural childbirth in the home. But a minority of these women suffered acutely and some of them died from obstetrical problems which have since been overcome, or from the dreaded Victorian plague of childbed fever. These tragedies of childbirth which afflicted a minority of unlucky women were largely responsible for the reasonable fears which surrounded childbirth in Victorian and Edwardian Britain.

6

The Tragedies of Childbirth

CHILDBIRTH was a natural process, but for an unlucky minority of women it was also dangerous. Maternal mortality rates remained high throughout the Victorian and Edwardian years. For much of this period five mothers died for every one thousand children born alive, and these figures did not significantly improve until the 1930s.[1] Moreover, deaths resulting from miscarriages and still births were not usually represented in the statistics. Thus, actual maternal mortality was much higher than the estimated five per thousand births. Women were well aware of the danger of death associated with childbirth. Many had sisters, mothers or friends who died in labour or shortly afterwards, and some even wrote their own informal wills during pregnancy.

General fears about death were often expressed before childbirth, and were justified by the mortality statistics. In 1874 Lady Acland reassured her stepdaughter, May Hart-Davis, that every thoughtful woman experienced fears about her first pregnancy, but God would bring 'strength for the time of trial'. When Maggie Acland became pregnant only three months after her wedding in 1879, she confessed to her sister-in-law: 'I get low in my mind and think that perhaps I may never see the dear old Home again.'[2] Mary Drew's mother prayed for 'a happy ending' to Mary's first pregnancy in 1886, while her sister commented: 'there is necessarily *some* trembling with *every 1st*, yet it is all in God's Hands.'[3] During her pregnancy in 1892 Edith Lyttelton wrote to her husband: 'how wonderful it all is, and how intense the meaning of Life and Death has become for me.' She could not quite believe she would create a perfect baby 'and live to hold it'.[4] The majority of women seem to have kept specific fears to themselves, or deliberately suppressed them. The women in this study did not discuss the danger of death from puerperal fever, though no doubt some of them thought about it. They accepted the dangers fatalistically and trusted in God, or they assumed a personal immunity, or they worried about problems they could actually hope to resolve.

Miscarriage was more dangerous for the majority of women than birth at full term. In the days before blood transfusions and antibiotics, miscarriages could cause the death of the mother as well as the foetus, or involve prolonged illness. Pregnant women who spent days on the sofa or weeks confined to bed were usually taking essential precautions against miscarriages.

It is impossible to obtain reliable statistics on miscarriages. Compulsory registration of stillbirths was not introduced until 1927 and even then a 'stillborn' child was only so defined after seven months in the womb. Before 1927 only babies born alive were registered. In 1885 William Farr hazarded a guess that the proportion of children born dead after seven months to total births was about 4 per cent, though other estimates in the *Lancet* were closer to 6 per cent. The rate of embryonic mortality before seven months was impossible to ascertain, though Farr assumed that mortality rates of embryonic life would multiply rapidly with every month back towards conception. The highest rate of foetal deaths would take place in the first three months of pregnancy. Farr provided some rare figures for nineteenth-century miscarriages, taken from the Westminster General Dispensary in 1818. Out of 400 pregnant married women, 128 had miscarried one or more times, giving birth in ten years to 556 live children and 305 dead embryos. Almost two-thirds of the miscarriages took place in the first three months.[5] A general practitioner, T. R. Allison, calculated in 1894 that 'eight women out of ten miscarry one or more times'. Dr A. L. Galabin in 1900 estimated the proportion of miscarriages to full-term deliveries as one in five. He thought that most middle-aged women who had borne children had at least one miscarriage or premature labour.[6]

In order to understand the dangers of miscarriage for Victorian and Edwardian women, and to place the subject in perspective, it is helpful to consider the risks in recent years. A British medical text of 1971 estimated that about ten per cent of all pregnancies terminated in spontaneous abortion, and an American text of 1977 gave an estimate of 12 per cent. These figures exclude the very early miscarriages in the first few weeks, which women are usually not aware of, and which constitute about 75 per cent of all conceptions. Threatened miscarriage is signalled by vaginal bleeding, for which the only treatment is still bed rest for three or four days. A large proportion of women are then safe, but the rest proceed through rhythmical labour pains to an inevitable miscarriage. The treatment still consists of morphia for pain, and ergot to encourage the uterus to expel its contents. Even today the most common result is an incomplete miscarriage, where the uterus fails to empty completely and the patient haemorrhages. This is still a common emergency, requiring urgent hospital attention for rapid blood transfusion followed by curettage to remove the remaining contents of the uterus. Without this treatment, blood loss or subsequent infection can be severe enough to cause the patient's death even now.[7]

The fears of Victorian and Edwardian women about miscarriage were more than justified. Blood transfusions were not generally introduced in British hospitals until after the First World War and the widespread use of antibiotics came only after the Second World War. Without blood transfusion and antibiotics, the dangers of death following incomplete miscarriage and haemorrhage were far greater. Infection could also be caused by medical intervention to empty the uterus if proper antiseptic precautions were not taken. Moreover the proportion of miscarriages to live births must have been higher than today, since women's diet and general health were inferior. An additional anxiety existed because of the difficulty in many cases of diagnosing pregnancy in the first three months, which were the critical months for miscarriage. During a period of uncertainty or ignorance about pregnancy, women were unlikely to take precautions to avoid miscarriage.

Victorian doctors understood only too well that miscarriages were dangerous and sometimes fatal. Dr Bull's popular advice manual warned in 1837 that 'There is no accident befalling female health which forms a greater source of dread, anxiety, and subsequent regret to a married woman than miscarriage.' Dr Ryan's midwifery manual said it was well known that a bad miscarriage was more dangerous than 'several natural labours at the full period'. At the end of the century, Dr Mary Scharlieb stressed that the mother's health and life were often at risk because of miscarriage:

[miscarriage] may immediately entail a long and serious illness, and may lay the foundation of prolonged ill health . . . The two great immediate dangers in abortion are severity of haemorrhage, and retention of some portion of the ovum, leading to blood poisoning . . . So great is this danger . . . that the services of a skilled attendant are really much more needed than they are in confinement at full term . . . All the forms of puerperal blood-poisoning—the haemorrhages, inflammations, and other troubles —are as likely to occur after miscarriage as after labour.

Miscarriage in the fourth and fifth months of pregnancy was the most serious because the placenta was then most likely to be retained in the uterus in an 'incomplete miscarriage', causing haemorrhage, blood-poisoning and peritonitis.[8] But doctors complained that they were usually only called in to deal with severe miscarriages when it was too late and they were helpless in cases of haemorrhage and septicaemia. Medical journals and texts therefore devoted little space to miscarriages, though advice manuals informed women how best to avoid them.

Most of the advice given to pregnant women by family and friends concerned the dangers of miscarriage. In 1869 Elizabeth King warned her daughter, Margaret Gladstone, during the second month of her pregnancy: 'You must be very cautious in travelling. A little want of care just now might do you serious harm for life. Many young wives are hurt from overdoing themselves and are delicate ever after just from what seemed a trifling imprudence.' Mrs King advised that the first three months were the most critical, and that women were 'more liable to go wrong' at their usual menstruation time: 'If there has been the slightest appearance at the periods you are liable to miscarriage.' Margaret should take gentle exercise, but should stop driving, visiting, receiving callers and teaching her Bible classes.[9] In the sixth month of her pregnancy, Margaret's doctor strongly advised her against risking the long journey from London to Scotland, and she heard 'from various ladies of so many misfortunes in similar cases'. Margaret concluded: 'it would be very sad if the poor little baby came too soon, dead, and a lifelong sorrow if it had anything wrong with it.' Moreover she noticed 'a great many premature and stillborn births announced in the paper', so she must not risk it.[10]

When Mary Drew was pregnant for the first time in 1886 at the age of forty, her friend, Lady Cowell-Stepney, advised her on how to avoid miscarriage:

I do hope you are staying quite in bed, or at least on a couch, till the next month is over. I know it is a fearful bore—but only think what many poor people like Blanche Kay-Shuttleworth have to do—(who are given to miscarriages). They go to bed quite at the first sign, and never get up till after the 4th month, when they rise, and have fine babies, and are none the worse for it. Shuttleworth has managed 3 in this way, after about 12 miscarriages.[11]

This was not indulgent fussing, since Mary nearly died from the miscarriage which followed soon after. When she was again pregnant in 1889, her doctors had good reason to warn Mary to be 'extremely careful, walk very quietly, be much on the sofa'. After the fourth month, Mary wrote: 'I don't feel a bit safe yet, but thankful to have passed my first anniversaries of illness.'[12] In 1912 Lady Selborne asked her daughter-in-law, Grace, to be more careful: 'a miscarriage with a first baby does often result in a great difficulty of having any others. Anyhow it is almost sure to ruin one's health for 3 or 4 years.' The greatest danger was over-fatigue, and Grace should always 'give in' and rest whenever she felt tired, no matter how inconvenient.[13]

The correspondence of pregnant women was full of the fears and dangers of miscarriage. Even at seven months, Lady Stanley in 1870 lived 'in fear of not going my full time', especially since she was still 'very seedy with pains and aches all over'.[14] Katharine Bruce Glasier in 1909 was relieved that her third child in its second month 'is well on the road to fruition in spite of that horrid flooding—which destroyed my nerve and brain power for over six weeks even more than it weakened my body'. She resolved to live 'like a nice old cow for the next six months at least'.[15] In 1907 Elsa, Lady Richmond, was 'plunged in the deepest gloom' by a threatened miscarriage during her first pregnancy. She reported: 'I began to dipe [bleed/menstruate] and according to rule I quickly went to bed and sent for the doctor. He was quite serious and said very likely the baby would leave me . . . I lie absolutely flat on my back.' A miscarriage was averted, but Elsa learned 'what having a baby really meant'. She also received some education from her doctor on the causes, symptoms and likely times of miscarriage.

This included the advice that 'being disgusting with your husband if carried too far' might produce miscarriage during the first three months.[16]

There were endless sad stories of women who had continual miscarriages. Lady Fanny Russell was often 'lying-in' in the 1840s and 1850s, because of threatened and actual miscarriages, with only four children born alive.[17] Lady Edward Cavendish was 'dreadfully low' in 1879 because she had 'just had her fourth dead child'.[18] May Harcourt wrote that Rachel Dudley 'has been again dreadfully ill and nearly died on the journey down from Scotland . . . I must say I think her pluck is wonderful. I am sure I wouldn't face it again if I had been as near dying as she was when she had that last still born baby.'[19] Beatrice Smith in 1881, at the age of seventeen, even dreamed that her stepsister Mary Codrington had borne two dead babies.[20]

These women generally coped bravely and competently with miscarriage. Louisa Antrim reported to Lady Minto on the experience of their sister, Victoria Dawnay, in 1890. The contents of the uterus 'all came away properly. We have seen it and think it a boy—but cannot quite tell.'[21] This was one of several surprising references to sisters or close female friends inspecting the dead foetus themselves, as well as having the doctor check the expelled contents of the uterus. They understood that the retention of fragments of the placenta could cause haemorrhage and septic infection. The following year Victoria Dawnay actually wrote to her sister, Mary Minto, while in the middle of another miscarriage: 'The afterbirth has not come away yet and meanwhile the pains are pretty bad.' She apologized for bothering her sister, but hoped she could 'look in some time'. Three days later she reported that she was 'perfectly well' but very tired of complete bed rest. The doctor was visiting her daily 'just as if I had had a baby. I suppose he does not want to be cheated of his £25.'[22] Convalescence after miscarriage consisted of '*rest* in the recumbent position, maintained for at least one week', just as after childbirth and for similar reasons.[23] For Victoria, the more serious consequences were mental rather than physical, as she suffered from severe depression for over a year after the two miscarriages.

The most detailed account of a dangerous miscarriage which has survived in these family papers is that of Mary Drew in 1886. The course of this miscarriage and subsequent illness was meticulously recorded in Mary's diary, first by Mary and then by her husband, Harry Drew, at Mary's request when she became too ill to write. This five-month illness was excluded from the published version of the diary, and no mention was made of the word 'miscarriage' or of a dead foetus in the original diary. Mary tried in vain to keep her pregnancy secret, in case it ended in miscarriage. Once that happened, she tried to conceal the cause of her illness, even from the privacy of her own diary, though her family and close friends were unable to prevent the news spreading further. The very lengthy account in the diary exemplifies the grave dangers of miscarriage even among the most privileged women with access to some of the leading medical authorities of the time.

On 1 September 1886 Mary Drew miscarried after almost four months of pregnancy and six months of marriage, at the age of forty. She had been exhausted after the 'dreadful journey' from London to the family home at Hawarden, near Chester, on 10 August 1886, especially since she had 'such heavy things to carry'. The next two days were hectic with church services, mother's meetings and 'rearranging furniture', despite the fact that she 'felt very bad' much of the time. The consequence was 'a serious threat of mishap' and a quiet week in bed on the doctor's orders. But on 24 August Mary suddenly 'got steadily worse in pain and discomfort'. A crisis was reached on 26 August, with much pain and bleeding and a high temperature. Dr Burlingham came three times that day, and telegraphed for a nurse from Chester. Next day Mary noted in her diary 'another crisis', with great pain and sickness. On 29 August, Mary's mother wrote as if the miscarriage was over: 'the mishap could not be kept off and there was much pain and fever last night. Dr B. is *pleased* today. We are keeping her as quiet as if it were a real confinement.' Yet on 30 August Mary herself noted cryptically that 'a very odd event happened to show all was not yet over', and mentioned 'a great startler' next day.[24] Mary's enigmatic comments presumably refer to the expulsion of the contents of the uterus in fragments over several days. The diary of Mary's maid, Auguste Schluter, was more enlightening: 'we have nearly lost my beloved Lady. On September 1st a wee boy was born dead. Lady Grosvenor and Lady Stepney both saw the sad little one before his burial.' Catherine Gladstone informed her husband that she had learned 'a great deal': 'yesterday when the doctors supposed all was over, *the* event happened with no *pain* and it moved me very much to see a *well formed* baby supposed to be nearly 4 months!!'[25]

Dr Burlingham's optimism on 29 August was quite misplaced as he evidently did not realize that Mary had suffered an incomplete miscarriage, with part of the placenta retained. During the first two weeks in September Mary's condition deteriorated, with high fever, pain and intermittent bleeding. Harry Drew noted in his wife's diary on 14 September that Mary's case 'baffles authorities', who disagreed about the appropriate medical treatment. Dr Dobie was puzzled and the only medical consensus was that it was 'a very mysterious case'. On 16 September Harry reported: 'tremendous bleeding leaving her quite prostrate and intense pains and sickness induced by Dr Dobie's medicine . . . It felt most helpless and heartbreaking.' More than two weeks after the miscarriage, Dr Dobie belatedly made his first examination; he concluded at last that 'some of the placenta was obstinately adhering' to the uterus and an operation was necessary to expel it. It is extraordinary that it took these two doctors two weeks to diagnose a condition as common as incomplete miscarriage, particularly given the case history and symptoms. Mary's sister, Agnes Wickham, was convinced that '*either* she was being wrongly treated or the Doctors were not on the right track'. Agnes believed 'there must be something left still—but when Doctors say it is all right one supposes they know best'.[26]

Dr Matthews Duncan was recommended for the operation, but as he was away, his substitute, Dr Griffiths, came instead. Meanwhile Mary's 'horrible pains' continued and she was not informed of the impending operation. She was given chloroform at 6.30 p.m. and the operation was over at 7.45 p.m. Harry Drew took the doctors' verdict at face value: 'operation very hard and most skilfully and completely done'. But after the operation Mary was 'quite prostrate' with sickness, which the doctors attributed to the chloroform but which only worsened with their medicine. By 18 September, Harry felt hope fading and the family recognized that 'our fear and foe possibly blood poisoning'.[27]

By the end of September Mary feared she had peritonitis, as she experienced high fever every afternoon, great difficulty sleeping and eating, and a continuous discharge. But Dr Dobie spoke vaguely of a 'chronic inflammation' which merely required·time and asserted that Mary was now safe. The surgeon, Dr Griffiths, sent a 'comforting letter' which left Catherine Gladstone 'most hopeful—there is yet a chance of its being slight—mere inflammation without abscess or remaining things left'.[28] But Mary herself was far from reassured and suggested sending for Sir Andrew Clark, the family's famous London doctor, who made two special visits from London in October. After examining Mary on 2 October he left written instructions about treatment for Dr Dobie, and had a private talk with Harry Drew: 'no longer in doubt as to mischief—inflammation in tissues around womb, extending over pelvis'. They hoped the inflammation would subside in time, but instead two lumps became abscesses. The illness was probably cellulitis, a form of puerperal fever, whereby infection of the pelvic tissue was accompanied by the development of large, painful pockets of pus (or 'abscesses') beneath the skin. The doctors continued with their mixed regime of poultices, laudanum, bromide, brandy, quinine, morphia, castor oil, and 'boiling fomentations' for stomach pains. Mary and Harry feared the worst, with justification, and Mary dictated her informal will to Harry, leaving her dresses, jewellery and books to friends and relatives. Harry found it especially heartbreaking to list their wedding presents in the will, so soon after the marriage. Towards the end of October the abscesses perforated, giving Mary gradual relief, and by the time Sir Andrew Clark returned in December she was much stronger. The doctors' bills were paid in January 1887 to mark her recovery: 'Dr Dobie £75, Dr Burlingham £30, chemists £10, nurse £15, and £105 to Dr Griffiths.'[29]

Mary Drew was extremely lucky to recover in 1887 after five months' grave illness, intensive nursing, doubtful medical treatment, and a medical bill for £235. In 1890 Mary gave birth to a daughter, but in May 1893 she had a second miscarriage. On the basis of Gertrude Gladstone's account, Mary was fortunate that this did not develop into another dangerous illness:

[Dr Dobie] made a careful examination, and found the womb was enlarged. He thinks the most probable thing is that some membranous stuff which might have to do with the after-birth is still there, and that it will *gradually* be expelled—*slowly* he says; it is not safe to take it away with violent measures . . . she must make up her mind to take care for a fortnight, to treat herself as if she had had a little confinement . . . she is taking Ergot which will help matters, and of course the syringing with Boracic Acid is continued, the nurse is careful . . . patience is *the thing*

required at present—it must run its course and take its own time—Dr
Dobie has known cases going on for 5 months.[30]

If Mary Drew had died after either miscarriage, a local cause
would probably have been cited on the death certificate, with no
reference to septic infection following an incomplete miscarriage.
Many women must have died from septic infection or haemorrhage after, miscarriage, but the extent of this common cause of
death was concealed. It is impossible to quantify the mortality
from miscarriages because it was rarely recorded on death
certificates and was not included in national statistics.

Women's secrecy about miscarriage meant that their illnesses
could appear to be psychogenic, since the real cause was unstated.
This probably explains the alleged 'delicacy' of many Victorian
women. For example, the Gibbs family letters in 1884 described
the prolonged illness of Beatrice Clarke, who was 'dreadfully
weak', could scarcely walk, suffered from 'shattered nerves' and
needed a full-time nurse. Only one letter in the family correspondence, marked 'confidential', divulged the secret of her illness in a
crucial sentence which the recipient only just failed to obliterate.
There was inflammation of the uterus after 'the last miscarriage',
when 'something had adhered to the womb';[31] her initial illness
was probably similar to Mary Drew's in 1886. In 1912 Lady
Selborne pondered the various medical problems of her daughter,
Mabel, Lady Howick. A confused list of symptoms included 'the
digestive machinery not working properly', and all were caused by
'the troubles which followed on her miscarriage'.[32] Lady Curzon
was dangerously ill in 1904 with peritonitis and phlebitis, only a
month after her second miscarriage. She survived two operations
only to die, allegedly of heart trouble, two years later at the age of
thirty-six.[33]

Edith Lyttelton and Molly Trevelyan each recorded details of
their miscarriages in the Edwardian period. Their accounts
illustrate the painful and traumatic experience so many women
endured, even when their lives were not in danger and they had
the best medical attendants available. In September 1902, when
Alfred was away in Newfoundland, Edith Lyttelton had a
miscarriage in her third month of pregnancy. Like Victoria
Dawnay, she described her feelings in a letter in the early stages of
the threatened miscarriage: 'I was terribly frightened at first, but

as the hours go on I am less so and full of hope that it was a mere warning . . . It is vital to keep absolutely flat and not to worry.' Edith was staying in Northumberland at the time and feared that she had precipitated the miscarriage by falling off her bicycle. When the 'unfortunate event' became inevitable she was relieved to discover that the foetus was malformed, so it was not her fault. She wrote to Alfred a week later:

I hope you think it was right to have Croome down—the local doctor was not at first *quite* sure if everything had come away, and he evidently desired it—I expect it will cost something. Croome did not operate—confirmed Mathison's opinion that from the very beginning the thing was all wrong and could never have come to a baby . . . He told me I must stay in bed at least a fortnight, and that in his opinion I ought not to have another baby until I have been what they call curetted—in other words scraped . . . I seem to be very well out of this scrape for he says that if it had gone on another month or two it might have been very serious indeed . . . The actual night when it all happened was horrible for tho' I had no pain there was considerable haemorrhage. The doctor hurt me rather and I nearly fainted and frightened both myself and the nurse.

Edith was determined not to wallow in sadness over the miscarriage, though it made it all the harder to bear the recent death of her young son.[34]

Molly Trevelyan was also fortunate in having a doctor who ensured that all the contents of the uterus were expelled, and that no septic infection followed. Even so, her miscarriage on 2 August 1911, in her third month of pregnancy, was a most unpleasant experience. The discharge slowly increased from 23 July and on her second visit the female doctor, Dr Williams, sent for Molly's mother and a nurse from Newcastle, 'as much to make me comfortable and happy as to catch the baby if it goes'. On 30 July Dr Williams said that her condition had become steadily worse and the foetus would almost certainly be lost. Molly wrote to Charles that she was bitterly disappointed, 'after our joy at his advent, and after this week of care, and particularly after the last 3 days spent flat on my back'. The prospect ahead was bleak, with the loss of their baby, followed by three weeks in bed, then 'having to lie up for the first three months' with the next baby.[35] Molly awoke in a pool of blood on 1 August 1911 and the nurse battled with the haemorrhage all morning. Dr Williams gave hot douches and ergot, but Molly's pulse rose to 120. The doctor decided to induce

170 *Childbirth*

the miscarriage: 'so she tewed [*sic*] at me with instruments for nearly an hour, hurting me very much. It had the effect of setting up labour pains, which went on till 10 o.c. and then stopped. Charlie sat by me all the evening and held my hands and consoled me.' The following day bleeding continued with occasional douches, and then great clots of blood: 'Dr. W. said the placenta was coming away in little bits', and that she would induce it again in the afternoon.

I had good cause to be afraid—for from 5 to 6 I suffered such pain as I hope never to have to go through again. The baby was lying loose in the uterus, and I had no power to expel it: and she brought it away piecemeal in very small bits. I determined I would not cry out, because I wanted Charlie to know that I was brave, because I loved him. But I cried silently all the time, and bit my arms and writhed about. Dr. W. would have been ready to give me chloroform but I knew that it was much better not to, with a chance of haemorrhage.[36]

Only afterwards was Molly given morphia for the pain. She spent ten days in bed, followed by a week resting in the garden. Dr Williams pronounced that the miscarriage was caused because the uterus was too low and put in a pessary to 'prevent it getting worse'.[37] Just a few days after Molly's ordeal, her sister, Elsa Richmond, had a threatened miscarriage:

I am not looking forward to the fact that all the beastly part is still to come but still I don't think it will be as bad for me as for you as [Dr] Hedley said that once it really began he would chloroform me and take the whole thing away, but he doesn't like to start doing that till it begins to come away.[38]

Elsa's miscarriage was averted, to the surprise of the family, but both women learnt a lesson about the extreme caution needed to avoid 'the most horrid illness on the face of the earth'. Exactly a year later, when Molly was pregnant again, she stayed in bed at the first signs of the ominous discharge: 'The horror of another experience like last summer is far greater than the dislike of being in bed, and I feel I shan't mind in the least spending so long in bed and on my back if only I can avoid a miscarriage.'[39]

MATERNAL MORTALITY

Maternal mortality rates remained high throughout the years from 1865 to 1914, despite the new knowledge of antisepsis. William Farr estimated that there were 5.4 maternal deaths for every thousand live births between 1847 and 1854. He calculated that in the thirty years from 1847 to 1876, on average five mothers died for every thousand children born alive.[40] The decennial averages for England and Wales between 1865 and 1904 varied between 4.6 and 5.1 maternal deaths per thousand live births. The probability was that three women in every hundred who bore six children would die in childbirth. The decennial averages fell to 3.9 per thousand between 1905 and 1924, but did not fall to one death per thousand live births until the end of the Second World War.[41] The drastic reduction in maternal deaths from puerperal sepsis was due to the introduction of sulphonamides from the 1930s and penicillin from 1941. These statistics for the years up to 1904 were grim, but they represent a significant underestimate of the actual maternal death rate, since they exclude deaths relating to still births and miscarriages. Moreover, registration regulations were lax before the 1880s and death certificates were frequently inaccurate, with the cause of death cited so vaguely as to be useless for classification. In order to improve the maternal mortality statistics, some hospitals, midwives and doctors failed to identify haemorrhages or infections as connected with childbirth, especially if the death took place some weeks after the delivery.[42]

Many women shared Lady Frederick Cavendish's concern about the maternal mortality rates. In 1876 she heard of yet 'another tragedy': 'I wish doctors would investigate the causes of the terrible delicacy of the "upper 10,000" women in childbirth.'[43] Her assumption that the upper classes suffered more than the masses was questionable, but her general sentiment was widely appreciated, as so many people had lost a wife, sister, mother or friend in childbirth. Among prominent politicians, for example, Joseph Chamberlain lost his first wife in 1863, five days after the birth of their second child. His second wife's death certificate in 1875 merely stated: 'Parturition 18 hours. Syncope sudden.' Presumably Florence Chamberlain died of shock or exhaustion during labour, and the child died with her. Sir William Harcourt's first wife, Thérèse, died when she gave birth to Lewis in 1863. Sir Charles Dilke's first wife, Katherine, died in 1874 after 'a sudden convulsion on the day following the birth of a child, primarily toxicohaemic condition of blood'. Lord Curzon's mother, Lady Scarsdale, died in 1875, at the age of thirty-seven. The immediate symptoms were blood-poisoning and exhaustion, but 'her constitution had been weakened by the bearing of eleven children in sixteen years'.[44]

(i) Puerperal fever

Causes of maternal death were divided into two general categories by the registrar-general. 'Accidents' included 'exhaustion', eclampsia and ectopic pregnancies, while puerperal fever was a confusing term which covered almost any kind of infection. From 1847 to 1874, puerperal fever was recorded as causing between 33 and 38 per cent of maternal deaths in England and Wales, though these figures undoubtedly represented a considerable underestimate. In the two decades between 1875 and 1894, deaths from puerperal fever accounted for 50 per cent of the total maternal deaths. Indeed, deaths from puerperal fever actually exceeded maternal deaths from other causes in the decade 1885–94. From 1865 to 1904 the maternal death rate from puerperal fever was approximately 2.2 per thousand live births, averaged over the period, reaching its height at 2.6 in the years 1885 to 1894. The maternal death rate from puerperal fever was only reduced to 1.6 per thousand live births from 1905 to 1914, while the significant drop to 0.17 only eventuated with the widespread use of antibiotics in the 1940s.[45]

There was considerable fear and confusion about puerperal fever in the nineteenth century, among both doctors and their female patients. Women are exceedingly vulnerable to infection following delivery because the expulsion of the placenta leaves a raw wound in the wall of the uterus which requires about a month to heal. Streptococcal bacteria can easily cause dangerous infections during this period, leading to high temperature, widespread inflammation of the abdominal cavity, blood poisoning, and death. Streptococcal organisms could produce a variety of symptoms, so that 'puerperal fever' was manifested in various frightening forms. In the early nineteenth century puerperal fever was still seen as a mysterious epidemic, but in the 1840s Semmelweiss and Wendell Holmes independently established that it was a contagious disease. The confusion surrounding its cause was only ended in 1879, when Pasteur published his conclusion that microbes in the lochia and blood caused the disease. Doctors were reluctantly obliged to recognize their role in spreading the disease from infected patients to parturient women. From the 1880s doctors attempted to combat the disease with antiseptic procedures, though with limited success, as the statistics illustrate. No cure for puerperal fever was found until the discovery of antibiotics.

Victorian women had every reason to fear puerperal fever, yet they rarely mentioned 'childbed fever' specifically, unless making a statement about a particular death. During pregnancy they talked only in very general terms about their fears of death, almost as if puerperal fever was equated with inevitable death. Miscarriages, by contrast, were discussed at length, but at least some practical preventive steps could be taken there, and death was far less certain. They were helpless and afraid in the face of puerperal fever, and responded with fatalism. Given the medical confusion on the subject until the late 1870s, and the doctors' conspiracy of silence, the women's reaction is explicable. When obliged to discuss puerperal fever, they used euphemisms and expected the worst. Families described such cases as 'erysipelas after confinement', or 'nervous fever', or even 'typhoid fever following the birth'.[46] Lady Derby heard 'from the wretched husband that there was but little hope' for Lady Carnarvon in 1875. She was suffering 'exhaustion and utter breakup from the effects of nervous fever which came on five days after her confinement'. Lady Derby knew no details but needed none to expect the worst.[47]

Margaret Gladstone died of puerperal fever on 16 August 1870, nearly a month after the birth of her baby on 20 July, and only a year after her marriage. This death is one of many thousands of similar deaths throughout the nineteenth century, but the details of Margaret's last illness were lovingly recorded in a journal kept by her mother, Elizabeth King. During her pregnancy Margaret occasionally discussed with her husband the possibility of death in childbirth. On New Year's Eve 1869 they talked freely of 'how I may die at the baby's birth and yet all will be well. And I felt as if I could leave even this intense and overflowing happiness on earth to be with Jesus.'[48] Margaret was in labour for only five hours on 20 July. 'She suffered a great deal on account of the great size of the child', but her pain was partially reduced by the chloroform which her husband himself administered. John Gladstone believed that everything was 'going on well' after the difficult confinement.[49]

Margaret was 'taken dangerously ill' twelve days after the delivery, starting with 'a terrible seizure' and ending in death two weeks later. A wet-nurse had to be obtained because Margaret did

not want to see the baby after 2 August.[50] Mrs King travelled
down from Edinburgh to nurse her daughter: 'It is not suitable for
John to have charge of a sick wife, a baby and such a number of
nurses and to talk to doctors so many times a day.' This was
the mother's role. Two regular sick-nurses were employed for
Margaret, as well as the wet-nurse and the monthly nurse to look
after the baby. Three doctors were involved in the case; two
consulting physicians, Dr Morris and Dr Hewitt, and the family
doctor, Dr Philip, who acted as spokesman for the trio.[51]

Margaret Gladstone seems to have suffered from a similar type
of infection to that which almost killed Mary Drew in 1886. The
death certificate subsequently stated: 'Uraemia and pyelitis with
slight pelvic Celluitis [*sic*] 14 days. Commencing 13 days after a
natural confinement.' The emphasis was placed on the renal
failure, without indicating that this was a symptom of 'slight'
cellulitis and that the major cause of death was puerperal fever.
Six days before Margaret's death, Elizabeth King wrote to her
husband:

Till yesterday afternoon the doctors gave no decided opinion about
Margaret's case. They have now discovered an internal abcess caused by
an injury at the birth which they think accounts for her illness—The
treatment is now directed to bring it to a head and when it breaks they
expect her to be better. Her pulse is always high varying from 100 to 125
and her mind is generally wandering . . .[52]

Five days later, Mrs King despaired: 'The sickness is so dreadful
and nothing does her any good. All you can do is to pray for us . . .
The abcess is disappearing without breaking, and the doctors now
think there is some disease of the kidneys.'[53]

These three eminent doctors presumably recognized that Margaret was dying from the dreaded contagious disease known as
puerperal fever, even though they knew nothing yet of its
microbiological character. No doubt the three doctors were also
well aware of their inadequacy. They took refuge in listing the
symptoms of the disease as if they were the cause. It sounded more
professional to blame an abscess caused by a birth injury or 'some
disease of the kidneys', and these diagnoses may even have given
some temporary comfort to Mrs King. The prescribed treatment
was opium, champagne, and brandy and soda every three
hours—a clear indication that the doctors knew they had no

remedy and could only ease the dying woman's pain and discomfort. On the other hand, they ordered a 'lamp bath', which caused Mrs King to 'quail at the thought of torturing the poor patient suffering lamb . . . all the applications [that] wore her out and disturbed her so.' The dying woman, most of all, recognized the futility of the doctors' prescriptions. The last time the three doctors stood round her death bed, Margaret whispered to her mother: 'they would like to learn from my case—let them.' Margaret did not see her baby daughter until the day she died, when she requested that she be dedicated to God.[54]

(ii) 'Other diseases and accidents'

Those women who died after too many pregnancies form a group which was also ignored in the maternal mortality statistics. Women died more frequently from excessive births earlier in the period, since average family sizes gradually declined with the slow acceptance of birth-control methods. Marriages of the late 1860s which lasted more than twenty years produced an average of 6.16 live births. This figure declined to 5.8 in the 1870s, 5.3 in the 1880s, 4.13 in the 1890s and 2.43 by 1915.[55] However, it must again be emphasized that these statistics ignore miscarriages and still births. So we do not know the total number of pregnancies, nor the actual numbers of women who produced more children than average. Certainly, birth-control propaganda underlined the dangers of bearing too many children as a powerful reason for artificially regulating family size. Though the medical profession publicly opposed contraception, a small minority, like Dr Henry Allbutt, wrote of 'the evil produced by over-bearing and excessive lactation'. Allbutt argued in 1886 that severe physical disorders could result from bearing children too rapidly and suckling them for too long: 'In the poor broken-down woman of thirty, prematurely old, few will be able to recognise the young, fair and happy bride.' The modern view is that the first five pregnancies become progressively easier and less dangerous for healthy young women; but the safety factor is reduced after the fifth child, and the risks of maternal death increase with each child thereafter. As early as 1859 Dr Robert Barnes warned other doctors that the risk of death rose rapidly after the fifth labour.[56]

Mary Lady Lyttelton provides a typical illustration of maternal death due to excessive childbearing. She died in 1857, and her death certificate merely recorded 'disease of the heart', with no mention of recent childbirth. Mary Lyttelton died at the age of forty-four, having borne twelve live children and suffered at least one miscarriage in the space of seventeen years. Breastfeeding did not noticeably increase the spacing between children in her case, and Mary called her regular pregnancies her 'yearly penance'. After the ninth baby she wrote to her sister, Catherine Gladstone: 'perhaps the 9th begins to give warning that I have had enough babies', since she was feeling weaker than usual. Within a year she had a miscarriage, the tenth child was born in 1854, and the eleventh in 1855. Her husband, Lord Lyttelton, later stated that this eleventh confinement marked the end of her days of 'vigorous health', especially as there was 'something not satisfactory at the confinement', and Mary became very ill afterwards. Sir Charles Locock, the leading gynaecologist of the mid-Victorian period, told Catherine Gladstone that another pregnancy would almost certainly cost Mary her life. Locock would have shown greater wisdom, responsibility and courage by warning Mary's husband, rather than her sister. If George Lyttelton ever knew of the warning, he did not act upon it, presumably sharing W. E. Gladstone's hostility to contraception.[57]

In 1856 Catherine learnt the news of Mary's final pregnancy, 'quite as a blow'. 'After a time of the greatest anxiety', in February 1857 the last baby, Alfred, was born. It became only too clear afterwards that Mary's heart had been progressively weakened. Only at this point did Locock inform George Lyttelton that 'the mischief was done', not then, but earlier. The doctors let it be known that 'the case was one of much obscurity and complication, upon which the doctors would not give an unhesitating opinion'. Lord Lyttelton for a while blamed Locock's stimulating treatment of port wine for over-exciting Mary's weak constitution, but possibly he needed to assuage his own guilt. Only years later did George admit that Mary's was 'a hopeless case from a very early date . . . a general break up of the constitution, of much longer standing'. It was also 'an extreme instance of the way in which doctors withhold the truth'. By July the heart condition was pronounced and Mary retired permanently to bed, with violent bilious attacks and increasing difficulty in breathing. Mary told William Gladstone on 16 August 'that she had long felt how this illness would end: that she could not recover'. Soon afterwards there was 'a fearful spasm in the heart' as she died in her sister's arms.[58] Meriel Lyttelton, Mary's eldest daughter, who bore the burden of caring for her motherless sisters and brothers, did not learn from her mother's experience. Meriel Talbot had ten children, though she was fortunate to survive until she was eighty-five. Her sister, Lavinia Talbot, had five children, while Charles Lyttelton fathered seven, but they were the only three children of the twelve Lytteltons to have large families.

In 1885 Laura Tennant married Mary Lyttelton's last child, Alfred. Laura herself died, aged twenty-three, on 24 April 1886, eight days after the birth of her first child. Laura was considered tiny and frail, and there is some evidence to suggest that she may have been in the early stages of tuberculosis. Her correspondence contained numerous references to death. Edith Lyttelton wrote later: 'It is curious how constant the idea of death is in her mind—metaphor and description seem to circle round death—it is almost as if she knew what was coming.' Laura wrote to Alfred soon after their marriage: 'I often think of death, my Darling, and wonder how long God is going to let us live together before one of us leads the way to the Anti-Chamber of Life.'[59] Pregnancy intensified her premonition of death: 'I always feel if I die in March, no woman ever had such a dawn to her married life . . . If I die I have been happy.'[60] When she was about five months pregnant, Laura wrote to Edward Lyttelton: 'I don't think I have done anything quite wicked enough to deserve such an awful punishment as to let the little thing live and me die . . . I think a great deal about it now and often find myself arranging everything, so as to leave all things neat and well.'[61] A month before her confinement she told Doll Liddell: 'the isles of the blest seem very near when there is a great possibility of death . . . I want you to choose something for me to leave you'.[62] Three weeks later, Laura confided in her sister, Margot, that she was fairly sure she would die. Margot argued in vain that their mother bore twelve children without chloroform and their two sisters had easy confinements. Margot was reluctantly persuaded to swear that she would read Laura's will aloud to the family gathered around her sister's deathbed.[63]

Laura's nine-pound baby boy was born on 16 April, 'after a time both terribly long and dangerous—the boy's life was only just saved'.[64] Her sister-in-law, Lucy Cavendish, described the ordeal:

'Poor darling Laura had a frightful hard business before an hour's work with instruments brought this immense boy into the world ... Almost immediately afterwards a horrid unusual haemorrhage set in from the liver. Sickness, every half hour or oftener.'[65] The Lyttelton family agreed that the trouble was partially explained by the large size of the baby and Laura's narrow pelvis. Interventionist obstetrics were obviously necessary in the decades before caesarian sections, though it is impossible to tell whether the post-partum haemorrhage was avoidable. Alfred Lyttelton wrote to Mary Drew the day his son was born: 'a fine son—a nine pounder—is the result of an awful night's anxiety. We had to have Matthews Duncan to help, for hardly anyone could possibly have had a worse time.'[66] Dr Matthews Duncan was one of the leading obstetricians of the day, and was assisted at various times over the next week by two other doctors, including Sir Andrew Clark.

The haemorrhage and sickness continued for five days after the confinement. Then on 22 April, Helen Gladstone reported: 'some extraordinary symptoms came on which puzzled them [the doctors] greatly, and now they say it is some very bad liver illness and nothing to do with the confinement'.[67] No doubt this medical approach reduced any blame which might be attached to the 'hour's work with instruments' and the 'horrid unusual haemorrhage'. Doll Liddell heard that 'the doctors don't seem to know what she died of'.[68] But the family was not inclined to attribute blame and agreed that the main problem was exhaustion and complete loss of strength. The death certificate merely noted: 'Childbirth 8 days. Haematomasis. Exhaustion.' Margot Tennant read Laura's will aloud to those gathered around the deathbed, as she had sworn to do, while Alfred looked suffocated, and efforts to deter Margot failed.[69]

Mary Drew mourned: 'impossible to exaggerate the tragedy-pathos of this event. I should imagine that not the death of any single person in the whole world could so deeply cut into the hearts and lives of so many people.'[70] After the funeral Mary wrote: 'it seemed too much—the little white bride, inside the coffin, and all the broken hearts around.'[71] It was not easy to adopt Catherine Gladstone's attitude to such a death: 'A beautiful time to die and wake on the *Easter* morn upon the Everlasting Throne.'[72] Two years later Laura's son, Christopher, died of tubercular meningitis. Alfred was 'comforted by the thought of his being with

my little Darling'.[73] But Laura's friends, Lady Cowell-Stepney and
Mary Drew, saw 'no comfort about his death'. They regretted the
'apparently utter waste of it all . . . it made her death seem so hard
and as if it were in vain'. It revived the 'keen misery' of Laura's
death and tore open the wounds again.[74]

Margot Asquith narrowly escaped the same kind of death as her
sister Laura. Margot was stepmother to H. H. Asquith's children
by his first wife, but she desperately wanted children of her own.
She struggled constantly with miscarriages and births made
dangerous by her narrow pelvis. Edith Lyttelton reported in
December 1894 that Margot was expecting a baby in April, the
anniversary month of Laura's death: 'I do wish it wasn't just then.
I think it will make her more nervous and it's altogether so
harrowing . . . she is so extraordinarily small . . . the chiefest
danger would be a very large child.'[75] Margot hoped that 'it may
be a girl and that I may live through it.' But she became very
depressed, concluding that it would not 'matter so much if I die . . .
death may not after all be so terrible'. Their fears were justified,
and the doctors had to sacrifice the baby to save Margot's life in
May 1895. She had to spend three months following the
confinement flat on her back in bed with phlebitis, and she was left
in delicate health for many years with insomnia and 'nervous
exhaustion'.[76]

Margot was not deterred; even though she lost three babies out
of five confinements, she did bear two live children, Elizabeth and
Anthony, in 1897 and 1902. She was 'always nervous—its my
nature quite as much as my past experience'.[77] Shortly before
Elizabeth's birth in 1897 Margot told Lord Rosebery: 'I should be
sorry never to have a child of my own but of course I know I am
not a good subject.'[78] Margot lost two other children shortly after
birth, in 1900 and 1908. During labour in 1900 she suffered such
agonizing pain that she was given a massive dose of morphia, and
she never saw the baby alive: 'she was mine for seven hours . . .
Henry carried the little coffin all the way in his arms.' Margot
wrote to Violet Cecil afterwards: 'My baby's death is a deep and
intimate sorrow. I have a passion for children and *longed* to give
Elizabeth a companion . . . I am not very well and my spirits have
gone to the devil . . . My illness and sorrow affected Henry
deeply.'[79] Afterwards, Frances Horner told Violet Cecil not to be
indignant at Margot's 'undefeated attempts': 'the only thing that

comforts her is to think she can try again . . . it was a bitter grief to them both and I was miserable for them; I don't know why it should go wrong so.'[80] Presumably it went wrong because Margot's pelvis was small, and caesarian section was still far too dangerous an operation.

INFANT MORTALITY

Examination of maternal death has already involved some discussion of infant mortality.[81] The most dangerous period for infants was the first year of their lives. Most still births and deaths within the first month were due to genetic causes, but deaths between one and twelve months were generally caused by infectious diseases. Infant mortality remained extremely high throughout the nineteenth century, and a substantial improvement did not take place until the 1920s. Between 1860 and 1900, over 14 per cent of infants born in England and Wales died in their first year.[82] In 1857 Dr R. Hall Bakewell condemned 'a system by which one-fifth of all who are born never see the first anniversary of their birth'.[83] The major causes of death for infants in their first year included gastro-enteritis, atrophy, tuberculosis, dysentery, diarrhoea, scarlet fever, measles and smallpox. Doctors could do little to cure such diseases in infants. The incidence of infant mortality for the professional and upper classes was substantially lower, as shown by Ansell's analysis of mortality rates for those classes in 1874. He found that eight per cent of these infants died before the end of their first year and that a further five per cent died before the age of five.[84] These improved figures were due to better diet, sanitation and living conditions, but they were still grim statistics for society's élite.

Lawrence Stone concluded that parents in earlier centuries refused to invest too much emotional capital in their children because such deaths were commonplace: 'The omnipresence of death coloured affective relations at all levels of society, by reducing the amount of emotional capital available for prudent investment in any single individual, especially in such ephemeral creatures as infants.'[85] Experts on death in the twentieth century have also tended to assume that the deaths of small children are more traumatic for parents in recent decades because they are so rare. Colin Murray-Parkes, a prominent psychologist, has recently

1 Molly Bell dressed for presentation at Court, 1899
(by kind permission of the Trevelyan family)

2 The engagement of Molly Bell and Charles Trevelyan, 1903
(by kind permission of the Trevelyan family)

3 Margaret Gladstone and Ramsay MacDonald before their marriage, 1896
(from the Ramsay MacDonald Papers at the PRO)

4 Margot and H. H. Asquith: after the wedding, 1895
(from Margot Asquith, *The Autobiography*, 1920)

5 Wedding of Maud Cecil and the future Lord Selborne, 1883
(*Illustrated London News*, 3 November 1883)

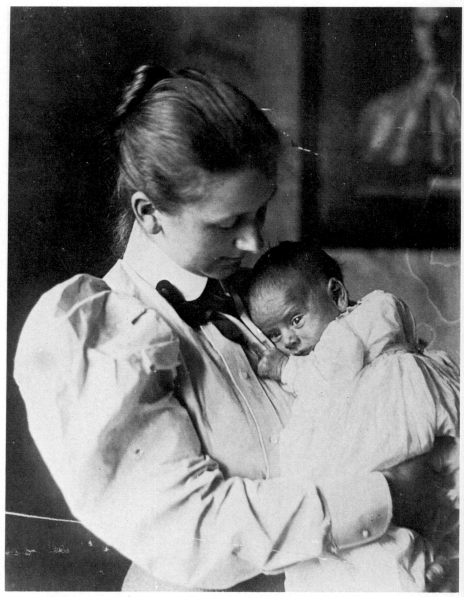

6 Margaret MacDonald with her baby, Alister, 1898
(from the Ramsay MacDonald Papers at the PRO)

7 Maud and Gwendolen Cecil, 1869
(Ms. Selborne 196, no. 5, reproduced by permission of the Bodleian Library)

8 Charles and Molly Trevelyan with their children, Pauline, George, and Kitty,
c.1910 (by kind permission of the Trevelyan family)

9 The Gladstone family at Hawarden, 1894 Back row, left to right: Stephen and Annie; Mary and Harry Drew; Herbert; Helen. Front: Catherine and William with their grandchildren (Mary Drew. *Catherine Gladstone*, 1919)

10 The Chamberlain family after Joseph's marriage to Mary Endicott, 1889
(The Illustrated London News Picture Library)

11 Evelyn Lady Stanhope, c.1888 (The
Stanhope Papers. By permission of the
Trustees of the Chevening Estate)

13 Laura Lyttleton, née Tennant
(Edith Lyttleton, *Alfred Lyttelton*, 1917)

12 Mary Gladstone, c.1880
(Lucy Masterman, ed. *Mary Gladstone.
Her Diaries and Letters*, 1930)

14 Margaret King during her engagement to
Dr John Gladstone, 1869 (from the Ramsay
MacDonald Papers at the PRO)

concluded that 'extremely severe and incapacitating reactions were found among mothers who have lost small infants.' Forty years ago, Geoffrey Gorer's sociological research led to the same conclusions, but he extended them to older children: such a loss was 'the most distressing and long-lasting of all griefs'.[86]

But to assume that parents suffered less when their children died in earlier centuries is to risk trivializing their emotions. To question this assumption raises the insoluble problem of measuring the relative intensity of grief in different individuals in different centuries. Yet there is an overwhelming mass of evidence testifying to the suffering of the Victorians and Edwardians on the deaths of their infants and young children. The anguish of thousands of mothers went unrecorded, but many probably responded like Margot Tennant's mother: 'She had suffered too much over the deaths of her first three to care for society . . . Sorrow had sapped her vitality: she had no worldliness and no illusions.'[87] Laurencina Potter already had eight girls when her two-year-old son died in 1864, yet 'the greatest sorrow of her life was the death of this little boy'.[88] Though she already had nine children, Mary Lyttelton was able to share her sister's sense of loss after a miscarriage in 1851: 'even I with so many should feel it very much'.[89] Decades later, in 1911, a friend who wrote to console Margaret MacDonald on the death of her son, David, understood that other children did not compensate for the loss of any one: 'if one had twenty children one could never in the least take the place of another—there would always be twenty yearnings and twenty gaps in one's heart'.[90]

It is also, perhaps, too readily assumed that the Victorians and Edwardians suffered less on bereavement because they had religion to console them. If the bare statements of some Victorians are taken at face value, then their grief does appear to have been made easier by their acquiescence in God's will and their belief in a better life hereafter. Thomas Acland was able to inform his sister of his daughter's death in 1851:

You will be grieved to hear that a slight ailment of our dear little Emma Cecily proved to be scarlet fever or some form of it, and convulsions coming her little life soon ebbed out—God be praised for All his Mercies which are great indeed—I feel this to be a serious call to us and beg your prayers that it may be blessed to us. Dear Mary is well, and able to do all that is required of her. I suppose the little one's remains will be laid by her sister's.[91]

W. H. Smith responded in similar manner on the death of his baby son in 1866: 'Poor Emily is in sorrow but it is a blessing we are one and that we are comforted by the assurance that our Father has permitted it and that He is both infinite love and infinite wisdom. . . . It is a sad blank in our nursery—a quiet little sorrow which will last with us for a long time to come.'[92] The Victorians had greater need of such religious consolation precisely because they had to come to terms with infant death so much more often than today. Deaths of children were the hardest to bear and they had to muster all the comfort available. Eva Knatchbull-Hugesson noted how her sister-in-law found some comfort on her baby's death in 1883 because he did not suffer: 'and also how much happier it would be for him not to have to go through this world'. Eva imagined the baby as 'a spirit with far more knowledge and comprehension than we have'.[93] These were sentiments frequently expressed in the attempt to console the bereaved or to accept death within one's own family. Parents who lost babies often recognized 'how very much greater the sorrow for those who have had to part with older children'.[94]

It would be a mistake to assume that religious belief always brought consolation. The words of condolence offered and received cannot reveal the depth of grief and can sometimes even conceal it. In 1914 Roundell and Grace Palmer lost their baby. Roundell's mother, Lady Selborne, wrote to another son:

I never think the doctrine of the immortality of the soul is the same comfort with regard to a baby that it is with regard to older people—at least from a mother's standpoint—because it is the body that she loves at that age—the affection is the instinctive animal affection, she wants to have it in her arms, to feel the little fingers clasping hers. She does not know what the soul is like yet, so she can only love that vaguely—but the other instinct is so strong that she suffers cruelly if she loses her baby.[95]

A month after the baby's death, Grace talked to her sister-in-law, Laura Ridding, 'about the sad little death quite freely and very intensely'. Her 'big London specialist' told her that 'these poisonous cases of septic pneumonia are rare, but when they come there is nothing can be done'.[96]

Even if religion provided inadequate consolation on the deaths of babies, its message that death was not final offered some comfort. But by the last decades of the nineteenth century, a number of these political families were unable to sustain their religious beliefs against the onslaught of science and secularism. In some cases, members of these new agnostic families turned to spiritualism to fight the finality of death. Edith Lyttelton's baby son, Antony, died very suddenly in 1902, after five days of an unspecified illness. Immediately afterwards Edith wrote: 'Alas, Alas, I can gather him no longer, though my arms weary for him, though my heart aches for him . . . The agony of our loss had grown and grown, until it seemed that such a thing could not be borne.' A few months later, Edith was avoiding social commitments because it was such 'a very short time since an experience and a grief which is never out of my mind for a moment and which haunts the hours of talk and social intercourse more than any others'. She felt that even Alfred 'hardly knows the daily and hourly struggle I have, to get on, and to put on a courageous front'. Many years later she still found it hard to write about 'the agony of that parting'.[97] But Edith found some consolation through spiritualism. The day before Antony's burial, 'when I looked upon his face, the child in it was gone . . . all at once, a wonderful peace and hope descended upon me'. She was certain that 'Antony's life is only a stage on a greater journey' and she learned that the mystery of sorrow can generate a sense of growth. 'The experience, the struggle, the light that came to me then' helped Edith immensely in coping with later sorrows, especially Alfred's own death in 1913.[98]

Agnostic or atheist families, like the Trevelyans, had to find their own ways of coming to terms with the deaths of infants. Robert and Elizabeth Trevelyan lost their baby daughter in September 1908 and their only remaining child, Paul, aged two, just six months later. The baby developed malignant jaundice soon after birth, and the doctor informed them that it would quickly prove fatal. Bessie 'took it very well: though she feels it very much, she is very self-controlled'. Both parents did their best to put on a cheerful front, but Robert's brother, George, was well aware of Bessie's 'mental suffering'. Bessie herself recognized that she would be more in need of moral support later on 'when depression and mental reaction is likely to set in'. Both parents admitted that 'it was fortunate it did not live longer so that they should have had time to get attached to it more strongly. But it is of course a bitter disappointment, and may prey upon their spirits later.'[99] The sadness was greater because the baby initially seemed so healthy. Six months later their two-year-old son, Paul, died of tuberculosis and internal ulcers in the bowels. Bessie tried to take comfort in the knowledge that Paul died 'very peacefully and easily with no struggle whatever'. Molly Trevelyan thought her sister-in-law 'amazingly brave—talks about him without a break in her voice'.[100]

George and Janet Trevelyan lost their five-year-old son, Theodore, in 1911, after a very painful illness with appendicitis. Molly's father, Sir Hugh Bell, understood their suffering: 'I think of the blank despair one feels when death comes and carries off our beloved—and how it seems as if one could not bear to go on living . . . Poor poor parents to have to face these coming weeks when the mere dimming of the memory, which is the way relief comes, adds to the grief one suffers from.' The poor mother would keep remembering those 'dreadful hours of suffering' for her boy. It would require great courage to face their life again, and there was 'bitter suffering' even in recovery.[101] Janet found courage in the realization that they would rather have loved and lost Theo 'than never to have known the joy of that darling life'. The 'joy and beauty of his little life will . . . illuminate the rest of our way'.[102] George Trevelyan appeared to the family to be hardest hit. At first he was shocked at the knowledge that Theo would 'never grow up'.[103] George confessed to his parents that he would 'never be *so* happy again', and he wished he was lying in the grave instead of his little son.[104] Charles recognized that it was a 'very sore blow' to his brother, who 'has been building much on Theo's future'. The parents would recover in time, but Charles thought it sad that they were unlikely to have more children: 'that would be the only thing to be any real compensation'.[105] After their 'honeymoon of grief and thought', communing with nature in the Lake District, the grieving parents returned to their 'only real comfort'—their two living children.[106]

Thus, pregnancy and childbirth could be experiences of great joy or great sorrow for Victorian and Edwardian families. The experience of tragedy was more widespread in the nineteenth than in the twentieth century, because of the more limited medical capacity to deal with miscarriage, puerperal fever and early infant mortality. If the picture for the privileged women was often grim, the prospects for the working-class poor were far worse. The problem of excessive childbearing was increasingly resolved by the more widespread use of contraceptives. The development of blood transfusions, caesarian sections and inductions were major steps towards a further reduction in maternal and infant mortality. The profound fears of tragedy in childbirth could only begin to diminish after the Edwardian period. However, our social memory still retains a heritage of women's anxiety, suffering, and sometimes their death.

PART THREE

POLITICAL WIVES

7
Roles and Attitudes

WIVES of Victorian and Edwardian politicians, unlike most women, performed several specific roles in addition to being wives and mothers. These additional functions carried social status as well as responsibility and a sense of public usefulness. Their social roles as political hostesses and mistresses of households were important to their husbands' careers, and their supportive political roles became more demanding in the second half of the nineteenth century with the growth of democracy and the influence of the women's movement. They were confidantes to their husbands, they participated in election campaigns, and, from the 1880s, many wives contributed to the women's political associations and the female suffrage campaign.

It has often been assumed that Victorian upper-class women had no need to fight for the vote since their position was already privileged and powerful. The anti-suffragist, James Bryce, asserted in 1884 that 'women already enjoy greater influence in other ways, both public and private, than the franchise would give them'. Scholars have appreciated the force of his argument. Gerda Lerner has pointed out that women have been excluded from political power for centuries, 'yet as members of families, as daughters and wives, they often were closer to actual power than many a man'.[1] Brian Harrison has also concluded that the upper-class woman often enjoyed extensive influence without the vote: 'For her, class loyalty was far more important than loyalty to sex. In a strongly hierarchical society with a small political élite, women could achieve much through personal influence.'[2] This chapter explores the major roles of Victorian and Edwardian political wives, the nature of their influence, and their attitudes towards the suffrage campaign.

MISTRESS OF THE HOUSEHOLD AND POLITICAL HOSTESS

The role of mistress of a large household could be very demanding, as Cynthia Asquith recalled:

It is a fallacy to suppose that any woman who ran a large and hospitable country house ever had a *light* job . . . However efficient and obliging, [servants] always tended to quarrel with one another, so that domestic politics were often inflamed and very preoccupying. And what a vast amount of organization keeping 'open house' involved![3]

The management of large households and sizeable estates, with the constant movement of staff, was comparable to running a substantial business. The size of households varied greatly according to wealth, status and numbers of children. Rich aristocratic establishments usually included twenty servants or more, with four housemaids and three or four laundry maids, four kitchen staff, the childrens' nurses and the male house and estate staff. Lady Constance Malleson described her family's 'twenty odd servants' sitting at family prayers in the 1890s in order of rank.[4] The Dukes of Atholl usually maintained a staff of about two dozen servants while the family was based at Blair in Scotland. During the London Season they employed about twelve servants in their London house, and left a dozen or more at Blair. The total number of Atholl servants retained in 1899, for example, ranged from twenty-two to thirty-two, as the numbers were temporarily increased to cope with particularly large house parties. The staff at Blair in 1900 included a home steward, a valet, an usher, an underbutler, two footmen, a housekeeper, a cook, the duchess's maid, four housemaids, four laundry maids, a stillroom maid, a dairymaid, a kitchenmaid, a scullery maid, a sewing maid, two coachmen and two stableboys. A few stayed in service at Blair for many years, but between six and eight left every six months and more than half the staff had less than two years' service.[5]

Below the level of these large aristocratic establishments the number of servants varied considerably. The millionaire iron-master, Hugh Bell, kept a staff of five to look after a family of seven.[6] The Campbell-Bannermans, who had no children, employed a range of servants, including a butler, two footmen, a cook and several maids.[7] The Asquiths lived well above their means to maintain a staff of fourteen servants at their imposing house in Cavendish Square, including a pair of footmen.[8] The Gladstone servants at Hawarden Castle in 1891 included a housekeeper, three housemaids, a cook who also served as kitchenmaid, and 'a boy for morning work, knives and boots'.[9] In 1895 Mary Drew mentioned the payment of 'board wages' for nine servants.[10] More representative of the majority of politicians were the James Bryces with four servants and the Charles Trevelyans with three (before the children came). The majority of upper-middle-class families in this study normally employed at least three or four servants. Few mothers gave their daughters practical training in household management. Beatrice Webb's mother was most unusual, because she expected each of her daughters to supervise the housekeeping at Standish for a year when they 'came out'.[11] Most new brides were untrained for the task, sometimes nervous, but willing to learn. Mary Lydia Hart-Davis probably only had one or two servants when she married in 1872 and acted as her own housekeeper. A year later she reported to her father, Sir Thomas Dyke Acland, that her husband was teaching her to 'keep accounts in a very orderly way': 'Still, I am sure I have a great deal to learn in housekeeping.'[12] Margaret King found herself with four stepchildren and a staff of eight servants when she married Dr Gladstone in 1869. She 'plunged deep into my new mistress duties' with enthusiasm and rapidly established a routine: 'I daily inspect the larder, carefully look over the books and accounts, and am made welcome by all the servants to know all about everything and take my own way.' She gave instructions each morning to the cook and the coachman: 'then I daily settle my housebook, write my business notes, and attend to any necessary things with nurse or housemaid.'[13] The management of household finances was considered a crucial part of the mistress's duties and Victorian wives could not afford to be helpless with the accounts.

Household management for political wives who kept two homes could be especially demanding. Moving large households with numerous servants and huge amounts of luggage between London and the country home required careful organization. Lord John Russell's family has been described as 'an army on the march'.[14] Meriel Talbot's diary for 1861 illustrates the complex logistics. The Talbots stayed at their own home at Falconhurst in Kent for a total of five months, scattered over nine visits; London was their base for four months, Meriel's parental home at Hagley in Worcestershire for two months, and a variety of other country homes for the remaining four weeks. They also travelled frequently between Falconhurst and London, making a total of twenty-five moves during the year.[15] Lady Carrington likewise supervised the frequent movements of her huge household between London and the country with quiet efficiency. It was vital to determine how many servants would be needed in the London house, who was willing to make the move, and what skeleton staff must be left to maintain the country house. Her diary entries gave no hint of the effort involved: 'the servants started for London by an early train and we followed'. Even the domestic upheaval involved in the 1885 move to Australia called for little comment: 'saw the maids in the morning and settled about Australia with them. Three laundry maids, 2 housemaids, 2 nurses have settled to come with us. Very nice of them.'[16]

Most of these women seem to have become capable household managers, but there were some exceptions. Lady Fanny Russell relied on her father, Lord Minto, to supply her with honest country servants from his own estate. She did not find it easy to balance the books and allowed herself to be overcharged.[17] Catherine Gladstone was rather chaotic, lacking organizational skills and a disciplined mind; but she cheerfully muddled through, with the willing help of daughters and servants dazzled by her immense charm. It is significant that the only woman in this study who expressed open dislike of household management was a spinster, Alice Balfour, sister of A. J. Balfour. Mary Drew noted that the Balfour household at Whittingehame was 'no light burden, for besides the numberless guests, there are 2 brothers who live here almost permanently with their wives and their children—8 children to house and feed and amuse.'[18] Packing and organizing the general exodus from Whittingehame to London was no mean feat; the Gerald Balfours alone sent seventeen boxes and six bicycles by goods train as their 'heavy luggage' in the 1890s.[19] As general controller of the household Alice was responsible for sending the servants south and preparing the London house for the family's arrival.[20] She was efficient but her resentment at the role was reflected in her officious manner, as perceptive guests realized: 'Smoking was allowed nowhere except in the grim smoking-room. All games and communal activities were banned on Sunday. Alice also had a mania for checking the number of spoons, forks and other cutlery.'[21] Her frustration at spending so much of her life at uncongenial tasks erupted in 1885, as she confided to Mary Gladstone: 'we are sending away almost all our domestics and going to live in a corner of the house. I like it partly because I don't like housekeeping, but still more because I cannot make up my mind that all these big households, with a lot of servants, who half the year have nothing to do but overeat themselves, are good things.'[22] Alice might have borne these domestic burdens more readily had she enjoyed a wife's compensations of status and affection.

Political wives also had an important role as hostesses, particularly if their husbands were prime ministers. This was especially so during the coalitions and fluid party politics of the two decades after 1846. Lady Palmerston was the only prime minister's wife in this period who was a famous political hostess in her own right.[23] As Lady Cowper she had already established this position before she married her second husband, Lord Palmerston, Foreign Secretary and Liberal leader. Her glittering parties no doubt assisted her husband's career in a period of political confusion, though they were scarcely the primary factor in his success. In the 1860s the Palmerstons moved to the central location of 94 Piccadilly, where guests were invited most evenings—including a considerable number of impressionable young men.[24] By contrast, Palmerston's long-term rival for the Liberal leadership, Lord John Russell, had a wife who disliked large parties and lacked the temperament of the skilled political hostess. The Russell family lived quietly at Pembroke Lodge in Richmond Park, so that Russell suffered some degree of isolation from his supporters.[25] As a social outsider, Disraeli was more dependent on his wife's skills than most rising politicians, and Mary Anne worked hard to overcome the Conservative Party's resistance to Disraeli's leadership. Her money, her house at Grosvenor Gate and her enthusiasm as a hostess all contributed to Disraeli's political security. They frequently entertained at Hughenden and in London and were gradually rewarded by return invitations to many country houses, even if they were never entirely accepted.[26]

The next generation of prime ministers' wives had less need to be skilful hostesses; the two-party system re-emerged after 1868 and party organization gradually superseded patronage with the increase in the electorate. Catherine Gladstone was indifferent to the social obligations of her husband's position and impatient of the etiquette of Society. Dull parties bored her, and she preferred to entertain personal friends rather than political supporters. Since Gladstone alienated party members by a similar social carelessness, it was left to their daughter, Mary, to try to

compensate for her parents' deficiencies.[27] Lady Salisbury and
Lady Campbell-Bannerman shared Catherine Gladstone's dislike
of indiscriminate entertaining for political profit, but they made
rather more effort to discharge their obligations. Lady Salisbury
kept in touch with the wives of her husband's colleagues through
parties in their London house, and gave more intimate house
parties at Hatfield for closer colleagues.[28] Lady Campbell-
Bannerman was handicapped by shyness and poor health, yet she
played the required social role in the last two decades of
the nineteenth century, giving several large dinner parties each
month during the Season.[29] Margot Asquith was the exception
among prime ministers' wives in the late Victorian and Edwardian
period, delighting in throwing brilliant dinner parties for famous
politicians. John Redmond may not have been the only politician
who 'particularly avoided the social functions which were conducted with such energy and ability by Mrs Asquith'. Elizabeth
Haldane commented that Asquith's marriage transformed 'the
social side of the party, for Mrs Asquith became a leading force in
its running'. It became less middle-class and nonconformist, and
began 'to mix with all sorts of people, welcomed so long as they
were interesting to talk to'.[30]

The advantages of being a good hostess were also evident for
wives of ministers and backbenchers with aspirations to office. Sir
Charles Dilke's first wife, Katherine, gave dinner parties for about
ten people once or twice a week while Parliament was sitting.[31]
Lady Harcourt was 'card writing for dinners all day and half the
night' in February 1883 on behalf of her husband, the Home
Secretary; she took it in her stride when he 'suddenly added 200
people to my House of Commons list'.[32] Lucy Masterman also
fulfilled her hostess role with pleasure, particularly as she enjoyed
the intellectual discussion and political debate which her social
skills facilitated. She explained the unusual failure of one
particular small dinner party: 'Bonar Law is a non-conductor, and
Simon a silent corner.'[33] A number of political careers were
enhanced, like Herbert Samuel's, because their wives were good
hostesses capable of making interesting conversation and helping
guests to mix easily.[34]

The social success and personal satisfaction of a political wife
obviously depended on her own temperament as well as her
husband's talents and popularity. Kate Courtney was the ideal

political wife who could fulfil her responsibilities with genuine enthusiasm, as her sister recognized in 1883:

Her life is a purely social one and not demanding much self-sacrifice or self-devotion. Her duty and her pleasure are identical. It is her duty to make herself and her home attractive to her husband's fellow politicians— and it has always been the greatest pleasure of her life to be on friendly terms with distinguished men and well-bred women.[35]

But the social life which was sheer enjoyment for Kate Courtney, Lady Palmerston or Margot Asquith could be an emotional strain for a wife with an unsuitable temperament, as George Cave's wife understood:

My husband was known and loved by both parties, and so things were easier for me than most wives of Members of Parliament; but unless you are of a hopeful disposition and have a certain sense of humour, politics might be a deadly thing to cope with, for it can take more out of you than almost anything I know and between whiles things are very dull.[36]

An accomplished political hostess could oil the wheels of her husband's career, as Lady Palmerston did so well. But having a good political hostess for a wife was not a major determinant of political success, though it made progress easier. A talented hostess could rarely push her husband's interests far beyond the bounds of his political capacity. Balfour became Prime Minister without a wife, while Gladstone dominated the Victorian era despite his wife's limitations as a hostess.

CONFIDANTES AND THEIR INFLUENCE

Though most women in this study were denied a formal education, many were widely read, articulate, and knowledgeable about politics. Lady Frances Balfour recalled that 'politics absorbed my generation'. The women grew up in a political atmosphere almost as pervasive as the men's; parliamentary leaders were their heroes and they espoused the cause of their family's party.[37] The Lyttelton, Gladstone and Talbot women corresponded intelligently and interminably about Irish Home Rule, the complex relationship between Church and State, and the iniquities of Conservative foreign policy. The women of the House of Cecil were often as formidable as their men in political debate at

Hatfield or Whittingehame. Mrs Caroline Grey's correspondence with her daughters, Lady Minto and Lady Antrim, contained summaries of political speeches and thoughtful analyses of foreign and defence policies.[38]

Political wives had more opportunity for political influence in the mid-Victorian period when party lines were fluid, but even then there were limits. Lady Cowper was not unusual among political wives in being 'a woman of immense activity of mind, varied interests and strong opinions'. But even she disliked interfering women who tried to influence politicians indiscreetly, as she revealed in a letter to her mother in 1842:

the less a woman has to do with eager, ardent, virulent politics, the better. She cannot help taking her husband's side, particularly if he holds high office; but I am sure neither party like political women, and Ladies Salisbury, Jersey, Palmerston and Co. have never been thought the better of for the line they took.[39]

Lady Cowper was correct when she noted that political wives could not avoid being partisan—by inclination, conditioning and discretion. The devotion of the Cecil women to Lord Salisbury matched that of the Gladstone women to the Grand Old Man. The views on political issues advanced by these women almost invariably echoed those of the statesmen who towered over their families; and where they did not, discretion prevailed. The women were unlikely to be critical, especially as they lacked the detailed inside information only available in Parliament or Cabinet.

Political wives usually attempted to influence their husbands in two areas only. Occasionally they tried to impose their own views about personalities. More frequently they sought to influence their husbands over particular posts or tenure of office. For example, before she became the second Lady Dilke in 1885, Emilia Pattison corresponded for many years with Dilke on political matters. In 1880 she warned him: 'Don't trust Harcourt, he would play you false tomorrow if he had anything to gain by it.' She also advised him to remain in the Liberal government, rather than lead a radical secession: 'Every day that you and Chamberlain manage to stay on with the present government you are reconciling people whom it is important to reconcile.'[40] Some wives, like Mrs Gladstone, persuaded their husbands to remain in office longer than was wise. Mrs Henry Fowler, conversely, recognized in 1905 that her husband needed rest after years of hard labour. After prolonged discusson they both agreed that he should refuse a senior position in favour of 'a much lighter though less important post'.[41]

Most political wives did not aspire to be more than the trusted confidantes of their husbands. Some, like Lady Harcourt, deliberately understated their influence. She told Sir William in 1903: 'I only report what I hear and do not express opinions'; yet she proceeded to write a perceptive analysis of Chamberlain as a formidable antagonist.[42] Kate Courtney was equally diplomatic in 1891: 'Mr Chamberlain asked me after dinner if I had "any influence over Courtney". I said "not much"—no-one has.'[43]

Lady Carrington was probably fairly typical of many upper-class wives of politicians in the House of Lords. Her interest in politics was focused on the areas of her husband's immediate involvement. In the first few years of marriage she tried to read parliamentary debates for an hour each day, and occasionally sat through 'dull' debates enlivened only by the fun of 'seeing Tannums [Carrington] sitting in his place'. In later years she rarely went to hear Carrington speak; more often she 'heard him say his speech' at home beforehand, then waited nervously to hear that he had acquitted himself well.[44] Her diary and correspondence indicate that Carrington was satisfied with devoted reassurance. On a rare occasion when he sought her advice over a difficult decision as Governor of New South Wales, she told him: 'put yourself into God's hands, as it were, and if you feel moved by a strong impulse one way or the other, act accordingly and do not fear any evil results'. Since everybody knew he was 'the dearest and kindest of men' he would always decide for the best.[45]

Wives who were not brought up in political families were often the most uncritical because they were so aware of their ignorance, but some were keen to learn. Edith Lyttelton, for example, the daughter of a businessman, resolved to abandon literary works for political texts after Alfred entered parliament. In 1895 she was 'reading up things generally on the Voluntary School Question— this in order to keep abreast of Alfred'.[46] The extent to which such a wife pursued a political education depended considerably on her husband's encouragement. Some husbands may well have chosen wives from outside political families partly because they preferred them to be ignorant. American wives were a special case because they usually brought wealth as well as ignorance of the British political scene. Mary Leiter was quickly forced to recognize her role after she married George Curzon. She told her father: 'George will do with his career what he chooses, and *nothing on earth* can alter his iron will. I have long since realized George's iron will, and never crossed it.' Margot Asquith criticized both Curzon's wives as passive accomplices 'who sustained him by their love but did little for him by their advice'.[47]

Prime ministers' wives obviously had the most opportunity to exercise political influence, but their comments were usually restricted to personalities and tenure of office, as with politicians' wives in general. Most prime ministers' wives enjoyed their husbands' total confidence. W. E. Gladstone gave Catherine 'the choice between knowing none of his political secrets and knowing them all but preserving absolute secrecy'. She chose political knowledge and was most discreet.[48] Other prime ministers do not seem to have posed the question in these stark terms, but they all reached the same conclusion, and all but one of the wives— Margot Asquith—preserved secrecy. Prime ministers needed a trusted confidante more than most politicians, and this was often their wives' most vital role.

Lady Palmerston had immense social influence which reinforced her husband's political position as prime minister. She acted as his trusted confidante and private secretary, willing to conciliate his colleagues and justify his actions when necessary. Since she believed his political views were always right and that the country needed him, she persuaded him to retain office on several occasions and to return after resignation, as in 1853.[49] Lady John Russell was Lady Palmerston's opposite in temperament, sociability and physical stamina, but their essential political roles were much alike. Lady Fanny Russell generally sympathized with her husband's views and enjoyed his full confidence. She had little time for 'the regular hardened lady politicians' who talked obsessively about political personalities and events. She preferred 'politics at a distance' and protected their private life at Pembroke Lodge in Richmond Park.[50] Lady Fanny has been blamed for her husband's 'infirmity of purpose' and continual threats of resignation. But his deficiencies of character originated years before their marriage, although she seems to have encouraged the vacillations over office which weakened the Aberdeen coalition and the Palmerston ministry which followed.[51]

Mrs Disraeli, Lady Campbell-Bannerman and Lady Salisbury all stayed out of public life but provided essential emotional support for their husbands. Mary Anne Disraeli was devoted to her husband and his career, though little interested in politics otherwise. He consulted her on most matters, appreciating her shrewd judgement and loving sympathy: 'She believed in me when men despised me.'[52] Lady Campbell-Bannerman was seriously ill for the last twenty years of her life, but her husband was very dependent on her support. She was the shrewder judge of character and her ambition for his career exceeded his own. The chief examples of her influence relate to his tenure of office. When the leadership question was in doubt in 1898, Lady Campbell-Bannerman pressed her husband to adopt a more aggressive stance in order to become Liberal leader. In December 1905 she urged him to stand firm against colleagues who sought to push him into the House of Lords, when it was crucial that the Prime Minister should lead from the Commons.[53] Lady Salisbury was a formidable woman of decided opinions, deep religious convictions and philosophical interests, all of which she shared with her husband. But her active involvement as a political wife was restricted to the role of political hostess for her husband's colleagues. She never made a public speech and disapproved of the new women's political associations.[54] She was a dedicated political wife who cared for her husband's physical and emotional needs, for the nation's benefit as well as her own. Her daughter-in-law, Lady Alice Cecil, paid tribute to Lady Salisbury's vital role in her husband's long career 'by her unhesitating acceptance of all responsibilities and putting the importance of his work before everything'.[55]

Catherine Gladstone was a mixed blessing as a party leader's wife, but an invaluable personal companion for her husband. Gladstone's marriage with Catherine Glynne relaxed and mellowed him. Her beauty, warmth, generosity and charm humanized her repressed and earnest husband. Catherine gave him uncritical devotion and became his totally trusted confidante. She delighted in the political limelight at 10 Downing Street. Her daughter, Mary, commented that she 'loves being inside the mainspring of history, and all the stir and stress and throb of the machine is life and breath to her'.[56] Catherine quickly became bored away from Downing Street: 'She is curiously dependent on excitement, it acts just like a tonic on her—when she is without it, she rather slips down the hill.'[57] Catherine enjoyed sharing Gladstone's electoral triumphs, driving along and waving to the crowds, with no inclination to take a more active role in campaigns. Only as a very old lady was she reluctantly persuaded to become president of the newly formed Women's Liberal Federation, but she avoided public speaking as far as possible.

Mrs Gladstone supported her extraordinary husband with a blind devotion, and hated being separated from him. The rest of the family was sometimes neglected because of her anxiety to protect his health and spirits. When her beloved William was exhausted she knew she must 'ask him next to nothing and pour oil'.[58] Family matters and minor problems were sometimes concealed from him to save additional worry: 'I think it is wisest not to puzzle Papa with every passing wind and pigman.'[59] She watched carefully over his health, stressing any medical warnings, as in 1881: 'Dr Clark entreats that after this great unusual strain you should rest without loss of time if it be only for a few days.'[60] She was even more protective of her husband in his extreme old age, as when he made a speech at Guildford in 1892: 'It is capital the public have not taken in the little derangement which brought *nausea*—and even thought Father was looking better!'[61]

Catherine Gladstone was fully satisfied by her role of confidante to the Prime Minister. She did not mind that Gladstone confided in her but rarely consulted her, particularly as she was basically uninterested in politics. She wrote to him on one occasion in 1884: 'So good of you to keep me well informed. It makes one quite understand matters.'[62] Catherine only ever entrusted these confidences to her daughter, Mary, or her beloved niece, Lady Frederick Cavendish, who were most discreet. She revered her husband's judgement too highly to disagree with any of his opinions on politics, or even to offer advice. On the very rare occasions when she did intervene, her intention was to reinforce her husband's views and strengthen his hand. In 1883, for example, she suggested that Lucy Cavendish might use gentle persuasion to bring her brother-in-law, Lord Hartington, into line over the parliamentary Reform Bill. But Lucy responded that 'it is *quite* impossible without being indiscreet'.[63] Catherine also intervened on rare occasions to conciliate a colleague alienated by her husband. In 1882 she wrote to Lord Rosebery 'unknown to my husband': 'Have you not surely taken in his affection and deep interest—Why do you not trust him?'[64] But she had no more success in persuading Rosebery to enter her husband's Cabinet than in cajoling Lucy Cavendish to influence Hartington.

Mrs Gladstone's influence was usually limited to attempts to keep her husband in power for as long as possible. Their only major disagreement in thirty-five years of marriage up to 1874 concerned his retirement from the party leadership. She believed his action was quite wrong, but at the same time felt most distressed at having to argue against him. It was 'a kind of agony' to be obliged to act otherwise than as 'a pillar to uphold and guide', but her remonstrances were useless against his determination. Six years later Catherine and Mary both wrote secretly to Lucy Cavendish, hoping that she might influence Hartington to step down as leader in Gladstone's favour.[65] But after Gladstone's triumphant election campaign, Hartington acquiesced in the inevitable return to power of 'the people's William', needing no feminine intrigues to guide him. Only in his extreme old age did Catherine's influence persuade Gladstone to remain in office against his personal judgement and inclination. A sympathetic observer, Kate Courtney, noted in her diary in 1892:

It is not very easy steering for the poor old man. And he is old—most evidently unfit for his difficult task which may finish him up any day. It is rather pathetic and almost repulsive that he should not be able to end his life out of this turmoil, but I suppose he would hardly wish it otherwise and they say Mrs Gladstone still less would.[66]

Catherine believed the country still needed her prophet, and preferred him to die in harness. Even when he 'set his heart' upon resignation she reminded him that there was still 'much to be done in Ireland' and pleaded with him 'to *wait* and *watch*' for some time longer.[67] Eventually, in February 1894, she could postpone the inevitable no longer: 'It is of no use saying that one's heart does not bleed'. She was moved to learn that ministers '*broke down in tears*' at Gladstone's final Cabinet, while he retained his dignity.[68]

Margot Asquith was the only prime minister's wife in this period who was indiscreet and gloried in tactlessness. Margot was a mass of contradictions. Vivacious, strong-willed, eccentric and opinionated, her loyalty could become stifling and her exuberance exhausting. Her contemporaries believed her remarkable insight into character was marred by her 'astonishing egotism' and her mistake of judging others by herself.[69] Margot's apparent independence of mind declined as Asquith's career advanced and her blind devotion eventually equalled that of Catherine Gladstone. She beçame intensely ambitious for Asquith, telling Balfour in 1900: 'he shan't wait on dummies like Campbell-Bannerman or apparitions like Rosebery for ever—I won't let him.'[70] In the early years of their marriage gossips claimed that Margot 'hurt Asquith's career by making him so lax in attending the House', and that she hunted too much instead of 'entertaining his party'.[71] Later she was held responsible for encouraging Asquith's enjoyment of high society and distracting him from official duties. None of these charges need be taken too seriously. Asquith would not have married Margot if he was not already fascinated by her brilliant social world, and Margot's personality was obvious from the start.

Her lack of discretion concerns the historian rather more, particularly as her husband was Liberal Prime Minister from 1908 to 1916. Unlike most prime ministers' wives she confided freely in other politicians, especially A. J. Balfour, prominent Conservative statesman and Prime Minister from 1902 to 1905. Margot even presumed to advise Balfour, as in 1897: 'I hope you will send Alfred Milner to S. Africa. I am sure the future out there will be most difficult and important and Milner would be of all men the most satisfactory to you'.[72] Just before the 1900 general election she confided in Balfour: 'I should think in our camp it will be a *humiliation!*' Some months later she told Balfour about a twelve-page letter from Milner concerning the Boer War: 'most private—which I would give anything to show you—his criticisms of the Generals and Army Medical Staff are most severe . . . it interests me always to tell you everything'.[73]

Asquith's colleagues were frequently burdened by the unsolicited advice of their leader's wife. Ministers occasionally received notes or postcards with scrawled pencil instructions from Margot concerning their statements or behaviour in Cabinet—with the additional instruction 'please burn'. Nor was Margot averse to working through ministers' wives. She sent Mrs Walter Runciman a highly confidential letter from the King's Secretary to Asquith, indicating hostile royal views on the women's suffrage question:

'I think neither you nor your husband should press any opinion just now on women's votes. It is not because I am strongly opposed to women having votes that I write this but because I would not like your husband to prejudice his position in the King's eyes.' Mrs Runciman was told not to mention this advice 'to a soul', including Asquith, and to return the letter.[74] Margot was an ingenuous intriguer and her intentions were transparent, since the Runcimans were sympathetic to female suffrage. When John Burns, a former trade union leader, entered the Cabinet in 1906, Margot told him to set an example of moderation to the new working-class members to reduce their distressing 'brag and bounce': 'violence and all round abuse is *such* a mistake . . . in this hour of victory let us be wise and self-controlled'.[75] Loulou Harcourt received similar unsolicited advice in 1910: 'I am *so* keen you should not be personal in your speeches. I did not like what you said of Arthur Balfour and payment of members . . . You have just got into a new office, and our party thanks to Winston and Lloyd George are *painfully* associated with personalities.'[76]

Margot Asquith's indiscretions were probably not dangerous, but this was no credit to Margot. She was fortunate in her friends, like Balfour, who made allowances and did not exploit her crass remarks and ill-timed confidences.They also disregarded many of her comments, as one of Asquith's biographers noted:

On people, her judgements were most often acute; on events they were almost invariably faulty. Those closest to her, including her husband, knew when to pay her heed and when to discount her categoric pronouncements. Those who knew her less well were alternately fascinated and appalled by her indiscretions.[77]

Moreover, Margot almost inevitably paid the price of her behaviour; politicians not only ignored her advice, but also became more cautious in their comments to her. Her husband almost certainly confided less in her after he became Prime Minister in 1908, though he was notoriously indiscreet in his later correspondence with one or two other women. Margot's fierce loyalty to Asquith seemed to increase after 1911 while his obsession with Venetia Stanley left her feeling lonely and excluded from political secrets. This explains her requests to ministers like Harcourt and Burns to provide her with detailed daily accounts 'of your frank and individual impression of your colleagues' at Cabinet meetings: 'I shall repeat *nothing*.'[78]

Margot Asquith was also untypical of political wives of the Edwardian period in her passionate opposition to the suffragist movement and her distaste for women's political associations. She adopted the role of devoted consort but broke the conventions so carefully observed by previous prime ministers' wives. She would have seemed more in character had she taken a leading part in the suffragist movement or the Women's Liberal Federation, like Frances Balfour or Maud Selborne. Margot's attempts to influence political affairs were usually ineffective and rather pathetic in a period when other strong-minded women were demanding more direct means of power. She too sought power, but her very perversity condemned her to an unsatisfying meddlesomeness.

Political wives automatically had more inside knowledge of high politics than the majority of women because of their social and marital position. Many were privy to political secrets in their role as confidantes, but there were clear limits to their influence. They could make politicians' lives more comfortable, could occasionally persuade them to stay in office longer, and could sometimes alter their opinions about individual personalities. But they had no role in political decision-making, even indirectly, and their influence on political issues was negligible. They were usually listeners rather than advisers; they acted as a safe sounding-board when colleagues could not be absolutely trusted. Only Margot Asquith attempted to push this role beyond its acceptable limits and thereby demonstrated its restrictions. Those women who sought more power in real terms turned first to the women's political associations and ultimately sought to give women the vote to gain a place in Parliament.

ELECTION CAMPAIGN WORKERS

The role of candidates' wives in election campaigns changed in nature and extent between 1870 and 1914. This was partly due to the general influence of the women's movement which altered conventional ideas about the realms of proper activity for women. It was also affected by the growth in the male franchise, the development of party organization and the end of 'old corruption' at elections. In particular, the 1883 Corrupt and Illegal Practices

Act transformed the nature of British elections by imposing and enforcing far more severe penalties for bribery, corruption and excessive expenditure. Women were suddenly welcomed as unpaid party workers since payments to election canvassers were forbidden. This stimulated the creation of women's auxiliary organizations in the 1880s, thus providing a legitimate supporting role for women in politics. The Women's Council of the Primrose League was founded in 1885, the Women's Liberal Federation in 1886, and the Women's Liberal Unionist Association in 1888.

Before 1883 the only electoral work in which women participated was canvassing, which was more important than platform speeches before the 1867 Reform Act. But Mary Anne Disraeli seems to have been unusual in her enthusiastic canvassing at Shrewsbury in 1841.[79] The role of Selina Mary Causton, later Lady Southwark, at the Colchester campaign in 1874 was probably more typical. She spent the time driving around in an open carriage with white horses: 'We called only upon the wives of our leading supporters, and bowed right and left as we passed backwards and forwards through the town.' She later claimed that it had been unusual for ladies to participate in canvassing even in 1874.[80] Constance Flower, later Lady Battersea, stayed in the local hotel watching the polling at Brecon for her husband, Cyril, in 1880. Her only contribution to the campaign was one sentence of thanks during the victory speeches.[81]

The role of candidates' wives and women supporters changed very slowly in the two decades after the 1883 Illegal Practices Act. Lady Frances Balfour was a formidable woman who subsequently became a force in the female suffragist campaign, but in 1885 even she had a limited view of the woman's role in election campaigns. She later recalled the Leeds campaign of her brother-in-law, Gerald Balfour:

It would never have occurred to him at that time that any woman could be of use in an election fight . . . one of Gerald's warm supporters was an Irishman and he asked Gerald if there was no female he could summon to his aid to be an 'ornament'. What other service in 1885 could a woman render? Gerald wrote to me, asking if I could come to Leeds and be with him till the end. I was more than willing, though my experience of election fighting was nil.[82]

Lady Frances Balfour was willing to be an 'ornament' in 1885 and other capable women were equally defensive about their electoral role. Elizabeth Harcourt apologized to Lord Rosebery in 1888: 'If you hear that I am doing *dreadful things* in the way of canvassing you will know that it is really because I want to sympathise with my boy in his work and *not* because I am a strong-minded woman!'[83] The Gladstone women did their share of canvassing, but otherwise their contribution consisted of 'driving endless miles, he [Gladstone] making speeches, all of us grinning and waving and nodding'.[84] Edith Lyttelton's contribution to the 1895 campaign was to go canvassing one day with Alfred, 'swelling with pride of him as he won all hearts'.[85] Kate Courtney was strongly committed to her husband's political career and became a leader of the Women's Liberal Unionist Association in the 1890s. Yet her involvement in Leonard's 1885 campaign in Bodmin was limited: 'I stand about all day with intervals of lunch and tea and sitting chatting with other ladies.'[86] The criticisms of the *Yorkshire Herald* in 1892 obliged Helen Pease to defend herself: 'It is not true that I talked politics to the York women—I know scarcely anything about politics.'[87]

Before 1900 only a few exceptional women took a more prominent and active role in elections. Sir Charles Dilke's first wife Katherine worked 'day and night' in 1874 to increase his majority by winning the support of influential canvassers. She wrote to one potential supporter:

Do you feel inclined to help me? . . . I am now thoroughly up in all the small details and I should like you to go to a few 'incurables' if you will . . . You know heaps of Lords! Can't you get one to canvass for us? It would be most impressive! . . . I think when it is over I shall be ashamed of my own 'cheek' but I find it answers.[88]

In 1885 Lady Randolph Churchill supervised her husband's campaign for Woodstock because he apparently lacked the time and energy to do so: 'Revelling in the hustle and bustle of the committee-rooms, marshalling our forces, and hearing the hourly reports of how the campaign was progressing, I felt like a general holding a council-of-war with his staff in the heat of a battle.' For two weeks she held daily conferences with their supporters at the Bear Hotel in Woodstock and visited doubtful voters with 'an arsenal of arguments'. Sir Henry James congratulated her on a victory which 'proceeded so very much from your personal exertions'.[89] But these were highly unusual wives in the Victorian period.

The major turning point for women in election campaigns was around the turn of the century. After 1900 women played a far more prominent role in helping to organize campaigns and took over a substantial share of the public speaking. Women needed a decade or so after 1883 to gain confidence and experience through their work in the women's auxiliary political organizations. Moreover their increasingly active role in election campaigns paralleled the gathering force of the women's suffrage movement; the one almost certainly reinforced the other. Lady Tullibardine, for instance, spoke as often as her husband, John, in the December 1910 campaign: 'we started at different ends of the constituency, and only took part in one joint meeting.'[90] Occasionally wives, sisters and daughters were obliged to substitute for incapacitated candidates, as was Lady Randolph Churchill, and found they could do an excellent job on their own account. Henry Fowler seemed on the verge of collapse at the start of the 1905/6 campaign and his two daughters intervened to ensure his safe return for Wolverhampton. They 'swallowed a mixed potion of prejudice and inclination, and dashed round the constituency, making speeches, and delivering his messages'.[91] Up to 1906 Elizabeth Haldane had been no more than a conscientious canvasser for her brother, Richard. But in January 1910 she was responsible for organizing his campaign at Haddington because of his illness. She planned the meetings, supervised the canvassing and spoke at a series of political rallies.[92]

Several political wives played a background role in their husbands' early campaigns but became valuable partners once they gained experience. Beatrice Samuel was unable to participate in the 1900 campaign because she was pregnant, but she compensated for that in the tough by-election in the Cleveland division of Yorkshire in 1902. Herbert Samuel wrote to his mother: 'No Member's wife could be a greater help to her husband than Beatrice is to me. She attended almost all my meetings and spoke at nearly all, and had half-a-dozen of her own as well.' Beatrice was a forceful public speaker who enjoyed participating at 'nine meetings in three nights', especially when 'Herbert says it helps him so much for me to be with him'.[93] Beatrice gained experience through her work on the executive of the Women's

Liberal Federation, as well as the Women's Industrial Council, with full support from her husband. He praised her achievement as a public speaker, assuring her that the more practice she gained, 'the more likely you are to become a useful member of your family'.[94]

During the early years of her marriage to Lewis (Loulou) Harcourt, May had little interest in politics and concentrated on raising her family. She enjoyed the social status of being a prominent politician's wife, but was terrified of having to take any active part herself. In 1904, for example, May merely had to support the vote of thanks at a woman's meeting in Bacup: 'it was *quite* awful but thank goodness I got through without an absolute breakdown'. Yet she was quite happy to accompany Loulou to nurse his Rossendale constituency in a decorative and supportive capacity at functions which were largely 'social affairs'.[95] She considered electioneering '*hateful work*' in January 1905: 'it is only a stern sense of duty which is dragging me to the Constituency as it is a case of "now or never" for me.' Having taken the plunge she gradually learned to swim, and grew into the job as more demands were made of her. May became accustomed to taking the chair at women's meetings in the constituency, though she still 'loath[ed] the role of a Public Woman standing on Platforms "saying a few words"'.[96] By the 1910 elections, she was quite capable and confident. Loulou was close to a nervous breakdown from overwork by December, so she went up to the constituency to campaign without him. May recounted a very busy week in the constituency 'making arrangements, seeing people, writing, visiting'. She spoke at two workers' meetings each evening, as well as several public meetings: 'It was simply awful but there is nothing for it but just to set one's teeth and go through with it.' She took over all the arrangements for the speakers from the agent, including correspondence, carriage arrangements and hospitality.[97] This was a considerable achievement for a wife who disliked the public role and fulfilled it only out of a strict sense of duty to her husband and his career. It illustrates how far such active participation had become a normal expectation of political wives by 1910, even when they disliked the work. Beatrice Chamberlain also became actively involved for the first time on Austen's behalf during the 1906 election: 'it was all very well for the women of the family to hold entirely aloof, but now that so

much good work is being done by women more or less behind the
scenes where it is very useful, it is rather mean to stand aside and
take no part'.[98]

Mrs Marjory Pease, wife of the progressive Liberal, Edward
Pease, was most unusual in expressing open resentment at the
restrictions of her electoral role. During the two 1910 campaigns
she played an important part in encouraging women workers and
speaking to women's meetings. She also stood in for the candidate
when he was delayed, speaking to the audience until he arrived,
before rushing off to perform the same function at the next
meeting, several miles away.[99] Evidently, Mrs Pease was a popular
speaker, but she became disillusioned during the second 1910
election, especially when the local committee ignored her ideas for
a stimulating campaign: 'I am *not* going to wear myself out doing
the work of an office boy!' She complained particularly about the
chauvinism of the local male Liberals who even opposed her
taking the chair at meetings:

It really was most shocking bad taste—none of the women stuck up for
me, though afterwards Mrs Hankey said how splendidly I went for the
men . . . The Liberals here are quite hopeless and I really am seriously
thinking of 'chucking' them . . . It is useless wasting time and energy here
when I can put work into other places where it is appreciated.[100]

In 1911 Mrs Pease was elected representative for her local
rural district council, where presumably her efforts were better
appreciated.

Other exceptional women who experienced Mrs Pease's frustration at their subordinate role in election campaigns may
well have redirected their energies into the female suffragist
movement. Election campaigns inevitably provided a training
ground for 'strong-minded' women like Frances and Betty Balfour
who became leaders in the suffragist movement. Political wives
became accustomed to playing a political role in their own right in
campaigning for male votes. It was scarcely surprising that in the
process some of them became convinced that they deserved a vote
themselves. As Kate Courtney argued in 1913:

From the day when politicians encouraged women to form political
associations to influence electors, they gave up the point that politics are
not our job. It is amazing to me that any man who does not believe in the
political freedom of women should ask them to help get him into

Parliament . . . I cannot understand the state of mind of a man who
encourages women to canvass electors (a doubtfully modest work),
organize meetings, speak at them, and even coax and bother electors to go
to the poll by every art they possess, but draws the line at the simple act of
voting themselves. It is nothing but stupendous egotism.[101]

VOTES FOR WOMEN

(i) Indifference and opposition

The majority of wives in political families did not become
passionately involved in the campaigns for or against votes for
women; on the whole they were less heated on this question than
their husbands. Many assumed that they already possessed more
important indirect political influence than the vote could give
them. They enjoyed the protection of class, wealth and privilege,
which could be more powerful than consciousness of gender.
Eleanor Cecil was pessimistic in 1910 about the prospects of
winning over society women and peeresses for the suffrage cause:
'The truth is they have so much power and influence already—or
think they have—and their instincts of self-preservation make
them as Anti [Suffrage] as the men.'[102] This was an overstatement,
because many upper-class women were indifferent rather than
actively hostile to the suffrage cause.

Even the minority of political wives who held strong views for
or against women's suffrage usually refrained from active involvement. The wives of Lewis Harcourt and James Bryce shared their
husbands' hostility to votes for women, but preferred to remain
silent. In 1906 Mrs Frederick Harrison asked Marion Bryce to take
a more prominent part in the anti-suffrage campaign by writing a
pamphlet. Mrs Bryce responded that 'as the wife of a member of
the Government it is not advisable for me to go into print but I will
help [her] with what advice I can'.[103] When Lord Curzon invited
May Harcourt to join the committee of the Anti-Suffrage League
in 1910, she discussed it 'most carefully' with her husband and the
Prime Minister, Asquith, who shared their views. Their decision
was that 'it is best for me not to join as it might tend to force the
wives of some of their colleagues into active operations in the
other camp'.[104]

At a more fundamental level many political wives in the 1880s
and 1890s still viewed the female suffrage campaign as con-

troversial and not yet respectable. They feared that involvement with it would prejudice their endeavours on behalf of women in other fields. Even as late as 1910, Adeline Duchess of Bedford reluctantly declined Lord Curzon's suggestion that she should sign a public appeal for the Anti-Suffrage League: 'I have kept apart from public movements because I am under the impression that such slight influence as I am able to exercise on questions that affect women in general might be weakened or impaired were I to take part in matters of controversy.'[105] Mary Bryce was most indignant in 1892 when leading suffragists accused those who were not involved of 'want of interest and sympathy in women's questions . . . most of us are far more interested in what concerns women, whether educationally or otherwise.'[106]

Many political wives devoted considerable time and energy to the more socially acceptable branches of the women's movement, and to the improvement of conditions for poor working-class women. The campaign for secondary and higher education for women spanned the political parties and attracted women of varied persuasions on the suffrage question—such as Lucy Cavendish, Helen Gladstone, Mary Bryce, Elizabeth Haldane and Eleanor Sidgwick. This campaign benefited middle- and upper-class girls, as did their efforts to admit women to professions like law and medicine. But most women in these families were also active in a large number of philanthropic causes in the interests of poor women.[107] As philanthropy became more organized from the 1880s, these women became more involved in the work of the Charity Organization Society and the University Settlement Movement. Most of all they were active in the women's political associations, which channelled their philanthropic efforts to the needs of poor working-class women.

Even radical and socialist wives were likely to give votes for women a second priority. Emilia Lady Dilke and Margaret MacDonald both believed women should vote, but felt that social and economic improvement for the mass of working-class women was more fundamental. Sir Charles Dilke's second wife, Emilia, became a leader of the Women's Protective and Provident League, created in 1874 to protect the industrial interests of working-class women. Her work at the Trades Union Congress helped to expose the exploitation of female labour.[108] Margaret MacDonald worked with the Charity Organization Society as a

girl, before she became a socialist and married Ramsay Mac-
Donald. In 1897 she joined the executive of the National Union of
Women Workers, which represented a broad spectrum of political
opinion, including Eleanor Sidgwick, Lucy Cavendish, Lavinia
Talbot, Mrs Fawcett, Mrs Arthur Lyttelton and Beatrice Webb.
Margaret MacDonald also joined the executive of the Women's
Industrial Council, where she examined the conditions of female
sweated labour and produced a series of detailed reports on
women's working conditions. Her correspondence reveals almost
nothing about her views on women's suffrage. Evidently she
shared her husband's belief that women deserved the vote because
of their unique role in the family, but socialist women should aim
first to improve the material conditions of their less privileged
sisters.[109]

The anti-suffrage movement was predominantly male. None of the
wives in this study took a leading part, despite the prominent
role of husbands such as Joseph and Austen Chamberlain, Sir
William and Lewis Harcourt, W. E. Gladstone, James Bryce and
H. H. Asquith. The women in their families had little to say on
female suffrage—indeed May Harcourt ignored it entirely in her
correspondence. Joseph Chamberlain told Beatrice Potter in 1884
that he refused to allow any discussion on the subject in his
house.[110] His veto was so effective that the Chamberlain women
usually avoided the issue in correspondence, except for occasional
echoes of the master's voice. His daughter, Beatrice, served on the
executive committee of the Anti-Suffrage League. When she
failed to complete the 1911 census forms correctly, she remarked:
'Oh dear! I don't want a vote.'[111] Austen Chamberlain's wife, Ivy,
attended a local mother's meeting in 1909 to persuade them to sign
an anti-suffrage declaration, having already enlisted her servants
for the cause.[112] Isolated remarks revealed the preference of some
political wives, such as Mildred Buxton, who 'very much liked Mrs
[Humphry] Ward and her anti-suffrage views'.[113] The attitudes of
other wives can be inferred from their comments on the female
role. Evelyn Stanhope, for example, read Mrs Fawcett's novel,
Janet Doncaster, in 1875, with considerable disapproval: 'the
heroine is meant for a model of the strong-minded female type . . .
Heaven forbid such a type of my sex should ever become
common!'[114]

A few political wives, such as Marion Bryce and Margot Asquith, were more outspoken against female suffrage, though usually in private. Gertrude Lady Acland was one of the few to take a more active role, but she was notably ineffective as president of the Devon branch of the Anti-Suffrage League. She confessed her failure to rouse the ladies of Devon to her cause: 'even the ladies who gave me their names have given no active support', and none of them felt equal to replacing her.[115] It was hard to stimulate the enthusiasm of women for a cause which extolled the inferiority of their own sex; they might passively acquiesce, but rarely acclaim. Given the nature of the anti-suffrage case, it was to be expected that many female supporters would be self-effacing wives. As Harrison noted, 'the woman Anti-[suffragist] preferred to act on her beliefs by shunning the limelight'.[116] It is impossible to know how many political wives who appeared indifferent to the whole suffrage debate may have been antis who quietly appreciated the privileges and prestige they enjoyed without the vote.

Brian Harrison has argued that 'No general charge of misogyny can possibly be sustained against most anti-suffrage leaders, for theirs is a story of much-loved and influential mothers . . . and adored wives.' Bryce is included in the former category, and Joseph and Austen Chamberlain, Curzon, Gladstone, Asquith and Bryce in the latter.[117] This conclusion is supported by my own study. Certainly the Antis included authoritarian husbands whose wives were loved but subordinate. George Curzon's affection for his wife increased with time, yet she was entirely excluded from his political concerns, except perhaps in India. Beatrice Potter was justified in her fear that Joseph Chamberlain would exercise domestic despotism. On the other hand the majority of pro-suffrage politicians took an equally conventional view of their wives' roles. Charles Trevelyan favoured votes for women but preferred to exclude his wife from his political concerns, except at election time. Indeed James Bryce's marriage might have been the perfect shared partnership, despite the powerful anti-suffrage opinions of both husband and wife. It would be difficult to argue that wives of anti-suffrage politicians were any more subservient than wives of pro-suffrage members.[118]

The anti-suffrage arguments have been skilfully examined by Harrison[119] and require only brief comment here. Their central thesis was well illustrated by the popular novelist, Mrs Humphry Ward, in 1909: 'there is in the State a natural "separation of powers" . . . answering to the natural differences between men and women; the life of women finds expression, first of all, in the home, in those ideals of wifehood and motherhood.' Men must rule politics at the centre, while women's influence should be indirect 'in proportion to education and character'. Mary Ward argued that many of the educational and legal grievances of women had been redressed by a Parliament of males, so that female suffrage was not needed to promote women's special interests.[120] Marion Bryce was the only political wife in this study to outline her anti-suffrage arguments at some length, following the same lines as Mrs Ward. The Gladstone and Lyttelton women agonized over women's suffrage in the 1880s, when the topic often dominated family conversation. Gladstone's Lyttelton nieces, Meriel and Lavinia Talbot, and Lucy Cavendish, finally endorsed their uncle's uncompromising position and signed the famous 'appeal against female suffrage' published in the *Nineteenth Century* in 1889.[121] Otherwise there was little discussion of the anti-suffrage case among the women in this study.

Very few anti-suffrage sympathizers before 1914 were self-conscious enough to worry that their arguments might sound complacent, privileged and self-serving. Beatrice Potter sometimes had that rare gift of intelligent self-awareness. In 1889 she analysed the criticisms advanced against her for signing the anti-suffrage appeal. Ben Jones of the Co-operative Movement had argued that 'she is satisfied with her own position, because she is rich and strong: she does not see that other women need the power to help themselves which would be given by the vote.' Beatrice charged herself privately with 'hopeless inconsistency', as a woman 'who is the personification of emancipation' but did not want the vote. By 1926 she could admit publicly that 'at the root of my anti-feminism lay the fact that I had never myself experienced the disabilities assumed to arise from my sex'.[122]

The anti-suffrage women shared the hostility of their suffragist sisters to the militant tactics of the Women's Social and Political Union, led by the Pankhursts. May Harcourt, Katharine Bryce and Lady Stanhope each expressed indignation at the violent activities of 1912, which they deemed 'silly and pointless' and 'too outrageous', and they approved of the severe sentences imposed.[123] Lucy Cavendish felt all women must recognize that the suffragettes were ruining their cause:

... by unsexing themselves—not only by disgusting waverers and turning friends against them, but by enraging the masses of the people in London and doubtless elsewhere. As an Anti-Suffragist I ought to be glad to see the smashers go from bad to worse and pull destruction on their cause. But I am too sick at the sight of the she-hooliganism to feel anything but shame.

Unlike many anti-suffragists Lucy Cavendish was reluctant to exploit the ammunition provided by the militants, preferring that moderate suffragists should make a collective repudiation of 'these hooligan methods'.[124]

(ii) The suffragists and the women's political associations

More political wives in this study were sympathetic to the pro-suffrage cause, but none were extremist and none belonged to Mrs Pankhurst's Women's Social and Political Union. They deplored militancy even more forcefully than the Antis because they believed such tactics damaged their cause. At a speech in Exeter in 1913, Kate Courtney condemned the use of violence: 'In dragging their womanhood through the mire, they had somewhat sullied the dignity of women.'[125]

Many pro-suffrage women started from the same assumptions as the Antis, but reached different conclusions. Mary Gladstone was converted in 1884: 'I am come round to female suffrage.' Whereas belief in 'separate spheres' led her Lyttelton cousins and her father to oppose women's suffrage, she decided that 'the difference in kind is so necessary' that both sexes must be represented.[126] As late as 1913 Margaret Hobhouse was pleased that her four sons were generous enough to support female suffrage: 'Men are stronger, more forcible, more enduring and will always rule . . . In fact the very weakness of women makes it necessary that they should have such protection as a vote would give them.'[127] Some suffragist women were persuaded by the more positive argument expressed by J. S. Mill. The Reform Act of 1884–5 enfranchised rural working-class male householders, yet excluded middle- and upper-class women. At the age of eighty-four, Mary Haldane wrote a letter to *The Times* in 1909 making this point. She had paid rates and taxes throughout thirty years of widowhood, but only her male servants could vote, though they paid no rates and taxes. She protested that she was considered fit to vote in school board and county council elections, yet forbidden to express her views on the laws these bodies administered.[128]

The women's auxiliary political associations created in the 1880s played an important role in politicizing women and served as a training ground in political activities and organization. The original function of the Women's Liberal Federation, the Women's Liberal Unionist Association and the Women's Council of the Primrose League was to organize women as unpaid party workers. It has been argued that these associations diverted the energies of many feminists into subordinate roles in party politics.[129] The evidence from the women in these political families, however, suggests a different interpretation. In the early 1880s it would be difficult to identify many 'feminists' among these political wives and most of them had not even considered the question of votes for women. But in the course of two decades from the 1880s the women's political associations encouraged women to debate the female suffrage question, and suffragists used the associations to educate other women. These auxiliary organizations helped to win for the suffrage cause the sympathy of those women with perhaps the least to gain by the vote but the most to contribute in terms of leadership and influence. By the time the female suffrage issue became a prominent national question in the Edwardian period, the attitudes of many upper-class women had been significantly changed—from indifference to active interest and limited participation.

Female members of politicians' families frequently joined the women's political associations. Suffragist leaders inevitably viewed these organizations as fertile ground for education and recruitment, but the main suffragist target was the huge Women's Liberal Federation. Liberalism and women's suffrage were closely linked and the majority of the Liberal parliamentary back-benchers were sympathetic. In the first ten Commons' divisions on women's suffrage after 1867, Liberals and Radicals contributed about 68 per cent of the total suffragist vote compared with only 30 per cent from the Conservatives.[130] The hard core of the back-bench opposition came from the Conservatives, though some of their most influential leaders—Salisbury, Balfour, Bonar Law and the Cecil brothers—supported women's suffrage. Conversely, the majority of the Liberal rank and file were sympathetic to women's suffrage, while four major Liberal leaders were adamantly opposed—namely Gladstone, Asquith, Rosebery and Sir William Harcourt.

The Women's Liberal Federation (WLF) could not escape the controversial question of women's suffrage, especially with Lady Aberdeen and Lady Carlisle as its formidable advocates. By 1890 the WLF had 133 local organizations and over 43,000 members, and Lady Carlisle was increasing the pressure to make women's suffrage a major plank of its platform.[131] Meanwhile Lady Aberdeen worked hard to enlist and retain the reluctant support of Mr and Mrs Gladstone. Catherine Gladstone was a valuable, if nervous, figurehead as first president of the WLF—her first personal involvement in politics in her own right, at the age of seventy-five. Lady Aberdeen pressed Mr Gladstone to address the 1891 annual meeting 'even though you do not feel able wholly to bless women's political work'. She pointed out that many of their local associations were angry at the lack of parliamentary progress over women's suffrage:

. . . this will be increased, I fear, if you cannot see your way to coming to the meeting on the 27th. And may I remind you that the Federation has up to now, refrained from putting Woman Suffrage [formally] among its objects. I and many others have done and are doing our utmost to prevent its being thus included . . . and *one* reason for our so acting has been the knowledge of your and Mrs Gladstone's feelings on the subject.[132]

Gladstone was induced to speak but was saved at the eleventh hour by an influenza attack. Mrs Gladstone remained as president of the WLF until 1893, in response to Lady Aberdeen's entreaties and her husband's need for the Federation's electoral support. After Gladstone's retirement, his successors, Rosebery and Harcourt, were just as uncompromisingly anti-suffragist, but they lacked wives and daughters who might be converted.

Lady Carlisle threw all her energies into making the WLF 'a power for suffrage', even before she became president in 1893.[133] She placed considerable pressure on moderate political wives within the WLF to make a public commitment for suffrage, as Lady Trevelyan discovered to her alarm in 1891:

. . . when I am *possessed* by a cause, I must back it to the very end . . . I want to urge on you the rightness of your making some public pronouncement in the Gazette or a platform to the effect that our Suffrage resolution seemed to you expedient and right and henceforward that you support that policy i.e. that the Federation should press forward the Suffrage. Please think over this: you are a leader—you cannot keep silence without misleading your followers . . . if such as *you* do not speak, why the clamour and the agitation will be left to the reckless extremists.[134]

By 1893 Lady Carlisle had succeeded. One of the stated aims of the WLF became the promotion of the parliamentary franchise for women on the same terms as men. The issue provoked great controversy and, though it was not made a test of membership, the anti-Suffragists seceded to form the National Liberal Federation. After 1893 the controversy shifted for the next decade to the issue of whether the WLF should help Liberal candidates who were opposed to votes for women. By 1902 they decided that the WLF as a Federation could not formally endorse such candidates, though local associations might do so.[135] Yet in 1905 Molly Trevelyan noted that the annual meeting was again devoted to an emotional debate about support for anti-suffrage candidates.[136] No members of the WLF from 1890 onwards, however moderate and cautious, could fail to appreciate the political significance of the women's suffrage question.

The links between the suffragist cause and the Women's Liberal Unionist Association (WLUA) were equally strong. The formation of the Liberal Unionist parliamentary group in protest at Gladstone's Irish Home Rule policy was followed by the creation of the women's auxiliary association in 1888. The first meeting was held at Kate Courtney's house:

Meanwhile some foolish people got up a scare among the Liberal Unionist men who are so alarmed at some of the women in our rising Association—because they have worked in other causes etc—that when Thursday (the next meeting) comes most of my ladies come to say their husbands won't let them join . . . However, old Lady Stanley comes manfully to the rescue and sweeps all the gossip and fears on one side, offers her house for the meeting and joins the working committee—Miss Fry, Lady Cunliffe, Mrs Fawcett of course are equally steadfast.[137]

The fears of suffragist influence were not unjustified since Mrs Fawcett and Miss Tod were both committed suffragists while Kate Courtney's husband, Leonard, had supported the issue in Parliament in 1884. The committee worked well together, gradually becoming 'fairly businesslike' and slowly creating branches on a national scale.[138]

By 1893 Mrs Fawcett and Miss Tod had drawn Kate Courtney and other WLUA members into the women's suffrage cause. Mrs Fawcett persuaded Kate to join her Women's Suffrage Appeal Committee, with members from all parties, and Kate looked forward to meeting active women from all groups, 'whether Liberal Federation, Extreme Temperance or Primrose League'. After the defeat of Gladstone's third Home Rule bill in 1893, Kate Courtney was concerned about the future role of their association, with no 'sufficient collective creed on other questions'. She did not want it 'to become a mere party organisation to help at elections' and discussed the problem with Lady Frances Balfour, 'one of our leading spirits' and another outspoken suffragist.[139] By 1897 several leading suffragists from the WLUA joined Frances Balfour, Mrs Fawcett and Miss Tod in forming the National Union of Women's Suffrage, which united sixteen suffrage societies in their demand for the vote on the same basis as for men. Kate Courtney subsequently remarked that the big women's political organizations first introduced large numbers of women to political work: 'from the moment that political leaders welcomed their help—stirred them to strenuous work, the exclusive masculine profession of the political world' was threatened.[140]

Wives of politicians had several distinct roles which carried status and responsibility in addition to their 'natural' functions as wives and mothers. Their actual political influence has tended to be exaggerated, though their role as confidantes often contributed substantially to their husbands' peace of mind. The function of reassuring listener changed little with the passage of time, though it varied greatly with different personalities. Otherwise the nature of the roles of political wives altered significantly in the fifty years before 1914. The social functions of political hostess and household manager gradually declined in importance while the political roles assumed greater weight. By 1910 political wives were expected to participate actively in electioneering rather than being passive ornaments, while the women's political associations taught them how to organize and campaign. The women's movement was partly responsible for these changes, since it slowly enlarged women's perceptions of their roles. The women's political associations also helped to educate upper class women about the suffrage question so that many changed from indifference or hostility in the 1880s to a more positive sympathy by 1914. The nature of the lives of political wives varied considerably from family to family, within the framework of these conventional social roles. That range of experience can best be understood through detailed case studies of the lives of individual women.

8

Experiences of Political Wives

IDEALS AND SACRIFICES

IN 1883 the future Beatrice Webb fell in love with a rising politician, but decided that she lacked the qualities of the ideal political wife. Joseph Chamberlain, twice widowed by forty-seven, and leader of the radical wing of the Liberal party, was eager to replace Gladstone as Prime Minister. Beatrice Potter was fully aware that Chamberlain took 'a very conventional view of women' and would soon realize that she was not the woman to 'forward his most ambitious views'.[1] Their few strained meetings ended at a party in January 1884, when the conflict between two highly independent minds was illuminated in an argument over women's status. Chamberlain said that he required 'intelligent sympathy' from women, since 'it pains me to hear any of my views controverted'. Beatrice translated 'sympathy' as 'servility' and feared that marriage to Chamberlain would destroy her intellectual individuality:

I shall be absorbed into the life of a man, whose aims are not my aims; who will refuse me all freedom of thought in my intercourse with him; to whose career I shall have to subordinate all my life, mental and physical . . . The outward circumstances of the life of a politician's wife would be distasteful to me, or rather they would be supremely demoralising . . . Once married I should of course subordinate my views to my husband's . . . He has pointed out to me plainly the hardships in the life of the wife of a man absorbed in public life.[2]

Yet Beatrice was tormented for years by her passion for Chamberlain which 'haunted me day and night'. Her married sisters warned her that such an ill-suited match would be 'a tragedy—a murder of your independent nature'. Kate Courtney saw no room in Chamberlain's nature for deep affection—only 'an intense personal ambition and desire to dominate at whatever cost of other people's rights'.[3] Another sister, Theresa Cripps, warned Beatrice to maintain a strong 'scientific bias' in her judgement of

Chamberlain: 'Mr Joseph is on the look out for a good wife, one who would forward, as you could do, his most ambitious views.'[4] When Chamberlain finally made an excellent marriage in 1888 to an aristocratic American girl, Beatrice bitterly reflected that 'she will see entirely through his eyes' and encourage his transformation from radical to Conservative imperialist. He would become 'a man of society—enjoying wealth, leisure, social position and a charming young wife'.[5] Beatrice Potter later married Sidney Webb and became a famous socialist and social scientist. She was an exceptional woman, while Chamberlain was more ambitious, more authoritarian and more able than most politicians. Even so, her comments reflect certain realities regarding the qualifications of an ambitious politician's wife.

Victorian and Edwardian political biographies seldom mention the wives, except for brief comments on their selfless devotion and loving dedication to their husbands' public duty. The portrait of Mary Anne Disraeli is typical: 'her passion for her husband's welfare marked her as the ideal wife for an overworked politician . . . her great capacity for love comforted him at all times.'[6] Henry Fowler's wife supported him constantly 'with the fuel of her untiring appreciation and approval. His views were hers . . . His ambition for a life of great public service was hers for him'.[7] Hugh Childers's biographer described both his wives as sympathetic, devoted companions and good housekeepers and mothers.[8]

These tributes need to be taken with a few pinches of salt, but evidence from contemporary correspondence and diaries suggests they are surprisingly close to the mark. Most of these political wives seem to have been strongly supportive and protective, their loving care strengthened by their total faith in the value of their husbands' services to the nation. Laura, Lady Selborne informed her son in 1876 that 'no other Cabinet will ever produce any equal to Father for integrity, Christian manliness and ability. He stands alone, as History will tell my Grandchildren.'[9] Kate Courtney illustrates the capacity of these wives to identify themselves entirely with their husbands' careers. She shared Leonard's commitment to unpopular causes and 'felt a strange triumph' when he resigned over Gladstone's parliamentary redistribution bill in 1884: 'I never thought my Husband a bigger man than I did that evening.'[10] Edith Lyttelton was another wife who had unlimited faith in the talents of her husband and played a prominent part in his decision to stand for Parliament in 1894: 'in my heart of hearts I believe if Alfred went into politics, he would have more effect on the House, and on the whole condition of politics than six Arthur Balfours.' She ,admitted that she found it impossible to criticize Alfred's ideas or his judgement: 'I do find it extremely difficult ever to think that he isn't quite blameless.'[11]

Women who aspired to be good political wives often had to make sacrifices, financial as well as personal. Ambitious young politicians with inadequate means needed wives with money. Otherwise both partners faced daunting problems in an expensive career. When Edith Lyttelton encouraged Alfred to stand for Parliament, she was well aware of the financial anxieties this would create. He was the youngest son of a distinguished family of limited means, and had to sacrifice all his earnings as a barrister, estimated at about £2,000 annually. Edith advised a move into a smaller and cheaper house nearer Parliament and promised 'to cultivate economy'.[12] Joseph Chamberlain's career also illustrates the high cost of politics. He would probably have become a millionaire had he continued as an industrialist, but he died comparatively poor because politics severely limited the time available for business. While still in office he contemplated giving up politics in order to retrieve his business losses. When he decided otherwise 'he warned the family that the result of continuing as we were must make serious inroads on his capital'.[13]

After the Liberals were defeated in 1895, even H. H. Asquith, the rising hope of the party, was obliged to return to his practice at the Bar, where he could earn well over £5,000 annually. Given his wife's expensive tastes he could not afford to be a full-time politician in opposition, even with Margot's annual allowance of £3,000 from her father. She was not averse to manipulating her influential friends to solve this financial problem. She appealed in 1898 to A. J. Balfour, 'as the person of *most* weight with papa', to write to her father, Sir Charles Tennant:

Tell him that in the interest of his family and the country he ought to make Henry independent of the Bar. Henry is making between £5000 and £6000 and he only wants to do the right thing by me and his family. At the same time his political career *cannot* be sacrificed and I for one would rather give up 20 Cavendish Square, live on the £3000 which papa allows us, than in any way spoil Henry's life. *You* better than anyone by flattering Henry's

224 *Political Wives*

future and abilities and appealing to papa's generosity could make him give us another £3000 a year. It would make very little difference to Eddy [her brother] whether he inherits £30,000 or £35,000 . . . As papa is unluckily for us a far greater Conservative than any of you, it would I think be a good thing to say to him that all the men of influence on your side feel that Henry is the only man to lead the house.

She coolly assumed that Balfour would comply with her astonishing request, as he did, but Sir Charles was evidently less malleable, particularly as he had just remarried. Over two years later she asked Balfour to join her in person at her father's London house, to push their case really hard, 'that papa may help us (which I know he is on the edge of doing)'.[14]

Politics was an expensive business partly because politicians had to live in London during parliamentary sessions and entertain their colleagues in a suitable manner. Rich politicians owned a family home in the country and a convenient house near Westminster. Balfour's family seat, for example, was at Whittingehame, near Edinburgh, and soon after coming of age in 1871 he purchased 4 Carlton Gardens in Pall Mall.[15] His Cecil cousins spent as much time as possible at Hatfield House, but the centre of their London life was their home in Arlington Street. Sir Henry Campbell-Bannerman inherited Castle Belmont in Perthshire and purchased a series of imposing London houses; in 1904,for instance, the sixty-three-year long-lease for 29 Belgrave Square cost £4,816, in addition to the annual rent of £170.[16]

Families living on more limited incomes had immense trouble maintaining two homes. Millicent Fawcett described their struggle to live on her husband's income as a Cambridge don while he was an MP: 'It was a tight fit, but it could be done, and was done without any Spartan privations. I was a dragon over every unnecessary expenditure.'[17] Some politicians with lesser means simply made London the family home throughout the year. Kate Potter searched for a suitable London house in 1882 before her marriage to Leonard Courtney: 'I should like you to have a pleasant easy walk to the House which would enable you to come back to dinner sometimes.'[18] Up to 1905 Richard Haldane and his spinster sister, Elizabeth, lived in a 'service flat' at Whitehall Court, but felt obliged to take a more impressive house in Queen Anne's Gate when he became a minister.[19] Haldane, like Asquith and Alfred Lyttelton, had surrendered his income from the Bar in the interests of politics. Herbert Samuel also lived in London, but rented furnished houses in his constituency each summer. When he attained Cabinet rank in 1910 the family moved from Gloucester Terrace to a larger house at 31 Porchester Terrace, more suitable for official entertaining.[20]

Some wives could not afford to join their politician husbands at Westminster. Politics could be a lonely business for Irish and working-class Lib-Lab or Labour members. Keir Hardie later paid tribute to his wife for maintaining their family in Cumnock, after he went to Westminster in 1893: 'During those first three years my wife kept my house going, kept my children decently and respectably clothed and fed on an income which did not even exceed twenty-five shillings a week.' Mrs Keir Hardie 'suffered much in health and spirit' from the long separations, but never reproached her husband.[21] Lloyd George, outstanding in so many respects, was also unusual in his domestic arrangements, though not from his own choice. Margaret Lloyd George disliked the life of a politician's wife in London and preferred to keep their five children at home in Criccieth. In 1897 he wrote sadly from London, accusing Margaret of neglect: 'I have scores of times come home in the dead of night to a cold, dark and comfortless flat without a soul to greet me. I am not the nature either physically or morally that I ought to have been left like this.'[22] Margaret did not respond to such appeals to share his political life, and after 1911 he established an alternative home in London with his secretary, Frances Stevenson.

Politicians' wives spent considerable time separated from their husbands, whatever arrangements were made about homes. Young wives discovered the trials of their role early in married life. Lucy Lyttelton became engaged to Charles Masterman in 1908 during a brief meeting in Westminster Abbey 'between the two debates'. They spent the first Christmas of their marriage apart, and on their first wedding anniversary 'Charles had to go off to Wales to examine ungotten minerals'.[23] Lady Grey commiserated with Connie Buxton in 1892: '[we] have got to begin new lives and don't look forward with pleasure to our husbands being a great deal away doing work in which we can't join.'[24] Mary Booth remarked on Margaret Hobhouse's role in 1886: 'what a lonely life she leads now that Henry is so devoted to his "parliamentary duties". She is wonderfully good about it; but it must be dreary in the evenings.'[25] Ideally, a political wife needed a strong constitution, numerous interests of her own and considerable tolerance for the demands of politics. Even Margot Asquith, who usually revelled in the political limelight, occasionally yearned for time alone with her husband, the Prime Minister, as in 1913:

I have ónly been alone with Henry and my children 3 weeks in 19 years. This has got on my nerves. It is really physical and the more I control the longing or the showing of it the *iller* I feel. We are always a trois on ships, in the hills, on official occasions, round the fire and at the altar. I long to take the Communion Service with Henry alone. I long to talk to him—to be with him.[26]

Some political wives found their role almost intolerable, though few seem to have adopted Margaret Lloyd George's extreme position. Lord John Russell's wife, Fanny, confided to her sister that her role as a political wife 'has always been awful'. The first decade of marriage in the 1840s was the greatest trial because she had to adjust to her new life as stepmother of six children, besides suffering a 'wearying state of health' because of miscarriages. She yearned for leisure in the country rather than 'the countless miseries of office' and dreaded the ordeal of becoming prime minister's wife: 'how entire the sacrifice must be of private happiness to public duty . . . the daily trial to us both of hardly meeting for a quarter of an hour between breakfast and bedtime.' When his government was defeated twenty years later in 1866 she was delighted: 'my joy in his release becomes greater every hour'.[27] Lady Campbell-Bannerman shared Fanny Russell's dislike of political life, for similar reasons of temperament and poor health. For twenty years she struggled against a disease which finally killed her in 1906 while her husband was Prime Minister. She hated the enforced solitude when he was busy at Westminster and spent many long evenings on the sofa, watching the clock, awaiting his return.[28] Mary Leiter, an American heiress, was shocked when she went to England·to marry George Curzon in 1895. He worked sixteen hours a day on official business: 'He sits and sits at those Foreign Office boxes until I could scream!' She was desperately lonely and bored since he excluded her entirely from his political life and she had no network of friends and interests of her own in a foreign country.[29]

The deprivation was not always one-sided; not all politicians were workaholics consumed by single-minded ambition. Sir Edward Grey shared Lord John Russell's preference for rural peace above public duty. G. O. Trevelyan was anxious during a brief respite from politics in 1877 that his wife should extend no more social invitations, 'for we really shall want all the time together of quiet that we can get'.[30] After a hectic political week in 1909 Herbert Samuel was delighted to spend a quiet weekend entirely at home 'for the first time for years'.[31] Four years later Henry Havelock-Allan decided to resign his seat at the next election: 'I've had enough of "lobbying", all night sittings, "snap divisions", and constant absence from my home and my estate.'[32]

For most political wives, the greatest sacrifice of all was banishment to the colonies, however elevated their husbands' status. Mildred Buxton spoke from personal experience in South Africa in 1915–16 when she warned: 'let no-one who is not adaptable be the wife of a Governor-General.'[33] Lady Ripon despaired in 1880: 'What I most feared and dreaded has happened. India has been offered and now doctors are deciding our fate . . . I am ashamed of my utter cowardice.'[34] Lady Antrim responded bluntly to news of Lady Carrington's destiny in 1885: 'Fancy, Lord Carrington going as governor to New South Wales. I cannot understand a real man taking that! . . . I am glad my husband is not ambitious. I *would not* go for 5 years to New South Wales—how horrible.'[35]

In some cases wives' fears of colonial service were justified. The health of Lady Cromer was seriously undermined after several years in Egypt, and Lady Curzon was gravely ill before she returned to India for the last time. Yet both women insisted that their husbands continue in their imperial roles, and both men placed ambition and duty before the health of their wives.[36] In similar circumstances Herbert Gladstone and Sir Thomas Fowell Buxton took the opposite course; Buxton resigned his post as Governor of South Australia in 1898 and Herbert Gladstone retired as Governor-General of South Africa sixteen years later.[37] Ireland was closer, but it was considered the graveyard of political reputations and often involved family separation. Lucy Cavendish's husband was murdered by terrorists the day after he arrived in Dublin as Chief Secretary in 1882. His successor, G. O. Trevelyan, found the strain of the post unbearable and his hair turned white in his one year of office. His wife, Caroline, received only a series of brief notes while he was in Ireland, saying that he found it impossible to write and could not explain what his work involved.[38] Thirty years later, Augustine Birrell suffered acutely when his wife was dying slowly from a brain tumour in England while he was obliged to spend long periods in Dublin.[39] Yet it must be said that some women, like Lady Aberdeen, flourished in a vice-regal role in both Ireland and Canada.

FIVE CASE STUDIES

This section examines the personal experiences of five very different political wives: two aristocrats and three women from upper-middle-class, industrialist and professional families. They span the Victorian and Edwardian political spectrum: Mary Trevelyan and Marion Bryce were Liberals, Lady Stanhope and Lady Selborne were Conservatives, and Mary Chamberlain was a Liberal Unionist. Three of these women either came from political families or were involved in politics before their marriage, while the other two were outsiders to the political scene—Mary Chamberlain as an American, and Mary Trevelyan because of her ignorance of politics before marriage. Lady Stanhope was an aristocratic wife whose political ambitions for her husband were unfulfilled.The husbands of the other four wives attained ministerial rank—Joseph Chamberlain was the most powerful, and Charles Trevelyan perhaps the most disappointed.

These women's lives were far more diverse and complex than the conventional tributes and passing references in political biographies have suggested. These case studies illuminate the sheer hard work, the frustration, and the element of luck involved in striving to become the perfect political wife'. Politicians usually required wives who were supportive, subordinate and even uncritical—as Beatrice Potter sadly recognized—yet the role of political wife was demanding in its own right. These women had to cope with an unusual combination of responsibilities—as housekeeper, hostess, political confidante, and election campaigner, at the least.

(i) MARY CHAMBERLAIN: THE SUBORDINATE ROLE
PLAYED TO PERFECTION

Joseph Chamberlain's third wife, Mary Endicott, is particularly interesting in the light of Beatrice Potter's bitter remarks on the difficulties of marriage to Chamberlain. Moreover, as an American, Mary's comments on her efforts to become a good British political wife provide a revealing outsider's view. Chamberlain's biographers disclose little about his first two wives, who died in childbirth: 'He had no time for a purely domestic life, and the common characteristic of his wives was that they were women devoted to his political activities'.[40] During his years as a widower, his eldest daughter, Beatrice, idolized her father and performed a similar supportive function, 'one great devotion' absorbing her whole young life.[41]

Mary Endicott adapted herself to the role of Chamberlain's wife in a way Beatrice Potter could never have done. Mary was many years younger than Chamberlain, but she earned the affection of stepchildren almost her own age because of her gentleness and sensitivity. Mary helped the family to bridge the gap between middle-class Birmingham and the fashionable upper-class world of Chamberlain's Liberal Unionist circle after 1886. Beatrice Potter noticed in 1884 that the two Miss Chamberlains were 'dressed with the dowdiness of the middle class'; they were 'homely hostesses' in Birmingham but ill at ease with the fashionable 'worldly wise' wives in London.[42] Mary was able to correct this state of affairs.

Mary Endicott fulfilled Chamberlain's expectations of the ideal wife for an ambitious politician.She had been trained in the social responsibilities of public life in the five years before her marriage in 1888, while her father was American Secretary of War. She was totally supportive, and never became actively involved in politics herself in the years before her husband's stroke in 1906. Lady Dorothy Nevill described her as 'the very opposite of the so-called advanced woman who dabbles in politics'.[43] Chamberlain's strong anti-suffrage views were accepted philosophically by Mary. She took her role seriously and was conscious at first 'that I shall have a great deal to live up to'. But her fears gradually evaporated as she found she revelled in the hectic life—'in fact I thrive on it'.[44]

Mary Chamberlain's first year of marriage was a social whirl of dinners, luncheons, receptions, and garden parties. The ritual of returning calls was especially time-consuming since so many

Birmingham ladies left their cards for the new mistress of High-
bury. Mary adjusted remarkably quickly to becoming mistress of
the two households in Birmingham and London. She wrote to her
mother in 1889, just before she gave a large dinner party:

I do not mind the preparation in the least, thanks to you and Washington.
Our cook is equal to the occasion which of course smoothes the way.
I have now assumed that part of the establishment and by degrees shall
take up the whole. A day or two ago I had my first experience of
dismissing a servant. There was no reason except total incapacity and I felt
very weak in the knees until I was face to face with her when my courage
revived, and it was not so bad as I expected.[45]

Mary acquitted herself to perfection in the social world of politics,
'taking especial pains to fulfil all my social obligations promptly, to
justify the good people of Birmingham in the extremely cordial
welcome they have given me.' She also had to learn a complex set
of new etiquette rules because of her American background.
Before her first Court presentation in 1890 she sent for a lengthy
treatise 'On Social Duties', detailing etiquette, dress and precise
rules for levees, drawing-rooms, dinners and Court functions.[46]
    Yet Mary Chamberlain was far from being a mere social
butterfly. She took an intelligent interest in Chamberlain's
political activities, accompanying him to meetings and rivalling
Mrs Gladstone's attendance in the Commons' ladies gallery. Mary
learned about British politics rapidly enough to become a well-
informed, if prejudiced, critic of parliamentary debates, as well as
a delighted observer of her husband's achievements. She listened
attentively as Chamberlain tried out his speeches on her at home,
'so anxious am I that he should be perfectly familiar with it'.[47]
Mary's unquestioning support was most needed during her
husband's controversial campaign for tariff reform from 1903.
His attack on free trade split the Conservative party and
Chamberlain resigned from Balfour's Cabinet to lead his campaign
independently. Mary wrote long, diplomatic letters to Betty
Balfour, the Prime Minister's sister-in-law, to keep communications open and avoid personal enmity: 'it is an infinite pleasure
to us both to know that this official parting has come with no trace
of misunderstanding . . . I have no fear that they will not be able to
work together, one from within, the other from without.'[48]
    Mary's greatest test came in 1906 when Chamberlain suffered a

serious stroke, from which he never recovered, though he remained in Parliament until shortly before his death in 1913. From July 1906 Mary gladly played a more active role, attempting at first to conceal the gravity of his illness in the vain hope that he might resume his political career. Shortly before his stroke she was sufficiently well informed to prompt him if he seemed in danger of breaking down during a speech. Afterwards she became his mouthpiece and his secretary. She wrote dozens of political letters on her husband's behalf explaining his current views, and set aside time each day to discuss political affairs with him. Increasingly she relied for support on her stepson, Austen, as it became impossible to conceal that Joseph was a semi-invalid. By 1909 Mary vetted all news to avoid upsetting Joseph 'by too much commotion'. As the years passed her correspondence with Austen increasingly gave her own opinions on politics rather than her husband's.[49] Mary was relieved when Joseph decided to resign from Parliament in 1913, with no prompting from her.[50] In these difficult years after 1906 Mary's intelligence, patience and diplomacy were exercised to the full. Walter Runciman noted at a dinner party in 1907 that Mrs Chamberlain 'had a good deal to say in a quiet way about political events and people . . . The poor creature probably has a weary, sorrowful life now.'[51] Joseph Chamberlain's ideal political wife was not a passive cipher when circumstances changed.

(ii) MARION BRYCE: A PARTNER IN POLITICS

Before her marriage to James Bryce in 1889, Marion Ashton, a banker's daughter, was heavily involved in committee work for the Hyde Women's Liberal Association. She sat on committees with her sister Margaret, to find employment for girls, to assist young teachers, and to help in election campaigns. She needed no further political education to share James's life as fully as possible. Marion rapidly established herself as an efficient domestic organizer who relished her new position as mistress of a London household. She was an excellent hostess who gave regular weekly dinner parties for James's colleagues and friends, and fulfilled her social obligations by making and receiving calls.

Marion Bryce gave James generous moral support. She was contrite about leaving him for a brief duty visit to her mother in 1890: 'I feel that if you are sad and tired my place is more than ever by your side.' She was politically ambitious for her husband, congratulating him in 1895 after a talk with Gladstone: 'I like to think of your taking all these opportunities while you may, and only regret that I may not share them personally.'[52] Marion acted informally as her husband's secretary and organizer, spending many hours copying out his speeches and offering constructive suggestions. She was the travel agent for all his journeys, making the most careful arrangements for his convenience, and helping to organize his visits to his South Aberdeen constituency. In 1895 she advised him that 'You ought to let it be known that you have arrived [in Aberdeen] and that you are ready to do business if required.'[53]

Marion was well informed on the political issues which concerned James. Their honeymoon in 1889 set the tone for subsequent married life: they read all the newspapers avidly 'to bring us up to the proper level of knowledge' of events in their absence, and they discussed political themes for his Aberdeen speeches.[54] They continued to exchange ideas on the issues of the day in the following years. Marion had an enthusiastic appetite for James's politics, and an endless flow of partisan encouragement. In 1903, for instance, she urged him to capitalize in his speeches on the chaos within the Conservative party, and considered that his 'way of knifing Balfour was rather *neat*'. She asked him to keep copies for her of the full press reports of all his speeches.[55]

The disruptions of political life were perhaps easier to bear because the Bryces had no children. Even so, in 1906 Marion found that life was often a trial for the wife of the Irish chief secretary. The cost of official life in Dublin made her anxious. In October 1906 she must pay 'the initial expenses about the house and the monthly books, and the horses etc., which will make a considerable hole in the cash'. She was 'struck with consternation' at the news that James was required in London for almost three months at the end of 1906 while she must persevere alone in Dublin: 'There is nothing going on in Dublin at present; no society, no work apparently in which I can take any part . . .I can't tell you, dearest, how hard it has been to me to be here all this time without you, and nothing but a sense of necessity and duty would have made me do it.'[56]

A few days later Marion had to face the shock of the proposal that James should become British ambassador to the United

States, before she had even adjusted to life in Dublin. James was enthusiastic about the new post but had considerable difficulty in convincing his wife that he was right to go. As she confided in her uncle, James would leave Ireland 'after a year's hard work of preparation for better things, and it looks rather like running away'. She put this point more diplomatically to her husband: 'I do not think you could properly throw up the Irish post now in the middle of everything.' But personal considerations weighed just as heavily. It was hard to leave their family and friends in England for an unknown life: 'The life socially would rather weary us—it is such an empty and expensive rush which is difficult to keep out of.' Marion concluded that 'it would not be well to take the post if offered . . . certainly not unless great pressure was put on you'.[57] James accepted the American post, despite Marion's arguments, and she stoically organized another major move. Early in 1907 she was back in London making preparations: 'I have been rushed all day, seeing servants and dressmakers, and arranging liveries etc. . . . I have seen two footmen who seem respectable and suitable . . . I have also seen a chef who may do, and a housemaid.' The American press subsequently regarded the Bryces as 'the most dignified and successful representatives of the court of St. James' for many decades, though the 'butterfly element' considered Marion too austere.[58]

Meanwhile, throughout these years Marion Bryce was on the executive of the Women's National Liberal Federation—the anti-suffrage organization which seceded from the Women's Liberal Federation in 1893. She was also engaged in promoting girls' secondary and higher education, and was much in demand as a public speaker, especially at women's meetings. Her personal views were staunchly anti-suffrage, like her husband's, but she avoided parading these opinions in public or taking an active role in the anti-suffrage movement. In 1906 Marion declined an invitation to write a pamphlet for the Antis, since this would be undiplomatic behaviour in a minister's wife. But she was quite sure of her objections to women's suffrage—arguments ignored by 'these noisy advocates and ignorant followers'.[59] Four years later she compiled an unpublished paper, arguing that women were incompetent to vote because of their separate domestic sphere, their unique maternal duties, and different mental capacities.[60] Marion Bryce remained adamantly opposed to the militant

suffragettes. She warned James in 1906,for instance, against seeing
a particular activist—'a thoroughly unscrupulous and prejudiced
woman who did not know what truth was'.[61]

The Bryce family illustrates the difficulty in identifying pro- and
anti-suffrage women in terms of political party or the nature of
their marital relationship. James Bryce was one of the most
prominent anti-suffrage leaders in the Liberal party, alongside
Asquith and Lewis Harcourt. Yet the caring and sharing nature of
the Bryces' marriage was perhaps its most outstanding characteristic. The Bryce family, however, also shows that a family united in
political persuasion could be deeply divided on women's suffrage.
James's brother Annan, his two spinster sisters, and his wife
shared his views. But Annan's wife, Violet Bryce, and Marion's
sister, Margaret Ashton, were equally strongly (and more actively)
committed to votes for women. Marion failed to convince her
sister that 'these extreme people do harm', and subsequently
concluded that amicable family relations were only possible if the
subject was avoided.[62] Violet caused greater problems because she
promoted her powerful pro-suffrage views from within the Bryce
family fold. After playing a significant role in Annan Bryce's 1906
electoral victory, she threatened to withdraw her support in future
unless her husband actively supported women's suffrage in
Parliament. She carried out this threat during the January 1910
election by deliberately prolonging a visit to America rather than
returning to support his campaign. The American press made
much of this 'family rift' over female suffrage. The *Washington
Post* headline was typical: 'Ambassador's Sister-in-Law Aloof
from Husband's Fight'. Violet told the press that she could not ask
women campaign workers to help elect her anti-suffrage husband,
though she denied that suffrage had 'broken up our family'. She
also declared war at the domestic level, as her sister-in-law, Mary,
reported in 1908: 'Violet won't have any one in the house who has
joined the *Anti*-Suffrage League. It is all very vexing.'[63] This
conflict of views created inevitable tensions, though family unity
ultimately prevailed.

(iii) EVELYN, LADY STANHOPE: A FRUSTRATED
POLITICAL HOSTESS

Evelyn, Lady Stanhope, represents a very different group of

political wives from the other four case studies. She was a prominent political hostess with ambitions for her aristocratic husband, who never became a politician of stature. After seven years as a Conservative MP, Arthur Stanhope became the sixth earl on his father's death in 1875. Disraeli's poor opinion of Stanhope was demonstrated by the lowly offer of the post of First Church Estates' Commissioner, managing the landed properties of the Church of England. Otherwise he had to content himself with his local estate commitments at Chevening, coupled with the post of lord lieutenant of Kent. Lady Stanhope's role as a political wife inevitably remained primarily social. She belonged to the wealthy 'hunting, shooting and fishing' branch of the peerage, unlike Lady Selborne and Mary Trevelyan whose links to the intellectual aristocracy were closer.

The Stanhopes maintained a suitable household to cope with their large Chevening estate and their lavish scale of entertainment. In 1874 their female staff included a housekeeper, three laundry maids, four housemaids, a cook and kitchenmaid, a dairymaid, stillroom maid and scullery maid. In addition, large numbers of male retainers maintained the house, stables and estates.[64] Lady Stanhope supervised the household with calm efficiency, besides mothering four children, and acting as estate manager in her husband's absence. In 1878, for example, she reassured him that the farm stock book was in order, the list of leases prepared, the new brick machine operating efficiently and the dairy wall cemented.[65] She had to be a skilful manager to organize the massive retinue of twenty or more servants and to superintend the frequent household movements between Chevening and London. She wrote to her mother in about 1875: 'We go up [to London] only from Monday till Friday next week, then return here [to Chevening] for ten days. So we only take up the menservants and two or three maids. All the cards are written and gone, so except arranging the rooms I have not much more to do.'[66]

Lady Stanhope was well known as an accomplished political hostess who threw successful dinner parties in their London home at Grosvenor Place at least once each week while Parliament was sitting. Outside the London Season she organized frequent weekend parties at Chevening,' often for twenty or more guests. She was privately critical of other people's entertainment which

did not meet her own high standards, as illustrated by a dinner
party at the Marjoribanks in 1870:

the dinner was spoilt by Lord Dufferin and one of the Bourkes failing to
appear, and by being *very* late and much too long: 4 entrees, 4 roasts etc;
and 5 different wine-glasses to everybody. F. Stanley went off to the house
directly after dinner so I had no talk with him; altogether I thought the
ladies too good for the men and the affair dull.[67]

Lady Stanhope took into account political diplomacy as well as
etiquette when she considered invitations. In 1884 she questioned
whether they were right to refuse the Richmonds: 'Of course it will
be dull, but I am not sure whether, as you run against him
constantly in the House of Lords, it is not wise to meet him half
way socially.'[68]

Lady Stanhope was reasonably well informed and keenly
interested in political affairs. She strongly supported her husband's
political endeavours and was more ambitious for him than his
talents merited. Early in his career in the Commons they discussed
how best he could make some impact on the House. She advised
against his trying to initiate a private member's bill, arguing that 'a
good speech on a topic already started is more telling.'[69] She
proved herself a capable backstage organizer and canvasser for her
husband's election campaigns before his elevation to the Lords in
1875. She learned before his 1870 by-election in Suffolk East that a
certain Mr Schreiber had relatives there: 'so I have been after him,
and he will do anything, especially whip up his people and see
them to the poll.' She also 'hooked Schreiber to work on the
Committee' besides 'being energetic' on polling day. Lady
Stanhope wrote to another man who might have 'voters among his
friends', and went out to Camberwell and Dulwich 'after more
voters'.[70] During Stanhope's 1874 campaign at Suffolk East, she
regretted she would be 'no use going about with you' since she was
still nursing her second child. Yet she helped write his letters and
organize canvassers, including Harriet Ashley, who 'used to win
all Ashley's Elections and delights in it'. She also announced a
useful private donation to the cause: 'That dear Mother of mine
wishes to give £100 towards Election expenses.'[71] Lady Stanhope
was more knowledgeable and capable than many other political
wives, but she had to come to terms with the fact that her husband
was a second-rate politician.

(iv) MAUD, LADY SELBORNE: AN INHERITED ROLE AND CONSERVATIVE INFLUENCE

Maud, Lady Selborne, daughter of Conservative Prime Minister Lord Salisbury and cousin of A. J. Balfour, was an exceptional woman by any standards. Independent and strong-minded, she shared the Cecil family's philosophical and political interests, and matched the intellectual powers of the talented Cecil men. Like her sister, Gwendolen Cecil, she would have made a capable politician a generation later, but seemed content in the earlier years of her marriage to concentrate on her childbearing role. Maud Cecil was one of the very few women in this study who had already formulated powerful political views before marriage and refused to alter them to suit her Liberal fiancé, William Palmer, Lord Selborne's only son. In 1883 William's sister claimed that Maud would convert to Liberalism after marriage. Maud wrote immediately to her fiancé to ensure that *'your* mind is *quite* free from error on the subject. Nothing is sure but death and taxes, but of all the improbable eventualities that is one of the most unlikely.' In case he harboured any other misapprehensions about her serious political commitment, Maud sent her fiancé a long letter that same week on 'what I should do if I were a man' to reform the evils of slum housing and bad sanitation.[72] In fact it was Willy Palmer who changed parties rather than his new wife, since he left the Liberal party in 1886 over Irish Home Rule, to join the Liberal Unionists in coalition with the Conservatives. Subsequently he became the Second Earl of Selborne in 1895, Under-secretary for the Colonies (1895–1900), First Lord of the Admiralty (1900–5) and Governor of the Transvaal (1905–10).

Maud Selborne was extremely well-informed on political issues and held strong views on most of them. An innate conservative, she believed that the Conservative party combined 'a regard for justice, order, and liberty' to a greater extent than any other party. In 1883 she was staunchly opposed to universal suffrage: 'You think an uneducated man can decide "by instinct" on some military, economical, or social difficulty?' Thirty years later she was less fearful of democracy because 'Anglo Saxon democracies in the Colonies appear to provide quite a decent government.' In the Edwardian period Lady Selborne was even prepared to contemplate individual proposals of 'piece-meal socialism' on their merits, except for the minimum wage and relief works for the unemployed. Despite her husband's position, in 1883 she thought the House of Lords 'a poor lot and I shouldn't mind their abolition.'[73] Lady Selborne's judgment of character was usually perceptive. She considered Curzon, for example, extremely able, but 'such an egoist—it will be very difficult to make him play for the side.'[74]

Maud Selborne was well trained by the Cecil family and knew that a woman's political influence had to be subtle to be effective. She never became one of those strident political women deplored by Lady Cowper. Yet she was willing to use her powerful family influence in an emergency, as in 1907 when she attempted to intervene in the Conservative party controversy over tariff reform:

> I talked to Milner after dinner while the others played bridge . . . I tried hard to persuade him to put himself a bit forward as leader of the Tariff Reformers and negotiate a truce with Bob and Linky [her brothers, Robert and Hugh Cecil] . . . I am quite sure the boys could come to an understanding with him.[75]

Lady Selborne sometimes acted as intermediary between her own family and her husband, placing the influence of the House of Cecil at Selborne's disposal. In 1907, for example, when the Colonial Office decided against publishing an important despatch by Selborne, Maud tried to have the decision rescinded. She told Lord Grey the story, hoping that 'as a cousin he might be able to appeal to the Elgin's better feelings'. If this failed 'I will get Alfred [Milner] or Arthur [Balfour] to try a question. I am rather in favour of doing it through the latter as he is so safe. He could get a man on the back benches to start the hare, and then take up the running, covering my tracks.'[76]

Lady Selborne considered the political education of her eldest son, Roundell ('Top'), a significant part of her role as political wife and mother. While Roundell was away at school and at Oxford, she sent him extensive letters of advice on political practice, principles and issues. She wanted him to 'go early into the House of Commons', immediately after Oxford, instead of spending the more usual ten years or so in the army or civil service first. This time would be more profitably spent 'in grasping the rules and procedure' of Parliament to prepare him for a successful political career. In 1908 Lady Selborne was concerned about Roundell's unwise choice of friends and his refusal to spend time at Hatfield with her influential brothers. The following year, however, Roundell began to respond more favourably to her training and sought an 'intelligent criticism' of his speeches from his mother. Maud assured her son that he had great facility for his age, but advised 'a certain decorum of speech' and intensive preparation, rather than talking without thinking, like F. E. Smith.[77] Roundell profited from his mother's teaching, and entered Parliament in 1910 at the comparatively early age of twenty-three, remaining there for thirty years until succeeding to the earldom.

Lady Selborne's participation in election campaigns followed the familiar pattern of increasing involvement after about 1900. By then her husband was in the Lords, but she lent her support to worthy candidates among her family and friends. She canvassed and helped organize meetings for W. G. Nicholson, who took over Selborne's Hampshire constituency in 1897. In the 1905 campaign she again gave sensible advice about capable canvassers, floating voters who might be swayed, and the most receptive locations for meetings.[78] Lady Selborne earned a high reputation in her family for effective organization of female electoral workers. In the December 1910 campaign, Robert Cecil sought his sister's support in his fight against Neil Primrose in Cambridgeshire. Lady Selborne thought Robert would have more chance of success if 'a decent organization had been started here three months ago'. But she did her best: 'I have been working the respectable quiet women all I can. I have got a little steam on but Whittlesea is a most tiresome place. They come to meetings and wear pink bows, but won't work.'[79] Eleanor Cecil thanked her sister-in-law: 'We should have done nothing with the women without you.'[80]

Given Maud Selborne's personality and political talents, it is scarcely surprising that she was one of the very few political wives in this study who became actively involved in the suffragist campaign. Although she was a Conservative, Lady Selborne's views were fairly representative of the majority of suffragist political wives from both major parties. Like many other political wives she was initially more interested in 'improving the position of women generally, and the vote seemed to me one means towards that end'. For many years she gave personal priority to campaigns for reforms in nursing, housing, female education and the promotion of female employment.[81] Yet she shared the views of her father, Lord Salisbury, and her Cecil brothers, on women's suffrage. Her short article for the *Nineteenth Century* in 1905 supported the grant of the franchise to women ratepayers, as generally responsible, mature property-owners. She argued that even if this led eventually to the franchise for married women, it would have no party influence or dangerous effects, since most married couples would vote the same way. Lady Selborne attacked the 'whigs, prigs and pigs' who objected that women were unsuited by their sex to vote, claiming that it would unsex them and cause a national disaster. She agreed that some functions were better suited to men, but politics was not one of these: 'Women can be politicians. Political ability, a capacity for the science of government, seems to be almost more common among women than it is among men.'[82]

It is perhaps surprising that Maud Selborne remained for so long outside organized suffragism. But for two decades she concentrated on raising her family and she was always reluctant to speak in public and take the limelight. In 1892 she rejected requests to address public meetings: 'I cannot do it, and I am too old to learn.'[83] Nobody believed her. She wrote humorously in 1907:

The suffrage societies still pursue me. I got a pink ticket by post the other day: 'Admit to the plinth of Nelson's column' inscribed upon it. But I remain deaf to all such temptations. Even if they offered me a seat on Nelson's cocked hat, I should have the strength of mind to refuse.

The Conservative Women's Suffrage Society finally succeeded in capturing her as president in July 1907.[84] For the next few years Maud Selborne and her sister-in-law, Eleanor Cecil, discussed policies and tactics. They endeavoured to persuade the Conservative Suffrage Society to protest publicly against the violence of the militant suffragettes. Many Conservative suffragists disapproved of the militants but feared to offend them, while some even privately hoped to profit by their deeds. The two women pondered the advantages of giving their 'forwards' some legitimate fighting to do, such as organizing a retaliation scheme against MPs who refused to help: 'Lots of women would be glad of a good excuse to get off political bazaars and such like.' They agreed that it was vital to win the favour of the 'quiet domestic women'. Once that was achieved they had almost won the battle, provided they could secure 'a competent politician to take the lead'.[85]

Lady Selborne used her excellent political contacts and persuasive skills in attempts to influence those 'competent politicians'. On several occasions she wrote to her cousin, A. J. Balfour, asking him to vote for particular suffrage bills and thus give heart to wavering Conservative suffragists.[86] Before the Conciliation Bill was introduced in mid-1910 to enfranchise women householders, Lady Selborne even appealed for support to the arch anti-suffragist, Austen Chamberlain. She tried in vain to persuade him that a limited suffrage bill would 'enlist the naturally Conservative force of property owning women on the Unionist side' and thus postpone universal adult suffrage for another generation.[87] Lady Selborne enlisted her husband's willing services to make several public speeches on behalf of the Conservative women's suffrage cause. In December 1911 she instructed Lord Selborne to persuade Bonar Law to speak for the Conciliation Bill, thus applying more pressure on Asquith: 'I wrote to Bonar Law to try to make him take some step in our favour, and he has promised me to see you and consult you about it. Ginger him up, if he sees you this week. Tell him it is no earthly use his trying to shirk the question.' Lady Selborne wanted it made clear that 'a large proportion of the Conservative party have always been in favour of giving votes to women.'[88] Her role in the suffragist movement was typical of her wider role as a political wife. She tried to keep a low profile, though she was sometimes pushed forward by others because of her powers of leadership, her wide knowledge of politics, and her influential family connections.

(v) MOLLY TREVELYAN: ASPIRATION AND ACQUIESCENCE

Mary (Molly) Trevelyan provides a contrast to Maud Selborne in many respects, not least because she was the daughter of a wealthy industrialist, rather than an aristocratic prime minister. Before her marriage she had less knowledge of politics than the other four women, but from 1903 she made immense efforts to educate herself politically and share her husband's work. Despite his advanced radical views, Charles Trevelyan did not encourage her to become politically active, except in the Women's Liberal Federation and in his own election campaigns. He preferred to keep the emphasis on the social role of the political wife, which Molly performed admirably.

The Trevelyans lived in Cambo House on the Wallington family estate, rent-free, when Parliament was not sitting. But they also regarded a London house as essential, so that Molly and the children would usually be with Charles during sessions. Within a year of marriage they built twin houses in Great College Street with their friends the Runcimans, owning the house and renting the land on long-lease at £200. They lived very comfortably in their ten rooms, with a cook, parlourmaid and housemaid, adding a nurse and nurserymaid when the children arrived.[89] Molly subsequently claimed that she was an incompetent housekeeper when she married at twenty-three, as she had never learned to cook or clean. Before the wedding she diligently took instruction from her mother, and together they calculated that it would cost £235 to keep the two Trevelyans and three servants for a year. Molly quickly learnt to organize the household efficiently, check all the accounts at the end of each year, and settle all bills and servants' wages. She did the cooking and housework on the servants' days off, and always took a large share of the care of her children.[90]

Molly Trevelyan was a superb political hostess who thoroughly enjoyed the social aspects of her role. She had received excellent training from her mother in managing social functions and was a good conversationalist with wide interests. During the London Season she gave small dinner parties for Charles's colleagues and their personal friends at least once a week. Their house was so close to Parliament that they had a division bell installed, allowing the politicians to rush off to vote between courses. Molly also loved organizing more formal parties or dances for forty or fifty people,[91] and was privately critical of other hostesses who were less capable. In 1904, for instance, the Trevelyans dined with the Alfred Emmotts: 'A beastly dinner, very long and ill cooked', whilst the St Loe Stracheys were criticized for failing to introduce guests properly.[92] The six months of each year spent in Northumberland were far more informal, though they often included visits from Charles's colleagues and their wives, especially the Runcimans and Samuels. Molly took an enthusiastic part in all their activities, from sixteen-mile walks to shooting, hunting and rock-climbing.

Molly Trevelyan had an idealistic view of her husband's political role which allowed her to cope with the separations involved in politics with equanimity. She was inspired and awed at first by

Charles's knowledge and commitment. She hoped for 'greatness' for him, and trusted she would 'never grudge any moment of the time you must of necessity spend away from me'. The frequent separations were often hard to bear, and she had mixed feelings about Charles gaining office in 1905: 'I hate to think that perhaps he may get Office; and yet I know that the whole duty of an M.P.'s wife is to hope he may. But I should see so little of him if he did.' Yet she concluded that she loved him enough to be unselfish about him, and would give him up to 'the people's good'. When Charles eventually did gain office in 1908, she rarely complained and generally kept her vow to be 'philosophical and happy' whatever the trials of political life.[93]

During her engagement and early marriage, Molly was anxious that her utter ignorance of politics would harm their relationship or act as a hindrance to Charles's career. Her family had entertained artists, archaeologists, industrialists and intellectuals, but rarely politicians. She frequently apologized for her ignorance, but said she was eager to learn and asked Charles 'to talk politics to me'. She continued her course in self-education in 1903, reading widely in history and literature with Charles's guidance.[94] Her aim was to understand the important political issues of the day, so that she could participate intelligently in his work: 'I like to know you on platforms and in *The Times*, as well as on moors and in drawing rooms.' Molly read all his speeches and visited the House fairly frequently to hear debates. During the 1905 election she helped him prepare notes for his speeches and in 1904 she proudly translated for him material on land reform from German: 'I never like to be doing other things when I can be of use to him.'[95]

Molly developed a sound grasp of political issues and rapidly proved her value as a political wife. On her first visit to her husband's Elland constituency in November 1903 she made a spontaneous speech at the opening of the new Liberal Club. Charles congratulated her on her excellent 'public manner' and told his mother that Molly revealed 'a delightful mixture of natural reserve and friendliness'.[96] By December 1904 she was invited to take the chair at Elland meetings of the Women's Liberal Federation, and spoke on land reform at the annual federation meeting. In May 1905 she was congratulated on a speech by the highly experienced political wife, Lady Aberdeen: 'It was charmingly done and very much to the point '. . . Both on public and on personal grounds I rejoice in you as a recruit.'[97] Molly took a remarkably active role in the 1905–6 election campaign, given her political inexperience and the fact that she was still nursing her three-month-old first child. For twelve days in January 1906 she attended three or more meetings daily, usually speaking for about twenty minutes at one or two meetings. The baby was brought by her nurse to various committee rooms, to be fed between meetings. On 4 January, for instance, she held two meetings of her own: 'Spoke quite well at both. Back to nurse Pauline at 4.30. Out at 6.15 to three meetings of Charles.'[98]

By 1906 Molly had gained confidence and began to see herself as Charles's partner rather than his adoring subordinate: 'we are equal friends and lovers—you are above me only because you are older and know more, not because you are better as a man or as a lover: no, I won't have anybody think I am not every bit as good as you are.' A few months later Molly told Charles that 'it will be easier to go on working together if you will take me as a co-worker.'[99] She assumed that Charles' progressive radical ideas encompassed greater equality in the marital relationship. Molly was also starting tentatively to offer Charles advice that was constructive but also mildly critical: '. . . don't be *too* vehement—other people have opinions which they think as good as yours . . . you'll carry more weight to back your opinion if you are calm.'[100]

But Molly's political education and aspirations for partnership were proceeding too fast for Charles. A crisis in their relationship was provoked by his misery and frustration at his own failure to obtain office between 1906 and 1908. After several months' depression, in May 1906 he confessed to Molly 'how he is left out of everything because no one wants him; the House is full of abler men than he . . . He believes himself a failure, with no possible future. It was terrible to see him cry, though he tried not to let me see.'[101] Up to this point Molly had underestimated Charles's need for personal achievement and overestimated his strength in meeting political disappointment. From now on she provided greater consolation, which he irrationally resented. Just at the time when a more confident and mature Molly was asking to become an equal partner, Charles was experiencing a serious crisis of personal failure. He seemed to regret his outburst of May 1906 and confided little more in Molly in the following months, despite continued depression. Six months later she learned that Charles had again been passed over for ministerial office, though his hopes had once more been high. She was 'sadly hurt' that he had not confided his bitter disappointment, and she spent a miserable evening composing a critical letter to him:

Don't you realise how the important side of your life is getting every day further from being a part of me? . . . I never doubt for one instant that you love me enormously, far better than anything else. But I am getting to see now that it is my beauty and my cheerfulness that are the reasons of that love. I think I can never now be to you what I so long to be—your chief friend in every way. Sonny, I do love you so, and it is not kind to leave me so much out of your life . . . I know that often, constantly, every day, I fail to come up to your standard of intelligence, and of political interest. I fail largely because there is so little point in caring for your interests, when you do not care to share them with me, nor to encourage my efforts, nor to show that you understand my desire to share in your life, by opening it to me and telling me every day the ups and downs . . . Dear, our life together can never be perfect until we can share everything . . . I fear that I am getting dull and narrow, caring for your daily welfare more than for the larger side of your existence.[102]

Molly was deeply disillusioned to find that progressive radical males (like most socialist males) still believed as deeply in the separation of the male and female spheres as did most conservative males. Gradually the Trevelyans ceased discussing politics at home because Charles became much too agitated and overrode Molly's opinions if she disagreed. In July 1907 Molly asked Charles in a letter if he intended to speak that day about the Scottish Land Values Bill: 'I shouldn't dare to mention it except in a letter, as I know you would be cross!' After 1907, even Molly's private diary gave little hint of her deep disappointment, though resentment occasionally surfaced. In 1908 she complained that Charles commanded her too roughly: 'I want to be fully your equal, obeying you when it is right, as you obey me, but not giving way slavishly.'[103] They quarrelled in February 1910 when Molly mentioned casually that she did not care for philosophy books, and Charles responded that he could have no serious discussion with a person 'so stunted' in ideas. Molly retorted that the real reason was that 'he talked the whole time. I boiled with indignation but I hope he didn't see it.'[104] After the negative response to her passionate letter of December 1906, she ceased striving for the perfect marriage which, for her, involved some measure of political partnership. This aspiration in itself illustrated the influence of the women's movement by the Edwardian period. Molly had hoped for a role as political wife which was far more a shared partnership than most. But she acquiesced in her husband's traditional attitudes, adopting a more passive role as political wife and concentrating her energies on her maternal and social duties. In July 1910 she embarked on a life's work in embroidery: 'I count that it is going to take me 30 years to finish it.'[105] The result was a magnificent tapestry now displayed over the chimneypiece in Lady Trevelyan's parlour at Wallington.

Molly continued to play the supportive role demanded by Charles. Throughout 1907 and 1908 he was 'dreadfully discouraged' about his failure to win office. His hopes were raised in spring 1908 because a Cabinet reconstruction took place when Asquith succeeded Campbell-Bannerman as Prime Minister. Molly felt so desperate on Charles's behalf that she tried to intervene herself. Her father, Sir Hugh Bell, said that he would 'pull strings', while she invited Churchill to tea 'to stir him up to help Charles to get a post'. Ominously Churchill did not come, and Reginald McKenna, invited to tea the following day, 'was very distant and noncommittal, and I felt it was no good'.[106] Molly lacked the experience and the network of influential contacts which Maud Selborne used so diplomatically yet so sparingly. When the bad news came, Molly and Charles 'tried to talk about it' but he needed to escape to Sicily for two weeks to recover alone from the blow. Molly meanwhile thought about her 'extraordinary man', his pride, his ambition, and his terror of failure: 'My poor boy! I will not ever let him think that he has not, or will not, succeed.'[107] She understood and loved her husband well enough to recognize his vulnerability and to see that her own ideal of an equal partnership was a threat to him. At last in October 1908 Charles was offered the post of Undersecretary at the Board of Education, where he remained for six years. It was one of the proudest moments of Molly's life when she visited the Commons to see 'my man on the front bench'.[108] But Charles had to serve an unusually long period in junior office in the same department, which became increasingly frustrating. These six years did, however, subsequently prove an excellent training ground for Cabinet office as President of the Board of Education in the 1920s. Ironically, Molly's sense of sharing her husband's political destiny was restored by his resignation in August 1914, in protest at the Liberal Government's declaration of war.[109]

From 1907 Molly Trevelyan acquiesced in her secondary and largely separate role as political wife, devoting her political energies to the Women's Liberal Federation. She became increasingly involved in WLF committee work and was much in demand all over the country as a WLF speaker. Her favourite topics included land values, old age pensions, the Government's record, 'the state as parent', and free trade. On one occasion in 1908 Molly made a speech at Shelf to about thirty women, 'then nursed Kitty before them all'. She became president of the WLF in Alnwick and spoke to them occasionally when the family was back in Northumberland. Molly also supported her husband in his constituency work at Elland, speaking at many of his meetings. On arrival in Elland there was usually 'a committee meeting of women for me and of men for Charles'.[110]

The general election of January 1910 gave Molly considerable scope for her political skills and enthusiasm since Charles was ill during the first stage of the campaign. She felt 'the thrill of battle in my veins' and assured Charles: 'you can feel quite safe in my arranging all the details of the campaign quite properly and not forgetting anything.'[111] She organized the campaign, arranged the meetings and prepared the publication of his manifesto. Molly was in her element addressing a series of meetings on Charles's behalf, as at Halifax:

I got up, and spoke perhaps for 20 minutes. I made a *really* good speech—rather a tub thumping speech, nearly all extempore . . . I spoke better than I should have done if you had been there, because I felt it was *my* show and I must speak for us both.

She delivered several extempore speeches on the Government's achievements: 'thumping good stuff *I* thought it and so did everyone else apparently'.[112] She also spoke on Charles's behalf to seventy men at his adoption meeting at Elland.

The 1906 pattern was restored for the second stage of the campaign in January 1910 since Charles had recovered. Molly addressed numerous women's meetings—often two or three a day. She was also needed to address overflow meetings while Charles spoke to the main meeting. Another important function was to keep meetings alive when Charles was delayed elsewhere and ensure that audiences did not leave. Sometimes Molly began a whole series of meetings, rushing off to start the next one as soon as Charles arrived. She also dealt with the rare heckler effectively, as when a youth interrupted her constantly at a Bradshaw meeting: 'My blood was up and I think I smashed him fairly well, on Tariff Reform.' On polling day she toured round from one booth to another all day, despite snow, hail and howling winds.[113] Her role in the December 1910 election was similar, though she did not have the opportunities provided a year earlier by Charles's absence.

Many years later, she recalled that she was 'a keen suffragist, but I detested the views and the methods of the suffragettes'.[114] Molly agreed with her mother-in-law, Caroline Lady Trevelyan, that 'in most revolutionary movements, there is always a party of violence, and [that] the cause and the constitutional advocates always suffer'.[115] Molly and Charles examined the anti-suffrage case carefully and attended a few of their meetings, before rejecting their arguments as 'absolutely fallacious'. Molly spoke for the moderate suffragist cause at a number of WLF and Elland constituency meetings, but she quickly tired of the rhetoric of the 'ardent suffragettes'.[116] On women's suffrage she was fairly representative of the majority of political wives, especially those on the Liberal side. She was not overly enthusiastic but was prepared on principle to give restrained support to the moderate suffragists.

Few simple conclusions can be drawn from the experiences of these five political wives. Their views on the suffrage question did not follow party lines. One Liberal was anti-suffragist while the other was moderately pro-suffrage. The Conservatives were equally divided, with Lady Selborne an activist for the suffrage cause and Lady Stanhope quietly critical. Mary Chamberlain kept silent on the question which so electrified her anti-suffragist husband. Only two of the five women held strong views on the suffrage question and only Lady Selborne became actively involved. The chief anti-suffragist among these women was a Liberal and the most prominent suffragist a Conservative. Marion Bryce, the anti-suffragist, played the most equal and active role in her husband's career.

Beatrice Potter was correct in her estimate of the qualities of the ideal political wife. All five wives in this chapter conformed to a degree she would have found unacceptable. Yet within the confines of the prevailing model of political wife, the scope varied according to several factors. The individual talents, political knowledge and family background of the women themselves were naturally important, as Maud Selborne illustrated so well. Impeccable political credentials as a Cecil gave her supreme self-confidence, which was combined with the acumen to use her skills tactfully and cautiously. But the extent to which the wife's talents could be exercised depended on her husband's political effectiveness, as Lady Stanhope discovered. It was also determined by her husband's view of their marital relationship, and the degree of initiative allowed to the wife. Marion Bryce played a satisfying part in an unusually equal partnership. By contrast, Mary Chamberlain and Molly Trevelyan were expected to acquiesce in the philosophy of 'separate spheres' and their responses were quite different. Mary Chamberlain had expected the subordinate and separate role and found contentment, though she proved she could operate efficiently within the male sphere when called upon after 1906. Molly Trevelyan, on the other hand, passionately desired an active partnership but had to acquiesce in her husband's traditional view of marriage; she had the greatest expectations and consequently made the greatest sacrifice as a political wife.

PART FOUR

SPINSTERHOOD

9

Dutiful Daughters, Desperate Rebels and the Transition to the New Women

THE Victorian spinster was judged by her contemporaries to be a human failure, condemned to a lonely life of futility, ridicule or humiliation. Recent studies of the middle-class spinster in Victorian society have concentrated on the minority who became governesses, writers or emigrant gentlewomen. Historians have neglected the majority of middle- and upper-class spinsters who performed a vital social role within the family. These spinsters were not brave or desperate enough to emigrate, and their families had sufficient means for outside work to be socially unacceptable. Such women were generally dependent on family charity, but it was not a one-way process. They frequently repaid any financial debt in kind, and the extent of the family's obligation to these women merits further analysis. Thousands of spinsters cared for ageing parents until their deaths; they acted as surrogate wives to bachelor brothers, without the personal rewards reserved for wives; they became resident maiden aunts, permanent child-minders and nurses, and unpaid housekeepers.

This final chapter will examine the roles of the middle- and upper-class Victorian spinster and the varying reactions to those roles, through a series of case studies. The spinsters were the women most rapidly relegated to family and historical obscurity. This was the result of their status which was determined by a predominantly male social value system. One spinster usually remained in each generation of the larger Victorian families, suggesting that this was the consequence of parental pressure. Very few of these spinsters left any historical record of their lives. Family papers were generally kept by the husband or sons of the married women, and most spinsters emerge only as occasional shadows in the background of their more fortunate married sisters' correspondence. In the vast majority of these family papers, the spinsters are represented only by passing references or rare letters of gratitude and condolence. But in a dozen families the lives of spinsters can be reconstructed to varying degrees, making possible an analysis of the special functions and problems of unmarried women in domestic life. Each spinster must be seen in the context of her own family, as part of a series of individual case studies, illuminating different aspects of spinsterhood.

Spinsters were not a new problem in the nineteenth century, though the Victorians wrote as if they had invented 'redundant women'. From 1600, between ten and twenty per cent of European women remained permanently single. At any one time, about one-third of all women under thirty were likely to be unmarried.[1] A correlation has even been suggested between the increase in witch-hunts in the sixteenth century and the rising numbers of spinsters. Women who lived alone, without the protection of husbands or fathers, could pose a threat to conventional society.[2] Lawrence Stone has argued that the rising numbers of unmarried women were 'a new and troublesome social phenomenon' in the eighteenth century; their numbers increased from about five per cent of all upper-class women in the sixteenth century to more than twenty per cent two hundred years later.[3]

The industrial revolution benefited working-class spinsters more than those from the higher classes. Industrialization opened up greater employment opportunities outside the home for working-class spinsters, especially in factories and domestic service where single women predominated. By contrast, the impoverished spinster of the middle class had little option but to teach. Any other occupation was considered socially unacceptable, and a limited education in the 'accomplishments' provided no vocational training. It was commonly assumed in the nineteenth century that the redundant women were chiefly concentrated in the upper classes, and that few working-class women remained permanently single.[4] It is more likely that the middle- and upper-class spinster was more conspicuous rather than more numerous.

The Victorians rediscovered the problem of the surplus female with the assistance of the statistical evidence provided by census material. The 1851 census caused considerable concern, revealing 1,407,225 spinsters aged between twenty and forty, and 359,969 confirmed 'old maids' over forty. In the years from 1851 to 1911, between twenty-nine and thirty-five per cent of all women aged twenty-five to thirty-five were unmarried; and between fifteen and nineteen per cent of women aged thirty-five to forty-five were unmarried. In 1871, 'for every three women over 20 who were wives, there were two who were widows or spinsters.' The problem of 'redundant women' was largely created by a natural demographic imbalance between the sexes. The 1851 census first highlighted the excess of females over males in the population, showing that for every one hundred males in England and Wales there were 104.2 females. This imbalance slowly but steadily increased after 1851, reaching 105.5 females to every hundred males by 1881, and 106.8 by 1911.[5]

The chief cause of this demographic imbalance was the higher death rate of males from birth onwards. Although more male babies were actually born between 1851 and 1871, this numerical advantage vanished by the end of the first year of life, and females outnumbered males in increasing proportions with each decade of life.[6] This preponderance of females existed in most European countries in the nineteenth century, and for the same reason. It is tempting to speculate that higher male mortality rates caused the excess of females reported in Europe since the sixteenth century; and that the imbalance was only corrected by advances in medical science after 1900 which increased the survival rate of male babies in the first year of life. Other factors contributed to the Victorian imbalance, though to a lesser degree than the high male death rates. Male emigration played a part, since three males emigrated for every one female, the figures in 1881 being 123,467 males to 40,840 females.[7] Males also served abroad in the armed forces and the colonial service. Among the upper classes there was also the increasing tendency to postpone marriage until the man's income allowed him to support a family at the appropriate social level. In his private actuarial survey of 1874, R. C. Ansell found that the average age at marriage for middle- and upper-class males who married between 1840 and 1870 was about thirty. This compared with the census figure of 27.9 years for the 1870s for the male population as a whole. Ansell found that over twenty per cent of the surveyed males married after the age of thirty-three, and his tables demonstrated the marked tendency to postpone marriage among the upper classes from 1840 onwards.[8]

Contemporary Victorian attitudes to spinsterhood established the cultural framework of rejection. Victorian social theorists, novelists and doctors reinforced ignorant social assumptions about the sexual, mental and physiological abnormality of spinsters. The radical publisher, Richard Carlile, was a progressive advocate of contraception, but even Carlile argued in 1838 that old maids belonged to 'a sort of sub-animal class', because deprivation of the passion of love produced 'a sad mental defect':

> It is a fact that can hardly have escaped the notice of anyone, that women who have never had sexual commerce begin to droop when about twenty-five years of age, that they become pale and languid, that general weakness and irritability, a sort of restless, nervous fidgettyness takes possession of them, and an absorbing process goes on, their forms degenerate, their features sink, and the peculiar character of the old maid becomes apparent.[9]

It was commonly believed that the sexually frustrated spinster was especially liable to hysteria, despite the opinion of some doctors that women lacked sexual feelings.[10] In the second half of the nineteenth century, the prolific writings of Herbert Spencer influenced social theorists and reflected contemporary prejudices. The contradictions in Spencer's arguments about unmarried women illustrate the inconsistencies in Victorian attitudes:

> The not infrequent occurrence of hysteria and chlorosis shows that women, in whom the reproductive function bears a larger ratio to the totality of the functions than it does in men, are apt to suffer grave constitutional evils from that incompleteness of life which celibacy implies.[11]

The arguments of writers like Spencer and Carlile re-inforced the resistance to spinsterhood of even the most intelligent females. Marion Ashton and Beatrice Potter, like Mary Gladstone, belonged to that large group of women who reluctantly resigned themselves to spinsterhood because they did not marry until their thirties. Women were considered 'on the shelf' if they were not married by their late twenties, even though the census statistics did not justify this common assumption. In 1889, Marion Ashton exulted that her unexpected marriage to James Bryce, at the age of thirty-six, would release her from the empty, repressed life of the single woman:

> I feel now (and have felt for a long time) as if my nature had been stunted and as if something that might have grown and expanded under other conditions was simply existing, would gradually wear out like my body, shrivel and grow old and decay.

The deepest pain in her 'struggle for duty' as a spinster 'was this load of self-repression' combined with the knowledge that half of her nature was being rejected. Had she remained unmarried, she felt she would have become cynical, hard and self-contained.[12] Beatrice Potter grew increasingly lonely as her seven elder sisters married, delighted not to waste their lives in 'single blessedness'. She was also somewhat resentful at being left 'quite alone to the home work and solitude'. For a decade before her marriage in 1892 to Sidney Webb she acted as her widowed father's hostess and companion. After her father's stroke in 1885 Beatrice sank into a near suicidal depression: 'Despair . . . Eight and twenty! living a life without hope . . . The position of unmarried daughter at home is an unhappy one even for a strong woman.' She dreaded the harmful effects of continued spinsterhood; the increasing numbers of women 'to whom the matrimonial career is shut' developed abnormal masculine qualities which were 'exceedingly pathetic'. The prospect of powerful women behaving like men horrified her: 'a female Gladstone may lurk in the dim vistas of the future'.[13]

Respectable middle-class Victorian spinsters were expected to direct their excess energies and frustrations into religion and philanthropy. Beatrice Potter feared that spinsterhood would starve the physical and emotional side of her nature: 'God knows celibacy is as painful to a woman (even from the physical standpoint) as it is to a man.' She recognized that if she remained a spinster, her sexual and emotional feelings 'must remain controlled and unsatisfied, finding their only vent in one quality of the phantom companion of the nethermost personality, religious exaltation'.[14] This was remarkably perceptive, anticipating Peter Cominos' modern explanation in terms of sexual sublimation through religion:

While gentlemen were urged to conquer their sexual instincts by complete sublimation through work, genteel women, barred from work and confined to the family circle, sublimated through religion, 'the only channel' through which the sexual emotions could be expressed 'freely without impropriety.' Women realized ideal-love in the religious sense.[15]

One other aspect of Victorian social thought which explains the restricted role of the spinster, was the belief in the natural separation of the spheres between the sexes. But the rationale for 'separate spheres' was based to a considerable degree on the female child-bearing role, which did not apply to spinsters. Yet the unmarried middle- and upper-class woman was restricted to the domestic sphere just as rigidly as her married sister. In many cases this meant subordination of the unmarried daughter to the will of the authoritarian father, especially if the mother had died: 'At least one [daughter] usually remained unmarried, the special servant for the father in his old age.'[16]

This concept of the spinster's primary duty was accepted unquestioningly by the most intelligent and able women. Frances Power Cobbe wrote in *The Duties of Women* in 1881 of the absolute obligation for daughters to care for their parents. In her own case, nursing her father for many years involved considerable personal sacrifice.[17] Beatrice Potter in 1883 rationalized her position as the eldest unmarried daughter, acting as mistress of her father's household after her mother's death:

It is almost necessary to the health of a woman, physical and mental, to have definite home duties to fulfil: details of practical management, and above all things, someone dependent on her love and tender care. So long as Father lives and his home is the centre for young lives, I have mission enough as a *woman*.[18]

Charlotte Brontë in the 1840s followed the same line of duty as Frances Cobbe and Beatrice Potter, trying to convince herself that 'the right path is that which necessitates the greatest sacrifice of self-interest'.[19] But Charlotte Brontë resented the frustration, loneliness and waste of her life in a remote village, doomed to care for a cantankerous father. Where Charlotte Brontë channelled her frustration into her novels, Lady Constance Lytton half a century later turned to the women's movement. Her earlier musical and artistic ambitions had been thwarted by the domestic demands of her parents on their spinster daughter. As late as the First World War, Vera Brittain still resented the expectation of subservient dependence at home 'which has always harassed the women now in their thirties and forties'.[20]

Victorian literary fiction is a rich source for stereotypes and assumptions about unmarried women. The dominant literary image of the spinster was victim and social failure. Victorian novels emphasized the sad fate of the ageing old maid, trapped in the parental home and treated like a dependent child until sour

middle age. The plight of Thackeray's Julia in *The Newcomes* was typical: 'Being always at home, and under her mother's eyes, she was the old lady's victim, her pin-cushion.' Mr Osborne in *Vanity Fair* tyrannized his middle-aged daughter, who became resigned to her fate as a 'lonely, miserable, persecuted, old maid'. Charlotte Brontë's personal anguish was revealed in *Shirley*, where she condemned the sheer waste of single women's lives, 'degenerating to sour old maids, envious, backbiting, wretched, because life is a desert to them'. Mrs Gaskell provided a rare portrait of a whole society of widows and spinsters in *Cranford*. Miss Matty's one chance of married happiness was sacrificed early on the altar of Cranford's concept of social respectability, leaving her with 'a mysterious dread of men and matrimony' as she joined other sad ladies suffering from repressed sexuality in a society without men. Even George Gissing's *The Odd Women*, with its emphasis on the independent new woman, provides ample evidence of the conventional stereotype of the spinster. The feminist Rhoda Nunn was well aware of the problems of the average spinster: 'A feeble, purposeless, hopeless woman . . . living only to deteriorate . . . due to the conviction that in missing love and marriage she had missed everything.'

Victorian social conventions and laws were based on the mistaken assumption that all women would marry. But, as Julia Wedgwood complained in 1869, 'women spend the best part of their lives in preparing for an event which may never happen.'[21] Charlotte Brontë's Caroline Helston protested in *Shirley*: 'what does it signify whether unmarried and never-to-be-married women are unattractive and inelegant, or not?' George Eliot, Dickens and Thackeray also ridiculed an education supposed to train spinsters for a life they were unable to lead. John Stuart Mill argued that the fundamental cause of the spinster problem lay in the defects of women's education; a single woman 'is felt both by herself and others to be a kind of excrescence on the surface of society, having no use or function or office there'.[22] Women without husbands were anomalies in a social system where marriage and motherhood were conceived to be the sole female vocations for middle- and upper-class women.

The following case studies suggest that the real problems of the spinster were rather different from those of the imaginary old maid portrayed by contemporary novelists and theorists. Harsh material considerations caused flesh and blood spinsters more suffering than sexual deprivation or 'premature physical decay'. They were usually financially dependent on male members of the family— often a sufficient explanation of their exploitation. Their social and economic position was exceptionally vulnerable, for they faced the possible loss of home, status and function in life with the death of a father or the marriage of a brother. Spinsters often had an ill-defined role in the family, with little recognition that they were individuals with interests, needs and identities of their own. The quality of the spinster's life varied with the stages in her life-cycle and also according to the nature of her familial relations. Angie Acland, for example, was contented in her earlier years, because of her affectionate relationship with her mother, but miserable during her subsequent years of service for an unappreciative father. The real hardship often came with bereavement of the parent and during the ageing process.

Three types of spinster emerge from this study. The majority accepted Victorian assumptions about single women and played the traditional role expected of them. These dutiful daughters were socially constrained and they tended to see themselves in terms of the stereotype, as passive, acquiescent and unhappy. The lives of the majority probably justified this poor self-image, though some, like the King sisters, did achieve a measure of contentment. There were extremes on either side of this stereotypical spinster. A tiny minority rebelled against the role which society and the family attempted to impose on them, and sought escape through invalidism, drugs or other desperate means which were often both self-destructive and disruptive of normal family life. At the other extreme, a rather larger minority had the capacity to transcend the stereotype of the unfortunate spinster. They carried out their domestic obligations efficiently, but also found fulfilment as independent 'new women'.

DUTIFUL DAUGHTERS: THE STEREOTYPICAL SPINSTERS

The stereotypical spinsters who acquiesced in their role will be examined first, using as case studies Sarah Acland, Elizabeth and Agnes King, Olive Maxse, Mary and Katharine Bryce, and Alice Balfour. The lives of Sarah Acland, the King sisters and Olive

Maxse illustrate the most common experience of such spinsters, caring for elderly parents over many years and losing their sole role in life when those parents died. Sarah Angelina Acland, known as 'Angie' by her family, was the only daughter of Sir Henry Wentworth Acland, first baronet and Regius Professor of Medicine at Oxford. Angie was born about 1840 into a large academic Oxford family, with a devoted mother and seven brothers. She had poor health from childhood, and also suffered from a fairly serious disability which left her lame, walking only with sticks. She was often sent away from Oxford as a child to climates more favourable for her health. It was not surprising that she remained single, since her poor health made her marital prospects bleak, and she was the only daughter.

After 1875 the happy family circle gradually collapsed, because of Mrs Acland's death and the sons' marriages. Angie's life grew emptier as her brothers left home and married. The great blow fell for Angie in 1878 with the death of her beloved mother. A year later she had morbid thoughts of following her: 'I miss her more and more, and shall be thankful if I may so do my work here that I may soon go to her.'[23] Her mother's death sealed Angie's fate. As the only daughter, she was now required to look after her father for the next twenty-two years until his death in old age. His health and comfort became the major considerations of her life, especially as she had promised her dying mother to 'do all in my power' for him.

Angie Acland's role was clearly defined from 1878 as her father's dutiful daughter, housekeeper and social secretary. She idolized her father, having immense admiration for his medical work and his academic reputation. But their relationship was formal, as if she were a business secretary rather than a daughter. He appeared to keep her at a distance as he went about his own busy life. Years later she recalled: 'As time went on I not only wrote out the cheques for [Father] to sign, but signed them all for him. My hands were full with the large and busy household and managing the stables.'[24] Her letters to Professor Acland always dealt first with his correspondence and appointments before she could 'trouble you with my affairs'. She consulted him on all decisions about her own movements, usually concluding, 'I hope you will think that all was done as you would have wished.'[25] She carefully compiled all the household accounts, sending them to her father for his correction and approval. Her tone was always subservient and submissive.

Angie's life was not happy, as her new sister-in-law, Caroline, recognized, when she offered to 'give you help and comfort and if it may be to brighten a little your life, which I well know is sad and difficult'.[26] Her father even played a part in dismissing Angie's personal maid, Marsh, for whom Angie had great affection. Angie was very dependent on 'Marshy' after her mother's death, confiding her few secrets to her. But Marsh left in 1880, despite Angie's plea to her father that he could still alter the decision, and that if Marsh went 'I think I should quite break down'. The loss to Angie was 'a real deep trial' and she resented her father's treatment of her faithful maid.[27]

The full recognition of the nature of spinsterhood came to Angie on the death of her father in 1900. He may not have made her happy, but he had given her life its purpose for twenty-two years. After the funeral Angie wrote to her brother William:

I shall never be the same again. I feel an old woman now that my only object in life is gone—and cannot imagine what I shall do—if I still have to live on. All my interest in life has so entirely gone during the long nursing of Father. My great comfort has been that he clung to me more and more to the end.[28]

William unwisely attempted to lift Angie out of her self-pity with a gentle reproach, provoking a sharp response from his sister: 'I do not think that I deserve your scolding or "think that things always go wrong". Of course you who have a comfortable home and a wife cannot the least realise what it is to lose Father and home and position in a moment.'[29] Angie felt uprooted at having to leave the old family home at sixty years of age and move to a cheaper house. Her physical ailments increased and she felt desperately lonely: 'I sometimes feel as if I could not be meant to live, circumstances all seem so against me.' She understood her main problem: 'No place can be happy which centres round self and I have nothing else round which to centre and no object in life.'[30] Fortunately her brothers helped her through the worst of the crisis, finding her a nurse-companion and giving her a £25 quarterly allowance. She also acquired some new sense of purpose through increasing involvement with the Acland Nursing Homes, though philanthropy could not entirely fill the void in her life.

Elizabeth and Agnes King were the spinster sisters of Margaret Gladstone, who died of puerperal fever in 1870. They shared Angie Acland's fate in that they devoted much of their lives to caring for elderly parents, but they escaped Angie's loneliness and frustration because they were clearly contented in each other's company. The King sisters were probably fairly typical spinsters, who only escaped the usual obscurity of such women because their niece happened to marry the Labour leader, Ramsay MacDonald. Their repressive, authoritarian upbringing drove their eldest sister, Margaret, to seek freedom in marriage, but the two younger girls were conditioned to stay at home with their parents, as old maids. The family had moved from London to Edinburgh in 1869, separating the two girls from their childhood friends and cousins. Agnes was fourteen and Elizabeth a few years older when their sister died the following year. From an early age they had to cope with their father's mental breakdown which started on his retirement in 1869. The Revd King's condition deteriorated rapidly, with the tragedy of his daughter's death in 1870 followed four years later by that of his son David at sea. Elizabeth King lamented that it was 'dreadful to witness his suffering' and despair. During these miserable years, Agnes and Elizabeth became more protective of their parents and 'so much use and comfort to them all at home'.[31] Even at the age of sixteen, Agnes was anxious about a very brief absence: 'I do not like the idea of you and Papa, neither of you very strong, without one of your children.'[32] Filial love and duty were powerful elements in the two daughters, supported by a deep religious faith. They had less spirit of independence than their sister Margaret, and the tragic circumstances tied them to the family home for life.

For twenty-six years after Margaret's death, they cared for both sick and elderly parents until Mrs King died in 1896. The surviving correspondence suggests that they accepted their spinster role with religious acquiescence, made easier by their affection for each other. They moved back to London in the 1870s to be near their childhood friends and their motherless niece, Margaret Gladstone. The devoted aunts found much pleasure in the time they spent with Margaret as she grew up, and later with her children. They lived on a small private income, Agnes passing the time painting pictures and gardening, Elizabeth attending classes in cabinet making, and both engaged in charitable work. In middle age the sisters increasingly fitted the stereotype of the fussy, ageing spinster, and their 'excessive self-absorption' bordered on rudeness.[33]

The love between the sisters made spinsterhood a tolerable state. Agnes was unable to cope with Elizabeth's prolonged final illness from 1911 to 1914, coinciding as it did with her niece's death after childbirth in 1911. The strain of nursing her beloved sister through an agonizing illness was too much. Inevitably she compared her own mental breakdown with that of her father forty years earlier, and like him she suffered a religious crisis. A series of 'prayers during the long struggle' revealed the intensity of her despair and grief at the impending separation from her sister: 'The trial I am going through is too great for me, my mind feels shaken from its foundation, and love, which has always been the mainspring of my life, love of God and love of my dear sister . . . seems drifting away.' She felt guilty about her suicidal thoughts, terrified her mind was going, and exhausted by insomnia and grief. She was unable to come to terms with her sister's 'great suffering', or the prospect of living without her: 'For more than fifty years my sister has filled [my thoughts]. Every joy has been a joy because it was a joy to her, every interest was an interest for and with her . . . I have no support and cannot stand alone.'[34] Elizabeth and Agnes King were more fortunate than most other spinsters who sacrificed themselves for their parents. After their parents' deaths they were content in each other's company and had sufficient means to live an independent life. Agnes's grief at Elizabeth's death was closer to that of a widow who had lost a husband, though the widow's social status would have been higher and she would probably have been able to transfer her affections to her children and a wider circle of friends.

Olive Maxse, elder daughter of Admiral Frederick Augustus Maxse, was another spinster who lived out the social stereotype. Olive's parents were separated in 1877, and Olive was the only one of the four children to remain unmarried. Her elder brother, Ivor, had a distinguished military career, while Leo became editor of the *National Review*. Olive's sister, Violet, married Lord Salisbury's son, Lord Edward Cecil, in 1894, and moved into higher echelons of society. Olive was left keeping house and caring for her father. The family papers reveal only fleeting glimpses of her life. She was sent to a boarding school and then to Paris, partly because the parental separation created an unsettled home life. Olive studied music in Paris for three years and declined to be presented at Court in London or to participate in the usual round of balls and parties. Instead, she chose to spend the years after her eighteenth birthday working at the piano in Paris.[35]

In the 1890s Olive was obliged to take on the traditional role of the spinster, as her father's health was declining and her sister and brothers were married. She nursed her father until his death in 1900, and cared for her ageing mother who lingered until 1918. Her small world was shattered by her father's death in 1900. Her loneliness and despair were much greater than her siblings', who had families to share their grief. Olive told Violet she was 'utterly heartbroken . . . I have lost everything . . . I cannot believe or think he is gone.'[36] Even before this crisis, she had been preoccupied with her own health as well as her parents'. She had suffered numerous unspecified illnesses which had necessitated water cures in Germany. Her father's death intensified her hypochondria, as her sister-in-law, Katherine Maxse, explained to Violet:

[Olive] is in the state that if amused and interested she becomes perfectly well at once—if with family alone and bored—or with nothing much going on she gets ill at once and will do nothing . . . I know it is a very common form for girls hysteria to take—and the Drs say there need be no alarm—unless she is so bored as to fancy herself really ill—when she might create it—This makes it clear how *fatal* it is for her to be alone with us or your Mother.[37]

Three months later, Frances Horner regretted that Olive had none of the 'fire of life . . . I tried my best to persuade her to go out . . . but she doesn't rush to meet the unknown a bit ever'.[38] There the evidence ends, though Olive remained a spinster until her death in 1955. She cared for her mother for the next eighteen years, and, as the adoring aunt, she enjoyed looking after Violet's two children while her sister was in Africa. Otherwise, the prognosis for Olive was poor; she had too many of the symptoms of the frustrated spinster, lonely and unhappy in a role she was unable to alter or transcend.

The Bryce sisters and Alice Balfour also fit the stereotype of the Victorian spinster, but in one significant respect they were more unusual than the women examined so far. Their lives of service were dedicated to their brothers, rather than their parents, and their brothers were the focus of their existence. After their father's death in 1877, Mary and Katharine Bryce transferred their affections to James, their younger brother. He became Regius Professor of Civil Law at Oxford in 1870, and ten years later began a long career in Parliament, winning a ministerial position in 1886. The two sisters doted on James, who was a surrogate husband to them both. They never married, despite social opportunities in their earlier years, and they clearly assumed that their brothers, James and Annan, would stay single also. Mary, as the elder sister, kept house at 35 Bryanston Square in London, and acted as hostess for her brothers. The sisters' letters to James might be mistaken for those of a wife, with many expressions of affection, as in 1887: 'Have we not much to be thankful for in our love for each other increasing as the years go on. My loving wishes dear one.' They constantly fussed over his welfare: 'take great care of yourself—of cold and getting out of railway carriage [sic] . . . do be particular about tidiness dearest.'[39]

The sisters also acted as social and business secretaries to James, managing his affairs and providing encouragement for his political and literary aspirations. They were delighted when in 1880 the news came that 'the Dear *Member*' had won his first seat, and were highly ambitious for his political future. They were concerned that his lecture tours abroad might endanger his political career. In December 1883, Katharine urged him to return from America as soon as possible, 'to make a noise for a week or two . . . on these burning questions of housing of poor etc. . . . You must keep in with the people down there.'[40] Mary meanwhile encouraged him to ingratiate himself with Gladstone by writing a book about America, which Gladstone said was needed just then: 'I mean to manage that you shall write it . . .' She was true to her word. Five years later she was busy organizing the publication of *The American Commonwealth* with Macmillan, and arranging to submit the book for a competition, and for A. V. Dicey to review it in *The Times*.[41]

The lives of the two sisters disintegrated with the unexpected late marriages of both brothers in 1889. By this time their beloved James was fifty-one and they were shattered by his marriage, even more than by Annan's. In January 1889 they were displaced by Annan's wife, Violet, as the new mistress of 35 Bryanston Square.

Violet was at first deceptively submissive, and Mary reported to James that 'Violet seems inclined to put confidence in me and consults me about everything.' But signs of tension existed already: 'Kath and I are in the studio all day and back drawing-room in the evening as we only meal with them.'[42] Three months later, the problems created by three mistresses in one household intensified. Katharine complained to James: 'I don't think Violet is very satisfactory, but I never had very much confidence in her. She is moody, and wants to get us all out of the way I think.'[43]

Unfortunately for the spinster sisters, James also deserted them for marriage only six months after Annan. Though they found Marion more acceptable than Violet, the sisters clearly could not cope with the collapse of their settled lives and went into a depression. By the end of 1889, family unity was completely disrupted and the spinster sisters left the family home. Only hints of the terrible rifts were recorded in their correspondence. Mary mentioned 'an unpleasant time' at Bryanston Square before they left, and feared that 'Annan will say all sorts of things about us which it would only vex us to hear.' Mary claimed that she restrained herself and said 'nothing against Violet except that I could not arrange the home matters with her for I found her manner tried me.' When James reproached the sisters in December for their behaviour, even threatening to cease communications, Mary replied:

While naturally shrinking from additional pain I have yet no wish to put myself out of your life. It is only that I realize more fully than you could do the new order of things and the necessity in the nature of things for the difference between the past and the present.[44]

Six months later, when jewellery disappeared from the family home at Bryanston Square, Violet convinced Annan that Mary had taken it out of spite. This led to a final breach between the Annan Bryces and the two sisters, and strained their relations with James.

The two sisters never recovered from this double shock. The transformation in their lives was immense and, already in their forties, they were unable to adjust. Their interest and sense of value in life had previously come vicariously through their brothers. But now Violet had displaced them as mistress of the household, and Marion took over their role as manager of James's academic and political affairs. Mary wrote sadly to James in December 1889, reminding him of their lifetime 'of perfect love and trust' together, accepting that the expression of his affection must be altered by his marriage, and confessing to 'torturing thoughts . . . that I have lived too long'. Six months later she sought solace from despair in religion:

Certainly life has lost for me much that made it not only sweeter but better for one's moral nature. And it is worse now than if it had come earlier when one had years to look forward to—a future in which the past could in some measure have been forgotten. But happily one has some work which can yet perhaps be done and if only one could more vividly and constantly realize God's presence and his purpose being worked out tho it is in much tribulation, the pain and sense of loss and of failure wd. not be so great as it often is.[45]

After 1889 their lives were like those of many other lonely, ageing spinsters. The change was reflected in their letters, which became far shorter and duller, with little to record and small reason for history to remember them. Mary became a companion nurse to her invalid mother until her mother's death in 1903, filling her letters with the smallest details of her mother's ailments. Mary took herself off alone for an annual holiday in Suffolk each year, which she devoted mainly to golf and cycling. She busied herself in committee work, joining the Executive Committee of the Women's Liberal Federation, and followed every step of James's career with letters of encouragement. Mary's response to the crisis was the more positive, aided by better health and fortified by her religious convictions. Katharine, by contrast, adopted the role of the invalid, though the precise medical problem was unclear. She frequently went off to take 'bath cures' abroad or to recuperate at the seaside, trying to give some meaning to an otherwise empty life.

Alice Balfour's case is sadder than that of the Bryce sisters. Her devotion to her brother was more obsessive, and her own talents were greater. Arthur Balfour never married, to release his sister from her chosen bondage, so she only ever attained prominence as the sister and housekeeper of A. J. Balfour, philosopher, scholar and Conservative prime minister. After their father's death in 1856, the three daughters and five sons were brought up at Whittingehame, the family estate in Scotland, by their domineering mother. Alice was a casualty of her mother's strict evangelical Christianity and concentration on her male offspring. The three sisters disliked each other and were 'unanimous in affection only to Arthur, Frank and Gerald—the three sons who did well in the world'.[46] Alice became mistress of Whittingehame in 1876, after the death of her mother and the brilliant marriages of her two sisters. She worshipped her eldest brother, Arthur, from childhood. He came of age in 1869, with a large fortune and abundant charm—the centre of a dazzling intellectual, social and political world. Arthur never married, though he was surrounded by beautiful and talented women who easily came under his spell. Alice's open adoration irritated her brother; on one occasion, when Alice dressed to please him, Arthur put up his eyeglass for scrutiny and pronounced: 'Alice, you look vulgar.'[47]

Alice Balfour acted as surrogate wife and general factotum for her famous brother. She had to manage the huge house at Whittingehame, with the two large families of their brothers, Eustace and Gerald, usually in residence, accompanied by their eight children and a constant flow of guests, besides the numerous servants. She also had to organize the whole household for the annual moves to London for parliamentary sessions, and entertain politicians while in London. All this was a great burden because Alice disliked household management and had to work very hard at it. Her excessively strict regime and her tendency to bossiness were possibly over-compensation for lack of natural gifts as a housekeeper, combined with a sense of resentment and insecurity. Her jealous possessiveness of her brother made his friends feel unwelcome at Whittingehame, and they found the household ruled by Alice oppressive.[48] Beatrice Webb, on the other hand, analysed the situation with considerable insight on a brief visit to Whittingehame in 1906. She described Alice as 'one of those sweet tempered, gentle-natured beings who are made to be oppressed— the slave of everyone but the *devoted* slave of her great brother.'[49]

Alice's life was made unbearable by an open feud with her suffragist sister-in-law, Lady Frances Balfour, who was unhappily married to Alice's alcoholic brother Eustace. A direct clash of personalities was intensified by the rivalry between the two women for Arthur's affection. The spinster sister, as his housekeeper, saw him more frequently, but was in a vulnerable and somewhat humiliating position. The sister-in-law received more real affection from him, which helped compensate for the inadequacies of her marriage to his brother. As Beatrice Webb noted: 'There is warfare between Alice and Lady Frances from "Prince Arthur's" soul to the question whether or not there should be a fire in September.'[50] Quarrels frequently erupted because Alice loved children and was accused of meddling with the upbringing of Frances's five. Arthur attempted to ignore the continual undercurrents of hostility within the family circle, unless they erupted into full-scale hostilities. The climax came in 1897, when Frances accused Alice of interfering in her husband's affairs. Alice was charged with 'disgusting conduct' and 'lack of breeding' because she 'cross-examined' the doctor about her brother's alcoholism. By Frances's account, Alice had been 'hunting Eustace with missives about his debts and the quantities of spirits drunk at Whittingehame'.[51] There followed a family crisis, described by A. J. Balfour as 'an outbreak which would do credit to a fishwife'. The effect of Frances on Alice was 'like a hot iron approaching a raw place', and Arthur finally issued his sister-in-law with an ultimatum. If Frances could not live in peace with Alice, then her family must visit Whittingehame only as occasional guests rather than habitual residents: 'By "peace" it must be distinctly understood that I do not mean "armed neutrality". Alice is your hostess: it is partly by her money that the Whittingehame life is rendered possible. For both reasons she has a right to cordial civility.' Arthur added that Alice was the chief victim of Frances's attacks and that she was not capable of fighting her own battles.[52]

The situation did not improve beyond 'armed neutrality' in the years that followed. In 1905, Betty Balfour reported from Whittingehame to her husband Gerald that Frances's 'presence with Alice destroys all sense of ease and comfort, and I feel as if the Whittingehame burden had been again hitched to our backs.' A few days later, Betty reported 'Frances in a very bad mind—generally abusive . . . in her fiercest mood about Alice . . .' Naturally the atmosphere in the house was 'odious'.[53] The feud between the two women continued after Eustace's death, with Frances expecting special treatment as a widow, though she had shown none to Alice as a spinster.

Not surprisingly, Alice was often miserably unhappy in a role which did not suit her, made worse by the violent family quarrels. She clearly envied other women their married state, as the letter she sent on Mary Gladstone's engagement in 1885 suggested: 'It is such a comfort to have one's duty in life put so plainly before one as yours probably will be in the future. It is one of the drawbacks of remaining unmarried that one has not those plain duties put before one.'[54] Alice would not have been human, given her love of children, had she not envied Betty and Frances their children. She also resented being taken for granted as housekeeper and hostess. The continual friction with Frances depressed her so badly that she gave in to 'great fits of gloom, especially at meal times'. In 1887 she unwisely confided her sense of failure to Lady Haddington, saying that she 'knew she bored everybody and [that] life was not worth having for her'. But the crux of Alice's despair was her complaint that she 'never got eno' love from those she cared for'. This came at a time when Alice was evidently getting on Arthur's nerves, and he was showing his irritation. Lady Haddington was too close to the truth for comfort when she told Alice that she had 'wasted her affection in a kind of idolatry'.[55] Mary Drew understood all of this when she wrote to Arthur Balfour, after a Whittingehame visit in 1899, asking him to show Alice more affection:

Alice's life is a grind and her adoring love for you is not enough in itself to give her the amount of happiness to which her goodness and unselfishness entitle her, . . . it *wd*. be *bliss*, if you could manage to sometimes give her a word of loving kindness and appreciation e.g. a little extra kiss, or touch, or word, or gift, showing that you think of her . . . she is far too loyal ever to complain, but her life is dust and ashes for 2 reasons, Frances' brutality and your coldness. You never write or utter to her except on business, and yr. time is too full to think much of her and she wears yr. mother's glorious jewels, and has plenty of money and luxuries and comforts and these things rather shut our eyes to the barrenness of her heart.[56]

Alice was a talented woman with pursuits of her own, but she was incapable of making a bold move towards an independent and happier life. She was a gifted artist who exhibited her paintings at the Royal Academy. She also took a keen and knowledgeable interest in music, and in natural history. Philanthropy provided some outlet for her maternal instincts and evangelical faith. She showed much concern for the welfare of the Whittingehame tenants, and shared Octavia Hill's belief in the beneficial effects of 'proper supervision' of the respectable poor in well-organized workhouses. Her considerable administrative skills and numerous contacts were put to good use in her foundation of a Nursing Association in East London in 1898 for the training of nurses. But her own talents and interests were usually subordinated to those of others. Maggie Cowell-Stepney, another sympathetic friend who understood the trials of women without husbands, sent Mary Drew a sensitive analysis of Alice's plight in 1904:

Oh yes we guessed it all, long before we went to Whittingehame—, though *then*, the desperate tragedy of it, made all one's blood boil. I often long for her to throw it all up, and him, for herself and her own soul, (as Ibsen advises). She has an enchanting life all ready for her—a real Artist's life—her painting is *professionally* good, and in her own line she would be in the first rank. But would she be happy away from him, and could she give him up, except to a wife?—If only he married happily perhaps she might.[57]

Alice never made this bid for personal fulfilment, and was listed in *Who's Who 1916* only as the 'sister of Rt. Hon. A. J. Balfour, M.P.'

The majority of middle- and upper-class Victorian and Edwardian spinsters accepted their lot. After all, their real choices were very limited. The degree of unhappiness they experienced depended on their individual circumstances and personality, but few of them appear to have been really contented and fulfilled.

DESPERATE REBELS: THE ESCAPIST SPINSTERS

Two minority groups, however—the independent 'new women' and the 'desperate rebels'—were not willing or able to accept the traditional role and status of the spinster in the appropriate submissive manner. The rebels could not tolerate spinsterhood and sought escape, demonstrated in the most positive and courageous form by emigrant gentlewomen like Mary Taylor.[58] But the forms of escape open to spinsters who accepted the authority of the paterfamilias, and who were trapped by family expectations and obligations, were necessarily limited. They could only protest through invalidism, hysteria, religious fanaticism and other types of self-destruction. For a number of these women, it was a short step from obsessive hypochondria to excessive dependence on drugs and alcohol.

The spinsters who sought escape experienced profound role conflict and used desperate measures to resolve a situation they could not tolerate. Helen Gladstone and Evelyn Murray retreated into invalidism. This was not uncommon for gifted Victorian spinsters, trapped in a social situation which prohibited the use of their talents. Alice James, for example, sister of the famous brothers, Henry and William, spent her forty-three years in psychosomatic invalidism. It can be argued that hysteria, chlorosis, and other classic Victorian female diseases sometimes arose out of role conflict, creating an alternative existence for women who found the conventional role impossible.[59] Helen Gladstone and Evelyn Murray both experienced harsh treatment because they refused to conform to their families' notions of respectable spinster behaviour. They needed a challenging role and occupation in life, but with no legitimate outlet for their intellect and emotions, they found ultimate refuge in invalidism, drugs and exile.

W. E. Gladstone's sister, Helen, was the daughter of a wealthy Liverpool merchant, and grew up in a family which regarded the frail invalid as its model of the ideal woman. Although Helen was born in 1814, several decades earlier than most other women in this book, she merits inclusion because of the intrinsic interest of her story, as well as for the parallels with Evelyn Murray half a century later. Helen was the last of six children, born when John and Anne Gladstone were middle-aged and had lost interest in young offspring, except for the precocious William, Helen's senior by four years. Mrs Gladstone was an intensely pious evangelical woman with a morbid obsession with death and suffering, and a narrow philosophy of man's natural depravity and the need for self-discipline. She was also a neurotic hypochondriac who gradually became a full-time invalid, served by a devoted husband and family. Helen was increasingly isolated and neglected in a home dominated by illness. She spent the years from 1823 to 1829 watching her beloved elder sister, Anne, die slowly of tuberculosis. When the two eldest sons also showed symptoms of the disease, Mrs Gladstone had a genuine outlet for her obsession with disease and death. Meanwhile, Helen received only sporadic education from inadequate governesses, while her three brothers were away at school and university. Helen had grown close to William while Anne was dying, but afterwards Helen was demoralized by William's unfavourable comparisons between herself and the idealized dead sister.[60]

In these circumstances, it was scarcely surprising that Helen gradually joined the family invalids, in search of attention. Though apparently a healthy child, she had been treated as delicate from birth. By the age of sixteen she was suffering from an unspecified illness, involving spasms and bowel problems and frequent consultations with doctors. She was dosed with medicine of all descriptions, but only laudanum provided relief. Laudanum, or tincture of opium, was widely used, habit-forming and dangerous. But the illness gave Helen a role in her family, and at last she became the focus of her mother's attention. She recovered briefly in 1835 to perform the first positive role of her life in caring for her dying mother, but rapidly reverted to invalidism afterwards. At the age of twenty-one she was the only child still living with the elderly father in his rambling new home at Fasque in Scotland. She was isolated in a splendid prison with no friends, little prospect of marriage and no hope of a career. The consumption of laudanum increased and she spent many hours of her futile days in bed. William criticized his sister's behaviour as self-indulgent and wilful, prescribing a rigid regime of self-discipline and prayer. He failed utterly to realize that a highly intelligent woman without a family or a function might share his own need for a worthwhile occupation.

From the age of twenty-four Helen rebelled more openly against her family, which was insensitive to her frustration, and made no effort to help her find any kind of positive role in life. In 1838, her father had the sense to send her abroad in an attempt to remove her from a destructive situation. However, she used her first freedom from family supervision to fall in love with a man who would have been considered most unsuitable by her family. But the parents of the Russo-Polish aristocrat of Greek Orthodox faith themselves considered the marriage unsuitable and the brief love affair was vetoed. Helen again became a recluse at Fasque, with no interest in life. She was an advanced opium addict by her mid-twenties, eating little and sleeping most of each day, regarded by William and her father as almost depraved. Her moody silence was broken only by quarrels over her extravagance on clothing. Helen was desperate: 'I am as a dead branch . . . offering no-one fruit or flower, for I am more beaten down than in any former illness.'

In 1842, she chose the most extreme form of defiance, by adopting the Roman Catholic faith, which William detested. William was self-righteous and shocked, not least by the press reports of 'the record of our shame', and had no appreciation of the support and consolation which the Catholic ritual provided for Helen. To his credit, John Gladstone refused to follow William's advice to expel Helen from the family home, but her expenditure and way of life at Fasque were more rigidly circumscribed. An attempt to establish a life for herself in Germany in 1844 ended in hysterical emotional scenes followed by a coma induced by a laudanum overdose. Presumably she could not cope alone, given her addiction, and the consequence was another emotional crisis designed to regain attention. Despite the strictest confinement on her return home, the family failed to keep opium and alcohol away from Helen, and her condition deteriorated, with symptoms of 'clenched hands, locked jaw, and inability to speak except in hysterical bursts'. Severe emotional scenes accompanied visits for medical treatment, reaching a climax in Edinburgh in 1848, when Cardinal Wiseman appeared to perform a miraculous cure with a sacred relic. William was inevitably profoundly disturbed by the public notoriety which Helen's cure achieved. The sustained improvement over the next three years resulted from continual attendance during her father's final illness, which for the second time in her life gave her a positive role as a nurse.

Helen was thirty-seven on her father's death in 1851, and she went almost immediately to Rome. She even had an audience with the Pope and requested him to pray for William. By 1855 she was in the care of a religious community in Rome, having relapsed once more into heavy dependence on opium. She finally became a professed nun—the ultimate challenge to her High Church brother. Helen became more stable during the last twenty years of her life. For some time in the 1860s she returned to London, reduced her drug intake, became cautiously reconciled to her brothers and rejoiced when William became prime minister. She died in 1880 in Cologne, aged sixty-five. Even at her death-bed, William tried to shake her conversion, convinced that it had been an opium-induced self-delusion. She saw herself as a victim of her male-dominated family, unable to perform the role expected of her as a female, but equally incapable of finding an alternative role which could provide fulfilment. Her rebellion against her fate took the form of opium addiction, while she sublimated her intellectual and emotional drives through religious exaltation. The insecurity of her life was probably determined as an adolescent. It was too late for her to learn to become independent afterwards, especially given the problems of her drug addiction and the self-righteous intolerance of William.

Fifty years later, the situation was no better for Evelyn Murray, one of seven children born to the seventh Duke of Atholl, and the last of three girls. The family papers reveal nothing about Evelyn till 1890, when she was twenty-two, and experiencing major problems with her health and her parents. She was reported as being very 'pulled down' because she had refused to take medicine, and then starved herself for a week. It may even have been a case of anorexia nervosa, in rebellion against her parents. Two years later, she was evidently suffering from 'persecution mania' after a nervous breakdown, following a dangerous case of diphtheria.[61] She was treated for a grave nervous disorder, which the doctors seem to have diagnosed as neurasthenia, an illness increasingly common in young, single upper-class women. As Lorna Duffin recently noted of neurasthenia: 'the diagnosis closely matched the dilemma which was faced by these women in their struggle to reconcile their desire for independence with the demands of family and society that they fulfil the conventional expectations of the female role.'[62]

Evelyn's parents were well aware that her hostility to them contributed to her illness. The Duchess admitted that 'if it had not been for me she could nearly have got over it'. Evelyn was an intelligent, strong-minded girl who had struggled for years against her parents to attain some sense of her own value and identity as a person. Her rebellion took the form of 'a sullen frame of mind' towards her mother, disregarding her parents' wishes, sitting up almost all night and 'remaining out after dark hours'. In 1892, the Duchess was again exasperated that her daughter failed to take advantage of the London Season: 'She is restless. She avoids Balls and goes to Battersea museum almost every day. She does not like riding out in a carriage. When will it end?'[63] The conflict between mother and daughter, and the regime imposed on the twenty-four-year-old Evelyn at Blair Castle, was illuminated further by an ultimatum from the Duchess to Evelyn in June 1892, establishing the conditions for Evelyn's continued residence at home: 'I *must* have *respect* and *obedience*. I do not want to stop your Gaelic or any of your amusements if you will do them in moderation and not neglect other duties . . . if you come home you will quite make up your mind to do *all* I wish in everything including your dress.'[64] Lady Evelyn failed to conform to her parents' stereotype of appropriate female behaviour. She was neither passive, docile nor obedient. She preferred reading late at night, visiting museums and learning Gaelic, to the social round that would win her a suitable husband. Evelyn's case was not helped at this point by the failure of her two elder sisters to marry. All three daughters were becoming something of a liability in a family where the future of the three more precious sons took priority.

The Duke and Duchess responded to Evelyn's prolonged ill health with anger and resentment, treating it as part of her general insubordination. Their reaction was to send her abroad, to relieve them of the problem. Evelyn resentfully opposed the first banishment in 1891: 'As you are so anxious to be rid of me almost the whole year round, you need never see me except at meals unless you wish and I will keep out of Mama's way as much as possible.' Her father's authoritarian reply to this hurt appeal for attention revealed a total lack of sensitivity: 'When your father decides to provide for you elsewhere for a time, you cannot insist on remaining at home.' Her mother complained that 'all this has caused me to take bad diarrhoea'.[65] Her grandmother wrote a harsh letter to Evelyn in exile:

If a daughter is a source of discomfort at home (instead of happiness and delight as *you might be*) a Father can send her away and she must live wherever he provides a home for her. It cannot be expected that you can be placed in a home as comfortable or congenial as the one from which you have by your own conduct exiled yourself . . . It is not for your own pleasure that you are living abroad. Your eventual return home will I believe depend on your own frame of mind. Should you come to see how undutiful, and unkind and cruel you have been to your mother—you should then write straight to her.[66]

This was hardly a wise letter to a lonely girl whom they thought to be suffering from a nervous breakdown.

An attempt at reconciliation failed in the following year, indicating once more that Evelyn was not prepared to live at Blair Castle on her parents' terms. By December 1892, the Duchess

accepted the doctor's 'sensible' view that Evelyn should 'go on a
long voyage in a sailing ship to Australia/New Zealand in charge of
a competent person—he says an entire change would benefit her
health'. If Evelyn objected, the doctor felt this voyage should be
enforced for medical reasons.[67] Emigration to Australia might
have been good for Evelyn, if only to give her a chance to establish
there a life of her own. Instead, she was sent into exile in Belgium,
knowing this time that she would never return to Blair Castle.

   Lady Evelyn remained in lonely exile in Belgium for the rest of
her life. Her identity was kept a close secret, and the few people
she ever met believed she was an orphan with no near relatives.
Constant reports were sent back to her parents by a 'lady
companion', and by a doctor who was treating her for insanity,
until he finally declared her cured. Evelyn refused to communicate
with either parent, writing only to her cousin, Emily Murray
Macgregor, and, from 1900, to her younger brother Hamish. She
even had a protracted dispute with her father over the extent of
her financial support: 'I wonder my father sent me away if he did
not wish to pay for it—perhaps it is too long ago for him to
remember that I was forced.' It was finally settled in 1896 that
Evelyn was to receive no more than £25 per month under any
circumstances, with an extra £5 to pay for her companion.[68] Even
as late as 1904 she protested against the Duke's continued demand
for receipts for payment of her companion: 'It seems a very
childish and unnecessary proceeding and was I suppose instituted
as an annoyance . . . as I am hardly a child by this time and on the
road to 40, I can surely be supposed to arrange my affairs at my
own discretion.' Evelyn arranged in 1907 that she should never be
required to communicate with him again and that he should be
contacted only on her death.[69]

   The futility and emptiness of Evelyn's existence were part of her
martyrdom. In 1899 she told her cousin Emily: 'As I always think
of the past everything here almost seems like a dream. It is almost
as if I wasn't living. Everything is so completely indifferent to me
that I hardly notice how the time passes.' She thought continually
about her estranged family at Blair and brooded on the injustice of
her father's treatment:

I have spent [my life] entirely wrapped up in my own thoughts and quite
oblivious to my surroundings, perhaps the fact of being completely unable

to take an interest in anything or anybody has saved me from falling into temptations into which many others would have fallen who have been left entirely alone and friendless at the age I was then—23 . . . my life might have been completely ruined in a very different way and I have only myself to thank that it has not been so. Papa knows enough of the world to know this and that is *one* of the reasons I could *never* write to him again not even now. A girl can have her life ruined when it would be nothing for a man and just these years between 20 and 30 should be the best of one's life.[70]

Evelyn's existence was far removed from such moral degradation. Her interests and human contacts were minimal. In 1911 she commented that 'my occupations are music and embroidery on a large frame', and she gave part of her allowance to the destitute. The only object of her affection was a pet parrot, her constant companion for sixteen years. She feared it was dying in 1910: 'My parrot is to me what an only child could be to someone else.' From 1899 her correspondence revealed the wish to die: 'I do so often feel as if I should just like to lie down and shut my eyes and die like that.'[71]

A final reflection on the tragedy and wasted potential of Evelyn Murray's life is provided by a letter to her brother in 1900:

If one stakes everything on one ideal as I did, if one has to give it up suddenly one's life is a blank. But for a boy it is very different, you will see more of the world than I had the opportunity of doing and will not have your mind warped by having to live in one groove.[72]

Evelyn initially had literary or possibly academic aspirations, which were thwarted by her parents; her rebellion was negative and finally self-destructive. Even though she was exiled, she made no effort to create a new life of her own, but lived within the confines of genteel martyrdom and neurasthenia.

THE TRANSITION TO THE NEW WOMEN

The final category of spinsters was a rather larger minority with the capacity to transcend the stereotypical role. They carried out their familial obligations efficiently, but also found fulfilment as independent 'new women' or 'bachelor women'. Most women in this category were exceptional in their circumstances, intellectual gifts and inner resources. Some were well endowed mentally, others had the advantagé of a good school education and a degree of financial independence, and most were fortunate in that domestic demands did not consume the greater part of their mature lives. The leaders of the women's movement who remained single naturally fell into this category. Constance Lytton, for example, turned to the suffrage movement as an outlet for her frustrations against society, and Emily Davies found fulfilment through the women's education movement. Others found a role in the more traditional female sphere of philanthropy. From the 1880s the women's movement at last made it easier for a minority of able and independent single women to find satisfaction in a career outside domesticity.

A growing body of literature from the 1860s onwards argued that single women had the capacity and the need to lead worthwhile lives. Frances Power Cobbe in 1862 contended that single women must learn to support themselves in independent lives of dignity. Josephine Butler in 1869 refused to admit that it was every woman's duty to marry: 'There is abundance of work to be done which needs men and women detached from domestic ties; our unmarried women will be the greatest blessing to the community when they cease to be soured by disappointment.' Harriet Martineau argued that women must become independent for practical, economic and demographic reasons. Barbara Leigh Smith believed that women must be trained for work and not expect to be supported by men 'if they are to stand as dignified, rational beings before God'.[73] By the 1890s numerous tributes were made to the achievement of single women, even by writers not entirely sympathetic to the goals of the women's movement. Lady Jeune noted in 1898 that modern thought and education had raised women intellectually, enabling thousands to choose their own careers and successfully pursue independent personal goals. Stephen Gwynn commented in the same year that ambitious women could now choose between marriage and a career, promoting the growth of a new class of 'ladies who live entirely by themselves and work for their living'.[74] George Gissing in *The Odd Women* in 1893 depicted Rhoda Nunn as the champion of the surplus women, aiming to train them 'for the world's work'.

Such writing provided support for a growing minority of courageous and independent 'new women'. Women in this category have already received attention because of the growing interest in the early leaders of the women's movement, such as Emily Davies and Frances Power Cobbe. The intention here is to consider briefly three women in these political families who fall within this category—Lady Gwendolen Cecil, Gladstone's daughter Helen, and Elizabeth Haldane. Lady Gwendolen is perhaps a borderline case in that her life essentially revolved around her famous father, but in some respects she was far more emancipated than most spinsters in political families. She was born in 1860 into an aristocratic family which respected individualism and eccentricity, even in its female members. Like most girls of her class, she was denied a formal education, despite her considerable intellectual and literary gifts. After her elder sister's marriage, when Gwendolen was twenty-three, she shared with her mother the responsibility of household and estate management at Hatfield, and there was no question of her leaving home. She was considered no great match, with her plain angular features and lack of interest in the doings of Society, and she made little effort to improve her chances of marriage. She was also assertive and self-opinionated—characteristics more readily appreciated by the Cecil family than most Edwardian husbands. Like all the Cecils, she preferred the company of her remarkable family to that of other people, so it was no great sacrifice to devote twenty years of adult life to her parents. If she suffered any emotional deprivation from single life at Hatfield, which seems unlikely, then it could be argued that her religious fervour provided the means of sublimation. But her correspondence suggests that she was somewhat cynical about love and marriage, and not strongly affected by sexual passion. There is no hint of sadness about her single state, rather a sense of relief at not being married.[75]

Spinsterhood conferred definite benefits on Gwendolen. As the daughter of the Marquis of Salisbury, leader of the Conservative Party and Prime Minister for many years, she had unusual advantages, which she exploited to the full. Like Gladstone's daughter, Mary, she had the extraordinary experience, for a Victorian female, of becoming confidential private secretary to the Prime Minister. She was exceptionally well informed about political affairs and could indulge her passion for politics in a family which included two prime ministers as well as several ministers and back-benchers. In a later generation she would probably have become an effective politician in her own right.

When Lord Salisbury died in 1903 she gained more personal and intellectual freedom, moving into a small 'spinster house' on the Hatfield estate. The major interest in her life became the official biography of her father—an arduous task, and considerable achievement, given the voluminous material and Gwendolen's lack of methodical training. Her other passions were philanthropy and architecture, which were united in her plans for building comfortable homes for old people, better mental hospitals and cheerful sanatoria for consumptives.

The life of Helen, eldest of Gladstone's three daughters, also revolved around the towering figure of her Prime Minister father. Earnest, reserved and deeply religious, she seems to have been even more overwhelmed by their formidable parents than were her sisters, with few friends, no formal education and little independent life outside the family routine. The situation changed dramatically in 1877 when Helen was twenty-eight, because the more extrovert younger sister, Mary, conceived her 'startling plan' that Helen should go to Newnham College, Cambridge. The arguments used to obtain parental consent reveal the limitations of Helen's previous life. She felt a great need of 'stirring up' through disciplined academic courses after many aimless years at home. Mary later reported to the family that Helen was transformed by Cambridge: 'her intellectual life is stimulated, her moral life strengthened and encouraged'.[76] The plan was so successful that in 1880 Helen became assistant to Eleanor Sidgwick, Vice-Principal of Newnham, and two years later succeeded her as Vice-Principal.

Cambridge provided personal fulfilment for Helen, but there was always a conflict with her view of her family duties. Mary accepted the full-time responsibility of caring for the 'Grand Old People' until her marriage in 1886, but she combined this with being her father's private secretary while he was Prime Minister. It was no great burden for Mary, who was a capable domestic manager and, like Gwendolen Cecil, delighted to indulge her passion for politics. But Helen worried in her early years at Newnham 'whether I ought to stay so much away from home', and she reiterated in several letters that 'if Mary was to marry or I was in any special way needed at home, I would give it up *at once*'.[77] The crisis occurred in 1886, when Mary unexpectedly married at the age of thirty-nine. Helen inherited primary responsibility for their parents and this involved far greater sacrifice for her than

Mary. Helen tried to respond unselfishly to Mary's marriage, but found the prospect of her new family responsibilities 'rather grim'. 'Home duties' were 'so pressing' that she made arrangements with Newnham 'for being a great deal at home', with the possibility of full retirement if necessary. The conflict of interests was intensified a few months later when Helen was invited to become the first Principal of the newly established Royal Holloway College, London. She agonized over the dilemma of career versus domestic responsibilities, circulating a memorandum to friends and relatives giving both sides of the case and requesting their views.[78] Nora Sidgwick was the only person to question Helen's assumption that a woman's primary moral obligation was to her parents, and the outcome was a foregone conclusion. Even Mary commented that, if Helen accepted the Royal Holloway post, 'it would be simply impossible for her to be much at home . . . she would be far more tied and bound than by most marriages'.[79] So Helen refused the Royal Holloway offer, and temporarily stayed on at Newnham with time off for 'home duties'.

Helen Gladstone felt obliged to make the personal sacrifice, even though she was much more effective and fulfilled at Newnham than in her filial capacity at Hawarden and Downing Street. She felt inadequate by comparison with Mary: 'I am not of much use to my Father while he is in office . . . I am not of any immense use to my Mother at any time, but at least I am available.'[80] She was bored by Society functions, found domestic duties tedious, and lacked Mary's organizing abilities on the home front. She tried to be a dutiful daughter, but she was temperamentally unable to transfer to her 'home duties' the independence and assurance she enjoyed at Newnham. Helen found the political responsibilities less of a strain, though she lacked Mary's natural flair and enthusiasm for politics. She took over Mary's work as personal secretary to the Liberal leader in 1886, and was 'a perfect tower of strength' in helping her elderly parents through the 1886 Home Rule crisis and the elections of 1886 and 1892. But her political role was almost entirely supportive and rarely gave her the fulfilment she found at Newnham.

The final sacrifice was required of Helen in the 1890s when her father became Prime Minister for the last time, and when she subsequently had to care for both parents through their last illnesses. Mary and Helen arranged to live alternately with their octogenarian parents in Downing Street during the 1893 session: 'Helen's having practically refused the Headship of Newnham privately before it was offered her, was done entirely to enable her to be of use to parents.' Helen left Cambridge for ever in November 1896, 'to take my share regularly of home duties'. She even allowed her father to glimpse the pain it caused her to sever her last links with Newnham: 'You will not think I have done this lightly or easily.'[81] Unfortunately for Helen, her resignation coincided with the Drews' move away from the family home at Hawarden, where they had lived since their marriage. Helen wrote a letter of utter depression to Mary: 'the prospect of Hawarden with only me, is one to me so almost hopeless (seldom able to satisfy Mama and with no time to do any work for Father—except the letters—almost always inefficient in my own eyes and everybody else's).' Helen was thus obliged to perform the usual spinster's role in caring for her father up to his death in 1898, and her mother until her death in 1900, but the declining health of both parents clearly depressed her intensely.[82] Her sense of filial obligation did not end even with their deaths, for subsequently she felt tied to Hawarden Castle to help John Morley with her father's biography. However, in 1901 she became Warden of the Women's University Settlement in Southwark and at last resumed her independent life. Though she was obliged to sacrifice a successful career at Cambridge, Helen Gladstone was more fortunate and had more opportunities than most other Victorian spinsters. She was able to enjoy ten years of Cambridge life, since her family responsibilities did not begin until she was thirty-seven. It is also worth noting that Gladstone was far more tolerant and under-standing in his attitude towards his daughters than towards his poor sister Helen.

Elizabeth Haldane was more emancipated than either Helen Gladstone or Gwendolen Cecil. She was a formidable lady with a powerful intellect, born in 1862 into a distinguished Scottish academic family. Her uncle and two brothers were Fellows of the Royal Society, while her eldest brother, Richard Burdon Haldane, was a distinguished philosopher and Liberal minister. An equally important influence was her father's death when Elizabeth was only fifteen, which freed her mother 'to do many things that she could not do before and to give expression to faculties hitherto latent'. Elizabeth was brought up by her mother, assisted by two spinster aunts—three loving and independent women leading fairly full lives. This strong female influence in Elizabeth's life was in marked contrast to the male-dominated families of most other spinsters examined here. Elizabeth suffered the disadvantages common to her sex only in that she received no formal education. The family was not wealthy, 'the sons had to be set up in life', and 'for an only daughter to leave a widowed mother was indeed considered to be quite out of the question'.[83] But her mother and aunts supported the women's movement even in the 1880s and encouraged Elizabeth to be intellectually active and personally independent. She organized a rigorous process of self-education through correspondence classes, combined with frequent discussion on philosophy and scientific thought with her Aunt Jane. Elizabeth was also fortunate as a young girl in that she spent three months each year with her brothers in London, where she was exceptionally well placed to meet interesting academics and politicians.

Against this supportive background, Elizabeth Haldane developed a strong sense of the potential for an independent female role in life. From an early age, she 'wanted to do for myself and not just to be the helper of others who were doing—a quite unbiblical ideal for any woman to have'. She was strong-minded and progressive in her opinions. There is no evidence that Elizabeth ever had any inclination to marry. She remarked later that she never knew the meaning of frustration, 'the disease which is supposed to attack unmarried women . . . life seemed brimming full and running over'.[84] Her mother commented in 1897 that marriage for Elizabeth 'would have been a hindrance. She has a self-sustaining nature'.[85] Even in politics she played more than a merely passive supporting role for her brother, Richard Haldane. She was not deeply interested in politics, but acted as his political hostess and kept house for him in London while Parliament was sitting—'making his house a real home to him'. Her fine mind and strong personality made her the equal of guests like Beatrice Webb, though some of their male visitors found her rather forbidding. But she also became more actively involved on Richard's behalf when necessary, canvassing and making speeches

at election time. Indeed, in December 1909 she herself actually
conducted the East Lothian campaign 'with great vigour' while
Richard was ill.[86]

Elizabeth also led a distinguished life of her own. She was an
accomplished philosopher and writer whose books included a *Life
of Descartes*, a *Life of George Eliot* and *A History of Nursing*, as
well as translations of the works of Hegel and Descartes. In 1906
she was awarded an honorary Doctor of Laws by St Andrews
University—a remarkable achievement for a woman with no
formal education. Elizabeth was also fully involved with social
work, nursing and philanthropy. She had endless energy and
organizing ability, rushing around enlisting patronage and support
for worthy causes. From 1892 she became a prominent fighter in
the movement to revise the Scottish Poor Law and improve
conditions in the workhouses, and gave evidence to the Royal
Commission on the Poor Laws in 1907. She was also a Manager of
the Edinburgh Royal Infirmary from 1892, and campaigned for the
registration of nurses and improvement in their hours and pay. By
1907 she was seen by the Local Government Board as an authority
on the financing and organization of hospitals.[87]

Elizabeth Haldane was an outstanding public figure in her own
right, with no need or desire to live vicariously through her
eminent brothers. She played a strong supportive role for her
bachelor politician brother, but unlike Alice Balfour or the Bryce
sisters, she never allowed it to dominate. She devoted much of her
life to her mother and her brother without any hint of sacrifice.
Admittedly, she was fortunate in that she did not have to nurse
elderly parents during her years of maturity and achievement,
since her father died when she was fifteen and her mother lived to
be over one hundred. Even so, Violet Markham regretted that
Elizabeth's life was so wholly devoted to the service of others;
'love and marriage had been laid on the altar of her mother and of
Richard', while her considerable accomplishments were always
restricted by family claims. 'Sacrifice had wrought in her a very
noble quality of life and character.'[88]

Victorian family life was founded on the primary values of social
and moral duty combined with parental authority. Many of the
spinsters in this study were talented, but the application of their
abilities was severely restricted by their male-dominated environment and by Victorian assumptions regarding the obligations of

unmarried daughters. Moreover, when the fathers or brothers were famous politicians, accustomed to exercising power at Westminster, the domestic pressures were often substantially increased. One of Helen Gladstone's Newnham students commented that 'one of the things that kept her such a very "unmarried" person was her ingrained attitude of daughter'.[89] Some of these women seem to have been conditioned to be spinsters from adolescence, especially if they were only daughters or their sisters appeared more likely to marry first on grounds of age or beauty. An assumption of spinsterhood was often reached by the mid-twenties and it was not easy to break that pattern, particularly when it was reinforced by family requirements. It is significant that two widows remarried for every spinster married in the age group over thirty during 1870 to 1872.[90]

The feminist Rhoda Nunn in George Gissing's *The Odd Women* contended that spinsters' lives were not 'useless, lost, futile'; but rather that 'the vast majority of women would lead a vain and miserable life because they *do* marry'. Elizabeth Haldane's aunt, Jane Sanderson, would have agreed with this up to a point. She knew that single women were often lonely, 'but it is far better to be single unless one is *truly* married'.[91] However, the vast majority of spinsters found it hard to endure the crippling assumption that they were social and emotional failures because they did not marry and could not have children. Even worse than their own presumption of failure, they had to bear the stigma of society. It is not surprising that only a minority found fulfilment and independence as single women. This last group, which transcended the stereotypical spinster role, were often fortunate in their intellectual endowments, social opportunities and strength of character. Usually they were free from family responsibilities for a sufficient length of time to establish their own lives. Most upper-class spinsters were overwhelmed by family obligations, reinforced by parental authority and widely accepted social conventions. The utter collapse of their lives could easily follow a father's death or a brother's marriage. Beatrice Potter believed that the best single women achieved a degree of nobility unattainable by their married sisters; but 'so few women have enough character to live an unmarried life, and not sink into a nobody, or still worse into a general nuisance'.[92]

Most Victorian and Edwardian women accepted the roles prescribed for them because of their gender and class. Their expectations of life were quite different from their brothers because of their assumed female destiny, as wives and mothers within the family. Middle and upper-class females were socialised from early childhood to occupy this separate and inferior sphere of domestic life. They were conditioned to subordinate their individual interests to the needs of husbands, children, parents and relatives. This book has documented the adaptability and the achievements of Victorian and Edwardian women within these social limits. These women merit recognition and respect for their stamina and resourcefulness, and their ability to make the best of their inherited social situation.

The lives of middle and upper-class women from 1860 to 1914 were quite different from the fictional stereotypes of the vacuous, passive ladies of leisure, frequently prostrated by boredom or hysteria. At least two decades of the lives of married women were usually devoted to child bearing and rearing, with the attendant risks of death or poor health from miscarriages, difficult births or puerperal fever. Their sense of danger was well founded and they generally endured pain and suffering with little complaint. These women also accepted the responsibilities of organising households and managing servants, as well as caring for elderly parents. Political wives had a further responsibility as political hostesses, and played an increasingly significant role in election campaigns. They were not regarded as the political equals of their husbands, but they were invaluable companions whose political role was primarily supportive.

These middle and upper-class wives enjoyed more contented and less repressed relationships with their husbands than the stereotypes of Victorian private lives have suggested. While their choice of marriage partner was restricted by parental and social requirements concerning the class and wealth of eligible males, they generally worked hard at their marriages, and led busy and often fulfilled lives. They were certainly fortunate by comparison with the majority of working-class women, with a comfortable cushion of wealth and social status. Political wives had no great personal incentive to try to transform the general position of women in society, but they became increasingly supportive of the campaigns for women's educational and political rights.

Spinsters were the most vulnerable and potentially the most unhappy members of middle and upper-class families. They had failed to achieve the status and emotional rewards of the wife and mother, and many spinsters were also deprived of opportunities to develop acceptable alternative roles. Yet some spinsters did become independent pioneering women, challenging the foundations of the Victorian doctrine of separate spheres for men and women.

The theory and practice of women's lives—whether single or married—have become far more varied and creative in the twentieth century, in part because of the achievements of the women's movement, as well as the changing economic conditions for female workers. However, many women have continued to perceive their primary roles as being within marriage and the family, rather than in the paid workforce, while increasing numbers of women have combined both roles. The exploration of women's private experiences and achievements within the family remains one of the continuing challenges for the historian.

Family Trees

1. THE GLADSTONE AND LYTTELTON FAMILIES

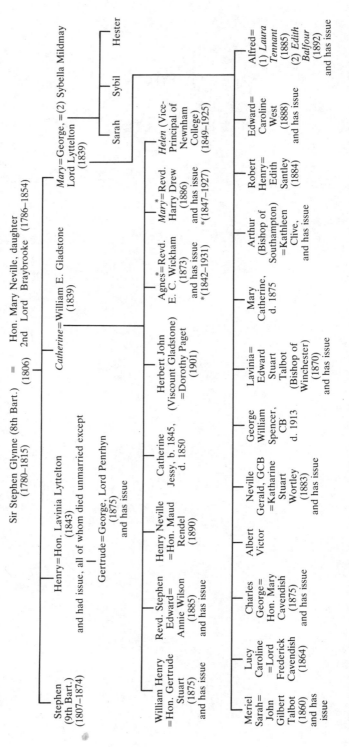

Sir Stephen Glynne (8th Bart.) = Hon. Mary Neville, daughter
(1780–1815) (1806) 2nd Lord Braybrooke (1786–1854)

Catherine = William E. Gladstone
(1839)

Mary = George, = (2) Sybella Mildmay
Lord Lyttelton
(1839)

Sarah Sybil Hester

Stephen
(9th Bart.)
(1807–1874)

Henry = Hon. Lavinia Lyttelton
(1843)
and had issue, all of whom died unmarried except

Gertrude = George, Lord Penrhyn
(1875)
and has issue

William Henry
= Hon. Gertrude
Stuart
(1875)
and has issue

Revd. Stephen
Edward =
Annie Wilson
(1885)
and has issue

Henry Neville
= Hon. Maud
Rendel
(1890)

Catherine
Jessy, b. 1845,
d. 1850

Herbert John
(Viscount Gladstone)
= Dorothy Paget
(1901)

Agnes * = Revd.
E. C. Wickham
(1873)
and has issue
*(1842–1931)

Mary * = Revd.
Harry Drew
(1886)
and has issue
*(1847–1927)

Helen (Vice-
Principal of
Newnham
College)
(1849–1925)

Meriel
Sarah =
John
Gilbert
Talbot
(1860)
and has
issue

Lucy
Caroline
= Lord
Frederick
Cavendish
(1864)

Albert
Victor

Charles
George =
Hon. Mary
Cavendish
(1875)
and has issue

Neville
Gerald, GCB
= Katharine
Stuart
Wortley
(1883)
and has issue

George
William
Spencer,
CB
d. 1913

Lavinia =
Edward
Stuart
Talbot
(Bishop of
Winchester)
(1870)
and has issue

Mary
Catherine,
d. 1875

Arthur
(Bishop of
Southampton)
= Kathleen
Clive,
and has issue

Robert
Henry =
Edith
Santley
(1884)

Edward =
Caroline
West
(1888)
and has issue

Alfred =
(1) *Laura
Tennant*
(1885)
(2) *Edith
Balfour*
(1892)
and has issue

[From Mary Drew, *Catherine Gladstone*, Nisbet, London, 1919, p. 293.]

2. THE CECIL AND SELBORNE FAMILIES

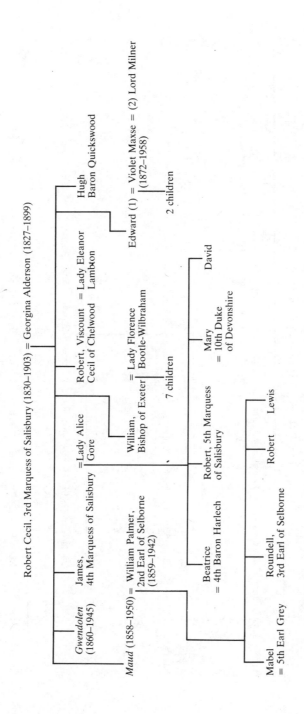

Adapted from K. Rose, *The Later Cecils*, 1975. by kind permission of George Weidenfeld and Nicolson Ltd.

3. THE MACDONALD, GLADSTONE AND KING FAMILIES

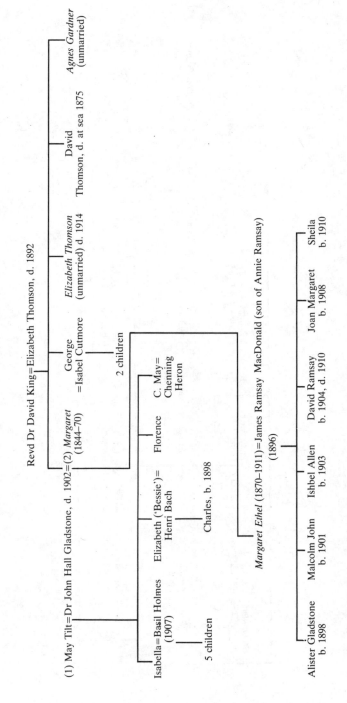

Adapted from the PRO guide to the MacDonald Papers.

4. THE CHAMBERLAIN FAMILY

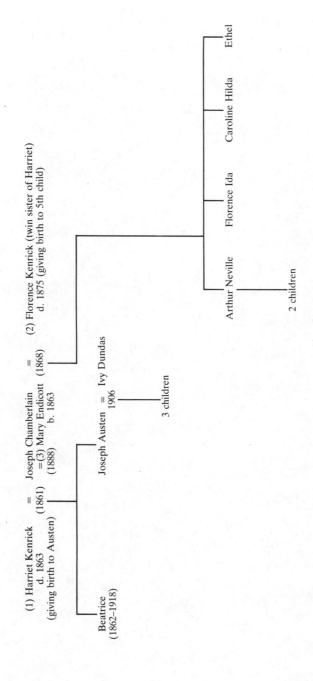

(1) Harriet Kenrick = Joseph Chamberlain = (2) Florence Kenrick (twin sister of Harriet)
      d. 1863   (1861)   =(3) Mary Endicott (1868)   d. 1875 (giving birth to 5th child)
(giving birth to Austen)   b. 1863

Beatrice   Joseph Austen = Ivy Dundas
(1862–1918)   1906

                                3 children

Arthur Neville   Florence Ida   Caroline Hilda   Ethel

2 children

Notes

THE place of publication is London, unless otherwise stated. A full reference is supplied for each published source in the footnote to its first citation in each chapter, rather than providing an over-long bibliography of secondary sources. The locations of the manuscript collections are listed in a section following the Notes.

ABBREVIATIONS

BL Add. MS	British Library, Additional Manuscripts
NLS	National Library of Scotland
PRO	Public Record Office
priv. pr.	printed for private circulation

Aims and Sources

1. M.Vicinus, ed., *A Widening Sphere*, Indiana, 1977, p. xi.
2. P. Branca, 'Image and Reality: the Myth of the Idle Victorian Woman', in *Clio's Consciousness Raised*, eds. Mary Hartman and Lois W. Banner, 1974, p. 181.
3. Brian Harrison, *Separate Spheres. The Opposition to Women's Suffrage in Britain*, 1978, p. 259.
4. M. Jeanne Peterson, 'No Angels in the House: The Victorian Myth and the Paget Women', *American Historical Review*, vol. 89, no. 3, June 1984, pp. 677–708.
5. Lady Constance Malleson, *After Ten Years. A Personal Record*, 1931, pp. 14–15.
6. Meriel Talbot's diary, end of year 1860, Talbot Papers, U 1612, F 108, ff. 111–12.
7. Maggie Acland to sister-in-law, Angie Acland, 16 Feb. [1879], MS Acland d. 144, ff. 9–10.
8. Beatrice Potter (Webb) diary, 24 Apr. 1883, Passfield Papers.
9. Mary Gladstone diary, 29 Dec. 1883, Mary Gladstone Papers, BL Add. MS 46261, f. 31.
10. Oliver MacDonagh, *The Inspector General Sir Jeremiah Fitzpatrick and Social Reform, 1783–1802*, 1981, p. 327.

Introduction

1. Frances Power Cobbe, *The Duties of Women. A Course of Lectures*, 1881, pp. 161–2.

2. Edith H. Fowler, *The Life of H. H. Fowler, First Viscount Wolverhampton*, 1912, pp. 598, 624.
3. J. M. Allan, 'On the Differences in the Minds of Men and Women', *Journal of the Anthropological Society of London*, 7 (1869), pp. cxcvi–cxcviii. See also P. Jalland and J. Hooper, *Women from Birth to Death 1830–1914*, Brighton, 1985, for extensive illustrations from medical texts and advice manuals.
4. Dr H. A. Kelly, *Medical Gynecology*, 1909, pp. 67, 72–3.
5. Dr L. A. Weatherly, *The Young Wife's Own Book*, 1882, pp. 28–31.
6. E. J. Tilt, *Elements of Health and Principles of Female Hygiene*, 1852, pp. 173, 175–6, 209, 219–21.
7. C. W. Saleeby, *Woman and Womanhood*, 1912, pp. 115–17.
8. J. C. Webster, *Puberty and the Change of Life. A Book for Women*, 1892, pp. 8, 28–31, 34.
9. E. H. Ruddock, *The Common Diseases of Women*, 1888, pp. 23–4.
10. Lady Muriel Beckwith, *When I Remember*, 1936, pp. 34–5.
11. B. L. Booker, *Yesterday's Child*, 1937, pp. 18–24, 72, 82. See also W. Peck, *A Little Learning*, 1952, pp. 30–1; S. Keppel, *Edwardian Daughter*, 1958, pp. 3–14.
12. Mrs Potter to Beatrice Potter, 30 July 1870, Passfield Papers, II, 1 (i), ff. 104–5.
13. Margot Asquith, *More Memories*, 1933, pp. 12–13; *The Autobiography of Margot Asquith*, 1920, p. 19.
14. Elizabeth Haldane to aunt, Jane Sanderson, 5 July 1885, Haldane MS 6015, f. 79.
15. Mrs Louise Creighton to Mrs Humphry Ward, 15 Dec. 1879, Ward MSS.
16. Kate to Beatrice Potter, 1873, Passfield Papers, II, 1 (i), f. 137.
17. Sir Philip Magnus, *Gladstone. A Biography*, 1954, p. 125.
18. E. S. Haldane, *From One Century to Another*, 1937, pp. 72–4.
19. Beatrice Potter (Webb) diary, see e.g. 3 July 1878, 30 Mar., 14 Dec/ 1879, 22 Jan. 1881, 8 Apr. 1884.
20. See e.g. Helen to Henry Gladstone, 30 Mar., 30 Aug. 1877, 17 Mar. 1878, Glynne–Gladstone MS 44/3; Mary to Henry Gladstone, 9, 11 May 1878, ibid., 43/2.
21. For useful general works on Victorian girls' adolescence and education, see Deborah Gorham, *The Victorian Girl and the Feminine Ideal*, 1982; Carol Dyhouse, *Girls Growing up in Late Victorian and Edwardian England*, 1981.
22. See M. Jeanne Peterson, 'The Victorian Governess: Status Incongruence in Family and Society', *Suffer and be Still*, ed. M. Vicinus, Indiana, 1972, pp. 3–19.
23. *Emma Lady Ribblesdale. Letters and Diaries*, ed. B. Lister, priv. pr. 1930, p. 41.

24. M. Fawcett, *What I Remember*, 1925, p. 38.
25. Maggie Harkness to cousin, Beatrice Potter, n.d. (1878), Passfield Papers, II, 1 (ii), ff. 128–31.
26. *The Diary of Lady Frederick Cavendish*, ed. John Bailey, 1927, 2 vols., I, pp. 7, 9, 11, 36.
27. *Mary Gladstone—Diaries and Letters*, ed. Lucy Masterman, 1930, p. 2.
28. Ibid., pp. 3, 12.
29. Mary Lady Trevelyan, 'The Number of My Days', undated TS, Trevelyan Papers, pp. 17–23.
30. Mary Drew to Catherine Gladstone, 16 Sept. 1898, Mary Gladstone Drew papers, BL Add. MS 46225, f. 335.
31. M. Buxton, *A Memoir*, n.d. [c.1966], pp. 32, 53.
32. May Harcourt to Lady Harcourt, n.d. [1912], MS Harcourt dep. 648, f. 73.
33. Cynthia Asquith, *Remember and Be Glad*, 1952, pp. 104–5.
34. Private boarding school education was too expensive for the lower-middle classes (see P. Branca, 'Image and Reality: The Myth of the Idle Victorian Woman', *Clio's Consciousness Raised*, eds. M. Hartman and L. W. Banner, 1974, p. 184).
35. Cecilia to daughter, Violet Maxse, 22 [June] 1887, Cecil-Maxse Papers, U 1599, C61/18.
36. Mrs Humphry Ward, *A Writer's Recollections*, 1918, pp. 96–7; Janet Trevelyan, *The Life of Mrs Humphry Ward*, 1923, pp. 8–16.
37. Louise Childers to her mother, 22 Jan., 22 May 1874; school bill, July 1874, Childers Papers, 19/23, 19/1.
38. B. Potter diary, 21 Sept. 1875.
39. Janet to sister, Dorothy Ward, 9 Mar. 1895, Ward Papers.
40. Miriam Pease to parents, 1900–1, from the Chateau de Dieudonne at Bornel, Gainford MS 518.
41. M. Buxton, *A Memoir*, pp. 14–17.
42. Lady Carrington's diary, 30 Sept. 1895, Carrington MS film 1100.
43. Katharine to brother, Graham Wallas, n.d. [c.1910], Graham Wallas Papers, Box 42.
44. Margaret Gladstone's journal, e.g. 8 Sept. 1887, 17 Nov. 1889, MacDonald Papers, PRO 30/69/911.
45. Lady Selborne's recollections, n.d., MS Eng. Misc. e. 964, f. 16.
46. Mrs C. S. Peel, *Life's Enchanted Cup. An Autobiography (1872–1933)*, 1933, pp. 31–2.
47. E. S. Haldane, *From One Century to Another*, 1937, pp. 72–3, 144.
48. M. Gladstone [MacDonald] journal, 3 Dec. 1891, MacDonald Papers, PRO 30/69/916.

49. Margaret King diary, 24 May 1869, MacDonald Papers, PRO 30/69/852, f. 53.
50. Helen to Henry Gladstone, 10 June 1877, Glynne–Gladstone MS 44/3.
51. E. S. Haldane, *From One Century to Another*, pp. 72–3.
52. Mary Gladstone diary, 14 Feb. 1883, M. Gladstone Drew papers, BL Add. MS 46261, ff. 5, 103–5.
53. Vera Brittain, *Testament of Youth*, 1980 (1st edn. 1933), p. 31.
54. *Mary Gladstone—Diaries and Letters*, ed. Lucy Masterman, p. 5.
55. Kenneth Rose, *The Later Cecils*, 1975, pp. 26–57.

Chapter 1: The Rituals of Courtship and Marriage

1. Leonore Davidoff, *The Best Circles*, 1973, pp. 41, 49 *et passim*.
2. Ibid., pp. 20, 25, 61; Q. H. Crewe, *The Frontiers of Privilege: A Century of Social Conflict as Reflected in 'The Queen'*, 1961, pp. 12–13.
3. Blanche Cripps to Beatrice Potter, 11 Feb. 1877, Passfield Papers, II, 1 (i), f. 219.
4. Sybil Lubbock, *The Child in the Crystal*, 1939, pp. 278–80.
5. Constance Battersea, *Reminiscences*, 1922, pp. 108–9.
6. Cynthia Asquith, *Remember and be Glad*, 1952, pp. 58–9. See also Davidoff, *The Best Circles*, p. 52.
7. *The Stanleys of Alderley*, ed. Nancy Mitford, 1968, p. 134; Lady Stanhope to Lord Derby, 1 Aug. 1887, Stanhope MSS, U 1590, C717/5.
8. Kate Courtney's diary, Jan. 1877 and n.d. [1875], Courtney Collection, vol. xxi, ff. 9, 3; B. Webb diary, 3 Aug. 1874, Passfield Papers.
9. Lady Constance Malleson, *After Ten Years. A Personal Record*, 1931, pp. 47–8.
10. Victoria Dawnay to sister, Louisa Antrim, 5 Feb. [1885], Minto MS 12427, f. 15.
11. *Earl Cowper, K.G. A Memoir*, by his wife, Katrine Cecilia, priv. pr., 1913, p. 107.
12. Mary to Henry Gladstone, 15 Nov. 1877, Glynne–Gladstone MS 43/2.
13. Mary to Catherine Gladstone, 16 Oct. 1876, M. Gladstone Drew Papers, BL Add. MS 46222, ff. 308–11.
14. Davidoff, *Best Circles*, p. 50.
15. Maud C. Braby, *Modern Marriage and How to Bear It*, 1908, pp. 76–7.
16. Sir Arthur Hardinge, *The Life of Henry Herbert, Fourth Earl of Carnarvon, 1831–1890* (3 vols.), 1925; Mrs H. Ward to daughter, Dorothy Ward, 7 Jan. 1892, Pusey House, Ward Papers.
17. Lady Carrington's diary, 10 Nov. 1887, Carrington MS film 1097.

18. Mary to Neville Chamberlain, 25 Nov. 1910, Chamberlain Papers, NC 1/20/2/4.
19. Lady Frances Balfour, *Ne Obliviscaris. Dinna Forget*, 1930, I, 121–3, 148–9, 370.
20. Lady Minto to her son, Gilbert John Elliot, Viscount Melgund, 8 July 1864, Minto MS 12367, f. 49.
21. *Dictionary of National Biography, 1912–21*, pp. 172–4.
22. Lady Minto to Bertie, 9 Oct. 1869, Minto MS 12367, f. 52.
23. Lady Macgregor to Lady Minto, 28 July 1870, Minto MS 12363, f. 246.
24. Lady Minto to Bertie, 15 Nov. 1873, Minto MS 12367, f. 229.
25. Lady Frances Balfour, *Ne Obliviscaris*, I, 159–60.
26. See e.g. Maud C. Braby, *Modern Marriage*, pp. 78–9.
27. A. S. Swan, *Courtship and Marriage and the Gentle Art of Home-Making*, 1893, pp. 12–13.
28. C. A. Hoff, *Highways and Byways to Health*, 2 vols., Philadelphia, 1893, II, 100.
29. Katharine Ramsay to Lord Tullibardine, 3 July 1897, Atholl MS 50/51.
30. Ibid., 6, 12 July 1897, 12 August 1898.
31. Ibid., 6 Sept. 1898, 15, 20 Apr. 1899, Atholl MS 51, 52/5.
32. Lady Cowell-Stepney to Mary Drew, 17 Mar. 1911, M. Gladstone Drew Papers, BL Add. MS 46250, ff. 117–18.
33. Col. Dundas to Austen Chamberlain, 8 May 1906, Chamberlain Papers, AC 1/8/8/49; Mary to Austen Chamberlain, 10 May 1906, ibid., AC 1/8/7/9; Sir Charles Petrie, *The Life and Letters of the Rt. Hon. Sir Austen Chamberlain*, 2 vols., 1939–40, I, 181.
34. Kate Courtney's diary, n.d. [1880], Courtney Collection, vol. xxi, f. 55.
35. M. Gladstone diary, 19–20 Dec. 1884, 25–7 Jan. 1885, M. Gladstone Drew Papers, BL Add. MS 46261, f. 69; G. Battiscombe, *Mrs Gladstone*, 1956, p. 192.
36. Lady Salisbury to son, Lord Edward Cecil, 26 Mar. 1894, Cecil-Maxse MSS, U 1599, C 709/32; Kenneth Rose, *The Later Cecils*, 1975, p. 193.
37. Maud, Lady Selborne to son Roundell Palmer, 1 Feb. 1908, Selborne Papers, MS Eng. hist. c. 978, f. 23.
38. Lady Cowell-Stepney to Mary Drew, n.d. [Spring 1902], M. Gladstone Drew Papers, BL Add. MS 46250, f. 7.
39. Helen Fox to Sarah Angelina Acland, 22 Nov. 1881, MS Acland, d. 144, f. 151.
40. S. A. Acland to Henry Acland, 30 Nov. 1875, MS Acland, d. 103, ff. 110–11.

41. Sarah Acland to S. A. Acland, 5 Apr. 1876, MS Acland, d. 140, f. 105.
42. *Earl Cowper, K.G. A Memoir*, pp. 187, 193.
43. Roundell Palmer, Earl of Selborne, *Memorials*, 1896, I, Part II, 19–20.
44. Laura Tennant to Spencer Lyttelton, 10 Jan. 1885, Chandos II, 2/2, f. 48.
45. *Emma, Lady Ribblesdale. Letters and Diaries*, collected by her daughter Beatrix Lister, priv. pr. 1930, p. 28.
46. May Burns to Sir William Harcourt, 14 Nov. 1898, MS Harcourt, dep. 669, ff. 1–2.
47. Mary Endicott to Beatrice Chamberlain, 26, 29 Mar., n.d. [1888], Chamberlain Papers, AC 4/9/5.
48. Katharine Ramsay to Lord Tullibardine, 9 Nov. 1897, Atholl MS 51.
49. Agnes Wickham to Henry Gladstone, 8 Jan. 1874, Glynne–Gladstone MS 42/5.
50. *Myself when Young. By Famous Women of Today*, ed. Margot Asquith, 1938, p. 229.
51. M. Mackay to fiancé, Alex Shaw, 24 July 1913, Craigmyle MSS.
52. *Lady John Russell*, eds. D. MacCarthy and A. Russell, 1910, pp. 64–5.
53. Maria Rogers to Henry Acland, 27 Nov. 1875, MS Acland, d. 103, ff. 95–6.
54. Louisa, Lady Antrim to Mary, Countess Minto, 15 Mar., n.d. [1897], Minto MS 12436, f. 48.
55. Mrs Burns to Lady Harcourt, 24 Nov. 1898, MS Harcourt, dep. 647, ff. 250–1.
56. *Margaret Cowell-Stepney: Her Letters 1875–1921*, ed. Blanche Elliott Lockhart, privately published c.1926, p. 292; Lady Cowell-Stepney to Mary Drew, 17 Mar., 12, 24 Sept. 1911, M. Gladstone Drew Papers, BL Add. MS 46250, ff. 117–18, 141–2, 146.
57. Jetta Barnett to Kate Potter, n.d., Courtney Collection, vol. iii, f. 125.
58. Mary Drew to Spencer Lyttelton, 13 Feb. 1895, M. Gladstone Drew Papers, BL Add. MS 46232, f. 235; Frances Balfour to Mary Gladstone, 4 Jan. 1886, ibid., MS 46238, f. 71.
59. Margaret Ashton to James Bryce, 12 Mar. 1889, MS Bryce Adds. 41.
60. Beatrice Webb diary, 5 Aug., 22 Jan. 1881, 21 Feb. 1889.
61. Margot Tennant to Mrs Gordon Duff, 21 May 1885, Chandos I, 4/4.
62. Margot Asquith to Violet Cecil, n.d. [1894], Cecil-Maxse MSS, U 1599, C 123/3.
63. *Emma, Lady Ribblesdale. Letters and Diaries*, ed. B. Lister, p. 124.
64. Albert Westland, *The Wife and Mother Medical Guide*, 1892, p. 5.

65. See e.g. Hoff, *Highways and Byways to Health*, II, 100.
66. May to Lady Harcourt, 13 Aug. 1909, MS Harcourt, dep. 648, f. 25.
67. See Lady Colin Campbell, *Etiquette of Good Society*, 1893, pp. 89–105.
68. Caroline Philips to G. O. Trevelyan, 9 Sept. 1869, Trevelyan Papers, GOT 117.
69. Cynthia Asquith, *Remember and be Glad*, pp. 125–7.
70. Maud Cecil to W. W. Palmer, 18 Oct. 1883, MS Selborne, Adds. 1, ff. 55–6.
71. Katharine Ramsay to Lord Tullibardine, 15 Apr. 1899, Atholl MS 52, no. 5.
72. Elizabeth Haldane to Jane Sanderson, 24 July 1885, Haldane Papers, NLS MS 6015, ff. 91–2.
73. Pencilled list by Mary Trevelyan of going away clothes, Jan. 1904, Trevelyan Papers, CPT.
74. C. P. Trevelyan to mother, Lady Trevelyan, 1 Dec. 1903, ibid.
75. Ivy to mother, Mrs Dundas, 20 May 1906, Chamberlain Papers, AC 6/6/1.
76. Lady Colin Campbell, *Etiquette of Good Society*, pp. 102–3.
77. Lady Muriel Beckwith, *When I Remember*, 1936, pp. 254–5.
78. Catherine Gladstone to Harry Drew, 11 May 1894, Mary Gladstone Papers, BL Add. MS 46225, ff. 166–7.
79. Sir A. Hardinge, *Life of Lord Carnarvon*, I, 181–4.
80. Lady Carrington's diary, 16 July 1878, Carrington MS film 1097.
81. Caroline Philips to G. O. Trevelyan, n.d. [1869], 15 Sept. 1869, Trevelyan Papers, GOT 117.
82. Maud Cecil to W. W. Palmer, 2, 6 Oct. 1883, MS Selborne Adds. 1, ff. 41–2, 50.
83. *Recollections of Lady Georgiana Peel*, ed. Ethel Peel, 1920, p. 159.
84. Stephen Hobhouse, *Margaret Hobhouse and Her Family*, 1934, pp. 98–100; Kate Courtney's diary, Oct. 1880, Courtney Collection, vol. xxi, f. 57.
85. Mary Chamberlain's diary, 12 Nov. 1888, Chamberlain Papers, C 5/1; Mary to Neville Chamberlain, 9 Jan. 1911, ibid., NC 1/20/2/5.
86. *Lady John Russell*, eds. MacCarthy and Russell, p. 47; Elizabeth Haldane to Aunt Jane Sanderson, 24 July 1885, Haldane MS 6015, ff. 91–2.
87. S. Olivier to Miss Davidson, 31 Jan. 1889, Wedgwood MSS, seen by kind permission of Mrs Edward Pease.
88. Mrs H. Ward to Dorothy Ward, 20 May 1903, Pusey House, Ward Papers.
89. Kate Courtney's diary, 23 July 1892, Courtney Collection, vol. XXVI, ff. 157–8.

90. Correspondence between John Bruce Glasier and Katharine Conway, 24, 26, 28 May 1893; J. B. Glasier to Miss Fraser, 26 June 1893, Glasier Papers I/1, 1893/25, ff. 37, 40, 43.
91. Lady Frances Balfour, *Ne Obliviscaris*, I, 184–5.
92. Olive Maxse to Violet Cecil-Maxse, 7 Dec. 1899; Eleanor Cecil to Violet Cecil-Maxse, 22 Dec. 1899, Cecil-Maxse MSS, U 1599, C 66/26, C 92/10.
93. L. Stone, *The Family, Sex and Marriage in England, 1500–1800*, 1977, p. 336.
94. May Harcourt to Lady Harcourt, 8 July 1899, MS Harcourt dep. 647, ff. 13–14.
95. J. W. Mackail and Guy Wyndham, *Life and Letters of George Wyndham*, 2 vols., 1925, I, 36.
96. Unidentified press cutting, 12 Nov. 1885, Childers Papers, 19/77; Catherine Gladstone to Lucy Cavendish, July 1884, Glynne–Gladstone MS 35/6.
97. *Lady John Russell*, eds. MacCarthy and Russell, p. 47; A. G. Gardiner, *Life of Sir William Harcourt*, 1923, p. 295.
98. *Recollections of Lady Georgiana Peel*, ed. Ethel Peel, p. 257.
99. *Earl Cowper, K.G.*, by his wife, p. 190.
100. Annie to Catherine Gladstone, 31 Jan. 1885, Glynne–Gladstone MS 30/6.
101. Margaret Mackay to Alex Shaw, 28 June 1913, Craigmyle Papers.
102. Caroline Philips to G. O. Trevelyan, 15 Sept. 1869, Trevelyan Papers, GOT 117.
103. Laura Lyttelton to Lavinia Talbot, 28 May 1885, Chandos II, 2/2, f. 43; and to Sybella Lyttelton, n.d., Chandos I, 2/19, item 40.
104. Kenneth Rose, *Superior Person. A Portrait of Curzon and His Circle in Late Victorian England*, 1969, p. 166.
105. Lady Cowell-Stepney to Mary Drew, 3 Dec. 1901, in *Margaret Cowell-Stepney: Her Letters*, ed. B. E. Lockhart, p. 222.
106. Mary to Catherine Gladstone, n.d. [*c*.17 Nov. 1875], M. Gladstone Papers, BL Add. MS 46222, ff. 254–6.
107. Blanche Cripps to Beatrice Potter, 31 July 1877, Passfield Papers, II, 1 (1) 217–18.
108. Marion Bryce to Mrs M. Bryce, 15 Aug. 1889, MS Bryce Adds. 41.
109. Caroline Philips to G. O. Trevelyan, 15 Sept. 1869, Trevelyan Papers, GOT 117.
110. Lady Cowell-Stepney to Mary Drew, 3 Dec. 1901, *M. Cowell-Stepney: Her Letters*, ed. B. E. Lockhart, p. 222.
111. B. Webb diary, 16 Aug. 1892.
112. Meriel Talbot's diary, 21 July 1860, Talbot Papers, U 1612, F 108; Lady Sherbrooke's pocket diary, entries for Feb. 1885, Sherbrooke Papers.

Chapter 2: Money and Marriage

1. L. Stone, *The Family, Sex and Marriage in England, 1500–1800*, 1977; E. Shorter, *The Making of the Modern Family*, 1976.
2. See esp. Stone, *The Family, Sex and Marriage*, pp. 180–91, 270–4.
3. See M. Anderson, *Approaches to the History of the Western Family 1500–1914*, 1980, pp. 39–64, for a useful critique of Stone and Shorter.
4. Ibid., p. 41.
5. H. V. F. Winstone, *Gertrude Bell*, 1980, pp. 35–7.
6. Louisa Lady Antrim to Mary Countess Minto, 30 Oct. 1907, 14 Nov. 1907, 2 Jan. 1908, Minto MS 12438, f. 225; MS 12439, ff. 19, 67.
7. Louisa Lady Antrim to Mary Countess Minto, 18 June 1906, Minto MS 12437, f. 74.
8. Evelyn Lady Stanhope to Lord Stanhope, 14–15 Mar. 1892, Stanhope MSS U 1590, C 513/11.
9. Louisa Lady Antrim to Mary Countess Minto, 2 Dec. 1896, Minto MS 12436, f. 39.
10. Evelyn to Arthur Stanhope, 24 Jan. 1874, Stanhope MSS U 1590, C 714/15.
11. *The Modern Marriage Market*, ed. Lady Jeune *et al.*, 1898, pp. 80–1.
12. Lady Frances Balfour, *Ne Obliviscaris. Dinna Forget*, 1930, I, 162–3.
13. A. J. Beveridge to mother, A. S. Beveridge, 24 June 1908, Beveridge Papers, II, a/90; José Harris, *William Beveridge*, 1977, pp. 68–70.
14. Mildred Stanhope (née Vernon) to sister-in-law, Evelyn Stanhope, 6 Dec. 1895, Stanhope MSS, U 1590, C 519.
15. May to Herbert Samuel, 23, 25 Aug., 8 Sept. 1897, Samuel MSS, B/6/18–19, 49.
16. Mary (Gladstone) Drew to Lady Cowell-Stepney, 22 Mar. and reply 31 Mar. 1911, Mary Gladstone Drew Papers, BL Add. MS 46250, ff. 120, 123–4.
17. Sir E. Cadogan, *Before the Deluge*, 1961, p. 159; Stone, *The Family, Sex and Marriage*, p. 274.
18. D. N. Thomas, 'Marriage Patterns in the British Peerage in the 18th and 19th Centuries', London, M.Phil. thesis, 1969, pp. 206–8.
19. Edith Gibbs to Vicary Gibbs, 25 June 1890, Gibbs Family Letters, MS 11021/29, f. 132; Lady Stanhope to Lord Derby, 3 Dec. 1889 and 12 Nov. 1886, Stanhope MSS, U 1590, C 717/6, C 717/4/67.
20. Lady Abercromby to Mrs Mary Haldane, [c.Feb. 1890], Haldane MS 6093, ff. 156–7.
21. Edith H. Fowler, *The Life of H. H. Fowler, First Viscount Wolverhampton*, 1912, pp. 20–3.
22. Beatrice Potter's diary, 31 Dec. 1890; Mary Playne to sister, Beatrice Potter, [Jan. 1892], Passfield Papers, II, 1 (i), 205–6.

23. Beatrice Potter's diary, 20 June 1891, 21 Jan. 1892, Passfield Papers.
24. D. Marquand, *Ramsay MacDonald*, 1977, pp. 45–7.
25. *The Modern Marriage Market*, ed. Jeune, pp. 73–4. See also J. A. and O. Banks, *Prosperity and Parenthood*, 1954, ch. 3.
26. Emilia Pattison (née Strong) to Charles Dilke, 10 Mar. 1885, Dilke Papers, BL Add. MS 43906, f. 44.
27. Mary (Bell) Trevelyan's diary, 1 May 1902; 18 Feb, 18 Oct. 1903, Trevelyan Papers.
28. Correspondence between Hugh Childers, W. M. Wilkinson (solicitor) and Stephen Simeon, July–Oct. 1885, Childers MS 19/45–78.
29. L. J. L. Dundas, Marquess of Zetland, *Lord Cromer: being the authorized Life of Evelyn Baring, First Earl of Cromer*, 1932, pp. 54–5.
30. Mary Bryce to brother, James Bryce, [*c*.1888], MS Bryce, Adds. 11.
31. John Jolliffe, *Raymond Asquith*, 1980, p. 94.
32. Mrs Humphry Ward to Arnold Ward, 23 Oct. 1907, Pusey House, Ward Papers.
33. Sir E. Cadogan, *Before the Deluge*, pp. 158–9.
34. Sarah Acland to son Henry, 18 Aug. 1875, MS Acland d. 46, ff. 147–9.
35. Henry Acland to son Henry, 26 Nov. 1875; Sarah Acland to Henry, 26 Nov. 1875, MS Acland, d. 103, ff. 85–90.
36. Agnes Acland to Fred Anson, 12–13 Oct. 1884, Devon Record Office, Acland–Anson MSS (2862 F 216 b).
37. Lucy Anson to nephew, Fred Anson, 24 June 1885, Devon Record Office, Acland–Anson MSS (2862, F 173 a).
38. Lady Colin Campbell, *Etiquette of Good Society*, 1893, p. 91.
39. M. Scharlieb, *The Seven Ages of Woman*, 1915, p. 68.
40. Quoted in P. Hollis, *Women in Public*, 1979, pp. 194–5; see also Lee Holcombe, 'Victorian Wives and Property', in *A Widening Sphere*, ed. M. Vicinus, Indiana, 1977, pp. 7–8.
41. Devon Record Office, Acland MSS (1148 M/add. 4/6).
42. William to Richard Rathbone, 1888, Rathbone MSS IX.8.48, IX.8.50.
43. Lady Selborne to son, Roundell Palmer, 8 Feb. 1906, Selborne MS Eng. hist., d. 444, ff. 85–6, 97.
44. Correspondence between Lord Blantyre and W. E. Gladstone on the marriage settlement of William and Gertrude Gladstone, 1875, Glynne–Gladstone MS 96/11.
45. Correspondence re marriage settlement between Agnes Gladstone and Edward Wickham, 1873, ibid.
46. Lord Blantyre to W. E. Gladstone, 31 July 1875, ibid.
47. M. Gladstone to R. MacDonald, 8 Sept. 1896, MacDonald MSS, PRO 30/69/778.

48. Hugh Bell to G. O. Trevelyan, 20 Sept. 1903, Trevelyan Papers, CPT 12.
49. Maud Cecil to W. W. Palmer, 7 Aug. 1883, MS Selborne Adds. 1, ff. 5, 8.
50. Mary to Catherine Gladstone, 29 Aug. 1873, Mary Gladstone Drew Papers, BL Add. MS 46222, ff. 182–3.
51. Laura Tennant to Alfred Lyttelton, n.d. [1885], Chandos II, 2/2.
52. Margaret Gladstone to R. MacDonald, 15 June, 8 Sept. 1896, MacDonald MSS, PRO 30/69/778.
53. Lady Stanhope to son Dick, 16 Mar. 1914, Stanhope MSS, U 1590, C 718/5.
54. 'History of the Onslow Family by the Fifth Earl', Onslow Papers 173/1/7, pp. 1919–20.
55. Sir Joseph Pease to Lady Alice Havelock-Allan, 10 Feb. 1886, Gainford MS 66; Jack Pease to Ethel Havelock-Allan, 17 May 1886, Gainford MS 517.
56. Helen to Olive Smith, Jan. 1876, Rend II, 12/2, Dilke–Enthoven– Roskill Papers.
57. Sir George Trevelyan to Hugh Bell, 19 Sept. 1903; Charles to Sir George Trevelyan, 20 Sept. 1903; Hugh Bell to G. O. Trevelyan, 20 Sept. 1903, Trevelyan Papers.
58. Hambleden MSS, MM 2–5.
59. Davidson to M. F. Leslie, 12 Feb. 1883, Childers Papers 25/20.
60. W. E. Gladstone to Barker, 26 Nov. 1873, Glynne–Gladstone MS 96/11.
61. Marriage settlement of Emily Evelyn Rathbone to Hugh Reynolds Rathbone, 19 Oct. 1888, Rathbone MS IX.8.46–47.
62. H. Pleydell-Bouverie, *From a Great Grandmother's Armchair*, 1927, p. 49.
63. Olive to Violet Maxse, 7 Dec. 1899, Cecil-Maxse MSS, U 1599, C 66/26. Lord Leconfield had a gross landed income of £88,000 in 1883 (W. D. Rubinstein, *Men of Property*, 1981, p. 194).
64. Evelyn Stanhope to father-in-law, Lord Stanhope, 20 June 1873, Stanhope MSS, U 1590, C 714/14.
65. Lady Londonderry to Lord Crewe, 8 Jan. 1895, Crewe Papers, P3 (14).
66. Chandos, 'Interwoven', 6/1/G; Nigel Nicolson, *Mary Curzon*, 1977, pp. 58, 72.
67. Edith to Kathleen Lyttelton, 10 Jan. 1898, Chandos I, 5/16; Mary Drew to Catherine Gladstone, 19 Jan. 1898, M. Gladstone Drew Papers, BL Add. MS 46225, f. 322.
68. Margaret Gladstone to Ramsay MacDonald, 15 June, 2 July, 8 Sept., 2 Oct. 1896, PRO 30/69/778; D. Marquand, *Ramsay MacDonald*, pp. 45–8, 51.

69. Margaret Mackay to Alex Shaw, 28 June 1913, Craigmyle Papers.
70. May Harcourt to Lady Harcourt, 31 Jan. 1902, MS Harcourt, dep. 647, f. 105.
71. Lady Stanhope to Lord Derby, 1 Aug. 1887, Stanhope MSS, U 1590, C 717/5.
72. Chandos, 'Interwoven', 6/1/K, 1892.
73. *Earl Cowper, K.G. A Memoir*, by his wife, Katrine Cecilia, priv. pr., c.1913, pp. 284–5.
74. Olive Maxse to sister Violet Maxse, 19 Oct. [1899], Cecil-Maxse MSS, U 1599, C 66/22.
75. May Harcourt to Lady Harcourt, [1909], MS Harcourt dep. 648, ff. 35, 37.
76. Lady Salisbury to son, Edward Cecil, 15 Mar. 1894, Cecil-Maxse MSS, U 1599, C 709/31.
77. Mary Gladstone to Alfred Lyttelton, 7 Dec. 1881, M. Gladstone Drew Papers, BL Add. MS 46233, ff. 239–40.

Chapter 3: Love and Other Complications

1. Constance Wilde to Juliet Mount Temple, 8 June 1890, Broadlands Estate Archive, 27 M60, C/IV/5/4 III.
2. Mary Gladstone to Alfred Lyttelton, 4, 7 Dec. 1881, M. Gladstone Drew Papers, BL Add. MS 46233, ff. 233–6, 239–40; M. Gladstone to Lavinia Talbot, 22 Jan. [1882?], ibid., MS 46236, f. 178.
3. Mary Drew to Lord Rosebery, 29 Feb. 1912, Rosebery MS 10015, f. 212; Lady Cowell-Stepney to Mary Drew, 12 May 1911, M. Gladstone Drew Papers, BL Add. MS 46250, f. 129; Helen Gladstone to Mary Drew, 5 Apr. 1911, ibid., MS 46231, f. 184.
4. Maud Selborne to husband, William, Lord Selborne, 27 Aug. 1908, MS Selborne, Adds 2, f. 201.
5. Baroness Ravensdale, *In Many Rhythms. An Autobiography*, 1953, p. 11.
6. Lady Selborne to son, Roundell Palmer, 10 Nov., 3 Dec. 1909, MS Eng. hist. d. 446, ff. 94–5.
7. Lady Cowper to son, Francis, 7th Earl, 7 Nov. 1870, *Earl Cowper, K.G. A Memoir*, by his wife, priv. pr., c.1913, pp. 194–5.
8. Mrs Sarah Acland to son Henry, 18 Aug. 1875, MS Acland d. 46, ff. 147–9.
9. Margaret Rogers to Angie Acland, n.d. [Dec. 1875], MS Acland, d. 144, ff. 3–4.
10. Mary to Catherine Gladstone, 17 Sept. 1881, Mary Gladstone Drew Papers, BL Add. MS 46223, ff. 85–6; Mary to Herbert Gladstone, 5 Nov. 1881, Glynne–Gladstone MS 51/2.
11. Jane Sanderson to sister Mary Haldane, n.d. [Feb.–Mar. 1881],

Haldane MS 6091, ff. 154–5.
12. S. Koss, *Haldane*, 1969, p. 10.
13. Elizabeth to mother, Mary Haldane, 18 Mar., n.d., [*c*.23 Apr.] 1890, Haldane MS 6046, ff. 235–6, 238–9; Lady Abercromby to Mrs Mary Haldane, 10 Oct. [1890], Haldane MS 6093, ff. 136–9.
14. Koss, *Haldane*, p. 10.
15. Correspondence between Sybella Lady Lyttelton and Lady Trevelyan, 7–9 Aug., 22 Oct. 1899, Trevelyan Papers, GOT 127.
16. Correspondence between Hester Lyttelton and Lady Trevelyan, 1900–1, ibid.
17. William Farr, *Vital Statistics*, 1885, p. 78; E. B. Duffey, *What Women Should Know*, Philadelphia, 1873, pp. 72–4.
18. Mary Paley Marshall, *What I Remember*, Cambridge, 1947, p. 10.
19. Lady Angela Forbes, *Memories and Base Details*, 1922, pp. 37–9.
20. Mary Drew to Lord Rosebery, 29 Feb. 1912, Rosebery MS 10015, f. 212; Lady Cowell-Stepney to Mary Drew, 12 May 1911, Mary Gladstone Drew Papers, BL Add. MS 46250, f. 129.
21. Cecilia to Violet Maxse, 28 Sept. 1889, Cecil-Maxse MSS, U 1599, C 61/34.
22. *Recollections of Lady Georgiana Peel*, ed. Ethel Peel, 1920, p. 158.
23. Mary Lygon to Lord Stanhope, 12 Feb. 1905, Stanhope MSS, U 1590, C 525.
24. Duffey, *What Women Should Know*, p. 75; Jane Sanderson to Mary Haldane, 6 Mar. 1881, Haldane MS 6091, ff. 141–2.
25. Louisa Lady Antrim to Mary Countess Minto, 22 Feb. 1901, Minto MS 12436, f. 179; Victoria Dawnay to Mary Minto, Dec. 1910, Minto MS 12431, f. 166.
26. Catherine Gladstone to Lord Rosebery, 22 Dec. 1884, Rosebery MS 10021, ff. 55–6.
27. Eveline Lady Portsmouth to brother, Lord Carnarvon, 27 Oct. 1876, Carnarvon Papers, BL Add. MS 61049.
28. B. Webb diary, 17 Mar. 1883, Passfield Papers; Kate Potter to Leonard Courtney, 25 May 1882, Courtney Collection, vol. III, ff. 29–30.
29. Duffey, *What Women Should Know*, p. 77; Lady Constance Malleson, *After Ten Years. A Personal Record*, 1931, p. 12.
30. Betty Balfour to A. J. Balfour, 22 Nov. 1894, Balfour (Whittingehame) MS 166.
31. Charty Ribblesdale to A. J. Balfour, 28 Oct. n.d. [1898], ibid.
32. *Earl Cowper, K.G. A Memoir*, by his wife, p. 17.
33. Mildred Buxton, *A Memoir*, priv. pr., n.d. [*c*.1966], pp. 22, 25, 27.
34. *Lady John Russell*, eds. Desmond MacCarthy and Agatha Russell, 1910, pp. 34–43, 47, 215.

35. See e.g. Duffey, *What Women Should Know*, pp. 87–9; A. MacDonald, *On the Bearings of Chronic Disease of the Heart upon Pregnancy, Parturition and Childbed*, 1878.
36. George H. Savage, 'Marriage in Neurotic Subjects', *Journal of Mental Science*, vol. 29, 1883, 49–54.
37. H. A. Allbutt, *The Wife's Handbook*, 23rd edn. 1894, 1st pub. 1886, p. 57.
38. See e.g. J. S. to G. E. Sneyd, 26 May 1880, Sherbrooke Papers, I.
39. Amelia C. Beal to uncle, W. H. Smith, 6 Sept. [*c.*1877], Hambleden MSS H 50.
40. M. Gladstone to A. Lyttelton, 7 Dec. 1881, M. Gladstone Drew Papers, BL Add. MS 46233, ff. 239–40.
41. D. D. Lyttelton to Kathleen Lyttelton, 5 Mar., 25 June 1890, Chandos Papers I, 5/16.
42. Lady Selborne to son, Roundell Palmer, 22 Dec. 1906, MS Eng. hist. d. 445, f. 166.
43. Frances Balfour to A. J. Balfour, 22, 26 Oct. 1889, Balfour Papers (Whitt.), MS 163.
44. William Rathbone to Randolph McKim, 15 Aug. 1894, and reply of 30 Aug. 1894, Rathbone MS IX, 8, 54–6.
45. Emilia to Charles Dilke, [*c.*1901], and note by G. T. Tuckwell, Dilke Papers, BL Add. MS 43906, f. 164.
46. Lady Trevelyan, 'The Number of My Days', undated TS, p. 53, Trevelyan Papers.
47. M. Scharlieb, *The Seven Ages of Woman*, 1915, pp. 66–8.
48. A. C. Beal to W. H. Smith, 6 Sept. 1877, Hambleden MSS H 50.
49. *Mary Haldane. A Record of a Hundred Years (1825–1925)*, ed. Elizabeth Haldane, 1926, pp. 88–90.
50. Wentworth Dilke to Sir Charles Dilke, 11 May 1896, Dilke Papers, BL Add. MS 43902, ff. 1–2.
51. Maud to William Selborne, 9 Sept. 1909, MS Selborne Adds. 3, ff. 76–7.
52. Mrs Humphry Ward to daughter Dorothy Ward, 20 May 1903, Pusey House, Ward Papers.
53. Duchess of Cleveland to Arthur Lord Stanhope, [13 Jan. 1878], Stanhope MSS, U 1590, C 522.
54. Helen to Henry Gladstone, 10 June 1877, Glynne–Gladstone MS 44/3; Lord Crewe, *Lord Rosebery*, 1931, pp. 117–20.
55. L. J. L. Dundas, *Lord Cromer*, 1932, p. 55.
56. Mary Chamberlain to mother, Mrs Endicott, 8 Feb. 1889, Chamberlain Papers, AC 4/3/57.
57. Walter Yates to Herbert Samuel, 25 Jan. 1896, Samuel Papers, B/6/10.

58. Lady Desborough to Monica, 30 June 1915, Desborough Papers, 1627, Box 1.
59. *Emma, Lady Ribblesdale. Letters and Diaries*, ed. Beatrix Lister, priv. pr., 1930, pp. 223–4.
60. A. G. Gardiner, *The Life of Sir William Harcourt*, 1923, p. 290.
61. B. H. Holland, *The Life of the Duke of Devonshire*, 1911, pp. 399–400.
62. *Recollections of Lady Georgiana Peel*, ed. Ethel Peel, 1920, p. 202.
63. Cynthia Asquith, *Remember and be Glad*, 1952, pp. 21, 68, 125–7.
64. 'Notes on Asquith's Life', n.d., A. G. Gardiner Papers, 3/7, pp. 8–10, British Library.
65. Margot Tennant to A. J. Balfour, 18 Nov. 1891, Balfour Papers, BL Add. MS 49794, ff. 48–9.
66. Margot Asquith to D. D. Lyttelton, n.d., Chandos Papers, I, 5/1.
67. A. G. Gardiner, 'Notes on Asquith's Life', A. G. Gardiner Papers, 3/7, pp. 8–10.
68. Margot Asquith to Mary Drew, 12 Oct. 1894, Mary Gladstone Drew Papers, BL Add. MS 46238, f. 223.
69. Margot Asquith to A. J. Balfour, 5 Sept. 1894, Balfour Papers, BL Add. MS 49794, f. 63.
70. Margot Asquith to Mary Drew, n.d., Mary Gladstone Drew Papers, BL Add. MS 46238, f. 239.

Chapter 4: Experiences of Love, Courtship and Early Marriage

1. Lady Lincolnshire's diary, 1877, Carrington MS film 1097.
2. Ibid., diary, 28–9 May 1878.
3. Ibid., diary, 25 Dec. 1878.
4. Agnes Wickham to Catherine Gladstone, 29 Sept. 1891, Glynne–Gladstone MS 30/10. This case study of Mary Gladstone is a revised version of part of an essay published in *The Gladstonian Turn of Mind*, ed. B. L. Kinzer, Toronto, 1985.
5. Mary Gladstone to Catherine Gladstone, n.d. [24], 28 Nov. 1870, Mary Gladstone Drew Papers, BL Add. MS 46222, ff. 145–7, 152. The Talbot sisters were Lady Brownlow, Lady Pembroke and Lady Lothian.
6. Mary Gladstone to Catherine Gladstone, n.d. [Oct. 1871], ibid., ff. 158–9; M. Gladstone to Lavinia Talbot, n.d. [Dec. 1885], ibid., MS 46236, f. 268.
7. Mary Gladstone to Catherine Gladstone, 23 Nov. 1876, ibid., MS 46222, f. 312; *Mary Gladstone: Her Diaries and Letters*, ed. Lucy Masterman, 1930, p. 144.
8. Mary Gladstone to Lavinia Talbot, Jan. 1879, Masterman, ed., *Mary Gladstone Diaries*, p. 144.

9. Mary Gladstone's diary, 5–6 Sept. 1881, ibid., p. 232; M. Gladstone to Lavinia Talbot, n.d. [Christmas 1885], ibid., p. 374.

10. Mary Gladstone to M. Cowell-Stepney, n.d. [19–20 Aug. 1879, Sept. 1883], Mary Gladstone Drew Papers, BL Add. MS 46249, ff. 23, 25, 133–5.

11. Mary Gladstone diary, 17 July, 23 Oct., 25, 29 Dec. 1883, 12–13 Jan. 1884, 24 Jan. 1886, ibid., MS 46261, ff. 18, 26, 31–2; MS 46262, f. 5.

12. Mary Gladstone to Lord Rosebery, 29 Dec. 1885, Rosebery MS 10015, ff. 97–8.

13. Agnes to Henry Gladstone, 4 Feb. 1886, Glynne–Gladstone MS, 42/5; Mary Gladstone to A. J. Balfour, 4 Oct. 1888, Balfour Papers, BL Add. MS 49794, ff. 185–6.

14. Catherine Gladstone to Lucy Cavendish, 26 Dec. 1885, Glynne–Gladstone MS 35/6.

15. Alice Balfour to Mary Gladstone, 31 Dec. 1885, Mary Gladstone Drew Papers, BL Add. MS 46238, ff. 90–1; Mary Gladstone Drew diary, 24 Jan. 1886, ibid., MS 46262, f. 5.

16. Mary Gladstone to Catherine Gladstone, 11 Dec. 1885, n.d. [c.6 Feb. 1886], ibid., MS 46223, ff. 228–9, 246–7; Mary Gladstone Drew diary, 2–3, 8 Feb. 1886, ibid., MS 46262, ff. 7, 10.

17. Mary Drew to Lavinia Talbot, 22 Mar. 1886, Mary Gladstone Drew Papers, BL Add. MS 46236, f. 271; Mary Drew to Catherine Gladstone, 21 May 1887, Glynne–Gladstone MS 30/12.

18. Margot Asquith, *The Autobiography of Margot Asquith*, 1935 (1st edn. 1920), pp. 1–23.

19. M. Gladstone to Lavinia Talbot, 5 Oct. 1882, Mary Gladstone Drew Papers, BL Add. MS 46236, f. 163.

20. Mary Drew to Catherine Gladstone, n.d. [19 June 1886], ibid., MS 46223, ff. 335–6.

21. A. G. C. Liddell, *Notes from the Life of an Ordinary Mortal*, 1911, cited in M. Asquith, *Autobiography*, pp. 24–5.

22. Sir Charles Petrie, *Scenes of Edwardian Life*, 1965, pp. 98–100.

23. E. S. Haldane, *From One Century to Another*, 1937, pp. 140, 171; A. J. Balfour, *Chapters of Autobiography*, ed. B. E. C. Dugdale, 1930, p. 232.

24. 'Interwoven' by Edith Lyttelton, unpublished typescript, 1938, Chandos Papers, 6/1/B (cited hereafter as Chandos, 'Interwoven', 6/1/A–H). 'Interwoven' is Edith (Balfour) Lyttelton's lengthy account of the dual courtships of herself and Laura Tennant with Liddell and Lyttelton, based on Liddell's diaries and the correspondence of the two women.

25. M. Gladstone to Lavinia Talbot, 5 Oct. 1882, Mary Gladstone Drew Papers, BL Add. MS 46236, ff. 163–5; 'Memoir of Laura Tennant by M. Drew', 1887, ibid., MS 46270, ff. 13–14.

26. M. Drew to Spencer Lyttelton, 9 Jan. 1890, ibid., MS 46232, ff. 196–7.
27. M. Gladstone to brother Henry, Oct. 1882, 6 July 1883, 12 Sept. 1883, 24 Oct. 1883, Glynne–Gladstone MS 43/2.
28. Chandos, 'Interwoven', 6/1/B.
29. Ibid.
30. Ibid., 6/1/C.
31. Ibid., 6/1/B–C.
32. Ibid., 6/1/C, G, I.
33. Ibid., 6/1/B.
34. Frances Balfour to A. J. Balfour, 23 Nov. [1884], Balfour Papers (Whittingehame) 164.
35. Chandos, 'Interwoven', 6/1/C.
36. Frances Balfour to A. J. Balfour, 6 Dec. [1884] and n.d., Balfour Papers (Whittingehame) 164.
37. M. Asquith, *Autobiography*, pp. 35–7; *Dictionary of National Biography 1912–1921*, 1927, pp. 349–51.
38. Laura Tennant to Doll Liddell, 4 Jan. 1885, Chandos II, 6/1/C.
39. Ibid., 30 Jan. 1885; Laura Tennant to Alfred Lyttelton, 31 Jan. 1885, and n.d., Chandos II, 6/1/E; I, 4/1.
40. Frances Balfour to Mary Gladstone, n.d., Balfour Papers (Whittingehame) 165.
41. Laura Tennant to Arthur Lyttelton, 27 Jan. 1885, Chandos II, 2/2, f. 19.
42. Laura Tennant to Alfred Lyttelton, 21 Apr. 1885, ibid., f. 32.
43. Alfred Lyttelton to Laura Tennant, 21 Apr. [1885], Chandos, 'Interwoven', 6/1/F.
44. Laura Tennant to Alfred Lyttelton, 9 Jan. 1885, Chandos II, 2/2, f. 18.
45. Laura Tennant to Alfred Lyttelton, n.d., Chandos I, 4/1.
46. Laura Tennant to Alfred Lyttelton and reply, 29 June 1885, Chandos, 'Interwoven', 6/1/F.
47. Ibid., 6/1/A, G.
48. Ibid.
49. Ibid., 6/1/I (Sept. 1889).
50. Ibid., 6/1/J.
51. Ibid., 6/1/K.
52. Ibid., 6/1/K–L.
53. Ibid., 6/1/J.; Margot Tennant to Mary Drew, 18 Mar. 1892 and n.d. [5 May 1892?], M. Gladstone Drew Papers, BL Add. MS 46238, ff. 208–10, 212.
54. Margot Asquith to Mary Drew, 29 Aug. [1913], ibid., ff. 245–6; Chandos, 'Interwoven', 6/1/J, K, L.
55. Chandos, 'Interwoven', 6/1/K–L.

56. Edith (DD) to Alfred Lyttelton, 25 Sept. 1895, Chandos I, 5/14.
57. H. V. F. Winstone, *Gertrude Bell*, 1980, *passim*.
58. Mary Lady Trevelyan, 'The Number of My Days', undated and unpublished typescript memoir, pp. 1–23. Lady Trevelyan's daughter, Dr Pauline Dower, kindly allowed me to consult this memoir.
59. Ibid., pp. 23–8.
60. Mary K. Bell diary, *passim*, Trevelyan Papers.
61. Ibid., 18 June, 8 July 1901.
62. Ibid., 18 Nov. 1901, 1 May, 30 June 1902.
63. Ibid., 15, 18 Feb., 15 June 1903.
64. Ibid.
65. Ibid., 25–8 June 1903.
66. Ibid., 4, 9 July 1903.
67. Ibid., 18 Oct. 1903.
68. Ibid., May 1911 (before entry for 16 May).
69. 'Notes on Charles by M.K.T.', n.d., Trevelyan Papers (possibly an early draft of 'The Number of My Days', pp. 50–3).
70. C. P. Trevelyan to Mary (Molly) Bell, 3 Mar., 21 June 1902; M. Trevelyan, 'The Number of My Days', pp. 39–40, Trevelyan Papers.
71. Mary K. Bell to Sybil Bell, 8 June 1902, ibid.
72. Mary Trevelyan, 'The Number of My Days', p. 40; M. K. Bell diary, 30 June 1902, 13 Feb. 1903, 27 Mar. 1904, Trevelyan Papers.
73. M. K. Bell to C. P. Trevelyan, 21, 26, 31 July, 14 Aug. 1903, ibid.
74. M. K. Bell diary, 19–24 Aug. 1903, ibid.
75. M. K. Trevelyan, 'The Number of My Days', p. 43.
76. M. K. Bell diary, 27 Mar. 1904, 13 Feb. 1903, Trevelyan Papers.
77. Ibid., 25 Aug.–8 Sept. 1903; M. K. Bell to C. P. Trevelyan, 30 Aug. 1903, Trevelyan Papers.
78. M. K. Bell diary, 15–20 Sept. 1903; M. K. Trevelyan, 'The Number of My Days', pp. 44–5; M. K. Bell to C. P. Trevelyan, 22 Nov. 1903, Trevelyan Papers.
79. C. P. Trevelyan to parents, 24 Sept. 1903; M. K. Bell to C. P. Trevelyan, 2 Oct. 1903, Trevelyan Papers.
80. M. K. Bell to C. P. Trevelyan, 6 Oct. 1903, ibid.
81. M. K. Bell to C. P. Trevelyan, 6, 17 Nov., 21 Dec. 1903, ibid.
82. M. K. Trevelyan, 'The Number of My Days', pp. 46–7; M. K. Bell to C. P. Trevelyan, 2, 4, 15, 27 Oct. 1903, Trevelyan Papers.
83. M. K. Trevelyan, 'The Number of My Days', p. 48; M. K. Trevelyan diary, 6–7 Jan. 1904, ibid.
84. Ibid.; diary, 1, 19 Nov. 1904.
85. M. K. to C. P. Trevelyan, 5 Feb. 1906, 14 Apr., 19 July 1907, 1 Mar. 1909, Trevelyan Papers.

86. Margaret King's journal, 14 Jan., 2 Feb., 12–13 Apr. 1869, Ramsay MacDonald Papers, PRO 30/69/852, ff. 4–5, 11, 15.
87. Ibid., 6 Mar., 26 Apr., 15 May 1869, ff. 18–19, 36, 47.
88. Ibid., 19 May 1869, ff. 50–1; Dr J. H. Gladstone to Margaret King, 20 May 1869, PRO 30/69/861.
89. M. King's Journal, 20, 26–7 May 1869, PRO 30/69/852, ff. 52, 54.
90. Ibid., 26–7 May, 6–8 June 1869, ff. 54, 58–9; M. King to Dr Gladstone, 29 May 1869, PRO 30/69/861.
91. Ibid.; M. Gladstone to Mrs E. King, 2, 29 Aug. 1869, PRO 30/69/852; M. Gladstone's Journal, 2 Aug. 1869, PRO 30/69/852, f. 85.
92. Mrs E. King to Mrs M. Gladstone, n.d. [late Sept. 1869], PRO 30/69/852, f. 111.
93. M. Gladstone's Journal, 30 Sept., 23 Dec. 1869, PRO 30/69/852, ff. 111, 139; M. Gladstone to Mrs E. King, 19 May 1870, PRO 30/69/852.
94. M. Gladstone's Journal, 26–8 July 1869, PRO 30/69/852, f. 82.
95. Ibid., 19 Aug., 1 Oct. 1869, ff. 93–4, 112; M. Gladstone to Mrs E. King, 7 Aug. 1869, PRO 30/69/852.
96. M. Gladstone's Journal, 23 July, 12, 30 Aug. 1869, PRO 30/69/852, ff. 80, 89, 98.
97. M. Gladstone's notes on the first few weeks of her married life, 21 Sept. 1869, PRO 30/69/852 (in envelope with bundle of diaries).
98. M. Gladstone's Journal, 11 Oct. 1869, PRO 30/69/852, f. 117.
99. M. Gladstone to Ramsay MacDonald, [2], 10 and 22 July 1896, PRO 30/69/778.
100. M. Gladstone to R. MacDonald, 23, 25 June, 10 July 1896, PRO 30/69/778; H. Samuel to M. Gladstone, 10 June 1895, PRO 30/69/886.
101. M. Gladstone to R. MacDonald, 23, 25 June 1896, PRO 30/69/778.
102. Bessie Gladstone to M. Gladstone, 22 Sept. 1896, PRO 30/69/887; M. Gladstone to R. MacDonald, 23 Sept. 1896, PRO 30/69/778.
103. M. Gladstone to R. MacDonald, 15 June, [2] July 1896, PRO 30/69/778.
104. Ibid., 30 June, [2], 3, 22 July 1896.
105. M. Gladstone's diary, 23 Nov. 1896, PRO 30/69/922.
106. Mr Cook (London School Board) to M. Gladstone, 28 Oct. 1896, PRO 30/69/887.
107. Isabella Holmes to M. Gladstone, 7 Nov. 1896, PRO 30/69/887.
108. M. MacDonald to Elizabeth King, 23 May 1897, PRO 30/69/950; M. L. Huggins to M. MacDonald, 6 Jan. 1903, PRO 30/69/896.
109. Annie Ramsay to M. Gladstone and reply, 27 July, 19, 23 Aug. 1896, PRO 30/69/775.
110. Peter Gay, *The Bourgeois Experience. Victoria to Freud*, vol. I,

Education of the Senses, 1984, p. 458.

111. Jane Hardy to Gathorne Hardy, 28 Mar. 1857, *Gathorne Hardy. First Earl of Cranbrook. A Memoir*, ed. A. E. Gathorne-Hardy, 1910, I, 96.

Chapter 5: The Joys of Childbirth

1. Mireille Laget, 'Childbirth in Seventeenth- and Eighteenth-Century France: Obstetrical Practices and Collective Attitudes', in *Medicine and Society in France. Selections from the Annales, Economies, Societies, Civilisations*, vol. 6, eds. R. Forster and O. Ranum, Johns Hopkins, Baltimore, 1980, p. 137.
2. See F. B. Smith's valuable chapter in *The People's Health: 1830–1910*, 1979, pp. 13–64. See also P. Branca, *Silent Sisterhood*, 1977, pp. 74–92, for a more general treatment based largely on health manuals. For recent work on childbirth in British aristocratic families in an earlier period see Judith Schneid Lewis, 'Maternal Health in the English Aristocracy: Myths and Realities 1790–1840', *Journal of Social History*, vol. 17, \ o. 1 (Fall 1983), 97–114.
3. Barbara Ehrenreich and Deidre English, *Complaints and Disorders. The Sexual Politics of Sickness*, Writers and Readers Pub. Co-op., London, 1976, 1st pub. New York, 1973, *passim*.
4. Lorna Duffin, 'The Conspicuous Consumptive: Woman as an Invalid', in S. Delamont and L. Duffin, *The Nineteenth-Century Woman*, 1978, pp. 26–7, 30–5, 50.
5. Lady Emily Hankey to daughter, Evelyn Lady Stanhope, 11, 14 Sept. [1882], Stanhope MSS, U 1590, C 577/4.
6. 'Elizabeth King's Journal of 1870 on the death of her daughter, Margaret Gladstone', MacDonald Papers, PRO 30/69/852. See Edward Shorter, *A History of Women's Bodies*, 1983, pp. 280–1, for a detailed examination of women's suffering.
7. Margot Tennant to A. J. Balfour, n.d. [late 1888], Balfour Papers, Add. MS 49794, ff. 35–6.
8. Margaret Hobhouse to sister Mary Playne, n.d. [1907], in Stephen Hobhouse, *Margaret Hobhouse and her Family*, 1934, p. 176; Kate Courtney's diary, 25 Aug. 1907, Courtney Collection, vol. xxxiii, ff. 27–9.
9. Lady Frances Balfour, *Lady Victoria Campbell. A Memoir*, 1911, p. 89.
10. Lady Constance Stanley to mother, 8 Nov. 1870, Hobbs MS 30/18.
11. E. Haldane to mother, Mary Haldane, 22 May 1882, and to her Aunt Jane, 3 Aug. 1885, Haldane MS 6046, f. 124, and 6015, f. 93.
12. Katrina to husband W. M. Conway, 23 Aug. 1900, Conway Papers, Cambridge University Library, Add. 7676, Conway E/150b.
13. Lady Evelyn Murray to brother, Lord Tullibardine, 12 Apr. 1911,

Atholl MS 82/83/1.

14. Lady Acland to stepdaughter, May Hart-Davis, 'Easter Day', 1879, Devon Record Office, Acland MSS (1148 M/21 (ii)/3).
15. Mary Drew to Catherine Gladstone, n.d. [*c*.20 April 1893], M. Gladstone Drew Papers, BL Add. MS 46225, ff. 42–3.
16. Lady Lyell to Lady Campbell-Bannerman, 27 Nov. [between 1895 and 1902], Campbell-Bannerman Papers, BL Add. MS 41246, ff. 261–2.
17. Marion Bryce to Mary Bryce, 29 Sept. 1904, MS Bryce Adds. 42.
18. Lady Cowper to son, Francis, Lord Cowper, 18 Jan. 1875, *Earl Cowper, K.G. A Memoir*, by his wife, Katrine Cecilia, priv. pr., 1913, p. 282.
19. Duffin, 'Conspicuous consumptive', p. 32. See also e.g. Ehrenreich and English, *Complaints and Disorders*, p. 10: 'medicine has treated pregnancy and menopause as diseases . . . childbirth as a surgical event'.
20. Wanda Neff, *Victorian Working Women*, 1966 (1st edn. 1929), p. 207.
21. Dr Thomas Bull, *Hints to Mothers*, 1837, p. 3.
22. Dr John T. Conquest, *Letters to a Mother*, 1848, p. 25.
23. Dr Albert Westland, *The Wife and Mother. A Medical Guide*, 1892, p. 62.
24. Dr Mary Scharlieb, *A Woman's Words to Women on the Care of their Health in England and in India*, 1895.
25. M. Gladstone to mother, E. King, 13 Nov. 1869, 14 June 1870, MacDonald Papers, PRO 30/69/852.
26. Mrs G. Smith to Mrs Gordon Duff, n.d. [1883], Chandos I, 4/5.
27. Edith Lyttelton to sister-in-law, Kathleen Lyttelton, 19 Aug. 1892, Chandos I, 5/15; May Harcourt to mother-in-law, Elizabeth, Lady Harcourt, 11 Aug. 1899, MS Harcourt dep. 647, ff. 17–18.
28. E. Ashton to daughter, Marion Bryce, 28 July 1891, MS Bryce Adds. 41.
29. Mary Drew to Lavinia Talbot, 20 Feb. 1890, M. Gladstone Drew Papers, BL Add. MS 46236, f. 303. For advice manuals on exercise during pregnancy, see e.g. H. A. Allbutt, *The Wife's Handbook*, 23rd edn., 1894, p. 12.
30. Mrs G. Smith to Mrs Gordon Duff, n.d. [1883], Chandos I, 4/5.
31. M. K. Trevelyan's diary, 1906, Trevelyan papers.
32. Frances Horner to Edith Lyttelton, 31 Jan. 1891, Chandos II, 3/5; Edith Lyttelton to Kathleen Lyttelton, 19 Aug. 1892, Chandos I, 5/15.
33. Lady Acland to stepdaughter May Hart-Davis, 17 Apr. 1874, Devon Record Office, Acland MSS (1148 M/21 (ii)/3).
34. M. Acland to sister-in-law S. A. Acland, 16 Feb. n.d. [1879], MS Acland d. 144, f. 12.

318   *Notes to Pages 139–143*

35. Evelyn Stanhope to husband Arthur Stanhope, 9 Feb. 1872, Stanhope MSS, U 1590, C 513/1.
36. K. B. Glasier to John B. Glasier, 1894, Glasier MSS, I, 1, 1984/10.
37. Louisa Antrim to Mary Lady Minto, 5 (2 letters), 7 May, 12, 18 Aug. 1884, Minto MS 12432, ff. 200, 203–4, and MS 12433, ff. 76, 79.
38. M. K. Trevelyan's diary, 1, 3, 8 May and 20 July 1904, 26 Feb. 1905; M. K. Trevelyan to sister Elsa Richmond, 19 Jan. 1905, Trevelyan Papers.
39. Mary Drew to Lady Cowell-Stepney, n.d. [*c*.8 April 1886], M. Gladstone Drew Papers, BL Add. MS 46249, ff. 212–13.
40. Lavinia Talbot to sister Meriel Talbot (both Lyttelton sisters married Talbot brothers), 26 Feb. 1875, Talbot Papers U 1612.
41. Lady Constance Stanley to mother, 5 Dec. 1870, Hobbs MS 30/23.
42. Mary Drew to Catherine Gladstone, 5, 11 July 1889, M. Gladstone Drew Papers, BL Add. MS 46224, ff. 175–6, 177–8.
43. M. Shaw to husband, Alex Shaw, 11 Aug. 1914, Craigmyle Papers.
44. Margaret Gladstone to Elizabeth King, 13 Nov. 1869, 14 Jan. 1870, and replies, MacDonald Papers, PRO 30/69/852.
45. J. M. Munro Kerr, R. W. Johnstone, M. H. Phillips, *Historical Review of British Obstetrics and Gynaecology, 1800–1950*, 1954, p. 10.
46. M. Buxton, *A Memoir*, n.d. [*c*.1966], p. 27.
47. Edith to husband Alfred Lyttelton, 20 Aug. 1895, Chandos I, 5/14.
48. Louisa Antrim to sister Mary Lady Minto, 21 Apr. 1884, Minto MS 12432, f. 188.
49. M. K. to C. P. Trevelyan, 27 Apr. 1908; M. K. Trevelyan's diary, 14 Sept. 1905, Trevelyan Papers.
50. Lucy Stanhope to sister-in-law Evelyn Stanhope, 17 Oct. 1872, Stanhope MSS, U 1590, C 590/4.
51. Margaret Gladstone to mother, Elizabeth King, 13 Nov. 1869, MacDonald Papers, PRO 30/69/852.
52. Lavinia Talbot to sister Meriel Talbot, 26 Feb. 1875, Talbot Papers, U 1612.
53. Margot Asquith to Mary Drew, 2 Jan. 1895, M. Gladstone Drew Papers, BL Add. MS 46238, f. 227.
54. Edith to Kathleen Lyttelton, 19 Aug. 1892, Chandos I, 5/15.
55. Mary Drew to Lavinia Talbot, 12 Aug. 1889, M. Gladstone Drew Papers, BL Add. MS 46236, ff. 300–1.
56. M. Gladstone to mother, Elizabeth King, 14 Jan. 1870, MacDonald Papers, PRO 30/69/852.
57. Mary Drew to Spencer Lyttelton, 13 Feb. 1895, M. Gladstone Drew Papers, BL Add. MS 46232, f. 236; M. Asquith to A. J. Balfour, 4 June 1897, Balfour Papers, BL Add. MS 49794, f. 73; Lady Alice

Cecil to Violet Cecil-Maxse, n.d. [20 Apr. 1900], Cecil-Maxse MSS, U 1599, C 77/12.

58. Lady Selborne to daughter, Mabel, Lady Howick, 24 Apr. [1908], Selborne Papers, 9M68/163 [Hampshire Record Office].

59. Mary Drew to Catherine Gladstone, n.d. [*c*.5 July 1889], M. Gladstone Drew Papers, BL Add. MS 46224, ff. 175–6.

60. M. Gladstone to mother, Mrs E. King, 14 June 1870, MacDonald Papers, PRO 30/69/852.

61. Lady Salisbury to Dr Acland, 30 Apr. n.d. [1870s], MS Acland, d. 74, ff. 6–7.

62. Meriel Talbot's diary, 16 June 1866, 14 Mar. 1870, 1 Sept. 1873, Talbot Papers, U 1612, F 111, F 114, F 118, F 121.

63. M. K. Trevelyan's diary, 8 Oct. 1905, 5 Nov. 1906, Trevelyan Papers.

64. Letters to the *Lancet*, 11, 18 Dec. 1841, 15 Jan., 26 Feb., 1842. See J. Jill Suitor, 'Husbands' Participation in Childbirth: A nineteenth century phenomenon', *Journal of Family History* (Fall 1981), pp. 278–93, for American evidence from marriage and health guides.

65. Sir A. Hardinge, *The Life of Lord Carnarvon*, 1925, I, 12.

66. *Lady John Russell*, ed. Desmond MacCarthy and Agatha Russell, 1910, p. 100.

67. Catherine Gladstone to Lucy Cavendish, 3 Jan. 1882, Glynne–Gladstone MS 35/5.

68. Meriel Talbot's diary, 19 June 1861, Talbot Papers, U 1612, F 110.

69. Katrina Conway to mother, 1 Oct. 1884, Cambridge Univ. Lib., Add. 7676, Conway F/43b + c.

70. Mary Drew to Alfred Lyttelton, Palm Sunday 1886, M. Gladstone Drew Papers, BL Add. MS 46234, f. 62.

71. M. K. Trevelyan's diary, 5 Nov. 1906, 30 Apr. 1908, Trevelyan Papers.

72. Lord Charles Nairne to Lady Minto, 9 Feb. 1910, Minto MS 12419, f. 119.

73. This accorded with the advice of influential medical manuals from the 1830s (though these did not include husbands). See e.g. Bull, *Hints to Mothers*, p. 129; Conquest, *Letters to a Mother*, p. 44.

74. See e.g. A. L. Galabin, *A Manual of Midwifery*, 1900, p. 204: 'especially among the Irish, the neighbours are fond of gathering in the lying-in room'.

75. Elizabeth King to daughter, Margaret Gladstone, 1 July 1870, MacDonald Papers, PRO 30/69/853.

76. Meriel Talbot's diary, 19 June 1861, 14 July 1862, 16 June 1866, 14 Mar. 1870, 1 Sept. 1873, 2 Nov. 1878, Talbot Papers U 1612, F109/F126.

77. See e.g. Lady Carrington's diary, 27 Sept. 1889, Carrington MS film 1099.
78. Ida Thomson to cousin, Margaret MacDonald, 24 Dec. 1910, MacDonald Papers, PRO 30/69/904.
79. *Lady John Russell*, eds. MacCarthy and Russell, pp. 99–100.
80. M. Gladstone to mother, E. King, 18 June 1870; J. H. Gladstone to E. King, 20 July 1870, MacDonald Papers, PRO 30/69/852.
81. Louisa, Lady Antrim to sister Mary, Lady Minto, 16, 17 Feb. 1884, 4 Jan. 1885, Minto MS 12432, ff. 57, 61; MS 12434, f. 10.,
82. Lady Antrim to Lady Minto, 1 June 1889, Minto MS 12435, f. 66.
83. Chandos, 'Interwoven', 6/1/L.
84. M. K. Trevelyan's diary, 7 May 1908, Trevelyan Papers.
85. Lady Emily Hankey to daughter Evelyn Stanhope, 30 July 1882, Stanhope MS U1590 C577/4.
86. Louisa Antrim to Lady Minto, 1 June 1889, Minto MS 12435, f. 66.
87. Victoria Dawnay to sister Lady Minto, 11, 18 Feb. 1910; Lord Charles Nairne to mother-in-law Lady Minto, 9 Feb. 1910, Minto MS 12419, ff. 119–21, and MS 12431, f. 88.
88. Helen Acland to sister-in-law S. A. Acland, n.d. [1890s], MS Acland, d. 144, ff. 161–2.
89. Louisa Antrim to Mary Lady Minto, 17 Dec. 1908, Minto MS 12439, f. 214.
90. E. Shorter, *Women's Bodies*, pp. 171–2, 271–3.
91. Dr Victoria Bennett, *Lectures to Practising Midwives*, 1911, p. 104. See also Galabin, *A Manual of Midwifery*, p. 219.
92. Dorothy Ward to Lady Trevelyan, 6 July 1906, Trevelyan Papers, GOT 124.
93. Florence Bell to daughter M. K. Trevelyan, 28 June 1908, Trevelyan Papers.
94. See e.g. Shorter, *Women's Bodies*, pp. 171–3; A. L. Galabin, *Practice of Midwifery*, 7th edn. 1910, p. 648.
95. M. K. Trevelyan to C. P. Trevelyan, 4 May 1906, Trevelyan Papers.
96. Lady Frances Balfour, *Ne Obliviscaris. Dinna Forget*, 1930, I, 235.
97. Victoria Dawnay to Lady Minto, 11, 18 Feb. 1910, Minto MS 12419, ff. 119–21.
98. Mary Drew to Alfred Lyttelton, 'Palm Sunday', 1886, M. Gladstone Drew Papers, BL Add. MS 46243, f. 62.
99. Lady Mary Beauchamp to brother, Lord Stanhope, 1873, Stanhope MS U1590 C518/1.
100. Annie Hicks to Margaret MacDonald, 1 May 1908, MacDonald Papers, PRO 30/69/901; see also e.g. Evelyn Lady Stanhope to Lord Derby, 15 June 1892, Stanhope MS U1590 C717/9, for use of the same euphemism.

101. Maud Lady Selborne to husband Lord Selborne, 15 Oct. 1908, MS Selborne Adds. 3, ff. 31–2.
102. J. W. Mackail and Guy Wyndham, *Life and Letters of George Wyndham*, 1925, I, 18 [Aug. 1863].
103. Alice Balfour's journal, 16 July 1898, Balfour MS (Whittingehame).
104. Louisa Antrim to Lady Minto, 15 Dec. 1884, and to Lord Minto, 12 Feb. 1891, Minto MS 12433, f. 219 and MS 12376, f. 128.
105. May Harcourt to Elizabeth Lady Harcourt, 16 Oct. 1905, MS Harcourt dep. 647, ff. 186–7.
106. Mary to Neville Chamberlain, 24 Jan. 1914, Chamberlain Papers, NC 1/20/2/9.
107. Lord Derby to Lord Stanhope, 14 Nov. 1880; Lord Reay to Lord Stanhope, 21 Nov. 1880, Stanhope MS U1590, C530.
108. The *South Bucks Free Press, Wycombe, Maidenhead and Marlow Journal*, 24 Apr. 1895, Carrington MS film 1116; Lady Carrington's diary, 24 Apr. 1895, MS film 1100.
109. Mary Haldane to son, R. B. Haldane, 18 Mar. 1911, Haldane MS 6009, ff. 46–7.
110. Lady Constance Malleson, *After Ten Years. A Personal Record*, 1931, p. 14 [c.1880s].
111. 'Lady Maud Selborne's childhood recollections', n.d., Selborne Papers, MS Eng. misc. e. 964, f. 7.
112. See e.g. Bennett, *Lectures*, pp. 109, 114–16, 124–5; Westland, *A Medical Guide*, pp. 63–9; W. D. Wiggins, *Midwifery for Midwives*, 1904, p. 140.
113. Meriel S. Talbot's diary, June–July 1861, Mar. 1870, Sept. 1873, Talbot Papers, U 1612, F 109, 118, 121.
114. Mrs Caroline Grey to daughter, Lady Minto, 1 Jan. 1885, Minto MS 12420, ff. 19–20.
115. Lady Carrington's diary, Apr.–May 1880, Mar.–Apr. 1881, Carrington MS film 1097.
116. Lady Salisbury to son, Edward, 11 Sept. 1895, Cecil-Maxse MSS, U 1599, C 709/35.
117. Betty Balfour to brother-in-law, A. J. Balfour, 6 Jan. 1903, Balfour MSS (Whittingehame), 281.
118. M. K. Trevelyan to C. P. Trevelyan, 3 Apr. 1908; Elsa Richmond to M. K. Trevelyan, 17 Nov. 1910, Trevelyan Papers.
119. M. K. Trevelyan's diary, May 1908; M. K. to C. P. Trevelyan, 4 June 1908, Trevelyan Papers.
120. Meriel S. Talbot's diary, 1 Sept. 1873, Talbot Papers, U 1612, F 121. On the decline in wet-nursing and the increasing criticism of the practice in the advice manuals, see e.g. L. A. Weatherly, *The Young Wife's Own Book*, 1882, p. 87; Branca, *Silent Sisterhood*, pp. 101–3.

121. Elsie (?) to cousin, Lady Minto, 6 Jan. 1885, Minto MS 12426, f. 64.
122. Betty Balfour to A. J. Balfour, n.d. [1886], Balfour (Whittinge-hame) 166.
123. Lady Salisbury to son, Edward Cecil, 30 Sept. 1895, Cecil-Maxse MSS, U 1599, C 709/36.
124. See e.g. Bull, *Hints to Mothers*, pp. 151–2, 168–9; Conquest, *Letters to a Mother*, pp. 76, 91–110; Weatherly, *The Young Wife's Own Book*, pp. 78–9.
125. Bennett, *Lectures*, pp. 219–24; Wiggins, *Midwifery for Midwives*, pp. 146–7.
126. Sir Charles Dilke to Ashton Dilke, 21 Feb. 1877, Dilke Papers, BL Add. MS 43902, f. 76.
127. Meriel S. Talbot's diary, 1861–78, Talbot Papers, U 1612.
128. *Earl Cowper, K.G. A Memoir*, p. 169.
129. Charlotte Danvers to son-in-law, W. H. Smith, 15 Aug. [1868], Hambleden MS G 28.
130. Louisa Antrim to Lady Minto, 4 Jan. 1885, Minto MS 12434, f. 10.
131. M. E. MacDonald to aunts, Elizabeth and Agnes King, 1 Aug. 1904 [wrongly filed under 1901], MacDonald Papers, PRO 30/69/894.
132. Bennett, *Lectures*, pp. 219–24; Westland, *A Medical Guide*, p. 73.
133. Olive Ilbert to M. K. Trevelyan, 2 Mar. 1905, Trevelyan Papers.
134. Mary Gladstone to Catherine Gladstone, n.d. [c.17 Nov. 1875], M. Gladstone Drew Papers, BL Add. MS 46222, f. 257.
135. See e.g. Bennett, *Lectures*, pp. 219–24; Wiggins, *Midwifery for Midwives*, pp. 146–7.
136. Lady Cowell-Stepney to Mary Drew, n.d. [2 Feb. 1913], M. Gladstone Drew Papers, BL Add. MS 46250, f. 180.
137. M. K. Trevelyan's diary, 1905 *passim*, Nov. 1906.
138. Ibid., 13–15 Feb. 1906.
139. Lady Colin Campbell, *Etiquette of Good Society*, 1893, p. 27.
140. *Emma, Lady Ribblesdale. Letters and Diaries*, ed. B. Lister, 1930, p. 100.
141. M. L. Hart-Davis to brother C. T. D. Acland, 23 May 1874, Devon Record Office, Acland MSS (1148 M/6/9).
142. Eleanor Cecil to sister-in-law, Violet Cecil, 28 Jan. 1900, Cecil-Maxse MSS, U 1599, C 92/14.
143. Lady Cowell-Stepney to Mary Drew, 12 Mar. 1913, M. Gladstone Drew Papers, BL Add. MS 46250, f. 182.
144. Catherine Gladstone to Lucy Cavendish, n.d. [Nov. 1885], M. Gladstone Drew Papers, BL Add. MS 46226, f. 79.
145. Lady Carrington's diary, 17 Apr. 1880, Carrington MS film 1097.

Chapter 6: The Tragedies of Childbirth

1. William Farr, *Vital Statistics*, 1885, pp. 270, 278; J. M. Munro Kerr, R. W. Johnstone, M. H. Phillips, *Historical Review of British Obstetrics and Gynaecology 1800–1950*, 1954, p. 259, table 1; F. B. Smith, *The People's Health 1830–1910*, 1979, p. 13.
2. Lady Acland to stepdaughter May Hart-Davis, 17 Apr. 1874, Devon Record Office, Acland MSS (1148 M/21 (ii)/3); Maggie Acland to sister-in-law S. A. Acland, 16 Feb. [1879], MS Acland d. 144, f. 12.
3. Catherine Gladstone to Mary Drew, n.d. [5 July 1886], M. Gladstone Drew Papers, BL Add. MS 46223, ff. 351–2; Agnes Wickham to Catherine Gladstone, 12 Aug. 1886, Glynne–Gladstone MS 54/9.
4. Edith to Alfred Lyttelton, 14 Nov. 1892, Chandos, 'Interwoven', 6/1/L; Edith to Kathleen Lyttelton, 6 Oct. 1892, Chandos I, 5/16.
5. William Farr, *Vital Statistics*, pp. 107, 189; see the *Lancet*, 26 Oct. 1872, for estimates of proportion of still-births.
6. T. R. Allison, *A Book for Married Women*, 1894, p. 29; A. L. Galabin, *A Manual of Midwifery*, 1900, p. 385.
7. G. D. Pinker and D. W. T. Roberts, *A Short Textbook of Gynaecology and Obstetrics*, rev. edn. 1971, pp. 93–5; Ralph Bension, *Handbook of Obstetrics and Gynaecology*, 6th edn., Los Altos, Cal. Lange, 1977, p. 260.
8. Dr Bull, *Hints to Mothers*, 1837, p. 98; Dr M. Ryan, *A Manual of Midwifery*, 1841, p. 307; Dr Mary Scharlieb, *A Woman's Words to Women on the Care of their Health in England and in India*, 1895, pp. 168, 181–2.
9. Elizabeth King to daughter, Margaret Gladstone, 14, 23, Nov. and n.d. [1869], PRO 30/69/853.
10. Margaret Gladstone to Elizabeth King, 15 Mar. 1870, PRO 30/69/852. *The Times* 'Births' columns in Jan. and June 1870 announced approximately one still-birth (or death shortly after birth) for every ten live births.
11. Lady Cowell-Stepney to Mary Drew, [Aug. 1886], M. Gladstone Drew Papers, BL Add. MS 46249, f. 249.
12. Mary Drew to Catherine Gladstone, n.d. [c.5 July 1889], M. Gladstone Drew Papers, BL Add. MS 46224, ff. 175–6; M. Drew to Lavinia Talbot, 12 Aug. 1889, ibid., MS 46236, ff. 300–1.
13. Lady Selborne to husband, Lord Selborne, 4 Aug. [1912], MS Selborne Adds. 3, ff. 155b–155c.
14. Lady Constance Stanley to mother, 28 Nov. 1870, Hobbs MS 30/22.
15. K. Bruce Glasier to M. E. MacDonald, 23 Sept. 1909, PRO 30/69/1376.
16. M. K. to C. P. Trevelyan, 20 Nov. 1907; Elsa Richmond to M. K. Trevelyan, 25 Oct., 12 Nov. 1907, Trevelyan Papers.

17. J. Prest, *Lord John Russell*, 1972, pp. 181–2.
18. Constance Stanley to Emma Talbot, 5 Sept. 1879, Hobbs MS 35/1/5.
19. May Harcourt to Lady Harcourt, 30 Oct. 1901, MS Harcourt dep. 647, ff. 77–8.
20. Beatrice D. Smith to mother, Mrs Emily Smith, 18 Sept. 1881, Hambleden MSS, L 15.
21. Louisa Antrim to Lady Minto, 19 Nov. 1890, Minto MS 12435, ff. 102–3.
22. Victoria Dawnay to Lady Minto, 10, 13 Jan. 1891, n.d. [1892], Minto MS 12428, ff. 21, 23, 139.
23. Dr A. Westland, *The Wife and Mother Medical Guide*, 1892, p. 42.
24. Mary Drew's diary, 10 Aug.–1 Sept. 1886, M. Gladstone Drew Papers, BL Add. MS 46262; Catherine to W. E. Gladstone, 29 Aug. 1886, Glynne–Gladstone MS 22/1.
25. Auguste Schluter, *A Lady's Maid in Downing Street, 1877–1890*, ed. Mabel Duncan, 1922, p. 141; Catherine to W. E. Gladstone, 2 Sept. 1886, Glynne–Gladstone MS 54/9.
26. Mary Drew's diary, 1–16 Sept. 1886, M. Gladstone Drew Papers, BL Add. MS 46262 (entries by Harry Drew from Sept.); Agnes Wickham to Catherine Gladstone, Sept. 1886, Glynne–Gladstone MS 45/9.
27. Mary Drew's diary, 16–30 Sept. 1886, M. Gladstone Drew Papers, BL Add. MS 46262.
28. Ibid.; Catherine Gladstone to Lucy Cavendish, 29 Sept. [1886], M. Gladstone Drew Papers, BL Add. MS 46226 f. 100.
29. Mary Drew's diary, Oct.–Dec. 1886, Jan. 1887, ibid., MS 46262.
30. Gertrude Gladstone to Catherine Gladstone, 2 May 1893, Glynne–Gladstone MS 30/4.
31. Edith Caroline Gibbs to brother, Vicary Gibbs, 16 Jan. 1884; Louisa Anne Gibbs to son, Vicary Gibbs, 4 Apr. 1884, Gibbs family letters, MS 11021/29, ff. 53–4, 98–9 (Gibbs/Lord Aldenham, Guildhall Library, London).
32. Maud to husband, Lord Selborne, 10 June 1912, MS Selborne Adds. 3, f. 158.
33. Nigel Nicolson, *Mary Curzon*, 1977, pp. 174–5, 208–9; Leonard Moseley, *Curzon: The End of an Epoch*, 1960, pp. 89, 113, 114–15.
34. Edith to Alfred Lyttelton, 19, 26, 30 Sept. 1902, Chandos II, 3/11.
35. M. K. to C. P. Trevelyan, 24, 25, 28, 30 July 1911; M. K. Trevelyan diary, 23–31 July 1911, Trevelyan Papers.
36. M. K. Trevelyan diary, 1–2 Aug. 1911, Trevelyan Papers.
37. Ibid., 3–14 Aug. 1911; M. K. to C. P. Trevelyan, 17 Aug. 1911, Trevelyan Papers.
38. Elsa Richmond to M. K. Trevelyan, 5 Aug. 1911, Trevelyan Papers.
39. M. K. to C. P. Trevelyan, 24–7 Aug. 1912, Trevelyan Papers.

40. William Farr, *Vital Statistics*, pp. 270, 278.
41. Kerr, Johnstone and Phillips, *Obstetrics and Gynaecology*, cite the following figures for natural deaths per thousand live births in table 1, p. 259: 1865–74 5.0; 1875–84 4.6; 1885–94 5.1; 1895–1904 4.6. These statistics were based on the annual reports of the registrar-general. See also F. B. Smith, *The People's Health, 1830–1910*, p. 13: 'Measured against each 1,000 live births, these figures represent rates of 6 per 1,000 in 1847, 4.3 in 1861, 4.9 in 1871, 4.8 in 1881, 4.7 in 1891 to 4.8 in 1901, to 4.03 per 1,000 in 1903.'
42. F. B. Smith, *The People's Health*, pp. 13–14; Kerr, Johnstone and Phillips, *Obstetrics and Gynaecology*, pp. 257–60.
43. *Lady Frederick Cavendish's Diary*, ed. J. Bailey, 1927, II, 194–5 (23–30 Jan. 1876).
44. Kenneth Rose, *A Superior Person. A Portrait of Curzon and His Circle in Late Victorian England*, 1969, pp. 37–8. Death certificates were purchased (at £4.50 each) from the General Register Office, London.
45. Statistics based on Kerr, Johnstone and Phillips, *Obstetrics and Gynaecology*, p. 259, table 1.
46. Meriel Talbot's diary, 15 Mar. 1860, Talbot Papers, U 1612, F 108; H. Pleydell-Bouverie, *From a Great Grandmother's Armchair*, 1927, pp. 52–5.
47. *Earl Cowper*, by his wife, priv. pr., 1913, pp. 282–3.
48. Margaret Gladstone's Journal, 31 Dec. 1869, PRO 30/69/852, f. 143.
49. Dr J. H. Gladstone to Elizabeth King, 20 July 1870, PRO 30/69/852.
50. Elizabeth King to sister-in-law, Margaret Henderson, 8 Aug. 1870, PRO 30/69/852.
51. E. King to David King, 10, 11 Aug. 1870, ibid.
52. Ibid., 10 Aug. 1870.
53. E. King to M. Henderson, 15 Aug. 1870, PRO 30/69/852.
54. 'Elizabeth King's Journal of her Daughter's Death, 1870', PRO 30/69/852.
55. Angus McLaren, *Birth Control in Nineteenth-Century England*, 1978, p. 11.
56. Dr Henry A. Allbutt, 'Evil produced by over-bearing and excessive lactation', *Malthusian Tract no. 4*, 1880, p. 2; Dr H. A. Allbutt, *The Wife's Handbook*, 1886, pp. 38–9; Robert Barnes, 'On the Risk to Life of First and Subsequent Pregnancies', *Transactions of the Obstetrical Society of London*, vol. 1, 1859, 314.
57. 'Memorandum on the death of Mary Lady Lyttelton, 1857', Mary Gladstone Drew Papers, BL Add. MS 46269, ff. 65–109b; Georgina Battiscombe, *Mrs Gladstone*, 1956, pp. 107–10; Betty Askwith, *The Lytteltons*, 1975, pp. 129–41.

58. Ibid.
59. Chandos, 'Interwoven', 6/1/B, E.
60. Laura to Katharine Lyttelton, n.d. [1886], Chandos I, 4/2.
61. Laura to Edward Lyttelton, n.d. [16 Dec. 1885], in 'Memoir of Laura Tennant by Mary Drew', M. Gladstone Drew Papers, BL Add. MS 46270, f. 76.
62. Chandos, 'Interwoven', 6/1/D.
63. Memo by M. Asquith on the death of Laura Lyttelton, 7 Nov. 1913, Chandos, 'Interwoven', 6/1/F.
64. Helen to Henry Gladstone, 22 April 1886, Glynne–Gladstone MS 44/4.
65. Lucy Cavendish to her brother, 'dearest old fellow' [Spencer Lyttelton?], Good Friday, 1886, Chandos I, 2/20, f. 44.
66. Alfred Lyttelton to Mary Drew, 16 April 1886, M. Gladstone Drew Papers, BL Add. MS 46270, ff. 79–80.
67. Helen to Henry Gladstone, 22 April 1886, Glynne–Gladstone MS 44/4.
68. Liddell's diary, Chandos, 'Interwoven', 6/1/D.
69. Memo by M. Asquith on the death of Laura Lyttelton, 7 Nov. 1913, Chandos, 'Interwoven', 6/1/F.
70. M. Drew's diary, 19–24 Apr. 1886, M. Gladstone Drew Papers, BL Add. MS 46262, ff. 18–19.
71. Mary to Henry Gladstone, 20 May 1886, Glynne–Gladstone MS 43/2.
72. Catherine Gladstone to Lucy Cavendish, n.d. [Apr. 1886], M. Gladstone Drew Papers, BL Add. MS 46226, f. 83.
73. Edith Lyttelton, *Alfred Lyttelton. An Account of His Life*, 1917, p. 161.
74. Mary Drew to Alfred Lyttelton, 21 May 1888, M. Gladstone Drew Papers, BL Add. MS 46234, ff. 114–15.
75. Edith to Spencer Lyttelton, 30 Dec. 1894, Chandos II, 3/16.
76. M. Asquith to Edith Lyttelton, n.d. [Jan. 1895], Chandos I, 5/1; M. Asquith, *Autobiography*, 1920, I, p. 287.
77. M. Asquith to M. Drew, 23 Nov. 1896, M. Gladstone Drew Papers, BL Add. MS 46238, f. 230.
78. M. Asquith to Lord Rosebery, 20 Dec. 1896, Rosebery Papers, NLS, MS 10109, f. 284.
79. M. Asquith, *Autobiography*, p. 287; M. Asquith to Violet Cecil, 29 Sept. 1900, Cecil-Maxse MSS, U 1599, C 123/1.
80. Frances Horner to Violet Cecil, 29 Sept. 1900, Cecil-Maxse MSS, U 1599 C 368/17.
81. This subject will be analysed more fully in my next book, *The Victorian Way of Death*, which will devote a chapter to the deaths of babies and young children.

82. Rosalind Mitchison, *British Population Change Since 1860*, 1977, p. 50.
83. Dr R. Hall Bakewell, 'Infant Mortality and its Causes', *The British Mothers' Journal*, June 1857, p. 141.
84. R. C. Ansell, *On the Rate of Mortality*, 1874, pp. 69, 71.
85. L. Stone, *The Family, Sex and Marriage in England 1500–1800*, 1977, pp. 651–2.
86. Colin Murray-Parkes, *Bereavement*, 1978, pp. 146–7; Geoffrey Gorer, *Death, Grief and Mourning in Contemporary Britain*, 1965.
87. M. Asquith, *Myself when Young*, 1938, p. 20.
88. Stephen Hobhouse, *Margaret Hobhouse and Her Family*, priv. pr. 1934, Rochester, pp. 25–6.
89. B. Askwith, *The Lytteltons*, p. 125.
90. M. A. Chitty to Margaret MacDonald, 12 Jan. 1910 [1911?], PRO 30/69/904.
91. T. D. Acland to sister, Lydia D. Acland, n.d. [1851], Devon Record Office, Acland MSS (1148 M/16/2).
92. W. H. Smith to 'Aunt Emily' Giberne, 7, 10 Feb. 1866, Hambleden MSS, E/1.
93. Eva Knatchbull Hugesson's diary, May 1883, Knatchbull MSS, U 951 F 30/5, pp. 72–8.
94. Mabel A. Allan to M. E. MacDonald, 9 June 1911, PRO 30/69/905.
95. Lady Selborne to son, Bobby Palmer, 18 Nov. [1914], MS Eng. lett. c. 454, f. 173.
96. Laura E. Ridding, 'Christmas at Blackmoor', n.d. [Dec. 1914], MS Eng. his. c. 1018, ff. 60–1, 65–7.
97. Edith to Alfred Lyttelton, 10 May [1902?], Chandos II, 3/11; Chandos, 'Interwoven', 6/1/L.
98. Edith Lyttelton, 'Antony', Chandos II, 3/21; Edith to Alfred Lyttelton, 8 Sept. 1902, Chandos II, 3/1; Chandos, 'Interwoven', 6/1/L.
99. G. M. Trevelyan to Lady Trevelyan, n.d. [Sept. 1908]; Robert Trevelyan to Lady Trevelyan, 15 Sept. 1908, Trevelyan Papers, GOT 189/2.
100. Elizabeth Trevelyan to Lady Trevelyan, Mar. 1909, Trevelyan Papers, GOT 189/2; Molly to Charles Trevelyan, 22 Mar. 1909, Trevelyan Papers, CPT.
101. Sir Hugh Bell to Molly Trevelyan, 19 Apr. 1911, Trevelyan Papers, CPT.
102. Janet Trevelyan to Lady Trevelyan, 23 Apr. 1911, Trevelyan Papers, GOT 189/3.
103. Molly Trevelyan to Lady Trevelyan, 20 Apr. 1911, ibid.

104. G. M. Trevelyan to Sir George and Lady Trevelyan, 19, 21 Apr. 1911, ibid.
105. C. P. Trevelyan to Lady Trevelyan, 19 Apr. 1911, ibid.
106. G. M. Trevelyan to Molly Trevelyan, 29 Apr. 1911, Trevelyan Papers, CPT.

Chapter 7: Roles and Attitudes

1. *Hansard HC Debates*, 12 June 1884, c. 168; Gerda Lerner, 'New Approaches to the Study of Women in American History', in B. A. Carroll (ed.), *Liberating Women's History*, Urbana, 1976, p. 351.
2. B. Harrison, *Separate Spheres. The Opposition to Women's Suffrage in Britain*, 1978, pp. 81–2.
3. Cynthia Asquith, *Remember and be Glad*, 1952, p. 4.
4. Lady Constance Malleson, *After Ten Years. A Personal Record*, 1931, p. 22.
5. Atholl MS 61.
6. Lady Trevelyan, 'The Number of My Days', n.d., TS, Trevelyan Papers.
7. J. Wilson, *A Life of Sir Henry Campbell-Bannerman*, 1973, pp. 124–5.
8. S. Koss, *Asquith*, 1976, p. 44.
9. Mary Drew to brother, Henry Gladstone, 19 Mar. 1891, Glynne–Gladstone MS 43/3.
10. M. Drew to father W. E. Gladstone, 12 Feb. 1895, ibid., 23/9.
11. Stephen Hobhouse, *Margaret Hobhouse and Her Family*, 1934, p. 37.
12. Mary Lydia Hart-Davis to father, Sir Thomas Dyke Acland, 28 May 1873, Devon Record Office, Acland MSS (1148 M/21 (ii)/13).
13. Margaret Gladstone's diary, 31 July 1869; M. Gladstone to mother, E. King, 28 Sept., 5, 14 Oct. 1869, MacDonald Papers, PRO 30/69/852.
14. John Prest, *Lord John Russell*, 1972, p. 182.
15. Meriel Talbot's diary, 1861, Talbot Papers, U 1612 F109.
16. Lady Carrington's diary, 11 May 1878, 4 Apr. 1885, Carrington MS film 1097–8.
17. Prest, *Russell*, p. 182.
18. M. Drew to C. Gladstone, 17 Oct. 1899, M. Gladstone Drew Papers, BL Add. MS 46225, f. 359.
19. Betty to Gerald Balfour, n.d. [*c*.1900], Balfour [Whittingehame] MSS, TD 80/19–271.
20. See e.g. Alice to brother A. J. Balfour, 22 Jan. 1903, ibid., 166.
21. C. Asquith, *Remember and be Glad*, 1952, pp. 177–8.
22. A. Balfour to M. Gladstone, 31 Dec. 1885, M. Gladstone Papers, BL Add. MS 46238, ff. 89–90.

23. For studies of the famous Victorian political hostesses, see e.g. O. W. Hewett, *Strawberry Fair. A Biography of Frances, Countess Walde-grave, 1821–1879*, 1956; S. M. Causton, *Lady Southwark. Social and Political Reminiscences*, 1913. A good bibliography on political hostesses is provided in H. J. Hanham (ed.), *Bibliography of British History, 1851–1914*, 1976, pp. 105–6. L. Davidoff, *The Best Circles*, 1973, presents a useful analysis of the social activities of such hostesses.

24. M. F. E. Ogilvy, *Lady Palmerston*, 1922, II, 170–2.

25. J. Prest, *Russell*, pp. 348–9; E. Lee, *Wives of the Prime Ministers*, 1918, p. 75; *Lady John Russell*, eds. D. MacCarthy and A. Russell, 1910, p. 112.

26. James Sykes, *Mary Anne Disraeli. The Story of Viscountess Beacons-field*, 1928, pp. 82–9, 106–13.

27. Georgina Battiscombe, *Mrs Gladstone*, 1956, pp. 97–8, 141.

28. Lee, *Wives of Prime Ministers*, p. 228.

29. J. Wilson, *Life of Sir Henry Campbell-Bannerman*, pp. 124–5.

30. Denis Gwynn, *The Life of John Redmond*, 1932, p. 355; E. S. Haldane, *From One Century to Another*, 1937, pp. 173–4.

31. Lady Dilke's lists of dinner engagements and guests for 'dinner at home', 1872, Dilke Papers, BL Add. MS 43902, f. 174.

32. Lady Harcourt to stepson, Lewis, 27 Feb. 1883, MS Harcourt dep. 671, ff. 19–20.

33. Lucy Masterman, *C. F. G. Masterman. A Biography*, 1968, p. 112.

34. John Edward Bowle, *Viscount Samuel. A Biography*, 1957, pp. 43–4.

35. Beatrice Potter (Webb) diary, 29 Aug. 1887, Passfield Papers.

36. Anne Estella, Countess Cave, *Odds and Ends of My Life*, 1929, pp. 159–64.

37. Lady Frances Balfour, *Ne Obliviscaris. Dinna Forget*, 1930, 2 vols., I, pp. 1, 57.

38. See e.g. Mrs Caroline Grey to Lady Minto, 29 Mar. 1885, Minto MS 12420, f. 95.

39. *Earl Cowper K.G. A Memoir*, by his wife, priv. pr., 1913, pp. 74–6.

40. Betty Askwith, *Lady Dilke. A Biography*, 1969, pp. 74–5.

41. E. H. Fowler, *The Life of H. H. Fowler, First Viscount Wolverhamp-ton*, 1912, pp. 620–1.

42. Lady Harcourt to her husband Sir William Harcourt, 9 July 1903, MS Harcourt dep. 634, f. 51.

43. Kate Courtney's diary, 3 Apr. 1891, Courtney Collection, vol. XXIV, f. 185.

44. See e.g. Lady Carrington's diary, 8 May 1877, 25 Feb., 5 Dec. 1878, 6 Jan. 1881, Carrington MS film 1097.

45. Correspondence between Lord and Lady Carrington, 1885–90, Carrington MS film 1153.

46. Edith to Spencer Lyttelton, 18 Oct. 1895, Chandos 11, 3/16.
47. Kenneth Rose, *Superior Person. A Portrait of Curzon and his Circle in late Victorian England*, 1969, p. 289.
48. G. Battiscombe, *Mrs Gladstone*, p. 37.
49. M. F. E. Ogilvy, *Lady Palmerston*, pp. 11, 161; Lee, *Wives of the Prime Ministers*, pp. 99–130.
50. Lady John Russell to sister, Lady Mary Abercromby, 3 Aug. 1848, *Lady John Russell*, eds. D. MacCarthy and A. Russell, 1910, pp. 101–2.
51. Prest, *Russell*, pp. xvi, 354–5, 366.
52. Lee, *Wives of the Prime Ministers*, pp. 131–55.
53. J. A. Spender, *Life of Sir Henry Campbell-Bannerman*, 2 vols., 1923, I, 22, 288; J. Wilson, *A Life of Sir Henry Campbell-Bannerman*, pp. 76, 131–2, 447–9.
54. Lucy Masterman,'Lady Salisbury', in Lee, *Wives of the Prime Ministers*, pp. 218–32.
55. Quoted in Kenneth Rose, *The Later Cecils*, 1975, p. 43. This book includes chapters on Lord Salisbury and all his children, but not his wife.
56. Lucy Masterman, ed., *Mary Gladstone. Her Diaries and Letters*, 1930, p. 424.
57. Mary to brother, Henry Gladstone, 2 Feb. 1883, Glynne–Gladstone MS 43/2.
58. Catherine Gladstone to Lucy Cavendish, July 1882, Glynne–Gladstone MS 35/5.
59. See e.g. Catherine to Mary Gladstone n.d. [8 Dec. 1882], M. Gladstone Drew Papers, BL Add. MS 46223, f. 106.
60. Catherine to W. E. Gladstone, n.d. [1881], Glynne–Gladstone MS 22/1.
61. Catherine Gladstone to Mary Drew, 10 Aug. [1892], M. Gladstone Drew Papers, BL Add. MS 46224, f. 411.
62. Catherine to W. E. Gladstone, 3 Jan. [1884], Glynne–Gladstone MS 22/1.
63. Lucy Cavendish to Catherine Gladstone, n.d. [c.Dec. 1883], Glynne–Gladstone MS 32/9.
64. Catherine Gladstone to Lord Rosebery, n.d. [1882?], Rosebery MS 10021, f. 39.
65. Battiscombe, *Mrs Gladstone*, pp. 156–60, 177–9.
66. Kate Courtney's diary, 1892, Courtney Collection, vol. xxvi, ff. 161–3.
67. Catherine to Henry Gladstone, n.d. [early 1890s], Glynne–Gladstone MS 37/19.
68. Catherine Gladstone to Harry Drew, 15 Feb., 3 Mar. 1894, Mary

Gladstone Drew Papers, BL Add. MS 46225, ff. 145–6, 149–50.

69. Edith Lyttelton's sketch of Margot Asquith, Chandos, 'Interwoven', 6/1/L; 'character sketch of Margot Asquith by Mary Drew', c.1918, M. Gladstone Drew Papers, BL Add. MS 46270, f. 323.

70. M. Asquith to A. J. Balfour, n.d. [1900?], Balfour (Whittingehame) 166.

71. Baroness Ravensdale, *In Many Rhythms. An Autobiography*, 1953, p. 30; Lady Angela Forbes, *Memories and Base Details*, 1922, pp. 113–14.

72. Margot Asquith to A. J. Balfour, n.d. [10 Feb. 1897], Balfour Papers, BL Add. MS 49794, ff. 74–5.

73. M. Asquith to A. J. Balfour, n.d., and 11 Sept. 1900, Balfour (Whittingehame) MS 166.

74. M. Asquith to Mrs Walter Runciman, 9 Dec. [n.d.], Runciman Papers, WR 302.

75. M. Asquith to John Burns, 17 Jan. [1906], J. Burns Papers, BL Add. MS 46282, ff. 39–40.

76. M. Asquith to Lewis Harcourt, 11 Nov. 1910, MS Harcourt dep. 421, ff. 157–8.

77. S. Koss, *Asquith*, p. 17.

78. See e.g. M. Asquith to L. Harcourt, 14 Aug. 1914, MS Harcourt dep. 421, ff. 201–2; M. Asquith to J. Burns, 14 Aug. 1914, J. Burns Papers, BL Add. MS 46282, ff. 160–1.

79. F. E. Baily, *Lady Beaconsfield and Her Times*, 1935, pp. 33–5; Sykes, *Mary Ann Disraeli*, pp. 66–7.

80. S. M. Causton (Lady Southwark), *Social and Political Reminiscences*, p. 94.

81. C. Battersea, *Reminiscences*, 1922, pp. 184–6.

82. Lady Frances Balfour, *Ne Obliviscaris. Dinna Forget*, II, 33.

83. Elizabeth Harcourt to Lord Rosebery, 21 June 1888, Rosebery MS 10087, f. 262.

84. See e.g. Helen to Mary Gladstone, 5, 11 July 1892, M. Gladstone Drew Papers, BL Add. Ms 46231, ff. 124–9.

85. Meriel L. Talbot to mother, Meriel S. Talbot, n.d. [1895], Talbot MS U 1612.

86. Kate Courtney's diary, 1 Dec. 1885, Courtney Collection, vol. xxii, ff. 35–7.

87. Helen Pease (wife of Alfred) to Elsie Pease, 6 July 1892, Gainford MS 517.

88. Katherine Dilke to Mr Hepworth Dixon, n.d. [1874], Dilke Papers, BL Add. MS 43902, f. 193.

89. Jennie Churchill, *Reminiscences*, 1908, pp. 124–7.

90. Katharine, Duchess of Atholl, *Working Partnership*, 1958, p. 60.

91. Edith H. Fowler, *The Life of H. H. Fowler First Viscount Wolverhampton*, 1912, pp. 496–7.
92. Elizabeth Haldane to mother, Mary Haldane, 20, 21 Jan. 1910, Haldane MS 6051, ff. 25–8. See also E. Haldane, *From One Century to Another*, 1937, pp. 123, 175, 194, 206–7.
93. H. Samuel to Beatrice Samuel, 12 Sept. 1900, Samuel Papers, A/157/51; Beatrice to Clara Samuel, 2 July [1902], ibid., B/3/63; Bowle, *Samuel*, pp. 43–4, 49.
94. Herbert to Beatrice Samuel, 2 Feb. 1905, 12 Jan. 1906, Samuel Papers, A/157/257, 310.
95. May Harcourt to Lady Harcourt, 3 Mar. 1904, n.d. [1905], MS Harcourt dep. 647, ff. 126, 148.
96. Ibid., 27 Jan 1905, 26 Nov. 1909, dep. 647, ff. 150–1; dep. 648, ff. 32–3.
97. Ibid., 3 Dec. 1910, dep. 648, ff. 50–1.
98. Julian Amery, *The Life of Joseph Chamberlain*, vi, 1969, 780–1.
99. Marjory Pease to Michael Pease, 20 Jan, May 1910, Wedgwood MSS.
100. Ibid., 19 Jan. 1911.
101. Lady Courtney's letter to the editor, press cutting, *Daily Mail*, 24 July 1913 (in response to a Liberal candidate who complained that the new Liberal Suffrage Society pledged its members not to work for anti-suffrage Liberal Candidates); Kate Courtney's diary, 24 July 1913, Courtney Collection, vol. xxxvi, f. 77.
102. Eleanor Cecil to sister-in-law, Maud Selborne, 26 Oct. 1910, Selborne MS Eng. lett. d. 424, f. 15.
103. Marion to husband, James Bryce, 4 Dec. 1906, MS Bryce Adds. 26.
104. May Harcourt to Lord Curzon, 5 Aug. 1910, Curzon Collection, MSS Eur. F.112/33, f. 156.
105. Adeline Duchess of Bedford to Lord Curzon, 17 July 1910, ibid., ff. 96–7.
106. Mary to brother James Bryce, n.d. [April, 1892?], MS Bryce Adds. 12.
107. See Frank Prochaska, *Women and Philanthropy in Nineteenth-century England*, Oxford, 1980.
108. See Betty Askwith, *Lady Dilke*, pp. vii–viii, 73, 190.
109. See Margaret E. MacDonald's papers, PRO 30/69/1366, 1368, 1378, 1380.
110. Beatrice Potter (Webb) diary, 12, 24 Jan, 22 Apr. 1884.
111. Beatrice to Ida Chamberlain, 4 Apr. 1911, Chamberlain Papers BC 3/2/47.
112. Ivy to Austen Chamberlain, 21 Jan. 1909, ibid., AC 6/2/48.
113. M. Buxton, *A Memoir*, n.d. [1966], pp. 41, 44, 50, 53, 60.

114. Evelyn Stanhope to father-in-law, Lord Stanhope, 8 July 1875, Stanhope MS U 1590, C 714/16.
115. Lady Acland to Christine Hamlyn, 7 Sept. 1910; Christine Hamlyn to Lord Curzon, 11 Sept. 1910, Curzon Collection, MSS Eur. F. 112/32, ff. 150–3.
116. Harrison, *Separate Spheres*, p. 111.
117. Ibid., p. 91.
118. Harrison comments that 'the biographers of Antis are unduly reticent, even by Victorian standards, about domestic life, perhaps partly because of their attitude to woman's role' [ibid., p. 254]. But the same reticence is found in most political biographies, whether the subjects were pro- or anti-suffrage. This can be explained more readily by the restricted political interests of the biographers than by their subjects' attitude to woman's role.
119. See Harrison, *Separate Spheres*, ch. 4, pp. 55–84.
120. Mrs Humphry Ward's speech in the debate with Mrs Fawcett, Feb. 1909, printed pamphlet, Pusey House, Ward Papers.
121. See e.g. Lavinia Talbot to Mary Gladstone, 12 Mar. 1884, M. Gladstone Drew Papers, BL Add. MS 46236, f. 214. Only about 12 of the 104 signatories of the 1889 anti-suffrage appeal were the wives of MPs.
122. Beatrice Potter (Webb) diary, [July], 29 June 1889; Beatrice Webb, *My Apprenticeship*, 2nd edn., n.d., pp. 9, 303.
123. May Harcourt to Lady Harcourt, 3 Mar. 1912, MS Harcourt, dep. 648, f. 64; Katharine to James Bryce, 15 Mar. 1912, MS Bryce Adds. 18; Lady Stanhope to son Dick, 7 Mar. 1912, Stanhope MS U 1590 C 718/4.
124. Lucy Cavendish to Mary Drew, 9 May 1912, M. Gladstone Drew Papers, BL Add. MS 46235, ff. 251–2.
125. Speech at Exeter by Lady Courtney, 24 Aug. 1913, press cutting, Courtney Collection, vol. xxxvi, f. 68.
126. M. Gladstone to Lavinia Talbot, 12 Mar. 1884, M. Gladstone Drew Papers, BL Add. MS 46236, ff. 209–10; M. Gladstone diary, 12, 24 Mar., 20 June 1884, ibid., MS 46261, ff. 40–1, 56.
127. M. Hobhouse to son Jack, 1913, Stephen Hobhouse, *Margaret Hobhouse and her Family*, 1934, p. 194.
128. M. E. Haldane, *A Record of a Hundred Years 1825–1925*, ed. E. Haldane, 1925, pp. 100–3.
129. Andrew Rosen, *Rise Up Women!*, 1974, p. 12.
130. Harrison, *Separate Spheres*, pp. 39, 27.
131. Lee, *Wives of the Prime Ministers*, p. 205.
132. Ishbel, Lady Aberdeen to W. E. Gladstone, 25 Apr. 1891, W. E. Gladstone Papers, BL Add. MS 44090, ff. 182–6.

133. See David Morgan, *Suffragists and Liberals*, Oxford, 1975, pp. 17–18.
134. Lady Carlisle to Lady Trevelyan, 5, 9 June 1891, Trevelyan Papers, GOT 126.
135. Morgan, *Suffragists and Liberals*, p. 18.
136. M. K. Trevelyan diary, 9 May 1905, Trevelyan Papers.
137. Kate Courtney's diary, 11 May 1888, Courtney Collection, vol. xxiii, f. 215.
138. Ibid., 5 July 1888, 1 Mar., June–July 1889, vol. xxiv, ff. 10, 60, 69–70.
139, Ibid., n.d. [Aug. 1893], 30 July 1895, vol. xxvii, f. 55; vol. xxviii, ff. 61–2.
140. Ibid., Jan. 1913, vol. xxxvi, ff. 47–8.

Chapter 8: Experiences of Political Wives

1. Beatrice Potter to sister, Mary Playne, n.d. [Oct. 1883?], Passfield Papers, II, 1 (i), 437.
2. Beatrice Potter (Webb) diary, 12, 24 Jan., 22 Apr. 1884, Passfield Papers.
3. Kate Courtney to sister Beatrice Potter, 23 July 1885, Passfield Papers, II 1 (i) 168–9.
4. Theresa Cripps to sister, Beatrice Potter, n.d. [1880s], ibid., 294–5.
5. Beatrice Potter (Webb) diary, 15 Nov. 1888, May 1891.
6. F. E. Baily, *Lady Beaconsfield, and Her Times*, 1935, pp. 150–2, 156–7; see also Elizabeth Lee, *Wives of the Prime Ministers*, 1918, pp. 137–8, 154.
7. E. H. Fowler, *The Life of H. H. Fowler, First Viscount Wolverhampton*, 1912, pp. 623–4.
8. E. S. E. Childers, *The Life and Correspondence of Hugh C. E. Childers*, 2 vols., 1901, I, 235–6, 258–9, 292.
9. Laura Lady Selborne to son, W. W. Palmer, 6 Mar. 1876, MS Selborne 98, f. 99.
10. Kate Courtney's diary, 1 Dec. 1884, Courtney Collection, vol. xxi, f. 121.
11. Edith Lyttelton to [Doll Liddell?], 6 Sept. 1893; Edith to Kathleen Lyttelton, 10 Feb. 1894, Chandos II, 3/11, ff. 12–13, 3/14.
12. Edith to Spencer Lyttelton, 30 Dec. 1894, Chandos II, 3/16; E. Lyttelton, *Alfred Lyttelton*, 1917, p. 212.
13. Mary to Neville Chamberlain, 20 Apr. 1910, Chamberlain Papers, NC 1/20/2/3. See also J. L. Garvin, *The Life of Joseph Chamberlain*, II, 1933, 497–500.

14. M. Asquith to A. J. Balfour, 18, 31 Dec. 1898, 22 July 1901, Balfour Papers, BL Add. MS 49794, ff. 89–90, 113–14; Stephen Koss, *Asquith*, 1976, pp. 43–4.

15. S. H. Zebel, *Balfour. A Political Biography*, 1973, p. 10; K. Young, *Balfour*, 1963, p. xiii.

16. J. Wilson, *C.B. A Life of Sir Henry Campbell-Bannerman*, 1973, pp. 124–5.

17. M. Fawcett, *What I Remember*, 1925, p. 55.

18. Kate Potter to fiancé, Leonard Courtney, 29 Aug. 1882, Courtney Collection, vol. III, ff. 130–1.

19. E. S. Haldane, *From One Century to Another*, 1937, pp. 215–16.

20. John Edward Bowle, *Viscount Samuel. A Biography*, 1957, p. 82.

21. William Stewart, *J. Keir Hardie*, 1921, pp. 13, 337.

22. *Lloyd George. Family Letters, 1885–1936*, ed. K. O. Morgan, 1973, pp. 112, 58.

23. Lucy Masterman, *C. F. G. Masterman. A Biography*, 1968, pp. 101, 124, 130.

24. Dorothy Lady Grey to H. H. Asquith, 21 Aug. 1892, MS Asquith 9, ff. 19–20.

25. Mary Booth to Beatrice Potter, 13 Mar. 1886, Passfield Papers, II, 1 (ii), 372.

26. M. Asquith to Edith Lyttelton, n.d. [1913], Chandos I, 5/1. It must be noted, however, that this letter was written in the middle of Asquith's obsession with Venetia Stanley, which certainly contributed to his neglect of his wife.

27. *Lady John Russell*, eds. D. MacCarthy and A. Russell, 1910, pp. 66–9, 72–3, 89, 206.

28. J. A. Spender, *Life of Sir Henry Campbell-Bannerman*, 2 vols., 1923, pp. 288–9; Lee, *Wives of Prime Ministers*, pp. 234, 238, 243–4.

29. Nigel Nicolson, *Mary Curzon*, 1977, pp. 83–5, 93.

30. G. O. Trevelyan to wife, Caroline Trevelyan, 30 July 1877, Trevelyan Papers, GOT 2.

31. H. Samuel to mother Clara Samuel, 28 Feb. 1909, Samuel Papers, A/156/303.

32. H. Havelock-Allan to mother, Lady Alice Havelock-Allan, 26 Oct. 1913, Gainford Papers [122].

33. M. Buxton, *A Memoir*, n.d. [1966], p. 33.

34. Lady Ripon to Lady Harcourt, n.d. [Apr. 1880], MS Harcourt dep. 89, ff. 34–5.

35. Louisa Antrim to Lady Minto, 8 Mar. 1885, Minto MS 12434, f. 67.

36. Nicolson, *Mary Curzon*, pp. 119, 187–8; L. J. L. Dundas, Marquess of Zetland, *Life of Evelyn Baring, First Earl of Cromer*, 1932, pp. 234–7.

37. G. W. E. Russell, *Lady Victoria Buxton. A Memoir*, 1919, pp. 167–8; Herbert Gladstone, *After Thirty Years*, 1928.
38. Correspondence between G. O. Trevelyan and wife Caroline, 1882, Trevelyan Papers, GOT 6.
39. P. Jalland, 'A Liberal Chief Secretary and the Irish Question: Augustine Birrell, 1907–1914', *Historical Journal*, 19, 2 (1976), pp. 449–50.
40. Peter Fraser, *Joseph Chamberlain: Radicalism and Empire, 1868–1914*, 1966, p. 112. See also J. L. Garvin, *The Life of Joseph Chamberlain*, I, 1932, 77, 175–6.
41. Beatrice Potter's diary, 30 Aug. 1886, Passfield Papers.
42. Ibid., 24 Jan. 1884.
43. Garvin, *Chamberlain*, IV, 272.
44. Mary Chamberlain to her mother, Mrs Endicott, 27 Dec. 1888, 8 Feb. 1889, Chamberlain Papers, AC 4/3/48, 57.
45. Ibid., 26 Sept., 24 Jan. 1889, AC 4/3/107, 53.
46. Ibid., 24 Jan. 1889, AC 4/3/53; file of correspondence about drawing room etiquette, etc., AC 4/8/1–16.
47. See e.g. Mary to Beatrice Chamberlain, 24 Oct., 7 Nov. 1897, Chamberlain Papers, BC 1/3/1–2.
48. Mary Chamberlain to Betty Balfour, 21 Sept., 26 Oct. 1903, Balfour Papers, BL Add. MS 49831, ff. 78–80, 82–7.
49. Mary to Austen Chamberlain, Chamberlain Papers, AC 4/2/1–75 (see e.g. 11 May 1909, 24 Feb. 1910, AC 4/2/57, 64).
50. Mary to Neville Chamberlain, 5 Mar. 1913, Chamberlain Papers, NC 1/20/2/8.
51. W. Runciman to his wife, Hilda, n.d. [c.1907], Runciman Papers, WR 303.
52. Marion to James Bryce, 7 Aug. 1890, 26 Mar. 1895, MS Bryce Adds. 21, 22.
53. Ibid., 28 June 1903, Adds. 25; 27 July 1897, Adds. 24; 30 May 1895, Adds. 23.
54. Marion to mother-in-law Mrs M. Bryce, 8 Oct. 1889, MS Bryce Adds. 41.
55. See e.g. Marion to J. Bryce, 21 Apr. 1896, 6–7 Oct. 1903, MS Bryce Adds. 23, 25.
56. Marion to J. Bryce, 31 Oct., 1 Nov. 1906, MS Bryce Adds. 26.
57. Ibid., 11 Nov., 5, 6 Dec. 1906, MS Bryce Adds. 26; M. Bryce to uncle, H. W. Gair, 24 Dec. 1906, MS Bryce Adds. 42.
58. Marion to J. Bryce, 22 Jan. 1907, MS Bryce Adds. 26; *Washington Post*, 13 Jan. 1910 (press cuttings, MS Bryce Adds. 59).
59. Ibid., 29 Nov., 4 Dec. 1906, MS Bryce Adds. 26.

60. Unpublished paper by Marion Bryce, 'On being asked an opinion on Women's Suffrage', 24 June 1910, MS Bryce Adds. 43.
61. Marion to James Bryce, 4 Dec. 1906, MS Bryce Adds. 26.
62. Ibid., I, 3 Sept., 29 Nov. 1906, MS Bryce Adds. 26.
63. *Washington Post*, 29 Dec. 1909, *New York Evening Telegram*, 31 Dec. 1909 (press cuttings, MS Bryce Adds. 59); Mary to brother, J. Bryce, 15 Dec. 1908, MS Bryce Adds. 17.
64. Servants' wages books, Stanhope MSS, U 1590, A 78/1.
65. Evelyn to husband, Lord Stanhope, 25 July 1878, Stanhope MSS, U 1590, C 513/3.
66. Evelyn Stanhope to mother, Emily Hankey, 12 Jan. [1875?], ibid., C 577/6.
67. Evelyn to husband, Arthur Stanhope, 28 May 1870, ibid., C 513/1.
68. Ibid., 24 June 1884, C 513/7.
69. Ibid., 24 Oct. 1871, C 513/1.
70. Ibid., 20, 24, 26–7 May 1870, C 513/1.
71. Ibid., 31 Jan., 2 Feb. 1874, C 513/1.
72. Maud Cecil to fiancé, W. W. Palmer, 21, 19 Oct. 1883, MS Selborne Adds. 1, ff. 62, 57–8.
73. Maud, Lady Selborne to son, Roundell Palmer, 16 Apr. [1908], n.d. [1909], Selborne MS Eng. hist. c. 978, ff. 76–8, 35–8; Maud Selborne to W. W. Palmer (Lord Selborne), 14, 16 Aug. 1883, 30 Apr. 1911, MS Selborne Adds. 1, ff. 23–5, Adds. 3, ff. 139–43.
74. See e.g. Maud Selborne to Roundell Palmer, 25 Jan., 16 Mar. [1908], MS Eng. hist. c. 978, ff. 20–1, 55; Maud to Lord Selborne, 23 Oct. 1908, MS Selborne Adds. 3, ff. 44–5.
75. Maud to Lord Selborne, 24 Apr. [1907], MS Selborne Adds. 2, ff. 135–7.
76. Ibid., 30 May 1907, f. 155. See also e.g. ibid., 27 Aug., 16 Oct. 1908, Adds. 2, ff. 199–200, Adds. 3, f. 37.
77. Maud Selborne to son Roundell Palmer, 29 Dec. 1906, 29 May [1909], MS Eng. hist. d. 445, f. 17; d. 446, ff. 81–2; Maud to Lord Selborne, 15 Oct. 1908, MS Selborne Adds. 3, ff. 33–4.
78. Maud Selborne to son, Roundell Palmer, 24 Dec. [1905], MS Eng. hist. d. 444, ff. 57–60.
79. Maud to Lord Selborne, 7, 8 Dec. 1910, MS Selborne Adds. 3, ff. 119–21.
80. Eleanor Cecil to Lady Selborne, 11 Dec. 1910, MS Eng. lett. d. 424, f. 19.
81. Maud Selborne to Roundell Palmer, 30 Jan. 1911, MS Eng. hist. d. 446, f. 136.
82. Maud Selborne, 'A Note on Women's Suffrage from the Common-

Sense Point of View', *Nineteenth Century*, vol. 58, Aug. 1905, pp. 306–7. See also Maud to Lord Selborne, 17 Nov. 1911, MS Selborne Adds. 3, ff. 146–8.

83. Maud to husband, W. W. Palmer (Selborne), 19 June 1892, MS Selborne Adds. 1, f. 110.

84. Maud Selborne to Roundell Palmer, n.d. [1906–7], 5 July [1907], MS Eng. hist. d. 445, ff. 94–5, 66–7.

85. Eleanor Cecil to sister-in-law, Maud Selborne, 3 Nov. 1909, 14 Nov. 1910, MS Eng. lett. d. 424, ff. 5, 17.

86. See e.g. Maud Selborne to A. J. Balfour, 3 June [n.d.], Balfour (Whittingehame) Papers.

87. Maud Selborne to Austen Chamberlain, July 1910, Chamberlain Papers, AC 8/6/4.

88. Maud to Lord Selborne, 7 Dec. 1911, MS Selborne Adds. 3, ff. 150–1.

89. M. K. Trevelyan, 'The Number of My Days', n.d., pp. 54–5, Trevelyan Papers; Molly to Charles Trevelyan, 13 Oct. 1903, Trevelyan Papers. (In 1904 the servants' wages (in addition to keep) were: cook £24 p.a.; parlourmaid £25 p.a.; housemaid £18. The children's nurse subsequently received £24 and the nurserymaid £10.)

90. 'The Number of My Days', p. 55; Molly to Charles Trevelyan, 29 Sept. 1903; see also e.g. ibid., 5 Jan. 1911.

91. 'The Number of My Days', pp. 56–7; M. K. Trevelyan diary, e.g. 27 Mar. 1911, 31 Jan., 7 Feb. 1908, 18 Mar. 1910.

92. M. K. Trevelyan diary, 14 Mar, 26 Apr. 1904, 19 May 1909, Trevelyan Papers.

93. Molly to Charles Trevelyan, 5, 22 Sept. 1903, 5 Dec. 1905; Molly Trevelyan to sister, Elsa Bell, 5 Dec. 1905, Trevelyan Papers.

94. Molly to Charles Trevelyan, 5 Sept., 15, 17 Nov., 19 Dec. 1903, Trevelyan Papers.

95. Ibid., 11 Aug. 1903; Molly Trevelyan to mother, Florence Bell, 19 Dec. 1905; M. K. Trevelyan diary, 3 Mar. 1904.

96. Molly Trevelyan to Elsa Bell, 30 Nov. 1903; C. P. Trevelyan to mother, Lady Trevelyan, 29 Nov. 1903, Trevelyan Papers.

97. M. K. Trevelyan diary, 10, 13 Dec. 1904 (see also 6 Nov. 1904); Ishbel Lady Aberdeen to M. K. Trevelyan, 11 May 1905, Trevelyan Papers.

98. M. K. Trevelyan diary, 4 Jan 1906.

99. Molly to Charles Trevelyan, 5 Dec. 1905, 18 Mar. 1906, Trevelyan Papers.

100. Ibid., 18 Feb. [1906?].

101. M. K. Trevelyan diary, 16 May 1906.

102. Molly to Charles Trevelyan, 15 Dec. 1906; M. K. Trevelyan diary, 15 Dec. 1906, Trevelyan Papers.
103. Molly to Charles Trevelyan, 10 July 1907; 25 Jan. 1908, Trevelyan Papers.
104. M. K. Trevelyan diary, 27 Feb. 1910.
105. Ibid., 20 July 1910.
106. Ibid., 6 Jan. 1908, 1, 7, 8 Apr. 1908.
107. Ibid., 13, 20 Apr. 1908.
108. Ibid., 9 Nov. 1908.
109. On C. P. Trevelyan's political career, see A. J. A. Morris, *C. P. Trevelyan, 1870–1958. Portrait of a Radical*, 1977 (esp. p. 117 on his resignation in 1914).
110. M. K. Trevelyan diary, see e.g. 15 Mar., 5 Oct. 1907, 6 Oct. 1908, 2 Oct. 1909, 27 Jan., 22 Nov. 1911.
111. Ibid., 4 Dec. 1909.
112. Molly to Charles Trevelyan, 5, 22 Dec. 1909; M. K. Trevelyan diary, 21 Dec. 1909, Trevelyan Papers.
113. M. K. Trevelyan diary, 5, 11, 17, 19 Jan. 1910.
114. Lady Trevelyan, 'The Number of My Days', p. 76.
115. Caroline Lady Trevelyan to son C. P. Trevelyan, 27 Nov. 1907, Trevelyan Papers.
116. Molly to Charles Trevelyan, 23 July 1908; see also e.g. M. K. Trevelyan diary, 30 Aug. 1909, Trevelyan Papers.

Chapter 9: Spinsters

1. S. R. Johansson, '"Herstory" as History', in B. A. Carroll, ed., *Liberating Women's History*, Urbana, 1976, p. 404. My chapter previously appeared in an earlier form in *Exploring Women's Past*, ed. P. Crawford, Melbourne, 1983, pp. 129–70.
2. E. W. Monter, 'The Pedestal and the Stake', in R. Bridenthal and C. Koonz, eds., *Becoming Visible. Women in European History*, Boston, 1977, p. 133.
3. L. Stone, *The Family, Sex and Marriage in England, 1500–1800*, 1977, p. 380.
4. See e.g. W. R. Greg, 'Why are Women redundant?', *National Review*, Apr. 1862.
5. *Census of England and Wales, 1851*, General Report, vol. 1, p. xliii; *Census of England and Wales, 1911*, General Report, table xxxi, p. 90; P. Hollis, *Women in Public: The Women's Movement, 1850–1900*, 1979, p. 33.
6. *Census of England and Wales, 1881*, General Report, vol. 4, pp. 15–16; B. R. Mitchell, *Abstract of British Historical Statistics*, Cambridge, 1962, p. 6.

340   *Notes to Pages 255–262*

7. Ibid.
8. *Census of England and Wales, 1881*, General Report, vol. 4, p. 24; R. C. Ansell, *On the Rate of Mortality at Early Periods of Life . . . and other Statistics of Families in the Upper and Professional Classes*, 1874, pp. 45, 83–5. See also J. A. Banks, *Prosperity and Parenthood*, 1954, *passim*.
9. Richard Carlile, *Every Woman's Book or What is Love?*, 1838, pp. 11, 35–6.
10. See Carl N. Degler, 'What Ought to Be and What Was: Women's Sexuality in the Nineteenth Century', *American Historical Review*, vol. 79, no. 5 (Dec. 1974), pp. 1467–90, for the view that there was a sharp difference of medical opinion on the nature of women's sexual feelings.
11. H. Spencer, *The Principles of Ethics*, 2 vols., 1892–3, I, 534.
12. Miss E. Marion Ashton to fiancé James Bryce, 11 Mar. 1899, MS Bryce, Adds. 21.
13. Beatrice Potter's diary, 22 Jan., 5 Aug. 1881, 19 Dec. 1885, 11 Feb., 28 May 1886; Beatrice Potter to father, Richard Potter, 8 Nov. 1885, Passfield Papers, II, 1 (i), 544–5.
14. Beatrice Potter's diary, 7 Mar. 1889, 10 Dec. 1886, Passfield Papers.
15. Peter T. Cominos, 'Innocent Femina Sensualis in Unconscious Conflict', in M. Vicinus, ed., *Suffer and be Still*, Indiana, 1972, p. 163 (citing Henry Maudsley, *The Pathology of Mind*, 1879, p. 164).
16. David Roberts, 'The Paterfamilias of the Victorian Governing Classes', in A. S. Wohl, ed., *The Victorian Family*, 1978, pp. 63–4.
17. F. P. Cobbe, *The Duties of Women*, 1881.
18. Beatrice Potter (Webb) diary, 5 Nov. 1883.
19. Margot Peters, *Unquiet Soul. A Biography of Charlotte Brontë*, 1977, p. 193.
20. Vera Brittain, *Testament of Youth*, 1978, pp. 401, 421–2, 536.
21. Julia Wedgwood, 'Female Suffrage' in Josephine Butler, ed., *Woman's Work and Woman's Culture*, 1869, quoted in Hollis, *Women in Public*, pp. 9–10.
22. Quoted in Stone, *The Family, Sex and Marriage in England*, p. 386.
23. S. A. Acland to father, Prof Acland, 20 July 1879, MS Acland d. 105, f. 56.
24. 'Memories in my 81st Year by Sarah Angelina Acland', MS Eng. Misc. d. 214, f. 86.
25. S. A. Acland to Prof Acland, 28 July 1880, MS Acland d. 105, ff. 60a–61b.
26. Caroline (Gull) Acland to S. A. Acland, 20 Dec. n.d. [1880s], MS Acland d. 143, ff. 150–1.

27. S. A. Acland to Prof Acland, 8, 28 July 1880, MS Acland d. 105, f. 40.
28. S. A. Acland to William A. Dyke Acland, 22 Oct. 1900, MS Acland d. 108, ff. 64–5.
29. Ibid.
30. Ibid., 18 Nov. 1900, 6 June 1901, ff. 67, 73–4, 99–100.
31. E. King to J. H. Gladstone, 20 Dec. 1874, PRO 30/69/861; M. Gladstone to sister Elizabeth King, 18 Feb. 1870, PRO 30/69/852 (Ramsay MacDonald Papers).
32. Agnes King to mother Mrs E. King, 18 Apr. 1872, PRO 30/69/970.
33. See e.g. May Gladstone to Margaret MacDonald, 25 Nov. 1903, 7 July [1904], PRO 30/69/896–7.
34. 'Prayers during the long struggle, AGK', 29 Feb. 1912, PRO 30/69/970.
35. Viscountess Milner, *My Picture Gallery 1886–1901*, 1951, pp. 19, 25.
36. Olive Maxse to Violet Cecil, 29 June 1900, Cecil-Maxse MSS, U 1599, C 66/34.
37. Katherine Maxse to Violet Cecil, 10 Aug. 1900, Cecil-Maxse MSS, U 1599, C 65/34.
38. Frances Horner to Violet Cecil, 29 Sept. 1900, Cecil-Maxse MSS, U 1599, C 368/17.
39. Mary to James Bryce, 30 Dec. 1887, MS Bryce Adds. 11.
40. Katharine to James Bryce, 19 Dec. 1883, ibid.
41. Mary to James Bryce, 10 Jan. 1884, 16 Nov. 1888, ibid.
42. Mary to James Bryce, 11 Jan. 1889, MS Bryce Adds. 12.
43. Katharine to James Bryce, 12 Apr. 1889, ibid.
44. Mary to James Bryce, 3 letters dated 4, 6 Dec., n.d. [1889], ibid.
45. Mary to James Bryce, 4 Dec. 1889, 9 Aug. 1890, ibid.
46. Kenneth Young, *Arthur James Balfour*, 1963, pp. 10–11.
47. Mary Drew to A. J. Balfour, 5 Nov. 1899, Balfour (Whittingehame) Papers, MS 164.
48. Young, *Balfour*, pp. 10–11, 133.
49. Beatrice Webb to Mary Playne, 12 Sept. 1906, Passfield Papers.
50. Ibid.
51. Frances Balfour to A. J. Balfour, n.d. [1897], Balfour (Whitt) MS 159; Frances to Alice Balfour, Mar. 1897, ibid., MS 162.
52. Alice Balfour to A. J. Balfour, 11 June 1897; A. J. Balfour to Frances Balfour (draft), 20 July 1897, Balfour (Whitt) MS 159.
53. Betty to Gerald Balfour, two letters of Dec. 1905, Balfour (Whitt) MS 273.
54. Alice Balfour to Mary Gladstone, 31 Dec. 1885, Mary Gladstone Drew Papers, BL Add. MS 46238, ff. 89–90.
55. Frances to Gerald Balfour, 9, 12 Oct. 1887, Balfour (Whitt) MS 283;

Frances to Arthur Balfour, 22 Oct. 1887, Balfour (Whitt) MS 163.
56. Mary Drew to A. J. Balfour, 5 Nov. 1899, Balfour (Whitt) MS 164.
57. M. Cowell-Stepney to Mary Drew, 22 Sept. 1904, Mary Gladstone Drew Papers, BL Add. MS 46250, ff. 28–9.
58. See e.g. A. J. Hammerton, *Emigrant Gentlewomen*, 1979.
59. See e.g. C. Smith-Rosenberg, 'The Hysterical Woman', *Social Research*, vol. 39, No. 4, 1972, 652–78.
60. The section on Helen Gladstone is based on S. G. Checkland, *The Gladstones. A Family Biography 1764–1851*, 1971, and material in the Glynne–Gladstone MSS.
61. Louisa Duchess of Atholl to Dowager Duchess of Atholl, n.d. [1890]; Dowager Duchess to Evelyn Murray, n.d. [1892], Atholl MSS 500, 480.
62. Lorna Duffin, 'The Conspicuous Consumptive: Woman as an Invalid', in S. Delamont and L. Duffin, eds., *The Nineteenth Century Woman*, 1978, p. 38.
63. Dowager Duchess of Atholl to Evelyn Murray, n.d. [1892]; Duchess to Dowager Duchess, 28 May 1892, Atholl MSS 480, 501.
64. Duchess of Atholl to daughter, Evelyn Murray, 30 June 1892, Atholl MS 501.
65. Evelyn Murray to Duke of Atholl, 10 Dec. 1891 and reply of 14 Dec. 1891, Atholl MS 63; Duchess to Dowager Duchess, 15 Dec. 1891, Atholl MS 1663.
66. Dowager Duchess to Evelyn Murray, n.d. [1892], Atholl MS 480.
67. Duchess to Dowager Duchess, 12 Dec. 1892, Atholl MS 1663.
68. Evelyn Murray to cousin, Emily Murray Macgregor, 3 Jan. 1896; Duchess to E. M. Macgregor, 17 Sept. 1896, Atholl MS 482.
69. Evelyn Murray to Duke of Atholl, 28 Jan. 1904, Oct. 1907, Atholl MS 64.
70. Evelyn Murray to E. M. Macgregor, 14 Mar. 1899, Atholl MS 66.
71. Evelyn Murray to E. M. Macgregor, n.d. [1911], 19 Dec. 1910, Atholl MS 66; Evelyn to Kitty Lady Tullibardine, 21 Sept. 1910, Atholl MS 82/83/1.
72. Evelyn to Hamish Murray, 8 July 1900, Atholl MS 489.
73. See Hollis, *Women in Public*, pp. 9–13, for useful extracts from the works of these women.
74. Lady Jeune *et al.*, *The Modern Marriage Market*, 1898, pp. 70–1; Stephen Gwynn, 'Bachelor Women', *Contemporary Review*, LXXIII, 1898, 867–8.
75. The material on Lady Gwendolen Cecil is based on Kenneth Rose, *The Later Cecils*, 1975, pp. 309–20.
76. Helen to Henry Gladstone, 30 Mar., 30 Aug. 1877, 5 July 1878, Glynne-Gladstone MS 44/3; Mary to Henry Gladstone, 9, 11 May 1878, ibid., 43/2.

77. Ibid.
78. Helen Gladstone's memorandum, 12 July 1886, and her letter to Martin Holloway, 13 June 1886, Glynne–Gladstone MS 135/22.
79. Nora Sidgwick to Helen Gladstone, 9 July 1886, Glynne–Gladstone MS 135/22; Mary to Catherine Gladstone, n.d. [c.19 June 1886], Mary Gladstone Drew Papers, BL Add. MS 46223, ff. 335–6.
80. Helen Gladstone's memorandum, 12 July 1886, Glynne–Gladstone MS 135/22.
81. Mary Drew to Henry Gladstone, 12 June 1892, Glynne–Gladstone MS 43/3; Helen to W. E. Gladstone, 2 Nov. 1896, ibid., 23/11.
82. Helen Gladstone to Mary Drew, 8 Mar., 22 Dec. 1897, Mary Gladstone Drew Papers, BL Add. MS 46231, ff. 150–2, 155–7.
83. Elizabeth B. Haldane, *From One Century to Another*, 1937, pp. 69–70, 72–3.
84. Ibid., pp. 15, 73.
85. Mary to R. B. Haldane, 24 Apr. 1897, Haldane MS 6008, f. 84.
86. R. B. Haldane, *An Autobiography*, 1929, p. 263; C. Addison, *Four and a Half Years*, 1934, I, 17; Lady Abercromby to Mary Haldane, 9 Feb. [1908], Haldane MS 6094, f. 73.
87. Information obtained from the Haldane Papers.
88. Violet Markham, *Friendship's Harvest*, 1956, p. 48.
89. *Newnham Letter*, Jan. 1926, 'Helen Gladstone: In Memoriam', p. 72, Glynne–Gladstone MS 135/124.
90. Registrar-general's 35th Annual Report, pp. xii–xiii, cited in William Farr, *Vital Statistics*, 1885, p. 80.
91. Gissing, *The Odd Women*, 1980, pp. 37, 59; Jane C. B. Sanderson to Mary Haldane, 9 Mar. 1881, Haldane MS 6091, ff. 143–5.
92. M. Harkness to B. Potter, n.d. [c. 1878], Passfield Papers, II, 1 (ii), 128–31.

Location of Manuscript Collections

ACLAND MSS, Bodleian Library, Oxford. All Acland MSS are located in the Bodleian unless the Devon Record Office is specifically cited.

ACLAND OF BROADCLYST MSS, Devon Record Office, Exeter, including the Acland–Anson Correspondence.

ALDENHAM MSS, Hertfordshire Record Office, Hertford.

ANCASTER MSS, Lincolnshire Archives Office, Lincoln.

ATHOLL MSS, Blair Castle, Scotland, seen by kind permission of the Duchess of Atholl.

BALFOUR MSS, British Library, London.

BALFOUR MSS, Whittingehame Tower, East Lothian, consulted in the National Register of Archives (Scotland) by kind permission of Lord Balfour.

BEVERIDGE MSS, British Library of Political and Economic Science, London.

BROADLANDS ESTATE ARCHIVE, Hampshire Record Office, Winchester, by courtesy of the Trustees of the Broadlands Estate.

BRYCE MSS, Bodleian Library, Oxford.

BURNS MSS, British Library.

CAMPBELL-BANNERMAN MSS, British Library.

CARNARVON MSS, British Library.

CARRINGTON MSS, Bodleian Library, Oxford (on microfilm).

CECIL-MAXSE MSS, Kent Archives Office, Maidstone, by courtesy of the Hardinge family.

CHAMBERLAIN MSS, Birmingham University Library.

CHANDOS MSS, Churchill College, Cambridge. (The Lyttelton family archive.)

CHILDERS MSS, Royal Commonwealth Library, London.

COURTNEY MSS, British Library of Political and Economic Science, London.

CRAIGMYLE MSS, seen by kind permission of Lord Craigmyle at his home in London.

CREWE MSS, Cambridge University Library, Cambridge.

CURZON MSS, India Office Library, London.

DILKE MSS, British Library.

DILKE–ENTHOVEN–ROSKILL MSS, Churchill College, Cambridge.

DREW MSS, British Library. (The diaries and correspondence of Mary Drew (née Gladstone).)

GAINFORD MSS, Nuffield College, Oxford.

GIBBS MSS (Vicary Gibbs), in the archives of Anthony Gibbs and Sons Ltd., deposited in the Guildhall Library, London.

GLADSTONE MSS, British Library.

GLASIER MSS, Liverpool University Library.

GLYNNE–GLADSTONE MSS, St Deiniol's Library, Hawarden, consulted in the Clwyd Record Office.

GRENFELL MSS, Hertfordshire Record Office, Hertford.

HALDANE MSS, National Library of Scotland, Edinburgh.

HAMBLEDEN MSS (W. H. Smith), Strand House, London.

HARCOURT MSS, Bodleian Library, Oxford.

HOBBS (DERBY/GATHORNE-HARDY) MSS, Corpus Christi College, Cambridge, by courtesy of Mr R. Hobbs.

LOWE (VISCOUNT SHERBROOKE) MSS, seen by kind permission of Mrs R. T. Sneyd, at her home in Hinton Charterhouse.

MACDONALD MSS, Public Record Office, London. These include the family papers of Ramsay MacDonald's wife, Margaret (i.e. the King and Gladstone families). (Ref: PRO 30/69.)

MILNER MSS, Bodleian Library, Oxford.

MINTO MSS, National Library of Scotland, Edinburgh. (Elliott–Murray–Kynymoud family.)

NEWHAILES (DALRYMPLE) MSS, National Library of Scotland, Edinburgh.

ONSLOW MSS, Surrey Record Office, Guildford.

PASSFIELD PAPERS, consulted in the British Library of Political and Economic Science by kind permission of the Passfield Trust and the London School of Economics and Political Science. References to the Beatrice Webb diary relate to the typescript volumes which I consulted in the LSE Library before the diary was published by Virago Press Limited.

RASCH MSS, Essex Record Office, Chelmsford.

RATHBONE MSS, University Library, Liverpool.

ROSEBERY MSS, National Library of Scotland, Edinburgh.

ROUS/STRADBROKE MSS, Ipswich and East Suffolk Record Office, Ipswich. (Ref: Hall.)

RUNCIMAN MSS, Newcastle University Library.

SAMUEL MSS, House of Lords Record Office, London. I am especially grateful to the Samuel family for their efforts to find Lady Samuel's correspondence before 1914.

SELBORNE MSS, Lambeth Palace Library. (Papers of the first Earl of Selborne.) (Ref.: MSS 1861–1906.)

SELBORNE MSS, Bodleian Library, Oxford. (Papers of the second and third Earls of Selborne.) (Ref.: MSS Selborne Adds; MSS. Eng. hist; MSS Eng. lett; MSS Eng. misc.)

SELBORNE MSS, Hampshire Record Office, Winchester. (Chiefly Lady Selborne's correspondence from South Africa.) (Ref.: 9M68.)
STANHOPE MSS, Kent Archives Office, Maidstone.
TALBOT MSS, Kent Archives Office, Maidstone.
TREVELYAN MSS, consulted at Newcastle University Library by kind permission of Dr Pauline Dower and the Trevelyan family.
WALLAS MSS, (Graham Wallas), British Library of Political and Economic Science, London.
WARD MSS, University College Library, London.
WARD MSS, Pusey House, Oxford.
WARING MSS, seen at the National Register of Archives (Scotland), by kind permission of Sir Ilay Campbell.
WEDGWOOD MSS, consulted by kind permission of Mrs Helen Pease, at her home in Cambridge.

The Lansdowne and Churchill Papers were closed, and I was not granted permission to see the Cecil Papers at Hatfield House or the Grosvenor Papers owned by the Duke of Westminster.

Index

birth control: acceptance and use of 175, 185; breastfeeding as method of 176; honeymoons and 36; ignorance of 121, 139; men's hostility towards 176; propaganda 175, 256

Blackstone, Sir William 59

Blantyre, Lord 61, 62; daughter, Gertrude *see* Gladstone (W. E. Gladstone/Hawarden Castle family); wife 62

Bleadon, Mr (clergyman) 85

Boer War 41, 202

Booker, B. L. 9; mother 9

Booth, Charles 34

Booth, Mary 34, 225–6

Bowland, Dr 148

Brand, Robert 88

Bright, Dr 136

Brittain, Vera 16, 258

Brodrick, St John 103

Bronte, Charlotte 258, 259

Brooks, Olive 56

Brownlow, Lord 101

Bryce, J. Annan 234, 266–7

Bryce, James 34, 43–4, 80, 189, 190, 210, 212, 213, 228, 231–4, 248, 256, 266–8

Bryce, Katharine 241, 234; *spinster case study* 260, 265–8, 286

Bryce, Mrs Margaret 268

Bryce, Marion (*née* Ashton; m. James Bryce) 34, 43–4, 80, 136, 210, 213, 214, 256–7, 267; *political wife case study* 228, 231–4, 241, 248, 249; mother 231; uncle 233

Bryce, Mary 56, 211, 234; *spinster case study* 260, 265–8, 286

Bryce, Violet (wife of J. Annan Bryce) 234, 266–7

Bryce family 233, 234, 267

Buccleuch, Duke of 42, 48

Bull, Dr Thomas: on breastfeeding 154; medical manual on antenatal care 137; on miscarriage 161

Burlingham, Dr 165, 166, 167

Burne-Jones, Edward 99

Burns, Mrs 33, 41

Burns, John 203, 203–4

Burns, May *see* Harcourt

Burrows, Dr 136

Butler, Josephine, on spinsters 280

Buxton, Connie (1st wife of Sydney Buxton) 83, 225

Buxton, Mildred (*née* Hugh Smith; 2nd wife of Sydney Buxton) 12–13, 14, 83, 141, 212, 227

Buxton, Sydney 83, 225

Buxton, Sir Thomas Fowell, Bt. (Governor of South Australia 1895–8) 227

"C. E.", Mr (hapless suitor of Margaret King) 122

Cadogan, Earl of 56

Cadogan, Sir Edward 52, 56–7

Cadogan, Henry (vetoed suitor of Gertrude Bell) 47

Cairns, Lady 50

Campbell, Lady Colin, etiquette manual 38, 58

Campbell, Lady Frances *see* Balfour (Whittingehame family)

Campbell, Pamela (mother-in-law of Percy Wyndham) 150

Campbell, Lady Victoria (sister of Lady Frances Campbell) 82

Campbell-Bannerman, Lady 136, 190, 194, 199, 226

Campbell-Bannerman, Sir Henry 190, 199, 202, 224, 226, 246

careers for girls (*see also* governesses) 17, 254, 280, 283, 284

Carlile, Richard 256

Carlisle, Earl of 55, 114

Carlisle, Lady 217, 217–18

Carnarvon, Evelyn Lady (*née* Stanhope; 1st wife of 4th Earl of Carnarvon) 38, 173

Carnarvon, Henry Herbert, 4th Earl of 38, 81, 173

Carnarvon, Henry John George, 3rd Earl of 53; daughter, Winifred *see* Herbert

Carrington, Lady (mother of Charles Carrington) 95

Carrington, Lady (Cecilia (Lily); *née* Harbord; m. Charles, Lord Carrington) 14, 25, 38, 138, 146, 151, 152, 154, 158, 191–2, 197, 227; *courtship case study* 94–6, 97; daughters (*see also* Wynn-Carrington) 14, 96, 151; mother 95, 96; sisters 38, 94, 95, 96, 158; son 151

Carrington, Lord Charles (Tannums) 25, 38, 95–6, 151, 197, 227; father 95

Weatherly, Dr L. A., on breastfeeding 154

Webb, Beatrice (*née* Potter; m. Sidney Webb) 4–5, 9, 10, 14, 16, 22, 23, 34, 40, 44, 53–4, 80, 82, 191, 195, 212, 213, 214, 221–2, 228, 229, 248, 256, 257, 258, 269, 270, 285, 287

Webb, Sidney 40, 44, 53–4, 222, 257; family 54

weddings 30, 31, 32, 35–41, 43, 58, 86, 89, 96, 101, 102, 109, 113, 120, 123, 125, 126, 128, 129, 159, 242; abroad 112; breakfast/tea (reception) 36, 37, 38, 40, 120; bride's and her parents' duties 36; bridegroom's duties 36; celebrated in churches 38, 40, 109, 120; celebrated on the estates of, or in, country houses 39–40; ceremony 36, 39, 40; choice of day 36; and christenings 157; and 'churching' the mother 158; common-law (unconventional) 40; non-religious ceremonies 39–40; presents 36–7, 39, 78, 112, 167; registry office 40, 120; trousseaux 36, 37–8, 112

Wedgewood, Julia 259

Wendell Holmes, Oliver 172

Wenlock, Lord 53; sister 53

West, Constance 30, 76–7; parents 76–7

Westland, Dr Albert, on childbirth 137

Who's Who 1916 48, 272

Wickham, Agnes (*née* Gladstone, W. E. Gladstone/Hawarden Castle family; m. Edward Wickham) 11, 32, 61–2, 63, 66, 68, 71, 97, 101, 140, 159, 166

Wickham, Edward C. 61–2, 66

widows, widowers, widowhood, widowerhood 29, 33, 69, 81, 86, 92, 111, 122, 215, 221, 229, 255, 257, 264, 270, 285, 287; sense of loss of child through marriage 33–4, 50–1, 79; in Victorian fiction 259

Wilde, Constance 73

Williams, Dr 169–70

Williamson, Dr 147

Willoughby, Lord 69

wills 60, 61, 69, 99, 159, 167, 177, 178

Wilson, Annie *see* Gladstone (W. E. Gladstone/Hawarden Castle family)

Wilson, Charles (2nd Baron Nunburnholme) 96

Wiseman, Cardinal 275

women's health (*see also* diseases, doctors, maternal mortality, medical treatment, miscarriages) 133–6, 161, 258; drugs and alcohol abuse (form of escapism) 47, 260, 272–6 *passim*; eugenics 84, 87; famous "woman's doctor" 136; hypochondria (cult of 'female invalidism') (*see also under* spinsters) 133–6 *passim*, 260, 265, 266, 272, 273, 274; ill-health and its symptoms 47, 109, 112, 135; illness as reaction to parental veto 47; invalidism 84–5, 134–5; prerequisite for marriage 46, 74, 79, 84–7, 93, 109, 112, 261; undermined by colonial service life 227; women's attitudes to doctors 134, 135–6, 141–2, 166; women's views on chloroform 147–8, 170

women's illnesses (*see also* maternal mortality) 134–5; anaemia 10, 156; breast cancer 135; cellulitis (*see also* puerperal fever) 135, 167, 174; chlorosis 256, 273; depression following infant death 183; depression following miscarriage 164; haematomasis 178; invalidism resulting from childbirth 152, 179; invalidism resulting from miscarriage 160, 162, 163, 168, 288; menstrual dysfunction 140; miscarriage *see* miscarriages; neurasthenia 276, 279; neurosis/hysteria 47, 137, 256, 265, 272, 273, 275; peritonitis 162, 166, 168; phlebitis 168, 179; prolapse 134; puerperal fever 135, 159, 161, 162, 164, 166, 167, 171, 172–5, 178, 184; pyelitis 135, 174; uraemia 174

women's movement 17, 49, 189, 204, 211, 246, 258, 280, 281, 285, 289; influence on electoral growth and reform 204–5; influence leading to transformation of women's accepted roles 17, 204–5, 219, 246, 280, 281; influence on marital choices 49; influence on secondary and higher education 14, 211

women's political associations (*see also*